The Essentials of Academic Writing

The Essentials of Academic Writing

Second Edition

Derek Soles

Soka University of America

WADSWORTH
CENGAGE Learning™

Australia • Brazil • Japan • Korea • Mexico • Singapore • Spain • United Kingdom • United States

WADSWORTH
CENGAGE Learning

The Essentials of Academic Writing: Second Edition

Derek Soles

Publisher: Lyn Uhl

Acquisitions Editor:
Margaret Leslie

Assistant Editor: Amy Haines

Editorial Assistant:
Elizabeth Ramsey

Senior Media Editor:
Cara Douglass-Graff

Marketing Manager:
Jennifer Zourdos

Marketing Coordinator:
Ryan Ahern

Marketing Communications
Manager: Stacey Purviance

Content Project Manager:
Corinna Dibble

Senior Art Director: Jill Ort

Print Buyer: Sue Carroll

Rights Acquisitions Account
Manager Text: Katie Huha

Rights Acquisitions Account
Manager Image: Jennifer
Meyer Dare

Photo Researcher: Kate Cebik

Production Service: Elm Street
Publishing Services

Text Designer: Elm Street
Publishing Services

Cover Designer: Wing Ngan

Cover Image: © 2008 Alamy Ltd.

Compositor: Integra Software
Services Pvt. Ltd.

For product information and technology
assistance, contact us at
**Cengage Learning Customer & Sales Support,
1-800-354-9706**
For permission to use material from this text or product,
submit all requests online at **www.cengage.com/permissions**
Further permissions questions can be emailed to
permissionrequest@cengage.com

Library of Congress Control Number: 2009923263

ISBN-13: 978-0-547-18133-2
ISBN-10: 0-547-18133-7

Wadsworth
20 Channel Center Street
Boston, MA 02210
USA

Cengage Learning is a leading provider of customized learning solutions with office locations around the globe, including Singapore, the United Kingdom, Australia, Mexico, Brazil, and Japan. Locate your local office at: **www.cengage.com/international.**

Cengage Learning products are represented in Canada by Nelson Education, Ltd.

For your course and learning solutions, visit **www.cengage.com.**

Purchase any of our products at your local college store or at our preferred online store **www.ichapters.com.**

Printed in the United States of America
1 2 3 4 5 6 7 13 12 11 10 09

To my beautiful daughters, Kate and MJ

Contents

3 Research Your Topic　　34

4 Make a Plan　　53

5 Write a Draft　71

6 Revise Your Essay　92

PART TWO   Sample Academic Essays with Instructional Notes and Commentary   194

PART THREE   An Anthology of Academic Writing   284

Alternative Rhetorical Contents

Model Essays Written by Students

Model Essays Classified by Rhetorical Mode

Expository: Examples and Details

Expository: Analysis and Interpretation

Expository: Compare/Contrast

Model Essays Classified by Discipline

Preface

This second edition of *The Essentials of Academic Writing* presents a completely new and updated anthology of readings and expanded coverage of academic honesty and visual literacy. At the same time, it preserves the philosophy and pedagogy upon which the first edition was based. There are three of these philosophical and pedagogical principles.

First, I believe that it is better to teach the fundamentals of the writing process thoroughly than all of its particulars superficially. Most first-year composition classes run for twelve to sixteen weeks, giving students adequate time to learn how to think about and research a topic, make a plan, draft effective paragraphs, revise, proofread, and document sources. These topics—the key components of the writing process—are covered thoroughly in Part One of *The Essentials of Academic Writing*. To illustrate the way in which a developing writer composes an academic essay, we follow the progress of one student, Hannah Goldman, as she works through each part of the process of writing an essay about the consequences of America's obsession with celebrities. Critical thinking and active reading, the corollary goals of any sound writing program, are covered in the context of the anthology of readings in Parts Two and Three.

Second, I believe a first-year composition course should prepare students to do well in all of their college courses that require writing. *The Essentials of Academic Writing* emphasizes instruction in writing the essays that undergraduate students will be required to write in their business, social sciences, natural sciences, and humanities courses. Chapter 1 introduces students to the concept of the academic essay. Chapters 2, 3, and 4 cover the prewriting process, emphasizing, respectively, the importance of knowing audience and purpose; the process of researching a topic; and the process of planning expository and persuasive essays. Chapter 5 offers advice on drafting effective introductory, body, and concluding paragraphs. Chapters 6 and 7 explain, respectively, effective methods of revising and editing academic writing. Chapter 8 covers the three most commonly used methods—MLA, APA, and *CMS*—of citing sources. Since instruction needs to be reinforced, each chapter concludes with a writing assignment and some exercises designed to reinforce the rules and conventions of excellent academic writing in a variety of disciplines.

Third, I believe that students should read very carefully, discuss, and analyze the kind of writing their professors would like them to produce. We do learn in part by imitating the behavior and the work of those adept in the skill we are trying to acquire. In their courses, undergraduates are usually required to research a topic, write an expository or persuasive essay on that topic, and cite their sources accurately and thoroughly. The readings in Parts Two and Three model the kind of writing that professors want their students to write or at least the kind of writing toward which professors would like their students to aspire. The readings are contemporary, well-documented examples of sound academic essays, some by students, most by experienced academics. The readings in Part Two are thoroughly annotated with instructional notes and commentary to help students understand the process writers invoke and the choices they make as they draft and revise. The readings in Part Three are followed by questions for study and discussion, designed to help students apply what they have learned in Part One and observed in Part Two. Journal prompts encourage students to explore further the issues raised in the paper and to consider, perhaps emulate, the ways in which the writers express themselves.

In essence, then, I believe that a writing program should teach students the essential components of the process of writing an academic essay and support and reinforce that instruction with authentic models and practical exercises. The second edition of *The Essentials of Academic Writing* attempts to realize this goal.

Acknowledgments

While I was writing and revising *The Essentials of Academic Writing*, I had indispensable help and support from Cengage editors and from a most astute group of fellow first-year-writing teachers.

When this project was in its formative stages and while I was writing and rewriting in response to reviewers' suggestions, I worked closely with Sarah Smith, Development Manager; Laura Barthule, freelance development editor; and Suzanne Phelps Weir, Executive Editor. They are experts at combining insight with diplomacy, a quality all writers wish for in an editor.

I am grateful, as well, to my colleagues who read various versions of the manuscript and offered such practical and intelligent advice. They are as follows: Joe Essid, Richmond College; Ned Bachus, Community College of Philadelphia; Michelle Auerbach, Front Range Community College; Leslie Henson, Butte College; Gail Corso, Neumann College; Michelle Ballif, University of Georgia; Maryanne Felter, Cayuga Community College; Ron Fortune, Illinois State University; Dorinda Fox, University of Central Florida; Marguerite Helmers, University of Wisconsin, Oshkosh; Georgina Hill, Western Michigan University; Marc Kemp, Shasta College; James C. McDonald, University of Louisiana at Lafayette; Sara McLaughlin, Texas Tech University; Lyle W. Morgan, Pittsburgh State University; Jonna Perrillo, New York University; Daniela Ragusa, University of Rhode Island; Althea E. Rhodes, University of Southern Indiana; Jennifer Richardson, Washington State University; Anna Ryan, Western Washington University; Greg Siering, Ball State University; Scott Slawinski, University of South Carolina; and Elizabeth A. Wardle, University of Dayton.

The Writing Process

To write a good college essay, you need to think about your topic, do some research, formulate a plan, write a draft, revise your work, and edit your work. You think about your topic by considering the needs and expectations of your readers, determining your purpose, and freewriting. You research by reading and making notes on books, periodicals, and Internet sites most relevant to your topic. You plan by jotting down main points in support of your thesis and subordinate points in support of main points. You draft by writing complete paragraphs. You revise by reconsidering the efficacy of the structure, the content, and the cohesion of your paper. And you edit by reviewing and reconsidering your grammar, sentence structure, diction, and punctuation.

An outline showing the components of the process of writing an academic essay looks like this:

I. Think About Your Topic
   A. Consider your reader
   B. Freewrite
   C. Determine your purpose
   D. Compose a preliminary thesis

II. Research Your Topic
   A. Books
   B. Periodicals
   C. Online sources
   D. Interviews and questionnaires

III. Devise a Plan
   A. The structure of an expository essay
   B. The structure of a compare/contrast essay
   C. The structure of a persuasive essay

IV. Write a Draft
    A. Effective introductory paragraphs
    B. Effective body paragraphs
    C. Effective concluding paragraphs

 V. Revise
    A. Reconsider overall structure
    B. Ensure content accommodates audience and purpose
    C. Check cohesion
    D. Improve style

VI. Edit
    A. Check grammar
    B. Check sentence structure
    C. Check punctuation
    D. Check diction and spelling

VII. Cite Sources
    A. The MLA method of parenthetical citation
    B. The APA method of parenthetical citation
    C. The *Chicago Manual of Style* method

Writing as a Recursive Process

Unfortunately, our outline is misleading. It is useful insofar as it neatly organizes the components of the process of writing an academic essay. But the writing process is not neat and well organized. Educators who have studied the processes of accomplished writers have come to the conclusion that writing is not a linear, well-organized, step-by-step process. While writers usually complete the components of the process just described, they do not do so in a systematic, orderly manner. We reflect upon our topic before we begin to write, but as we write, we continue to reflect and often alter our plan based on these new thoughts and insights. We revise and edit *while* we draft, not only after we have completed and are reviewing a first draft. We read and make notes on sources before we write, and then, after we have completed a draft or two, we might discover a valuable new source that forces us to revise again the content of the essay. Writing is not a linear but a *recursive* process.

For clarity and convenience, Part One of this book is organized in the way our outline is organized, but it contains frequent reminders of the recursive nature of the writing process. After defining and providing examples of academic essays in Chapter 1, this book guides you through the components in the process of writing an effective academic essay, teaching you, specifically, how to do the following:

- **Think about your topic.** As a successful writer, you will take time to reflect upon, to mull over, to consider the subject of your essay. Such reflection is ongoing. It occurs both before and throughout the processes of drafting and revising. It is an essential component of the writing process, fostering as it does an understanding of your purpose in writing and of the needs and expectations of your readers, while helping you formulate a central focus, a controlling idea, a thesis. Several effective methods for thinking systematically about a topic are covered in Chapter 2.

- **Research your topic.** Whenever you are assigned to write an academic essay, you must research your topic. You can access many journals and reference books online; books also are increasingly available online, but most are still stored in print form in libraries. Your research will provide information that can be integrated into an essay to render it well developed and authoritative. You must know how to access information, how to evaluate sources, and how to summarize information contained within these sources. Research strategies are discussed in Chapter 3.

- **Plan your essay.** Planning is an essential component of the process of writing expository, compare/contrast, and persuasive essays. Planning is more than constructing a system of headings and subheadings to use before beginning your draft. It is a continuing process. Those series of points you arrange in a system of headings and subheadings are really only a start. The act of writing stimulates thinking, and as a result, that preliminary outline likely will change and evolve. Planning is an essential part of the process because it helps establish a structure for the essay. Planning expository, compare/contrast, and persuasive essays is discussed in Chapter 4.

- **Write a draft.** Planning outlines your essay's beginning, middle, and end; drafting transforms the outline into sentences and paragraphs. The essence of drafting is writing an effective introductory paragraph (or paragraphs for a longer essay), a series of well-developed body paragraphs, and an effective concluding paragraph (or paragraphs for a longer essay). Writing effective introductory, body, and concluding paragraphs is discussed in Chapter 5.

- **Revise.** Revision is the process of making global changes to a written text, that is, a process of reconsidering, moving, reshaping, and developing whole paragraphs and/or of altering the entire structure of a written work. The revision process is ongoing. You will revise while you draft and while you read and reread a draft. Revision is covered in Chapter 6.

- **Edit.** Editing is the process of reviewing, changing, and correcting words and sentences within a written text. The editing process includes checking for and correcting errors in grammar, sentence structure, diction, spelling, punctuation, and mechanics. It is, like most components of the writing process, ongoing. It is not something you do only after drafting and revising. You will edit while you draft and as you read and reread a draft. Editing is covered in Chapter 7.

- **Cite sources.** Academic essays require research (covered in Chapter 3), and research sources have to be properly acknowledged. Professors take seriously the importance of acknowledging and citing any and all sources you use to authenticate and develop your ideas. Chapter 8 describes three widely used and well-established methods for citing sources thoroughly and accurately.

Reading Academic Writing

Writing is a process best learned by doing, so the focus of this book is on mastering the components of the writing process. But we can also learn by studying the work of accomplished academic writers, especially if that work is accompanied by notes and annotations that explain what the writer is doing and why he or she is doing it effectively. Part Two of this book is an anthology of five good academic essays with instructional notes and commentary designed to show you how the authors have used the components of the writing process to create an effective finished product. Part Three presents eight additional academic essays followed by questions for study and discussion designed to further enhance your ability to recognize and consider the elements of effective academic discourse.

There are also four examples of exemplary student academic writing in this text. "Some Social and Psychological Consequences of Celebrity Worship" by Hannah Goldman is presented as a case study in the components of the process of writing an academic essay. "Saving the Vancouver Island Marmot" by Adam Black is one of the annotated essays in Part Two. "The Qualities of a Grade A Essay" by Edna Bell serves as our example of an essay cited using the MLA method; "Is Chocolate Good for You?" by Tersa Lyons is a literature review cited using the APA method.

The Process of Writing an Academic Essay

PART ONE

CHAPTER 1

What Is an Academic Essay?

An academic essay is a written text, rarely fewer than 500 words or more than 5,000 words in length, on a topic related to a course taught at a school, college, or university. Given the number and variety of courses offered, there are thousands of possible topics for an academic essay. Good academic writing has a clear beginning, middle, and end; is written in Standard English; and projects a forceful and confident voice. Good academic writing, in other words, has ISCE: intelligence, substance, clarity, and energy. An essay projects intelligence when it contains insightful ideas and cites authoritative sources; it is substantial when ideas are developed in enough detail so readers grasp the knowledge the writer is conveying; it is clear when its grammar, sentence structure, organization, punctuation, and diction are sound; it has energy when the writer uses a strong and confident voice in a fluid and vigorous style.

Academic essays and reports fulfill a purpose. They present the findings of a research study or project; they present factual and objective information about any number of topics; they make a case for or present an argument in favor of any number of propositions. That purpose is often encapsulated in a thesis or thesis statement, which the bulk of the essay will develop and elucidate.

Professors often draw a distinction between an expository and a persuasive academic essay, and often specify, in their assignment handouts, which of these two academic "rhetorical modes" they want their students to use as they compose their texts.

An **expository (or informative) essay** presents to its readers interesting, informative, and important knowledge that elucidates, supports, and justifies a central or controlling idea, known as a thesis. This thesis is usually a matter of fact. An expository essay about the process of photosynthesis or the side effects of Prozac or the climate of Seattle is not likely to provoke a prolonged argument. These essays present primarily factual information.

A **persuasive essay** also presents its readers with knowledge in support of a thesis, but this thesis is a matter of opinion. The persuasive essay is also known as the argumentative essay, though some professors do draw a slight distinction between the two, asserting that a persuasive essay goes a slight step beyond an argument in more overtly trying to alter belief or encourage a course of action. An essay in support of drilling for oil in the Arctic National Wildlife Refuge or in opposition to school vouchers or in support of gun control presents an argument and, as such, will likely both vex and intrigue readers who believe otherwise.

The distinctions between the two modes often blur. One person's fact is sometimes another person's opinion. An expository essay about the reasons why the U.S. government decided to send troops to Vietnam in the mid-1960s might discuss two reasons about which there is widespread agreement but one reason about which even the experts disagree. An expository essay about the hazards of global warming will not resonate with a reader who is suspicious of the essay's premise. To an extent, the form (or "mode," as it is often called) of an essay is in the eye of the beholder. It is true that an informative essay tries to teach and a persuasive essay tries to convince. But teachers will persuade sometimes, and advocates will inform.

An academic essay is not a personal narrative, but it might contain a personal anecdote in support of its thesis. If a writer is developing an argument in support of tougher drunk driving laws, and if that writer has a friend or a relative who was injured or killed by a drunk driver, the writer might describe the incident and its effect on him or her as a way of intensifying the argument. Personal anecdotes are common and can be effective, especially in persuasive writing.

Academic essays almost always require research. To acquire the information you will need to support, elucidate, and defend the thesis of your essay, you likely will have to attend lectures, read books, surf the Internet, and read articles in scholarly journals. The nature of your research will depend upon your topic. If your essay is on the most recent research into the human genome, you likely will use the Internet and the most recent journal articles to find the information you need; books will be less useful to you because by the time a book about current scientific research is published, its information can be dated. If, in contrast, your essay is about the role of the African-American soldier in the Civil War, books might be the best and most reliable sources available to you.

Writers must acknowledge in the body of their essays and again at the end of their essays the source of any information they are using in their essays. There are very specific ways, sanctioned and required by colleges and universities, of acknowledging sources used in an academic essay. The two most common methods (discussed in Chapter 8) were developed by international professional organizations, one by the Modern Language Association (MLA) and the other by the American Psychological Association (APA). The *Chicago Manual of Style* (also covered in Chapter 8) recommends another method, also widely used within the academic community. Essays about English and foreign literatures and languages are usually cited in the MLA method. Social science essays—especially psychology and education—are usually cited in the APA method. History and economics are among the disciplines that frequently use the *Chicago Manual of Style* method. Some journals have designed their own citation system and require their authors to use it.

An academic essay must conform to the rules and the conventions of the academic discipline—the subject—for which it is written. The social sciences, the natural sciences, the humanities, technology, and business all have their own subset of discourse conventions. These discourse conventions are discussed in general terms in the following sections. At least one example of an essay from each discipline is included in Parts Two and Three of this book, along with commentary, instructional annotations, questions for study and discussion, and journal prompts designed to help you learn how to write effectively within each discipline.

Writing for the Social Sciences

The social sciences include anthropology, cultural studies, economics, education, political science, psychology, and sociology. Social scientists conduct empirical research into their particular areas of expertise. An educator, for example, might conduct a study comparing the effectiveness of two methods of improving reading comprehension among economically disadvantaged twelve-year-olds; a psychologist might design and conduct a study to investigate the effect of aging on memory loss. They would write an essay or a research report describing the results of their studies. Parts Two and Three offer several examples of such reports, including "Getting Inked: Tattoos and College Students" by Laura Manuel and Eugene P. Sheehan.

Social scientists generally prefer writing that is concise, to the point, and clearly organized. They usually write in the third person, even though third person does often mean using the somewhat less efficient passive voice. Usually, a social scientist will write, "This study was conducted at the University of Washington," not "I conducted this study at the University of Washington." Social scientists tend to write using the jargon common in their fields of expertise, reasoning that their readers will be familiar with it. If they are writing for a general, as opposed to a specific, publication, however, or if they are writing a textbook for undergraduates, they will lighten up on their use of jargon or include a glossary of terms. Graphs, charts, and illustrations, which offer an effective visual summary of the results of their research, often appear in the work of social scientists. Their papers often include a system of headings and subheadings, in the interest of clarity. They often include an abstract at the beginning of their paper; an **abstract** is a one-paragraph summary of the nature of the study and its findings. Social scientists usually use the APA method of parenthetical citation to cite their sources.

As an undergraduate social science major, you will be expected to complete a variety of writing assignments. You likely will be asked to write a **literature review,** which is an essay that summarizes important research on a particular topic. The literature review is a component of research studies, the section in which the authors put their own study in context by reviewing related work done earlier on the subject of their investigation. It is also a separate assignment, a common one in social science courses. One of the student essays in this book—Tersa Lyons's "Is Chocolate Good for You? A Review of Some Online Sources"—is an example of a literature review.

You also might be asked to write a wide variety of **expository essays** about the relationship between the individual and society, about different cultures, about the effect of a particular variable on human behavior, about methods of teaching and learning, about the function and dysfunctions of the human mind, or about various political and economic doctrines. This book provides several examples of academic expository essays/reports, including "Faculty and College Student Beliefs About the Frequency of Student Academic Misconduct" by Hard, Conway, and Moran and "What Predicts Adjustment Among College Students? A Longitudinal Panel Study" by Pritchard, Wilson, and Yamnitz.

You also might write a wide variety of **persuasive essays** in which you argue the advantages of one psychological theory over another, of one social or political or economic system over another, of one learning or teaching style over another. An essay recommending ways in which the social security system could be streamlined and made more cost-effective is an example of a persuasive social science essay. Why the new economic policies of the Chinese government will adversely (or positively) affect the U.S. economy; why Freud's concept of the Oedipus complex is flawed; why Asian students outperform other races on measures of mathematical ability; why Marxism has failed (or succeeded) in Cuba—these are other examples of argumentative essay topics that professors in the social sciences often assign. In this book, examples of academic arguments include "Fixing the Borders (Without a Wall)" by Michele Wucker.

Much academic writing, of course, **blends the two modes of exposition and argument.** Academic writers often undertake a study or a literature review and, on the basis of what they have found, develop an argument. This book presents several examples of expository/persuasive essays and reports, including "Are Drinking Games Sports? College Athlete Participation in Drinking Games and Alcohol-Related Problems" by Grossbard, Geisner, Neighbors, Kilmer, and Larimer. In "Meeting Her Maker: Emily Dickinson's God," Jay Ladin adds an interesting narrative dimension to his study of student responses to Dickinson's religious poetry.

The **case study** is another common social science assignment. The case study is usually an account of how a single individual responds to a particular situation: a teaching style, a psychological survey, a conflict within a group, or some other stressful or significant sequence of events. An education professor, for example, might examine closely the schoolwork, behavior, and social interactions of a single dyslexic child, both to help that child and to develop hypotheses about dyslexia in the hope that this one case study might help in the diagnosis and treatment of other dyslexic children.

Writing for the Sciences

The sciences include astronomy, biology, chemistry, computer science, geography, and physics. Scientists usually value a clear and concise writing style that uses sentences that are typically shorter than sentences used by humanists and social scientists. They use the jargon of their fields when they know their readers will be familiar with that jargon, but avoid it or provide definitions if they are writing textbooks for undergraduates or essays for general readers. They use the third-person point of view and passive voice—writing, for example, "The temperature of the solution was then raised by 9 degrees Celsius," as opposed to "I then raised the temperature of the solution by 9 degrees Celsius." They make extensive use of charts and graphs. They often use a system of headings and subheadings to improve clarity.

Scientists use a variety of methods to acknowledge secondary sources they have used in their papers or reports, but in general, they prefer a footnote or endnote system to a parenthetical citation system. The Council of Biology Editors, the American Chemical Society, and the American Institute of Physics all have style manuals, which explain the discourse conventions within their disciplines.

Scientists write fewer argumentative essays than do social scientists and humanists, dealing as they do more with fact than opinion. Obviously, there are controversial issues in the world of the sciences, but the natural scientist becomes something of a social scientist when he or she leaves the laboratory to reflect upon the ramifications of scientific experiments and advancements upon society as a whole. In Part Two, the student essay "Saving the Vancouver Island Marmot" by Adam Black is an example of an essay that summarizes and synthesizes scientific research to support a thesis.

If you plan to major in one of the sciences, you will write expository essays about ecosystems; animal physiology and behavior; the life cycles of plants and animals; the origins and development of the universe; quantum theory and relativity; atoms and molecules; electrolytes, electrolysis, and electrochemical cells; evolution; and genetics. The expository essay that explains a process—photosynthesis, chemical and physical reactions, evolution—are especially prevalent in the natural sciences.

One of the most common writing assignments in the sciences is the **lab** or **research report,** which presents the results of an experiment. A scientist has a premise or an assumption—in the language of the research report, a

hypothesis—he or she wants to test. The lab or research report begins, as all such reports do, with a statement of this hypothesis. The hypothesis typically is followed by a review of other reports (the literature review), which presents the results of a test of the same or similar hypotheses. The hypothesis and the literature review form the **introduction** to the report. The introduction typically is followed by a clear and detailed description of the **methods** the scientist used in conducting the experiment and an explanation and description of any materials he or she used in the course of conducting the experiment. Accuracy and precision are essential in this section of the report; readers (likely other scientists) want to be confident that the correct procedure was followed, and they might even want to duplicate the study. The methods section is typically followed by the **results** section, wherein the writer presents the data—which are usually numeric or quantitative—that reveal precisely what the scientist learned in the course of testing the hypothesis. The data are usually summarized with the help of a variety of graphs, charts, and tables. Finally, in the **discussion/conclusion** section of the report, the writer indicates whether the experiment has validated the hypothesis, discusses the study's implications, and describes what additional research is necessary to continue exploring the validity or lack thereof of the report's hypothesis.

As a science student, you also might be asked to write a literature review or a summary of all of the research published about a particular hypothesis. The literature review is usually organized chronologically; that is, the writer begins his or her review with a summary of the earliest experiment related to the hypothesis and ends with a review of the most recently conducted study. The literature review usually comments, as well, upon the overall implications of the studies considered as a whole. Note that a literature review, usually in a briefer form, is also a part of a laboratory or research report.

Writing for the Humanities

The humanities include the fine arts, history, languages, literature, philosophy, and religion. Humanists, like all academics, value a clear and concise style of writing, but they tend to value sentence variety more than their counterparts in the social sciences and sciences do. They try, perhaps more than their colleagues in other disciplines, to give some flair and energy to their writing.

Here, for example, is a passage from Jay Ladin's article, presented in full in Part Two on pages 223–237 "Meeting Her Maker: Emily Dickinson's God":

> I was both delighted by my students' ability to connect Dickinson's work to their personal experiences, and startled by the effectiveness of that connection. Rather than oversimplifying the complexities of the text, reading Dickinson through the lens of their religious experience had made my students more effective, subtler readers than they would have been had they adopted the humanist framework I offered them.

Compare that passage with this passage from Philip Mote and Georg Kaser's paper, presented in full in Part Three on pages 412–425, "The Shrinking Glaciers of Kilimanjaro: Can Global Warming Be Blamed?":

> Melting, sublimation and the warming of ice require energy. Energy in the high-mountain environment comes from a variety of energy fluxes that interact in complex ways. The Sun is the primary energy source, but its direct effect is limited to daytime; other limiting factors are shading and the ability of snow to reflect visible light. Energy can nevertheless reach the glacier through *sensible-heat flux*.

The two passages are the same length, but the humanist writes two sentences to the scientists' five. This is a common distinction between the humanist and the scientific writing style. Scientists favor simple sentences; humanists, complex. In addition, the humanist adds narration to his or her expository essay and writes in the first person—"I was … delighted." The scientists use the third-person point of view. Instead of writing, "Hardy had invited me to join him," for example, they write, "Hardy had invited Kaser to join him." The humanist style is academic but less formally so than the social or natural scientist's.

Humanists use a variety of citation systems. Literature and language scholars usually use the MLA method for parenthetical citation, while historians prefer the *Chicago Manual of Style* method of footnotes or endnotes.

As a humanities major, you will write a wide variety of expository (or informative) essays in which you will express your knowledge of topics related to works of literature, philosophical systems, historical events and circumstances, painting and sculpture, and tenets of world religions. Examples of well-written humanities essays in this text include Michele Wucker's "Fixing the Borders (Without a Wall)" and Valerie Wee's "Resurrecting and Updating the Teen Slasher: The Case of *Scream*."

The writing you do if you are taking a class in a foreign language will differ from the writing assignments you typically will undertake in other humanities classes. In introductory language classes, the purpose of writing assignments is more to help you learn the language than to present information or to advance an argument. Your professor likely will ask you to write responses to questions based upon fairly simple readings, to compose a simple friendly letter, or perhaps to keep a diary or journal. As you become more fluent in the language, the assignments will become more sophisticated, and if you major in a foreign language, you eventually will be expected to compose essays in that language that approximate the demands of a writing assignment in any other humanities course. In some cultures—in Asian and Arabic cultures, for example—the concept and the convention of argument differ from our own, so you will have the additional challenge of composing essays that are not only intelligent, substantive, clear, and energetic, but also appropriate within a specific cultural context.

Writing for Business

Business schools offer courses in accounting, finance, human resources, management, and marketing. In business writing, the style is dictated by the genre and the audience. Advertising copy directed at the general public needs to be clear, lively, and direct. Prospectuses, business letters, and annual reports have to have a fairly formal but still readable style, since they are read by both the general public and specialists in the field. Interoffice memoranda and e-mails can be less formal but must be clear and to the point. A businessperson may use acronyms and the jargon of his or her field when writing something that will be read only by his or her peers but should avoid specialized language when writing for the general public. One of the annotated readings in Part Two, "Is the United States Losing Its Productivity Advantage?" by Mary Amiti and Kevin Stiroh, presents a good example of a business paper.

Business majors often begin their program of study believing that their professors won't require much writing from them. In fact, the reverse may be closer to the truth. Business majors do a lot of writing, and businessmen and -women do even more. Hardly a month passes without a major newspaper somewhere quoting a CEO who is critical of his or her new employees because they don't possess the communication skills they need to be successful.

Even in a field such as accounting, which we think of as more concerned with numbers than letters, good writing skills are essential. Accountants regularly write reports that explain, summarize, and interpret a company's balance sheet. Clarity and accuracy are obviously crucial to such reports. Accounting firms often ask job applicants to respond in writing to complex questions as part of the interview process. And there is a written component to many of the exams would-be accountants must take to become certified.

If you plan to major in business, you will have to learn how to write a prospectus, an annual report, a marketing report or survey, an interoffice memo, a job description, and various forms of letters. Your professors also likely will ask you to write an expository and/or a persuasive essay to complete the requirements for their courses. Essays about the training and hiring practices of various companies, the management styles of successful business executives, the marketing campaigns of various businesses, and the ethics of the auto industry, for example, are commonly assigned in business courses.

Writing for Technology

Computer scientists, educational technologists, engineers, and others employed in high-tech industries do a tremendous amount of writing in the course of their careers. Senior engineers and high-tech executives often stress the importance of written communication skills to success in their industries. They value clear language, cohesion, concision, logic, structure, good grammar, and correct punctuation in the reports, letters, and proposals they demand from their employees. Written texts produced by computer scientists, engineers, and other technologists typically are replete with charts, tables, graphs, and other visuals. The ability to compose clear and meaningful visual aids is essential to success in technical writing. Writers rely on them to help their readers understand the often very complex information they are trying to convey. For the same reason, technical writing, more than other genres, relies on numbered, point-form, or bulleted information to convey meaning clearly, concisely, and precisely.

Here, for example, is the first paragraph from a paper called "Configuration of OFDM Transmission Techniques—Based on Algorithms Developed Using Concept of UML and Matlab," from the journal *Computer Sciences and Telecommunications*:

> A mobile radio channel is characterized by a multipath fading environment. These reflected delayed waves interfere with the direct wave and cause intersymbol interference (ISI), which causes significant degradation of network performance. A wireless network must be designed in such a way as to minimize these adverse effects. For broadband multimedia mobile communication systems, it is necessary to use high bit rate transmission of at least several megabits per second. However, if digital data are transmitted at a rate of several megabits per second, the delay time of the delayed waves exceeds 1 symbol time. Because the delayed waves interfere with other symbols, the effects of this interference must be eliminated in the received signal. There are several ways to achieve this goal, such as using adaptive equalization techniques at the receiver is one way to equalize the received signal. However, in practice, achieving this equalization at several megabits per second with compact and low cost hardware is quite difficult.[1]

Clearly the authors of this paper are writing for a highly specialized audience. Still, the authors organize their work in an elaborate system of headings and subheadings, and on nearly every page of the paper, there is a table, figure, graph, or chart designed to help readers comprehend the complex technical information the authors are presenting.

If you are a student in computer science, engineering, or another high-tech field, you likely will receive instruction and practice in writing project proposals, project progress reports, user manuals, technical descriptions of machinery or computer hardware, project feasibility studies, and business letters. Technological projects are usually collaborative, so you also likely will learn some strategies for writing collaboratively and productively with one or more colleagues. You also will need to know how to adapt your writing for different audiences, since an

1. R. Goel and P. K. Bansal, "Configuration of OFDM Transmission Techniques—Based on Algorithms Developed Using Concept of UML and Matlab," *Computer Sciences and Telecommunications* 1 (2007): 14–21.

audience of fellow technologists has very specialized knowledge that a general reader does not have. And you will have to learn, as well, how to effectively integrate figures, charts, tables, graphs, and point-form bulleted information into written communication.

Technical reports usually begin with an introduction that explains the problem or the circumstances that generated the need for a report. The introduction also quickly orients readers to the subject of the report and presents its purpose. The introduction usually is followed by the summary, which briefly presents the main results of the report and the recommendations the author is making based upon his or her findings. The body of the report presents the detailed information, accompanied by the necessary charts, graphs, tables, and figures, which are clearly referenced in the written text of the report's body. Typically, about 75 percent of the report consists of the detailed, well-substantiated, clearly explained information contained within the body. Depending on the report's length, the body might be subdivided into a literature review, analysis, discussion, or other subsections. Next comes the conclusion section, wherein the authors present the results of their investigation and analysis. The report ends with recommendations the authors make based upon the conclusions they have reached. In short reports, the conclusions and recommendations are often presented together. In some longer reports, a source list is included, presented as footnotes or in a recognized bibliographical format—technologists use various acceptable methods of citing sources. In addition, longer reports are often preceded by a letter of transmittal from the reports' authors to the reports' commissioners, reminding the commissioners of the circumstances or problems that generated the need for such a report.

Conclusion

As we have seen, each academic discipline has certain conventions that govern the way written information within that discipline is presented. It is important that you know these conventions and apply them in your own writing. The style and structure of a botany report on the effect of global warming on deciduous trees in the Pacific Northwest, with its charts and graphs, headings and subheadings, and short, clear, precise sentences will be quite different from an anthropology essay about family dynamics among Pacific Northwest Native Americans in the seventeenth century.

It is equally important, however, to realize that basic qualities of good writing are valued in all academic fields. The academic writing you do as a college student and, later, as a businessperson, teacher, lawyer, architect, economist, scientist, computer programmer, or psychologist should confirm that you are knowledgeable about your subject, that you have thought about, read about, and researched your topic. It should be, in a word, intelligent. It should be substantive, offering details, examples, definitions, causes, effects, comparisons, contrasts, and anecdotes that develop the points and ideas you are presenting. It should be written in Standard English and, hence, be free from errors in grammar, sentence structure, diction, spelling, and punctuation. And it should have some energy and style, some confidence and forcefulness. ISCE: intelligence, substance, clarity, and energy—these are the fundamental elements of good academic writing.

The purpose of the rest of this book is to help you learn about those elements and produce sound academic essays.

WRITING ASSIGNMENT

Most college textbooks represent decent examples of academic writing. Study a recently published textbook written about a subject that interests you. You might use a textbook from a class you are currently taking. Write a paragraph in which you evaluate a chapter or an excerpt from this book based upon the discussion of the elements of good academic writing you have just read. Study the way in which sources are cited in the book. Determine if the citation method is MLA, APA, or something else. Explain how you can tell which citation method the author of the textbook is using.

EXERCISES

Write a paragraph that describes an object that has special significance to you, an object that you treasure: your car, a piece of jewelry, an item of clothing, your TV or CD player. Then rewrite this paragraph from the perspectives of any two of the following: a marketing major, a sociologist, a chemist, a football coach, a sculptor, a poet.

COLLABORATIVE ACTIVITY

In a small group, discuss your experiences writing academic essays. Talk about the process you go through as you write; exchange views on what you consider to be an interesting and effective writing assignment; consider why the ability to write well is so valued at colleges and universities.

JOURNAL PROMPT

Reflect upon the amount and the type of writing you will have to do when you graduate from college and begin to work. If you have not yet selected an occupation you wish to pursue, select one that at least holds some interest for you.

CHAPTER 2

Getting Started: Consider Topic, Audience, Purpose

The first step in writing an academic essay—what is often called the **pre-writing** stage—involves selecting and reflecting upon your topic, considering the needs and expectations of your readers, and establishing your purpose. You must, of course, keep the needs and expectations of your readers in mind and continue to refine your purpose while you draft your essay. But if you consider your TAP (topic, audience, and purpose) before you begin to draft, you will generate some ideas you can use to develop your essay and will begin to develop the voice and style you want to use to complete the assignment successfully.

Reflect upon Your Topic

If you are like most students, you begin work on an academic essay immediately by annotating the assignment sheet containing the list of topics your professor has given you. You circle the number of the topic that most appeals to you, underline a key phrase or two, and make a few preliminary notes about main points to cover and references to check. Perhaps then you put a question mark beside another topic or two that you could turn to if your first choice doesn't work out. Perhaps in other topics you find information that might provide some insights into the topic you have chosen.

If your teacher wants you to choose your own topic, you likely will undertake a different strategy. You may browse through your lecture notes and textbooks, underlining and highlighting sentences and phrases that interest you, trying to find preliminary connections between and among them, connections that might eventually lead to an interesting and feasible topic.

These are good strategies, good places to begin. The simple process of annotating your assignment sheet or selecting your own topic will center your assignment, encourage you to come up with some ideas to develop your topic, and help you focus the research you eventually will have to carry out.

Your topic, whether your teacher assigns it or you choose it, likely will contain key words that will help clarify the nature of the assignment. Read the assignment sheet and list of topics carefully. Look for terms such as *describe, explain, define, discuss, compare and contrast*, and *analyze*. To **describe,** in the context of an academic essay assignment, is to put into words the characteristics of your subject: Describe the architecture of homes designed by Frank Lloyd Wright. To **explain** usually requires the delineation in words of a process: Explain the process of photosynthesis. To **define** involves identifying the group to which a concept belongs and then distinguishing it from other members of that group; if you had to define the term *democracy*, you would identify it as a form of government and then illustrate how it differs from other forms. To **discuss** usually presupposes causes: Discuss the causes of World War I. To **compare and contrast** requires you to point out the similarities and differences between the two items that are the subject of your essay: Compare and contrast the themes and styles of "Ode to a Nightingale" and "Ode on a Grecian Urn." To **analyze** is to examine closely one or more of the component parts of a process or an action or an artifact (often a written text), usually as part of the larger process of analyzing the whole: Analyze Tiger Woods's long-iron game.

Stick to your topic and focus on that key word contained within it. If you are asked to compare and contrast "Ode to a Nightingale" and "Ode on a Grecian Urn," do not discuss the life of John Keats, except insofar as it might be relevant to the main topic. If you are asked to discuss the causes of World War I, do not compare and contrast the peace settlement of World War I with the peace settlement of World War II. Teachers often complain that a recurring problem in student writing is a tendency to drift away from the topic.

● Freewriting

Having considered carefully the wording of your topic, you are ready to do some brainstorming, freewriting, and other creative thinking activities designed to help you come up with information and insights that might eventually be useful in developing the paragraphs in your essay. **Freewriting** is a form of brainstorming on paper. It is a technique designed to help unblock the creative process by forcing you to write something—anything—about the subject of your assignment. The process is as follows. Using your assignment as a prompt, you write nonstop for a limited period of time, usually about ten minutes. You write whatever comes into your mind without worrying about spelling, grammar, or any other aspects of "correct" writing. No one but you sees your freewriting. After the ten minutes are up, you read your freewriting and extract from it ideas and information that might be useful to you as you write your essay. You can use these ideas as additional prompts and freewrite again and even a third time if you feel the exercise will yield results. (For an example of freewriting done as part of the prewriting process for an academic essay, see—on page 28—the freewriting Hannah did when she began working on her essay about our celebrity culture.)

W5 + H1 Questions

There are several variations on the freewriting process—other activities designed to do the same thing: to generate ideas. Journalists are taught the **W5 and H1 strategy,** which is a method of asking and answering the questions *who, what, when, where, why,* and *how* as they are developing and reporting a story. This strategy can be adapted to academic writing as well. When you have selected your topic, make up a list of W5 and H1 questions about it. Who will be reading this essay? What does he or she want from me? Who are the important people relevant to the topic? Where did important events related to my topic take place? What do I want to accomplish? When did the events relevant to my topic take place? Why did events transpire as they did? Why is this subject important? How will my reader evaluate my work? Some of these questions you will be able to answer, and at least parts of those answers eventually will find their way into your essay. Some questions you will not be able to answer, but by asking them, you at least will begin to focus your research.

Webbing

Webbing is a similar strategy, one that exploits our ability to generate ideas through free association. In the middle of a piece of paper, write and circle the topic or the concept of the paper that has been assigned to you. Jot down ideas as they occur to you and arrange them randomly around your topic or central concept. Circle each idea and draw lines between and among them and the central concept to illustrate their various relationships to each other. This linking process is especially valuable because it can reveal relationships between ideas that might not otherwise have occurred to you, relationships that might help you see an effective structure for your essay.

Suppose, for example, that you are a business major taking a marketing course. You are assigned to write an essay about how toy manufacturers market dolls. Such a topic requires research, of course, but before you begin the research process, you might try a web as a way to provide some focus and impose some structure onto your topic. Write and circle, in the center of a blank page, the phrase *marketing dolls* and see what connections you can make. (See the example on the next page)

Consider Your Reader

Writing an academic essay is a process of analyzing and synthesizing knowledge, a way of helping us to know and understand our topic in a meaningful, complex,

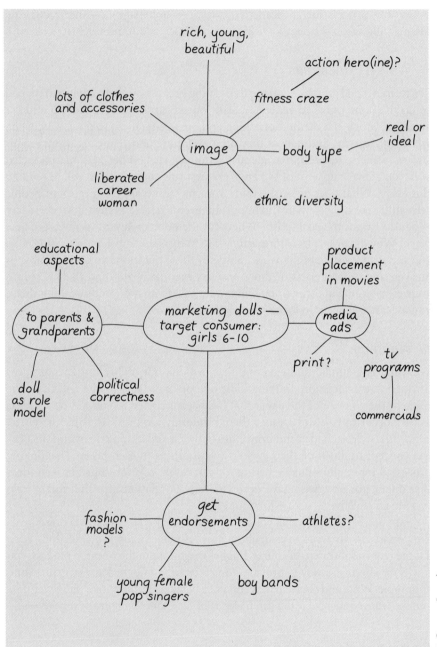

and intense way. Writing is so important a school subject—one of "the three R's"—because it requires active learning: You learn a lesson thoroughly when you have to express your knowledge of its content in writing.

You don't, however, write academic essays only for yourself. Other invisible but important participants are involved in the process: your readers. You write an essay to inform your readers, to provide them with information you want them to have or that they have requested. Or you write to convince your readers that your position on a debatable issue is valid. It is important that you consider the needs and expectations of your readers before you begin to write and while you draft, revise, and edit. Your readers will influence the content and the style of your text and, on some level, will judge its quality.

● Readers Influence Content

Your primary reader is your teacher. You might share your essay with a classmate, a friend, a tutor in your writing center, or a family member and get his or her input before you hand in your essay. Your professor might show your essay to a colleague or share it with the rest of the class. After you graduate, you might write for an employer, an employee, or a professional organization to which you belong. Throughout your life, you will write for a variety of readers, and you will have to remember that different readers require different information, even about the same subject. An article about the new Chrysler engine written for an automotive engineer would be quite different from an article on the same subject written for a car salesperson or a potential customer. For now your primary reader is your teacher, and it is his or her needs and expectations you must meet.

Those needs and expectations should be evident from the assignment sheet or from class discussion about the nature of the assignment. If they are not, it is important to find out from your professors what their expectations are. Professors might want original ideas or some evidence you have a solid understanding of the course content already covered. They might want you to tell something about the topic they do not already know, or they might want your take on one of the debatable issues discussed in class. Know what your reader wants, try to achieve those goals while you write, and your work will have a clearer focus.

It will help, as well, to know how long your reader expects your essay to be. Length will determine the level of detail you are expected to provide. An economics professor, for example, could ask for a 1,000-word or a 5,000-word essay on the law of supply and demand; the length would dictate the level of detail you would include in such an essay. Meet or exceed slightly the required length. If you do not, your ideas likely are not developed in the detail your professor wants.

Finally, clarify any important aspect of the assignment your teacher may not have made clear. Question anything not clear to you: Do you want us to include a plot summary along with our analysis of the story? How many sources do you expect us to cite? Are there sources you particularly recommend? How many words do you want? May we use subtitles? The more you know about what your reader wants, the more successful your writing will be.

● Readers Influence Style

Style identifies the manner in which you present information to your readers. If you are sending an e-mail to your friend, your writing style will be informal; your sentence structure might be fragmented; you may use slang; you will not be overly concerned about spelling.

The readers of your academic essays, in contrast, are well-educated women and men working with you in an academic setting. They will expect you to present your information in a mature and relatively formal writing style. You should not be flippant or sarcastic in an academic essay, nor, at the other extreme, should you be pedantic. Try to strike a balance with a style that is smooth and natural but appropriate for a well-educated reader.

Most of your textbooks should be written in such a style and might provide you with a model to emulate. Here, for example, is a paragraph from the essay "The Qualities of a Grade A Essay" by Edna Bell, a student in a school of education. The entire essay is on pages 166–169.

> The second quality of a Grade A essay, report, or article is that it meets the needs and expectations of its readers or "audience," to use the term many composition scholars prefer (Lunsford and Straub 179). Writers for newspapers, magazines, journals, and book publishers have an implied contract with their readers that they will present certain information, at a certain rhetorical level, in a certain style. Student academic writing is usually read and assessed by teachers and professors, who expect students to obey the rules of Standard English (Blaauw-Hara). They want to see smooth and logical transitions between and among sentences within a paragraph and paragraphs within the essay or report as a whole. They don't want to see errors in sentence grammar, sentence structure, spelling, or punctuation. They want academic voice and academic style. Academic voice is formal and steady, not ostentatious, not flippant, not sarcastic, while academic style is generally clear and concise, specifically aligned with the discourse conventions of the discipline. Scientists, for example, writing for an academic audience typically use a comparatively clear and simple sentence structure; they will use the language of their discipline, assuming that their readers share their knowledge of that language. Humanists also will use the special language—the jargon—of their discipline but typically will favor more complex sentence structure and often a less formal style.

Note, first, the length of the paragraph. At 224 words, it is longer than the typical paragraph in a letter, e-mail, newspaper, or popular magazine, but not much longer than a typical paragraph in an academic journal. It has nine sentences, with an average length of 25 words. The sentence structure is varied: the first sentence is simple; the second, complex; the third, complex; the fourth, simple; the fifth, simple; the sixth, simple; the seventh, complex; the eighth, compound; and the ninth, compound. The voice is clear and formal but not ostentatious. The paragraph is typical of the style of solid academic undergraduate writing.

● Readers Judge Quality

A friend who receives your e-mail will not judge your sentence structure, paragraph structure, spelling, or grammar. Your friend just wants the news, a casual, friendly response to his or her questions, a diversion.

Those who read your writing in an academic or business setting will judge its quality. Other students might be invited to read and respond to a draft of your essay, to make suggestions about how to make it better. In the future, colleagues and bosses will read your work and, at least indirectly, will judge its quality, especially if it does not give them the information they require.

For now, the primary judge of the quality of your writing is your professor, who will pass ultimate judgment on your work by giving it a grade. You are well advised to try to find out everything you can about the criteria your professor will use to assess your work. If your professor provides you with a list of the criteria, work closely with it as you write and revise your essay. Studies indicate that students who understand the criteria on which their writing will be judged write better essays than students who do not know how their teachers will evaluate their writing.

If your professor does not have a set of evaluative criteria or, for one reason or another, cannot provide students with one, at least keep in mind, while you draft, revise, and edit, those basic criteria for good academic writing we have already discussed: intelligence, substance, clarity, and energy. Try to write an intelligent and informative essay that is well supported with details, facts, and examples, clearly expressed in a strong and confident voice.

Establish Your Purpose

After you have considered the needs of your reader, consider your purpose in writing this academic essay. We write for many reasons: We write a letter to exchange news with friends; we write a poem to express our feelings; we keep a journal to record daily observations.

Academic writing has usually one of two purposes: to provide information that a teacher has requested or to advance an argument about an issue related to the subject you are studying. In other words, academic essays generally are written in either the **expository** or the **persuasive** rhetorical mode.

● Expository Mode

An expository or informative essay presents complete and accurate information about a specific topic. If you are asked to discuss the causes of the conflict in the Middle East, to explain how to treat a victim of a heart attack, to define poststructuralism, to compare and contrast Freudian and Jungian methods of treating obsessive-compulsive disorder, or to explain the rules of basketball, you will write an informative essay. The purpose of an informative essay is to provide your reader with information he or she has requested or can use.

There are several different patterns by which expository academic essays are typically developed. One or any combination of these patterns may be used to structure and develop an expository academic essay. Usually, one pattern will dominate, but others will be present. There may also be some elements of a narrative or persuasive mode within an expository framework.

One common expository mode is the **process analysis,** which details the parts of a process and their relationships with each other. If your health sciences professor asks you to write an essay about the circulation of the blood through the body or about how the body converts carbohydrates into energy, you will write a process paper. If your physical education professor asks you to write an essay about teaching children how to swim, you will write a process paper.

Another common expository mode is the **cause and/or effect essay.** Your economics professor, for example, might ask you to write an essay in which you explain the causes of inflation or the effects inflation has on a certain community. Your European history teacher might ask you to explain the causes of the Crimean War or to discuss changes to (the effects on) the map of Europe that resulted from the war. Your marketing professor might ask you to write an essay about why an advertising campaign for a fast-food restaurant failed or to write about how the failure affected the management structure and practices of the company. For a major paper, professors often combine the cause and effect modes: What causes inflation, and how does inflation affect an industrialized society? What caused the Crimean War, and how did the war change the map of Europe? Why did the marketing campaign fail, and what effect did the failure have on the company as a whole? In "Are Drinking Games Sports? College Athlete Participation in Drinking Games and Alcohol-Related Problems," printed in Part Two, Joel Grossbard and his research colleagues speculate on the possibility of a causal relationship between participation in college sports and alcohol abuse.

A third expository mode is the **comparison/contrast essay.** Compare and contrast the developmental theories of Jean Piaget and Jerome Bruner; compare and contrast Immanuel Kant's and Johann Goethe's concept of free will; compare and contrast the marketing campaigns of McDonald's and Wendy's. Professors often use compare/contrast assignments because these challenge the analytical ability of their students, who have to juggle and ultimately synthesize similarities and differences between two objects or concepts. The compare/contrast mode demands a fairly sophisticated organizational structure. For a good example of a compare/contrast essay, see "Faculty and College Student Beliefs About the Frequency of Student Academic Misconduct," by Hard, Conway, and Moran, in Part Three.

A fourth expository mode is the **analysis/interpretation essay.** Analyze and interpret Book I of John Milton's *Paradise Lost*, the foreign policy of President Clinton, the presidential campaign strategies of Barack Obama, Vincent van Gogh's *Starry Night*, Henry VII's role in discrediting Richard III, the advertising campaigns of hybrid cars: If you have been a college student for more than two years, you undoubtedly have encountered assignments similar to these. Analysis is the process of dividing your subject of study, your topic, into its component parts. Interpretation is the process of assessing and describing how those parts coalesce into a coherent whole and cause the enterprise you are analyzing to succeed or to break down. To write a successful analysis/interpretation essay, then, you need to define the distinguishing features of the whole, divide the whole into its component parts, analyze the parts, and interpret the relationship of the parts to the whole. In "From Sex to Sexuality: Exposing the Heterosexual Script on Primetime Network Television," in Part Three, Janna L. Kim and her colleagues analyze the gender content of several popular television programs and draw certain interpretations—about these programs' obsession with masculine sexual prowess, female sexuality, the nature of contemporary sexual politics—from that analysis.

A fifth expository mode is the **problem/solution essay,** topics for which are typically framed in the form of questions. Why did fourth-graders from poor families score low on a nationwide math test, and how can educators improve math education for this group? Why is Iran a threat to our national security, and how can we reduce this threat? Why did it take the Democratic Party so long to select a candidate for the 2008 presidential election, and what can the party do to make the process more efficient in the future? These essays have two parts: a full explanation of the nature of the problem, followed by an analysis of solutions and their likelihood of success. The student essay in Part Two, "Saving the Vancouver Island Marmot," is a good example of a problem/solution essay.

Problem

Once abundant in central and southern Vancouver Island, the marmot has become an endangered species.

Solution

Fortunately, British Columbia's Ministry of Environment and the general public are aware of the problem and want to implement an aggressive program to save *Marmota vancouverensis* from extinction.

A sixth expository mode is the essay developed by **details and examples.** Of course, details and examples are important components of all modes of academic discourse, but some academic essays have as their primary developmental system a series of facts, details, and examples. What hockey teams use the neutral-zone trap effectively? What are the most challenging mountains to climb? Who is the leading U.S. sportswear designer? These are examples of topics that require a thesis and details to support the examples.

Knowledge of the modes of the expository essay can help you structure an essay successfully and stay on topic. But remember that an academic essay is often a combination of several modes, even though one usually predominates.

● Persuasive Mode

The purpose of a persuasive essay, in part, is to present information to your readers. But its primary purpose is to convince or persuade your readers that your views on a particular controversial topic are valid and legitimate. If you are asked to discuss the causes of the civil war in Kosovo, you will write an informative essay, but if you are asked how you feel about NATO's involvement in the war, you will write a persuasive essay. If you are asked to write an essay synthesizing the reasons why Islamic fundamentalists attacked the World Trade Center, you will write an informative essay, but if you are asked to write an essay in support of or in opposition to military action in Saudi Arabia as part of a campaign to end terrorism, you will write a persuasive essay. If you are asked to define and explain the process of poststructuralist criticism, you will write an informative essay, but if you are asked if you believe poststructuralism is a viable method of literary analysis, you will write a persuasive essay.

Often academic essays straddle the expository/argumentative border. Valerie Wee's essay, "Resurrecting and Updating the Teen Slasher: The Case of *Scream*," in Part Three is clearly an argument. The first sentence of the abstract notes, "The author. . . disputes," and the second begins, "She argues." But the first third of the essay is expository, in that the author traces the history of the slasher genre, reviews the literature on slasher films that preceded the *Scream* series, and summarizes the plots of the films in the series. She then proceeds to advance her argument, the core of which is that the *Scream* films are not conservative and reactionary but advance a feminist agenda.

Hannah is taking a sophomore-level course in cultural studies. To fulfill the course requirements, Hannah must write an academic essay of approximately 1,500 words on a topic related to the content of the course and of interest to her. Hannah enjoyed most the unit on popular culture, especially her professor's lecture on the general public's obsession with even the most trivial aspects of the lives of celebrities. She decided she would like to do her essay on this topic. She knows this is a broad topic and that, as she proceeds, she will have to narrow her focus. For now, she is considering several possibilities: the history of celebrity obsession, the role of the media in perpetuating a celebrity culture, the dangerous role of the paparazzi, celebrities as role models for college students, the reasons why the public is obsessed with celebrities, and the effect this obsession has on celebrity watchers.

Hannah considers her reader:

My reader is my cultural studies professor. I am writing my essay on an aspect of popular culture but I am writing for an academic audience, so the content of my essay and its voice and style will have to respect the traditions of academic discourse. I am going to have to do a lot of research for this essay, and my prof will expect me to use reliable and authoritative sources. There will be a lot of unreliable and less than authoritative sources on celebrity obsession—probably thousands on the Internet, so I will have to be careful to verify the qualifications of the authors whose work I use. Prof. Ellis requires MLA format and five to ten sources.

Hannah determines her purpose:

What do I want to accomplish with this essay? I don't think our obsession with the lifestyles of the rich and famous is healthy. Do I want to write an argument about the need to live our own lives and to not live vicariously through other people? Or I could do an expository essay tracing the history of how we have treated celebrities in America, say, from 1900 to the present. Or maybe limit it to film stars. That would make an interesting historical essay that might trace the way we have idolized or reviled film stars from the 1920s to the present day. But I think at this point that I am most interested in the reasons why there are so many television programs and magazines about rich and famous people. What need are we trying to fulfill? I think people obsessed with celebrities have self-esteem issues. This approach would combine the informative and persuasive modes. There must be a lot of commentary about the effects of celebrity worship on our personality and on the way we relate to others—our family, friends, coworkers.

Hannah tries some freewriting:

At seven o'clock on any weeknight, I can watch at least 3 tv shows about the lifestyles of the rich and famous—what they are wearing, who they are dating, what kind of trouble they are in with the law, when their babies are due, what their houses are like, what kind of car they are driving . . . half an hour later I can watch another 3. When I go to Borders or Barnes and Noble, I can't even count the number of magazines I can read that focus on celebrities. Why have we gone so crazy? Why are we so obsessed with these people? Does the media create a celebrity culture and do we just go along like sheep? Or is the media just responding to our inherent interest in rich and famous and beautiful people? Are we lacking something in our own lives? Faith? Love? Why do we do this? How can I narrow down a topic so I can write an essay about this? Should I write an argument—we need to stop this madness. Should I do a literature review? I could do an informative essay about some aspect of the topic. I could zero in on a certain type of celebrity—athlete, pop star, television star, film star. Even politicians are fair game these days. There is some psychological need we have, some need we need to fulfill that explains all this. I'm guilty too. Maybe I could write something about the reasons why I watch these shows and at least browse through theses magazines. Those tabloids are at the checkout counter at the grocery store. No one admits buying them but their circulation is huge. Maybe there is a topic there. Maybe there is a certain demographic—do poor people buy these tabloids? Does everyone regardless of race or class? I think women buy them more than men. I'll check this out. Housewives. What about age?

Hannah considers a preliminary thesis:

At this stage of the process, Hannah is considering three possible central ideas for her essay:

- Historical approach: Ever since the 1920s, America has been fascinated by the lives of its film stars, but today this fascination has evolved into an obsession.
- Identity-based approach: People who are obsessed with the lifestyles of the rich and famous are lacking something in their own live—friends, self-esteem.
- Media-based approach: The media has created a dangerous and vicious cycle, whereby it responds to the public's demand for information

about famous people and then fuel the demand by intruding more and more into every aspect of the lives of celebrities, destroying their right to privacy and even threatening their safety.

At this point these thesis statements are in draft form. The one Hannah chooses will be clearer and more refined when it appears in the final draft of her paper.

Compose Your Thesis Statement

The end of the beginning of the writing process is the composition of the thesis statement. The thesis statement is an expression of the central or controlling idea of your entire essay. It is the essence of your academic essay, what would be left if you put your essay into a pot and boiled it down to its most essential component.

Your thesis might be very specific and incorporate the main point you want to make about your topic plus the supporting points. Here is an example of such a thesis statement for an informative essay about taking effective photographs:

To take good pictures, a photographer must pay attention to composition, lighting, and point of view.

Such a thesis is effective because it provides your reader with a blueprint, a mini plan of the body of your essay. It suggests to the reader that those three points— composition, lighting, and point of view—will be developed in more detail in subsequent paragraphs.

For a more complex essay—a persuasive essay, for example—a detailed thesis might be difficult to compose and hard to understand. For such essays, you might prefer a more general thesis, as in the following example:

If he were judged by today's standards, the narrator of John Donne's poem "The Flea" likely would face a charge of sexual harassment.

This thesis has a persuasive edge to it, which means the writer will have to acknowledge and refute opposing points and then develop and support his or her own argument. Here a general thesis is preferable because a blueprint thesis would have to encompass so much, it would seem unwieldy.

Professors often assign broad topics and expect students to narrow the topic down to a viable thesis. Broad topics are good in that they allow you to compose a thesis of interest to you and to write about whichever aspect of the topic you want to write about. But they do require you to have a strategy for narrowing a topic down to a workable thesis. For such assignments, the invention strategies discussed for reflecting on your topic—especially freewriting—work effectively. You can also narrow a topic effectively by thinking about the topic in the context of the rhetorical modes, discussed earlier in this chapter. Does the topic lend itself to a compare/contrast approach? A process analysis? An explanation of causes and/or effects?

Khaliq is a business major taking a course in business ethics. His professor wants a term paper "related to the theme of the course." The course has focused on recent cases of ethical malfeasance in certain American corporations and on laws, old and new, that attempt to curtail ethical violations. As Khaliq reviews the content of the course and freewrites about aspects of the course that interest him, he is struck by the number of laws Congress has had to pass to regulate business practices. He knows that new laws will probably be needed to regulate Internet businesses, and he considers the Internet and the law as a possible topic. But he knows this idea is still too broad. As he walks around his campus, he notices that outside the bookstore, tables are set up and piled with fake Louis Vuitton purses, Burberry scarves, and other faux designer merchandise on sale for a small fraction of the cost of the originals. He is surprised the vendors can sell this merchandise with impunity and wants to find out if what they are doing is legal and, if it is, if laws need to be developed to prevent the sales of fake goods. Using LexisNexis as his first source, he begins to research the topic. What he finds surprises him. It is illegal for a retailer to sell designer goods that he or she claims are real. But it is not illegal to sell "knockoffs," which are imitations of the real things the vendors admit are imitations. In fact, Khaliq learns that knockoffs do not have an adverse impact on the sales of the original products and may even increase their appeal. His topic becomes "Why Laws Against 'Knockoff' Products Will Never Be Passed."

● Placement of the Thesis

The thesis statement is often the final sentence of the introductory paragraph. Here, for example, is the introductory paragraph for an essay called "Prototypes for the Characters in Shakespeare's Sonnets." Note the clear thesis statement that concludes the paragraph:

> William Shakespeare was a master at describing and developing characters who are so complex and intriguing that they have become a part of our shared cultural heritage. Most literate people in the English-speaking world, indeed the whole world, know of Lear, Othello, Falstaff, Hamlet, Macbeth, Romeo, and Juliet. Many of Shakespeare's characters seem so real, in part, because they were based upon historical figures, even if the playwright did take some dramatic license in depicting these people, their motives, and their actions. Similarly, the people who appear in Shakespeare's famous sequence of 154 sonnets are rendered so authentic that many scholars, encouraged by Shakespeare's tendency to base his characters on real people, have suggested that, taken together, the sonnets tell a story based on the poet's own experiences and that the characters in the sonnets have real-life prototypes.

The thesis might be expressed in the form of a question, which the rest of the essay will answer. Here is the first paragraph for an essay about gender and pronoun agreement:

> There is no doubt that the feminist movement has influenced the English language. Only the most linguistically conservative have problems now addressing a woman, directly or in a letter, as "Ms." Sexist words such as police_man_ and fire_man_ have given way to police officers and firefighters. Restaurants hire servers now, not waiters and waitresses; airlines hire flight attendants, not stewardesses. But one problem with gender-neutral language remains. <u>How should writers use singular pronouns to refer to a singular gender-neutral noun they use in a sentence?</u>

The thesis might be spread over two sentences if the essay is long and complex. Many academic essays do not even contain a recognizable single-sentence thesis in their introductions, but the essay's central idea will certainly be implicit within the essay's introduction, especially when the essay's title helps establish a context for the introduction. Jermaine had to write a definition essay for his first-year composition class. He chose to define the term *racism*, and he titled his essay "Not Our Fathers' Race War." Here is his opening paragraph:

> A half century ago, racism in America was transparent and undeniable. Indeed, the legal system, especially in the South, institutionalized racism with laws that enforced segregation. African-Americans were denied entry into white schools, churches, and restaurants and were herded to the back of buses and subways. The Civil Rights Movement gradually abolished segregation laws, and if it is not yet completely color-blind, the American legal system now presupposes racial equality. Yet some argue that racism is alive and well, even if it is expressed in more subtle ways. Geraldine Ferraro, a prominent liberal Democrat, once a vice presidential candidate, has been, to her amazement, vilified and branded a racist for saying Barack Obama is a contender for the presidency because he is African-American. On the cover of *Vogue* magazine, basketball great LeBron James has his left arm around supermodel Gisele Bundchen; he is bouncing a basketball with his right hand, and he is screaming. Gisele is smiling, but the scream has some social commentators accusing *Vogue* of racism because that scream combined with LeBron's size and his menacing body language perpetuate the stereotype of the large black man as a sexual threat to a small white woman.

Jermaine's thesis is that the term *racism* has become difficult to define because, now more than ever before, it is in the eye of the beholder. Words and actions with no intentional racial animus are being interpreted as racially insensitive. There is not a single sentence in this paragraph that states the thesis in so many words, but through the examples Jermaine presents, his thesis is implied.

Note, finally, that at this stage of the writing process, your thesis statement is preliminary. As you think more about your topic, do some research, and write a few paragraphs, your central focus might change, and you might return to the beginning of your essay and alter your thesis. Eric, a business major, was writing an essay about the drawbacks of collaborative management. He wanted to make the point that a company is best off with a single strong leader, a person who has the charisma, vision, and work ethic that inspires employees and brings out the best in them. He knew he was going against current conventional wisdom that stressed the value of a collaborative approach—the "there is no *I* in team" approach. His early attempts at formulating a thesis were heavy-handed, criticizing as they did political correctness, arguing that democracy was fine for a government but counterproductive to business, and suggesting that a benevolent dictatorship was an ideal model for business leadership. His professor pointed out to him that he risked alienating readers, offending them even, if he appeared to question political correctness and support dictatorship in any form. He needed a less threatening, wittier opening to undercut so controversial a topic. After writing and rejecting several possibilities, Eric finally settled on the following:

> In today's business climate, collaborative management is held in high esteem, business executives reasoning that teamwork involves all in decision making and fosters a happier and hence more productive work environment. But a camel, the old saying goes, is a horse designed by a committee. When too many people are making decisions, arguing for their own point of view, and ultimately being forced to compromise, productivity declines, morale suffers, and decisions are delayed. Although in theory an enlightened and democratic concept, in practice collaborative management is less effective than management by a single person, one who inspires confidence, has some vision, and wins the loyalty of employees.

Conclusion

In writing, as in so many other activities, a strong start helps assure a smooth journey and a solid finish. You dramatically improve the chances your work will be well received if you take some time—before you draft—to consider the needs and expectations of your readers. Your work will be substantive if you take some time during the prewriting stage to generate relevant information. And if you are certain of your purpose before you begin to draft, your writing will project that rhetorical confidence good writers strive for and expectant readers appreciate.

WRITING ASSIGNMENT

Write an essay of approximately 500 words in which you describe "the typical reader" of a magazine with which you are familiar. The articles in the magazine, the ads, and the letters to the editor will give you valuable clues about the target audience at which the magazine is aimed. Include in your essay such information as the gender, age, interests, and personality of the typical reader. Note that this assignment calls for an expository essay.

EXERCISES

1. Use the methods discussed in this chapter to generate ideas for an essay on each of the following topics:
   - A person who has had a significant influence on your life
   - Typical characteristics of the dysfunctional family
   - The benefits of school uniforms
   - A review of a restaurant where you have eaten recently
   - Strikes by professional athletes
   - Sexual harassment
   - A topic already assigned to you in another course you are taking (make up your own topic if you have not yet been given an assignment)

2. Design an essay topic for each of the six expository modes discussed in this chapter.

COLLABORATIVE ACTIVITIES

1. In a small group, select an interesting topic, and design a web with this topic at its center. Make sure your topic is specific and focused, not vague or too broad.

2. Create a thesis based on one of the topics in Exercise 1. In a small group, read your thesis out loud, and then discuss ways to make it more focused.

JOURNAL PROMPT

In your journal, discuss why you think it is important to consider the needs and expectations of your readers before you begin to draft an essay and while you write and revise your essay. Assume for this journal entry that your reader is one of your professors.

CHAPTER 3

Research Your Topic

I n Chapter 2, you learned how important it is to consider the needs of your reader, determine your purpose, and think about your topic before you begin a draft of your essay. By doing this, you will begin to focus your topic and will acquire some ideas and information you might ultimately incorporate into your essay. But you will need more. You will have to find out what other people, especially the experts in the field, have to say about the subject of your essay. In other words, an academic essay requires research. Research will provide you with much of the information you will need to develop the ideas you present in your essay. Research also lends that aura of authority to your work, which your readers, especially your professor, will expect.

There are many sources writers can consult to find the information they need. The research source depends, to a certain extent, on the academic discipline for which the research is being conducted. To complete most of the academic essays assigned to you, you will have to read books and journal articles and download and read information from the Internet. You might also have to or want to interview people who will have information about the topic of your essay; it would be quite a coup, for example, to interview a poet or a novelist whose work you were explicating. Social scientists often use information from questionnaires they have designed and distributed; psychologists and sociologists observe and analyze the behavior of individuals and groups and use their "field notes" that result as a research source. In this chapter, you will learn how to find in books, articles, and Internet sources the information you need and how to use interviews, questionnaires, and observation as research sources.

Books

To find book titles that will provide some of the information you will need to discover and develop the ideas you will present in your essay, check your course outline to see if your professor has included a bibliography or a list of further readings relevant to the course material. If he or she has, and if the list includes a title that sounds relevant to your topic, do all you can to find the book and see if it contains relevant information. Study also any bibliographies or lists of further or related readings at the end of textbook chapters or at the end of the textbook itself. Most textbooks contain bibliographies, lists of related readings, or both. You should be able to determine from the titles if these works are likely to contain information that will help you develop the ideas in your essay.

Once you have a list of a dozen or so promising titles, go to your library and check your card catalog to see if your library has the books and if they are available. University libraries are computerized, so you must go to a terminal (sets of which are usually located throughout the library) and follow the instructions (which should be close by) as to how to find out if your library has the book you need. The process usually involves typing in the author's name and the title. You can probably access your university's card catalog from your dorm or, possibly, with a password and the requisite electronic access, from any location off campus.

If your library has the book, the computer screen will tell you where in the library the book is located by providing you with a **call number.** The call number is a series of letters and numbers indicating where in the library the book is stored. If, for example, the call number of the book is PE 1471.S65 1997, you find the bookshelf with a label on the end of it indicating that books with a PE call number in the 1400s are located upon this shelf. In large libraries you may have to go up one or several flights of stairs to find the letters and numbers you are looking for. There should be signs in the library directing you to the appropriate floor. The information on the computer screen will indicate whether the book is in or has been signed out and, if it has been signed out, when it is due back. If it is not due back for a long period of time, you can usually put a recall on it and get it sooner. If the book title does not come up on the screen, indicating the library does not have the book, you can sometimes access a copy through interlibrary loan if your library has reciprocal lending privileges with other libraries, as most university libraries do.

If you do not find any specific titles from course outlines or textbook sources, you will have to do a keyword or subject search. Instead of typing authors' names and book titles into the library computer, try typing in various versions of the subject of your essay. If, for example, you are taking a music history course and have to write an essay on the English madrigal, type in the word *madrigal* as a subject search, and you are bound to get some leads. You also can type in authors' names as subjects rather than as names, so for your madrigal essay, you could find sources by typing in the names *Orlando Gibbons, Thomas Weelkes,* or other English madrigal composers. Begin by making your subject search as specific as possible, so you get the most relevant information. Avoid making your search too broad, because the number of books you can access is likely to overwhelm you. Keyword searches are a good way of helping you zero in on the specific information you require. They can become quite sophisticated and involve combining words you might not necessarily think of combining. Your university librarian can help, and he or she will be happy to do so. Librarians have access to directories of keywords that can pinpoint information in a way you might not be able to.

Remember, as well, to check reference books such as encyclopedias and biographical and other specialized dictionaries. Such books are useful if you need an overview of your topic. The online edition of the *Encyclopaedia Britannica*, for example, includes a brief history of the madrigal, tracing its origins in fourteenth-century Italy and describing its popularity in sixteenth-century England. It offers links to other sites where, usually with just a click of your mouse, you can find additional information.

Periodicals

Periodicals are texts published at regular intervals: daily, weekly, monthly, quarterly, or yearly. They include newspapers, magazines, and academic journals. Some periodicals—mainly newspapers and magazines available at a newsstand—are aimed at the general reader. They are usually published daily, weekly, or monthly. Newsmagazines such as *Time* and *Newsweek*, social-issue magazines such as *The Atlantic* and *Harpers,* and subject-specific magazines such as *Psychology Today* and *National Geographic* are some general-audience periodicals you might use while researching an essay. It is possible, though less likely, you would need information from lifestyle magazines such as *Vogue, Cosmopolitan, GQ, Elle,* or *Esquire.*

Many periodicals are for readers with a specific academic interest. They tend to be published quarterly or every other month. Business majors will spend time scanning the pages of the *Harvard Business Review, Journal of Business, Business America, Business and Society, Business Quarterly,* and *Columbia Journal of World Business,* to name a very few of the periodicals in that field. Prospective English teachers will have to familiarize themselves with the *English Journal, Research in the Teaching of English, College Composition and Communication,* and *Teaching English in the Two-Year College.* Physics majors will use the *Journal of Chemical Physics, American Journal of Physics, Journal of Atmospheric and Terrestrial Physics,* and *Trionic Physics* to conduct their research. There are thousands of academic journals, at least one about any topic you can imagine.

Journals are invaluable sources of information for your academic essays. The advantage they have over books is their currency. Because they are published so regularly, the information in them is usually up-to-date.

To find a journal article that will provide you with information you might be able to use in an academic essay, you need to access your campus library database. It will likely offer you access to search engines such as Academic Search Premier or Wilson Select Plus. By typing keywords into the appropriate spaces on these sites, you will be rewarded with a list of articles related to your keyword, the journal in which the article is published, and often a link to the entire article, which you can then read or, if you think it will an especially valuable research source, print out. These search engines have an invaluable "Advanced Search" option, which allows you to refine your keywords or authors' names, limit the nature of your sources to, say, academic journals only, and limit your time range, even to the last few months, if you require the most up-to-date sources.

If, for example, you searched for "English Madrigal" in the Academic Search Premier Data Base, you would be offered a choice of about seventy relevant sources, a recent one in the Spring 2008 issue of *Musical Times*, the oldest in the March 1949 issue of *Modern Language Quarterly*. Most of these articles are on PDF files and can easily be read and printed. If you refined your search to academic journals only, you would have thirteen hits, the first ten of which are as follows:

1. MUSIC RECEIVED. Notes, Mar2007, Vol. 63 Issue 3, p706–714, 9p;
    (*AN 23975098*)
    PDF Full Text (76K)

2. Songs of Sundrie Natures (1589). By: McCarthy, Kerry. Notes, Jun2006,
    Vol. 62 Issue 4, p1049–1052, 4p; (*AN 20519862*)
    PDF Full Text (43K)

3. Psalmes, Sonets, and Songs (1588). By: Turbet, Richard. Notes, Mar2006,
    Vol. 62 Issue 3, p803–806, 4p; (*AN 20478449*)
    PDF Full Text (39K)

4. A NEWLY DISCOVERED EDITION OF WILLIAM BYRD'S PSALMES,
    SONETS & SONGS: PROVENANCE AND SIGNIFICANCE. By:
    Smith, Jeremy L. Notes, Dec2005, Vol. 62 Issue 2, p273–298, 26p;
    (*AN 19577362*)
    PDF Full Text (304K)

5. Reading the Revels. By: Dempsey, Jack. Early American Literature, Dec99,
    Vol. 34 Issue 3, p283, 30p; (*AN 2574510*)
    HTML Full Text PDF Full Text (1.6MB)

6. On Peter Riley's Lyric Excavations. By: Tuma, Keith. Chicago Review,
    1997, Vol. 43 Issue 3, p8, 10p; (*AN 9711193850*)
    Cited References (19)
    HTML Full Text

7. The hidden editions of Thomas East. By: Smith, Jeremy L. Notes, Jun1997, Vol. 53 Issue 4, p1059, 33p, 3 charts, 3bw; (*AN 9706252051*)
    Times Cited in this Database (1)
    HTML Full Text

8. Bringing the past into music classrooms. By: Snedeker, Jeffrey L. Music Educators Journal, Sep93, Vol. 80 Issue 2, p37, 5p, 4 charts; (*AN 9312061374*)
    HTML Full Text

9. WE BEN CHAPMEN. By: Hala, James. Explicator, Spring88, Vol. 46 Issue 3, p3, 2p; (*AN 7207444*)
    PDF Full Text (105K)

10. Chaucer's PROLOGUE. By: Renn III, George A. Explicator, Spring88, Vol. 46 Issue 3, p4, 4p; (*AN 7207445*)
    PDF Full Text (216K)

Note that the full text of each of these articles is available so you can click on the link to download the PDF or HTML full-text file. If the full text is not available, you might have to find the journal you need in the stacks of your library or request it through interlibrary loan. Consult your college or university librarian, if this is the case.

The Internet

The Internet is a valuable and widely used research resource. There is a warehouse of information stored in cyberspace, and it is easy to access. First you need to log on to the Internet, usually done by clicking the appropriate icon on your computer screen. If you know the Uniform Resource Locator (URL) of the source you are seeking (the URL is that string of letters and numbers usually beginning **http://www**), you can type that in your browser's Address text box (found at the top of the opening screen) and press the Enter key (or, if you are using a Macintosh, the Return key). If you do not have a URL, you can use a **search directory** or a **search engine,** which uses a computer program to search for keywords found in files and documents on the Internet. Useful and widely used search engines include Google and Yahoo. A comprehensive list of search engines is available at **http://www.searchenginewatch.com.**

If, for example, you used Google to search for *Thomas Weelkes,* the English madrigal composer, you would get over 50,000 hits. These include the Wikipedia article on Weelkes and other encyclopedia articles about him, as well. They include titles to books about Weelkes and information about where to purchase them and titles to CDs of Weelkes's music and information about where to purchase them. You will be directed to sites where you can listen to his music instantly. You will be directed to sites where you can see paintings of him and of the churches where he worked as an organist.

You must, however, exercise caution when accessing information from the Internet. Anyone can publish anything on the Internet. Unfortunately, this includes misinformation and disinformation. Some information on the Internet is biased; some is misleading; some is simply incorrect. You must make certain the website you are using is authoritative.

One clue to a website's trustworthiness is the last three letters of its URL. URLs that end in **.gov** (for *government*) or **.edu** (for *education*) are usually trustworthy, since their point of origin is typically a university or a government agency. URLs for sites that end in **.org** (for *organization*) are often biased. The website of the National Rifle Association (**http://www.nra.org**) is not a good site on which to look for unbiased information about gun control; the website of Greenpeace (**http://www.greenpeace.org**) is not going to give you unbiased information about environmental issues. URLs for sites that end in **.com** are commercial in nature and often try to sell you something, though there are reputable information sources that end with these letters, for example, the *New York Times* (**http://www.nytimes.com**) and the *Wall Street Journal* (**http://www.wsj.com**). URLs that end in **.htm** are usually personal-opinion webpages, which are sometimes very biased and unreliable.

A website should not be anonymous; if it is, be somewhat suspicious about its content. Verify that the author is an authority in his or her field before you use the site as a research source. A professor with a Ph.D. affiliated with an accredited university is usually a reliable source of information. The name and address of the university should be included, sometimes in a header or footer. If the site provides any indication that contributions have been *refereed*—that is, screened by an editorial board before being accepted on the site—you can usually be confident the source is valid and reliable. In summary, if you do not have a way of authenticating Internet information, do not use that information in your academic essay.

Interviews

Research can involve more than words on paper or a computer screen. Interviews also can be excellent sources of information. If you are writing an essay on the benefits and drawbacks of the North American Free Trade Agreement (NAFTA), you might get useful information from participants in a NAFTA conference and the leaders of the protest taking place outside conference headquarters. Interview the author of the novel you are reviewing, and you might get insights other critics missed. Interview the local Catholic priest for a perspective on church reform different from the one you are likely to get from articles in the *Washington Post*.

In some disciplines, especially in the social sciences, interviews are an important source of information.

How do you conduct a successful interview, one that is going to elicit from your subject the kind of information you need? You can take a formal approach and ask your subject specific questions you have prepared in advance. Alternatively, you can take an informal approach, prepare nothing, and simply engage your subject in a conversation that, you hope, will reveal the information that you need. Or you can choose an in-between approach and conduct a semi-structured interview, one that, although guided by a set of basic questions you need answers to, asks questions in no specific order and encourages responses to evolve into a conversation. The last approach is the most common and generally is considered the most effective.

It is important to arrange a specific place where and a time when the interview will take place. Do not expect the interviewees to come to you; instead, meet them at a time and place convenient to them. Tell the interviewees beforehand why you want to interview them and what the questions will be. The meeting will be more relaxed and productive if your subjects know what to expect. If you want to record the interview, request permission before the interview takes place. Avoid engaging your subjects in debate, but don't shy away from tough questions.

If, for example, you are interviewing that leader of the NAFTA protest, and your ultimate purpose is to elicit information about how and why a protest might degenerate into confrontation, you might begin by asking questions such as these:

- Why have you organized this protest demonstration?
- What do you hope to accomplish?
- Who primarily are you hoping to influence?

Then you could ask the more substantive questions:

- Are you prepared to take the kind of forceful action that will interrupt or end the conference proceedings?
- Do you have any plan to rouse the protestors and encourage violent acts if the conference participants and their political leaders ignore your protest?
- Under what circumstances, if any, are you prepared for physical confrontation to get your message heard?

Be polite and solicitous at all times while you conduct your interview. Be well prepared. Use the W5 + H1 heuristic (*who, what, when, where, why,* and *how*) discussed in Chapter 2 to help you generate relevant questions. Assure your interviewees that you will cite the interview appropriately in your essay.

Questionnaires

Researchers, especially social scientists, also acquire information from questionnaires that they distribute usually to the subjects participating in a study. Questionnaires are a cost-effective method of gathering data, especially now that they are easily distributed via e-mail. Many questionnaires do require confidentiality, however, so they are often mailed out to participants in the study.

It is essential that you define precisely the objectives of the questionnaire before you design and distribute it. Without a clear objective, a questionnaire can contain questions that waste participants' time, complicate the work of the researcher, and compromise the data. Suppose, for example, that a college is considering offering a diploma in technical writing, and the committee proposing the diploma decides to send a questionnaire to potential employers. An objective such as "The purpose of the questionnaire is to determine whether Sundance College should offer a two-year diploma program in technical writing" could result in a cumbersome and unfocused questionnaire that participants are reluctant to complete and return. A clear and specific objective—"The purpose of the questionnaire is to determine whether graduates of a two-year technical writing program at Sundance College could find work within the Tri-City Region"—would generate a shorter and more focused research tool that participants are more likely to respect and respond to.

There are two types of questions a researcher can include on a questionnaire. *Closed-format* questions offer participants a choice of answers for each question:

How many technical writers does your company currently employ?

   a. none
   b. one or two
   c. three or four
   d. more than four

Open-format questions offer participants the chance to provide a brief written response:

Briefly describe the projects your technical writers have participated in during the past twelve months.

With the help of computers and scanners, closed-format questions are easy to tabulate and analyze. Open-format questions require more time to process but provide richer information for the researchers to use. Most questionnaires use both types, though it is wise to limit open-format questions to those that are the most important and relevant to your study. You want as high a response rate as possible, and participants are usually more willing to respond to questionnaires that do not make too many demands on them.

Questions must be clear, succinct, and unambiguous. They should be phrased in such a way as to ensure that all respondents understand the question in the same way. Vague and hypothetical questions rarely elicit useful information. It is better, for example, to ask, "How many technical writers will your company likely be hiring over the next three years?" than to ask, "Do you think all companies need to hire technical writers?" Your questionnaire should include questions that elicit personal information only when such information is crucial to the validity of the results of your study. Responses to these questions should be optional.

Having considered her audience and her purpose, done some freewriting, and considered a few preliminary theses, Hannah begins to research her essay on the fascination our culture has with celebrity lifestyles.

Hannah decides against doing a search using a comprehensive search engine such as Google or Yahoo. She knows that, if she does, she will be overwhelmed by sources and that many of them will not be authoritative and reliable. She decides, instead, to begin by using one of the research databases to which her college library subscribes. She has four choices: Academic Search Premier, EBSCO EJS, ProQuest Research Library, and Wilson Select Plus. She knows that each database will access similar sources, and that Academic Search Premier is a well-respected database, so this is the one she chooses.

On the first search line, Hannah types "celebrity" (without the quote marks) and, on the next line, "culture" (without the quote marks), and she learns that there are 19,674 sources on her topic. Obviously this is too many, so she decides to go to the advanced search option and limit the dates, since it is our *contemporary* obsession with celebrity she wants to focus on. She limits her time frame to 2002 until the present. Now she has 11,078 sources from which to choose—still too many.

She decides she will add the word "obsession" (without the quote marks) to the third search line. Now her sources are reduced to 983, still a lot. Academic Search Premier gives Hannah the option of limiting her search to academic journals, and she considers doing so. But she decides against it. She knows that there will be good newspapers and good popular magazines with valuable information about her topic. So she decides she will begin to scan the titles of the sources Academic Search Premier has provided. She reasons that the titles will provide a good indication as to whether or not the sources are worth reading in full.

Because Hannah wants the latest information on her topic, she knows that newspaper, magazine, and journal articles will be her best sources.

But since she originally planned to begin her search at the year 2002, she has a hunch there will be books on her topic, published since then, so she decides to do an online card catalog search for books in her college library that are related to her topic. She does a keyword search, simply using the word "celebrity" (without the quote marks), and she finds two books whose titles sound very promising: *Framing Celebrity: New Directions in Celebrity Culture*, edited by Sean Redmond and Su Holms, and *Fame Junkies: The Hidden Truth Behind America's Favorite Addiction* by Jake Halpern. The former is a collection of essays, and Hannah will reference four of them in the final draft of her paper.

Hannah prepares her preliminary bibliography:

Hannah is now ready to prepare her preliminary bibliography. This is not a list of the sources Hannah *will* cite in her paper but a list she *might* cite. She has to read the sources first to determine the extent to which they will help her establish and achieve her goals.

Hannah's first-year composition teacher gave her some good advice. He told Hannah to put even her preliminary bibliography in the proper citation format, the one the professor has requested. Doing it now saves time later and will eliminate the frustration of having to sign a book or journal out again or check online again for bibliographical information.

Here is Hannah's preliminary bibliography, in the MLA format her professor wants. Of course, the sources she actually uses will be shorter and will form her Works Cited list in the paper's final draft.

Preliminary Bibliography

Carlin, Flora. "Seeing by Starlight." *Psychology Today* Aug. 2004: 8+. Print.

Chaudhry, Lakshmi. "The Diana/Whore Complex." *The Nation* 27 Aug. 2007: 22–25. Print.

Coleman-Bell, Ramona. "'Droppin' It Like It's Hot': The Sporting Body of Serena Williams." *Framing Celebrity: New Directions in Celebrity Culture*. Eds. Sean Redmond and Su Holms. London and New York: Routledge, 2006. 195–206. Print.

Halpern, Jake. *Fame Junkies: The Hidden Truth Behind America's Favorite Addiction*. Boston: Houghton Mifflin, 2007. Print.

Hecom, Dale. "Satisfaction Rates Among Women Undergoing Celebrity Influenced Cosmetic Surgery." *Southwest Journal of Contemporary Culture* 3.3 (2005): n. pag. Web. 9 Feb. 2008.

Feasy, Rebecca. "Get a Famous Body: Star Styles and Celebrity Gossip in *heat* Magazine." *Framing Celebrity: New Directions in Celebrity Culture*. Eds. Sean Redmond and Su Holms. London and New York: Routledge, 2006. 177–194. Print.

Franco, Judith. "Langsters Online: K.D. Lang and the Creation of Internet
   Fan Communities." *Framing Celebrity: New Directions in Celebrity Culture*.
   Eds. Sean Redmond and Su Holms. London and New York: Routledge,
   2006. 269–284. Print.
Gilsdorf, Ethan. "Celebrity Gossip's Siren Call Grows Louder." *Christian Science
   Monitor* 12 Jan. 2007. Academic Search Premier. n. pag. Web. U. of
   Athabaska Lib. Athabaska. 15 March 2008.
Redmond, Sean. "Intimate Fame Everywhere." *Framing Celebrity: New
   Directions in Celebrity Culture*. Eds. Sean Redmond and Su Holms. London
   and New York: Routledge, 2006. 27–44. Print.
Rosenstein, Bruce. "The Good, Bad and the Ugly of America's Celeb
   Obsession." *USA Today* 1 Dec. 2003: 1B. Print.
Weir, Jill. "Why We Are Celebrified." *CultureCow.com* 18 Mar. 2006. 8 Feb.
   2008. n. pag. Web.

Hannah prints out the six articles. Then she scans all of her sources.
Next, she reads carefully and makes notes on the ones she thinks will help
her as she drafts her essay. In the end, she will cite, in the final draft of her
paper, eight of the eleven sources she first identified as promising.

Incorporating Research

Once you have gathered information from sources—the information that you
will use to develop the ideas in your essay—you must decide whether to quote
that information just as it appears in the source or to paraphrase it. It is a good
strategy to include some direct quotes in a research paper, especially when the
quote blends with your own voice and clearly elucidates the point you are making. It is a very poor strategy to use a lot of direct quotes connected together by
transitional sentences. This "cut and paste" method yields an essay that is imper-
fectly organized and dissonant. Too many voices do to an essay what too many
cooks do to the broth. It is usually better, then, to paraphrase.

● Direct Quotes

If the information you want to quote directly takes up four lines or less in your essay,
enclose the quote in quotation marks and integrate it into the text of your essay.

Nielsen disagrees, insisting that "diplomacy is always worth the risk" and
arguing that "a delay of two months does not give a nation without nuclear
weapons enough time to acquire them" (35).

If the direct quote is more than four lines, separate it from the rest of the text and
do not enclose it in quote marks, unless the source itself contains them.

The narrator is typically described as a love-struck adolescent with his first crush on the older sister of his friend. But his anxious intensity suggests that he is more obsessed with Mangan's sister than infatuated with her and his obsession is spiritual in nature:

> Her name sprang to my lips at moments in strange prayers and praises which I myself did not understand. My eyes were often full of tears (I could not tell why) and at times a flood from my heart seemed to pour itself out into my bosom. I thought little of the future. I did not know whether I would speak to her or not or, if I spoke to her, how I could tell her of my confused adoration. But my body was like a harp and her words and gestures were like fingers running upon the wires. (Joyce 62)

Summarizing

Rather than quote directly, writers of academic papers often summarize or paraphrase a passage from a source. A paraphrase, described in the next section, is a recapitulation of an original passage, expressed in the distinctive voice and style of the essay writer doing the paraphrasing. A summary is simpler. It maintains the style of the original but reduces the original to its essence. Consider, for example, these two passages:

Original

It is an enduring mystery of the Bush White House that no one seems to know exactly when, how or why Bush decided to invade Iraq in 2003. But no such confusion clouds how the surge of 2007 was hatched. In December 2006, even as the Iraq Study Group was urging the President to begin a staged withdrawal from Iraq, another group of experts was putting together a very different plan. Fred Kagan of the American Enterprise Institute and retired Army General Jack Keane began calling not for a pullout but for an escalation of troops—a one-time infusion of combat soldiers to push the insurgents out of Baghdad. The Kagan-Keane plan found an eager audience at the National Security Council and with Vice President Dick Cheney. Within days, the plan had been sold to Bush, who pulled out a lot of stops to persuade the Pentagon—as well as colleagues in Congress. One Republican lawmaker, having watched his party lose control of both houses because of the war just a few months before, told Bush in a White House meeting that he would support the surge but that the strategy was a little like throwing a Hail Mary on fourth down. At about the same time, Bush told General David Petraeus, the top U.S. general in Iraq, that he would be getting additional troops.

(From "The Surge at Year One" by Michael Duffy,
Time *Magazine Online, Jan. 31, 2008)*

Summary

In December 2006, the Iraq Study Group was urging the President to withdraw from Iraq. At the same time, others in support of the war argued in favor of an escalation of troops. President Bush sided with those in favor of the surge. Although one Republican lawmaker professed support of the plan but worried about its chances for success, the President told the top U.S. general in Iraq that more troops would be forthcoming.

The original contains 225 words, and the summary 74. The summary is about a third the length of the original, which is the highest original-to-summary ratio you want.

Paraphrasing

Paraphrasing is the process of revising a passage from a written text so that the revised version is written in the manner and style of the paraphraser and not the original author. Writers paraphrase information to make certain that information clearly develops their ideas and to maintain the stylistic integrity—the voice—of their work.

To paraphrase a source effectively, make sure you understand the original completely. Read the original carefully several times; then try to write the paraphrase without consulting the original. In this way, you will be more likely to put the original into your own words and produce a paraphrase that will blend in with your essay clearly and effectively. Then check your paraphrase against the original to make certain you have not altered the meaning of the original. Remember that you want the paraphrased information to blend seamlessly into your own work. Remember too that your paraphrase will often be longer than the original, because you might need to establish a context within the paraphrase for your reader. The context often includes the name of the original author, the circumstances under which the author wrote the passage you are paraphrasing, and an explanation, elaboration, or clarification of some of the ideas in the original.

Here is an example of the evolution of an effective paraphrase. Kay was working on an essay about the influence of Bible interpretation on religious reform and wanted to use this information from *Pears Cyclopaedia* (103rd ed. 1995).

The wholesale vending of indulgences by the papal agents had incensed the people, and when Luther denounced these things he spoke to willing ears. After much controversy, the reformers boldly propounded the principles of the new doctrine and the struggle for religious supremacy grew bitter. They claimed justification (salvation) by faith, and the use as well as the authority of the Scriptures, rejecting the doctrine of transubstantiation, the adoration of the Virgin and Saints, and the headship of the Pope. (J46)

First Kay simply substituted her own words for some of those in the original:

> The selling of absolution from sin by the pope's agents angered the people, and when Luther criticized indulgences the people listened. After much controversy, the reformers touted the principles of the new doctrine and the struggle for religious power grew bitter. Reformers claimed justification (salvation) by faith, and the use as well as the authority of the Bible, rejecting the doctrine of transubstantiation, the worship of the Virgin and Saints, and the supremacy of the Pope.

Kay realized this version did not complement her own writing style and did not support her thesis as strongly as she needed it to. She read the original a few more times and then put it aside so her paraphrase would be in her own style and would stress Luther's appeal to the Bible, which is the point most important in defense of her thesis.

> It was not difficult for Luther to undermine the Pope's authority. The people resented the Pope's agents who sold indulgences to the highest bidder. When Luther began to question Papal supremacy, the worship of the Virgin and the saints, and the doctrine of transubstantiation, the people were predisposed to listen. The struggle grew bitter, but Luther further justified his intransigence by appealing to the authority of the Bible and, in so doing, won over many converts.

Here are two other original passages followed by effective paraphrases. Study them carefully to get a sense of what you need to do to put someone else's words into your own.

Original
He that hath wife and children hath given hostages to fortune; for they are impediments to great enterprises, either of virtue or mischief. Certainly the best works and greatest merit for the public have proceeded from the unmarried or childless men: which both in affection and means have endowed the public.
(From "Of Marriage and Single Life" by Francis Bacon)

Paraphrase
Even Francis Bacon, writing some four hundred years ago, denounced the value of family life, advancing the extraordinary argument that family actually inhibits success. A man with a wife and children, wrote Bacon, is less likely to be productive than the single man; indeed, words

and deeds that have truly benefited society have come from single or childless men.

Original
Secondly, the poorer tenants will have something valuable of their own, which by law may be made liable to distress, and help to pay their landlord's rent, their corn and cattle being already seized and money a thing unknown.
(From "A Modest Proposal" by Jonathan Swift)

Paraphrase
Swift's second argument is even more heart-rending. Even the poorest couples, he notes, can have children and will have, therefore, tangible assets which they can sell to pay their rent and other debts. Into this argument Swift injects another attack against the treachery of absentee landlords, attacking their practice of claiming all of the corn and cattle of their tenants without compensation.

Remember that a paraphrase must be cited just as a direct quote from a source is cited. The information does not become yours just because you express it in your own words. You need not acknowledge information about a topic you possessed before you wrote an essay or report about that topic, but you do need to acknowledge all of the information you learned about a topic in the course of writing an essay or report about it.

● Plagiarism

If you do not acknowledge all of the sources from which you borrowed information—whether you quoted directly from these sources or paraphrased information—you are likely guilty of the serious academic offense of **plagiarism**. Plagiarism is the failure on the part of a writer to recognize the work of others. It is the theft of one writer's knowledge or direct written text by another writer, an attempt by one writer to imply to readers that he or she has created work that was actually taken from another. Because work on such a wide variety of topics is readily available on the Internet, plagiarism has become an increasingly common and serious problem. Fortunately, the Internet is not only a source of the problem but also a source of the solution, since it is as easy for a professor to detect plagiarism through the Internet as it is for a writer to download an essay on the assigned topic. In most schools, plagiarism is punished incrementally: For the first offense, the student fails the assignment; for the second, the course; and for the third, the offending student is at serious risk of being expelled from the college.

For a thorough discussion of plagiarism and other forms of academic misconduct, see, in the anthology of readings in Part Three, the report "Faculty and College Student Beliefs About the Frequency of Student Academic Misconduct" by Hard, Conway, and Moran. In that essay, the authors not only define plagiarism, but also identify specific behaviors that constitute plagiarism. You may be guilty of plagiarism if you engaged in any of the following conduct:

- Submitted another's material as your own for academic evaluation
- Prepared work for another student to submit for academic evaluation
- Worked with another student on material to be submitted for academic evaluation when the instructor had not authorized working together
- Copied sentences, phrases, paragraphs, tables, figures, or data directly or in slightly modified form from a book, article, or other academic source without using quotation marks or giving proper acknowledgment to the original author or source
- Copied information from Internet websites and submitted it as your own work
- Bought papers for the purpose of turning them in as your own work.

Citing Sources

The extent to which the academic community takes seriously the proper acknowledgment of secondary sources is indicated by the elaborate citation systems it has developed. The Modern Language Association, for example, has a 292-page *MLA Handbook for Writers of Research Papers*, now in its seventh edition, which explains how to cite sources correctly if you are writing an essay in the humanities. Similarly, the American Psychological Association publishes a 439-page *Publication of the American Psychological Association*, now in its fifth edition, which explains how to cite sources correctly if you are writing an essay in the social sciences. The University of Chicago publishes another guide to citing sources, *The Chicago Manual of Style*, now in its fifteenth edition.

These three methods for citing sources thoroughly and accurately are described in detail in Chapter 8. That chapter also includes two model student essays, one that uses MLA Style and one that uses APA Style.

Conclusion

Undoubtedly, you have heard expressions such as "all flash and no substance" and "too much sizzle, not enough steak." If used to describe a speaker or writer, they would criticize someone who looks good, sounds good, and writes clearly but whose ideas are lame and insubstantial. Writing that is glib and superficial might be effective in some circumstances—to sell soap or to prompt a response to a personal ad, for example—but it is antithetical to academic writing. Academic writing is prized for its depth and substance. Read the books, scholarly articles, and websites written by the leading authorities in the subject you are writing about, and integrate your work with theirs—properly acknowledged, of course. In academic writing, flash is optional; substance is essential.

WRITING ASSIGNMENT

Find some information in popular magazines and on the Internet about one of the following topics. Write an essay of approximately 750 words on the topic you select. (Your instructor might simply want you, at this stage, to gather the information.) Cite correctly the sources you use. See Chapter 8 for more information on citing sources.

- Why _____ is an outstanding (select one) actor, recording artist, talk show host, basketball (or football, hockey, etc.) player, clothing designer, or novelist
- A product I would never buy
- Why soap operas are so popular
- Why "professional" wrestling is so popular

RESEARCH EXERCISES

Select a topic of interest to you. (If you are currently working on an essay for one of your other courses, you may use that essay's topic, if your instructor approves.)

1. List five periodicals that are likely to contain information relevant to your topic.

2. Look up your topic in a reference book—in print or online—that includes bibliographies at the end of its entries. Then look up and record the call number of one of the books mentioned in the bibliography. Find the book in the stacks. Read the first chapter of that book, and write a brief summary of its contents.

3. Find on the Internet a source of information relevant to your topic. Write a brief summary of its contents.

PARAPHRASING AND SUMMARIZING EXERCISE

Summarize and paraphrase the following passages:

If we were a people much given to revealing secrets, we might raise monuments and sacrifice to the memories of our poets, but slavery cured us of that weakness. It may be enough, however, to have it said that we survive in exact relationship to the dedication of our poets (include preachers, musicians and blues singers).

(From "Graduation" by Maya Angelou)

The films' plots essentially examine the issue of trust in romantic relationships, using the slasher film conventions as an allegory through which we explore the turmoil of female adolescence. Sidney's horror at discovering that she had unknowingly dated the boy who raped and killed her mother may be read as a metaphor for every teenage girl's fear that she does not really know her boyfriend.

(From "Resurrecting and Updating the Teen Slasher: The Case of Scream*" by Valerie Wee)*

When in 1999 President Bill Clinton (not George W. Bush) finally decided to intervene militarily to stop the genocidal war in Bosnia—an intervention that had been called for by French public opinion for months and months—the same French people were quick to tell pollsters (by the huge margin of 60 percent) that "the Americans did it for their own political and military interests," with a meager 24 percent granting the possibility that they might have done it "for human rights and democracy." Clearly, for most French people, even in the ragged, oil-free hills of Kosovo, the greedy Yankees were conducting war and business as usual—that is, according to the preset global perception that French anti-Americanism has nurtured for so many decades.

(From "Global Anti-Americanism and the Lessons of the 'French Exception'" by Philippe Roger)

With his commission revoked by the governor of Cuba, Cortés arrived on the mainland as a rebel against both the governor of Cuba and the king of Spain. Much of what he did concerning the great Aztec Empire was an attempt to justify his initial act of insubordination and win back royal support. Cortés burned his ships so that his troops were forced to go with him. Then he founded the city of Vera Cruz, whose town government, which was his own creation, offered him a new commission to proceed inland to Tenochtitlán. He quickly found allies among native groups that for their own reasons wished to see the Aztec Empire destroyed.

(From Western Civilization: The Continuing Experiment, *by Thomas F. X. Noble et al., Houghton Mifflin, 1999)*

COLLABORATIVE ACTIVITY

Working with two or three classmates in a small group, design a questionnaire for a study designed to help solve a problem—parking, traffic, crime, recreation—at your college or in the community it serves. Establish a clear objective for the study, and identify the group or individuals to whom you would send the questionnaire.

JOURNAL PROMPT

What kind of information have you looked for on the Internet? How successful was your search? How did you conduct the search? If you have never used the Internet to buy a product or a service or to acquire information, explain the reasons why you have never done so. Explain the advantages and disadvantages of the Internet as a research source.

CHAPTER 4

Make a Plan

In this book, planning follows thinking and researching as steps in the writing process, and, indeed, most writers probably do most of their planning at this point. But planning really begins when you annotate your assignment sheet and choose a topic, and it continues while you write and revise your essay. Always remember that planning an academic essay is an ongoing process, not a single step along the road to the production of a text. You likely will alter your plan as you draft and revise your essay, because the drafting and revising processes often stimulate the production of additional ideas and information that you might want to incorporate into your essay. Your plan is made of clay, not granite. You will want to mold it throughout the writing process to change it as you discover new insights into and new information about your topic.

Planning is an important component of the writing process. It is at this point that a writer begins to decide what information needs to be included and establishes the order in which that information can be presented most effectively. I say "begins to decide" because good writers continue to consider content and order as they write; they may add, delete, or reorder information. All of these decisions—what to include, what order to present information in, what to change while drafting is under way—depend upon the writer's commitment to fulfilling his or her purpose and meeting the needs and expectations of his or her readers.

Many writers, at the planning point in the process, produce a point-form summary of the main ideas and supporting ideas they want to include in their essay. Some writers produce a detailed plan in complete sentences divided into any number of headings and subheadings; some writers produce a brief, point-form plan. You can use a system of numbers and letters to indicate main headings and subheadings or simply indicate these with dashes and indentations.

From Chapter 2's discussion of reflecting on the purpose for writing, recall that academic essays usually are written in either the expository (also known as the informative) or the argumentative (also known as the persuasive) mode. The mode you choose will determine your plan. Planning an **expository essay** is usually a fairly straightforward process, because the plan is often implicit in the topic. Planning one form of the expository mode, the **compare/contrast essay,** is a bit more complicated. And the **argumentative essay** requires a strategy and some information not usually included in an expository essay. To write a sound argumentative essay, you need to know this strategy and the information required for an effective argument.

Planning an Expository Essay

In Chapter 2, you learned about the various developmental patterns for expository academic essays: process analysis, cause and/or effect, comparison/contrast, analysis/interpretation, problem/solution. The outline you develop as a prewriting activity (remember, your outline will evolve as you draft and revise) will depend upon the developmental pattern you choose, which, in turn, will depend upon the way in which your topic is presented. If, for example, the topic on your assignment sheet reads, "Explain how and why the polar bear became an endangered species, and discuss what needs to be done to ensure its survival," your outline will be based upon a problem/solution format: Here is the problem (the polar bear is becoming extinct); here are the solutions (end global warming, protect its habitat, do more research, start a fund-raising campaign).

Remember also that an essay might require more than one developmental pattern. If, for example, your topic is the role of complex carbohydrates in a well-balanced diet, you are writing primarily an effects essay: How do complex carbohydrates affect diet and nutrition? But certainly you need to invoke other patterns of development as you compose and revise. Definition is one important aspect of the essay in that you have to define key terms such as *calorie, carbohydrate,* and *fiber.* The details/examples pattern is another important aspect of the essay in that you have to provide *examples* of foods that contain complex carbohydrates and add *details* about the chemical and nutritional content of these foods, before describing how these foods affect human metabolism.

Hannah is ready to make a preliminary plan for her essay about the modern-day obsession with celebrities. Writing is a recursive process, so Hannah's plan will continue to evolve as she drafts and revises. She won't be certain what her final plan will look like until she is working on her final draft. But a preliminary, working plan is a good reminder of the importance of structure in an essay and gives the writer some idea of what information will go in what sections and paragraphs of the essay.

Hannah's working title:

The Benefits and Drawbacks of Our Celebrity Culture
Note this is a working title and is not the one Hannah will ultimately use.

Hannah's working thesis:

When she began to research her essay, Hannah thought her suspicions would be confirmed: People who are obsessed with the lives of celebrities are lacking something in their own lives, and such people need to work on establishing bonds with "real" people, or they risk their psychological health. She was thinking her thesis might be along these lines:

> People who are obsessed with the lives of celebrities have low self-esteem and difficulty forming bonds with others.

But what she learned from her research was more complicated: Some of her sources suggest that gossip actually has a social function. Moreover, celebrity watchers often want to look as good as the celebrities they watch, so they can be motivated to adopt a healthier lifestyle.

Hannah's suspicions were not wrong—most of the sources she read did note that celebrity obsession can be unhealthy, even dangerous. But others noted that gossip is useful insofar as it is fun and diverting and helps people form social bonds. Hannah realizes her thesis has to be more sophisticated. It has to point to the deleterious effects celebrity worship can have on self-esteem and socialization but also acknowledge that, for many if not most celebrity watchers, it is a harmless diversion. Her working thesis becomes:

> For most people a fascination with the lives of the rich and famous is a harmless diversion, but for some it can threaten self-esteem and inhibit the ability to connect with others on a social level.

Hannah's tentative plan:

At first, Hannah decides she will build her essay around these two points—self-esteem and social bonding—and show how an interest in celebrities both increases and decreases self-esteem and social bonding. As she reflects upon this plan and begins her first draft, however, she sees a flaw: This plan might suggest that celebrity worship is equal parts a positive and negative influence in our culture. What she really wants to say is that, while there may be some benefits to celebrity worship, there are more downsides. Her research confirms that this is so.

She decides, then, to change her plan. She will begin by talking about the benefits of an interest in celebrity lifestyles and then talk about the drawbacks. Since there are fewer benefits, the first part of her essay will be shorter than her second. And since she wants to focus on the drawbacks, she will put them in the more rhetorically powerful second position. Here, then, is Hannah's working plan for an essay she is now thinking of calling "The Benefits and Drawbacks of Our Celebrity Culture":

I. Benefits
   A. Empowers women who are main consumers of celebrity gossip
   B. Motivates us to look better, so leads to healthier lifestyle
   C. Source of conversation with others; hence builds social bonds

II. Drawbacks
   A. Anti-feminist—does not empower women—perpetuates stereotypes about beauty and worth
   B. Diminishes self-esteem—can't live up to the ideal celebrities represent
   C. Distracts attention away from more important things in life—family and friends
   D. Can become dangerous obsession and psychologically damaging

Planning a Compare/Contrast Essay

The compare/contrast essay, in which you are asked to discuss the similarities and differences between two related subjects (two literary works, two economic systems, two political systems, two psychological theories, two marketing strategies), is commonly assigned in most college and university courses. Professors assign the compare/contrast essay often because it requires students to master two aspects of course content: to analyze each and then to establish some form of synthesis between them. The compare/contrast essay demands a higher level of thinking than some other expository modes do. There are two ways of organizing a compare/contrast essay: the common-traits method or the similarities/differences method.

The **common-traits method** is the best method to use if you are writing primarily an informative essay, one in which you want to point out similarities and differences between two entities without suggesting that one is superior to the other. If you are comparing and contrasting two cities, for example, you might isolate common traits of climate, ethnic diversity, and architecture and discuss each trait in the context of the two cities. As another example, suppose you are comparing and contrasting the talk patterns of men and women. You want to compare the reasons why men talk with the reasons why women do; you want to compare the places women tend to talk with the places men do; and you want to compare what women talk about with what men do. The plan for such an essay might be as follows:

Thesis: Men and women communicate in essentially different ways and are often at odds with each other as a result.

I.   Why Men and Women Talk
   A.   Women to build bridges, establish cooperation, negotiate relationships—to build rapport with others—"rapport-talk"
   B.   Men not to distance themselves from others but to preserve independence—talk is more competitive—talk to negotiate and maintain status—"report-talk"

II. Where Men and Women Talk
   A.   Women more communicative at home, on the phone, around the breakfast table
   B.   Men more silent at home—stereotypically buried behind the newspaper at the breakfast table—their silence a source of frustration to wives, as wives' chatter a source of distraction to men—men more communicative in public

III. What Men and Women Talk About
   A.   Women of internal matters—share secrets, discuss relationships, personal appearance—use personal anecdotes to support an argument
   B.   Men of external matters—sports—more likely to tell jokes in public—use logic to defend argument and find women's argumentative style inadequate—believe many of the things women talk about unworthy of the energy it takes to utter them

Conclusion: Men complain that women change topic or shift focus before a conversation is finished; women counter that they need to personalize discussion if it is to resonate with them.

(Adapted from "Rapport-Talk and Report Talk,"
by Deborah Tannen. In You Just Don't Understand.
Harper Collins, 1990)

This compare/contrast essay offers no judgment about whose conversational style is superior. That is not its purpose. Its purpose is simply to compare and contrast communicative styles along gender lines and to offer a wide range of examples, often in the form of anecdotes, to support your views. For this reason, such an essay would be organized with the common-traits approach because the author reflects upon why and where men and women talk and what they talk about.

The **similarities/differences method** is the best one to use if your compare/contrast essay has a persuasive edge to it, that is, if your purpose is to suggest that one of the two items you are comparing and contrasting is superior to the other.

Benazir was planning a compare/contrast essay about the whole-language method and the phonics method of teaching reading to young children. She wanted to convey her opinion that the whole-language method is superior. Here is her plan:

Title: Two Methods of Teaching Children to Read

(Preliminary) Thesis: Educators are divided over how to teach children how to read, though the weight of the evidence now favors the whole-language method.

 I. Similarities
  A. Both methods have the same aim.
  B. Both methods are validated by research.
  C. Most teachers use both methods, at some point.

 II. Differences
  A. The educational theory underlying each method is different.
  B. Children enjoy the whole-language method more.
  C. Teachers enjoy teaching the whole-language method more.
  D. The whole-language method is more authentic.
  E. The whole-language method teaches not only reading but also values and attitudes.

Conclusion: While both methods of teaching reading are effective, the whole-language method offers additional benefits that the phonics method does not.

Take a moment to compare the two outlines in this section. Note that the common-traits outline contains three main divisions specifying, without value judgment, the "why, where, and what" of girl talk or "rapport-talk" and then of boy talk or "report-talk." The similarities/differences outline, in contrast, has only two main divisions: how the methods are similar and how they are different. Note that under the "Differences" heading, the persuasive edge emerges, as the writer begins to highlight ways in which the whole-language method is superior. The common-traits outline has no such argumentative edge.

Planning an Argument

An argumentative academic essay is a written text that makes a claim or asserts a thesis on an issue about which there is disagreement, provides clear evidence in support of the claim or thesis, and summarizes and refutes evidence in opposition to the claim or thesis. Here we use *argument* and *persuasion* as synonymous terms, though some professors draw a distinction between the two, asserting that an argument does not necessarily urge a change in outlook or behavior while a persuasion does, and that therefore an argument is more dispassionate than a persuasion. The distinction might be valid, but the qualities of effective persuasions and arguments are similar enough that the two modes can be considered together. The ultimate purpose of a persuasive/argumentative essay is to convince readers that your opinion on an issue is thoughtful and reasonable and therefore valid.

Arguing convincingly and persuasively is an art that requires careful planning and a good knowledge of various argumentative strategies. An argument is more complex than an exposition. Both arguments and expositions assert a thesis and present details, facts, anecdotes, statistics, causes, effects, comparisons, contrasts, and examples in a series of paragraphs in support of that thesis. Both cite authoritative sources to support and develop a thesis. But an argument has a different purpose. While the expository academic essay informs and teaches, the argument attempts to convince readers of the validity of one side of an issue and—equally important—the invalidity of the other side; in its persuasive incarnation, it may urge readers to change their own minds, even commit themselves to a course of action. To present a convincing case, an argumentative academic essay takes shape in a way an exposition does not.

To support an expository thesis, for example, you have to present all important and relevant information. When you write an argument, you must not be deceptive, but you can be selective in the information you present to strengthen your case, stressing those points that strongly support your thesis and downplaying those that do not. Suppose, for example, you are arguing that health care should be a right and not a privilege, and that the government should provide health care coverage for all legal U.S. residents. You might not mention the long waits for surgery in countries that provide universal health care coverage, or you might at least downplay their significance. In an expository essay comparing and contrasting the Canadian and U.S. health care systems, you would include such information as a matter of course to meet the expectations implicit in the expository mode.

In addition, argumentative essays often include an emotional appeal, rarely part of an exposition. You can sway an audience by appealing to its emotions. As part of an argument in support of a particular political candidate, you might point out that this candidate is from a poor, minority background and so deserves a break more than does the candidate's rich and privileged opponent. Or, as part of an anti-handgun essay, you might tell the story of an innocent child tragically killed in a drive-by shooting. There is a fine balance here, of course. Emotional appeals must be measured. If you are too dramatic and too sentimental, your chances of alienating your readers become greater than your chances of winning them over.

Finally, an argument includes an acknowledgment and refutation of the opposing point of view, which an exposition does not. You might think that you weaken your argument if you openly admit there is another side to your case, but in fact you strengthen it. If you do not admit openly that there is another side, your readers will still know that there is. They will conclude that you are afraid to raise those issues that weaken your argument; you will lose credibility, and the strength of your case will diminish. This strategy of acknowledging the opposition also strengthens the voice of your essay. You appear fair, honest, and trustworthy, and you (and therefore your argument) are more likely to be taken seriously. And remember that you are acknowledging the opposition in order to refute it, so you are supporting, not undermining, your thesis.

Dwight wanted to present an argument defending Black liberation theology (BLT) against charges that it is a racist and divisive movement within the Christian church, against charges that it is, in fact, anti-Christian. He talked about the success that BLT churches have had recruiting new members at a time when attendance rates at most Christian churches are declining precipitously. He described the many successful programs BLT churches have sponsored to feed the homeless, raise scholarship money so minority students could attend college, and build affordable housing. He pointed out that BLT churches have preached against sexual promiscuity and praised the sanctity of the family, both important Christian values. He did not shy away from criticisms that the rhetoric coming from the pulpits of BLT churches was often incendiary and anti-white, nor did he deny that such rhetoric is a part of the culture of Black liberation theology churches. Instead, he made the elegant argument that the pastors were using a tried-and-true rhetorical strategy—hyperbole—less to provoke anger among white people or even prove their arguments than to underscore their passion for reform. He further refuted the opposing position by making the clever case that the Black liberation theology sermon is a form of theater, a one-act play, which the parishioners recognize and accept as creative nonfiction. Dwight made a strong case for his thesis and buttressed it further by acknowledging and refuting the opposing point of view.

A strong argument, then, requires not only solid facts, evidence, statistics, examples, and details but also a strategy for planning and for presenting such information in a way that maximizes its credibility. Some leading philosophers and scholars have developed sophisticated systems of presenting the kind of evidence writers need to develop and support an argument. Some basic knowledge of these systems will help you gather the information you need to argue effectively and to plan a strategy for presenting the information clearly, and will suggest methods of conveying that information convincingly.

● Aristotle: Logos, Ethos, Pathos

Aristotle believed that an effective arguer uses logic and reason to support and advance his or her case, conveys an impression of trustworthiness and sincerity to win the audience's respect and attention, and appeals to the audience's feelings and emotions to draw them in on a personal level to support the position the arguer is advancing. Logos, ethos, pathos—these are the three foundations of an effective Aristotelian or classical argument.

Logos

To Aristotle, an effective argument is a logical argument. A logical argument presents evidence, refutes opposing viewpoints, and avoids logical fallacies. A logical argument incorporates statistics, facts, and quotes from experts to convince readers of the veracity of the writer's thesis. It also anticipates and avoids errors in logic, which undermine the evidence the writer is presenting. **Logical fallacies**—that is, errors in logic—usually present overly simple arguments in support of complex problems or insufficient evidence in support of a point.

Hasty Generalization. Suppose, for example, you are a new student in the College of Education, and you have gone to your first two classes. The professors in both classes are not exactly lively and inspiring. You e-mail your friend, telling him that education professors are all dull. You have a flaw in logic here, usually known as the **hasty generalization.** You have drawn a conclusion, made a general statement, based on insufficient evidence. You cannot generalize based on a sample size of two.

Post Hoc Ergo Propter Hoc. An editorial in a national newspaper argues for a ban on violent video games such as Grand Theft Auto because a fifteen-year-old boy hijacked a car and threatened the driver with a handgun, right after playing the game. The game might have been one factor, but usually a complex set of experiences, behaviors, and personality traits cause serious crime. You cannot argue that the game *caused* the crime. This logical fallacy is called **post hoc ergo propter hoc,** which in Latin means "after this, therefore because of this." You can argue that one event or action contributed or may have contributed to another, but avoid claiming that one event or action caused another.

False Analogy. Suppose you argue that all exams should be open-book because, in the real world, doctors, lawyers, businesspeople, and others must consult books in order to do their work effectively, and one of the purposes of a college education is to prepare students for the real world. This is a **false analogy.** College prepares students for the real world, but it is not the real world. A test measures knowledge more than it measures the ability to perform a certain task. To equate surgery, say, to a written exam is to make an inaccurate comparison, to draw a false analogy.

Ad Hominem. You oppose a senator's proposal to extend government-funded health care to poor minority children because that senator is a liberal Democrat. This is a common logical fallacy known as **ad hominem,** which is Latin for "against the man." Instead of dealing with the argument, you preempt any discussion by basically saying, "I cannot listen to anyone who does not share my social and political values." You indeed may decide you don't like the argument the senator is making, but it is your job to poke holes in the argument, not to engage in a personal attack.

Straw Man. A similar logical fallacy is known as the **straw man.** Suppose, for example, you are making the case for your belief that the spirits of dead people can continue to communicate with the living. As part of your argument, you claim that people who don't share your views are atheists. It is likely true that atheists have problems believing in a spiritual existence after death, but not true that only atheists disagree with you. Nor is it relevant. It is an attempt to run away from opponents by pretending they are insubstantial people—straw men. An effective argument does not deflect or avoid opponents but acknowledges and confronts them.

Either/Or Fallacy. The military dictator of a third-world country defends his management style by arguing that denying a few freedoms is better than anarchy. This is an example of the **either/or fallacy,** which suggests that there are only two solutions to a problem and that it is better to choose the lesser of the two evils. Obviously, there are several systems of government that fall between the extremes of dictatorship and anarchy.

Slippery Slope. You argue against drilling for oil in environmentally sensitive areas of Alaska, claiming that, next, mining companies will demand mining rights, then hydroelectric companies will insist on building dams, and soon the Alaskan wilderness will be destroyed. This is the **slippery-slope** fallacy. Rather like the post hoc fallacy, it illogically implies a series of inevitable and drastic consequences that result from an action or policy. Unless you have evidence that mining engineers are preparing to petition the government the moment oil companies get permission to drill, avoid this "Where will it all end?" strategy.

Ethos

Aristotle also believed that an effective argument is an ethical argument. An ethical argument is calm, firm, but rational and conveys a sense of respect for the readers' intelligence and for the opposing point of view; an unethical argument is loud and obnoxious, angry, shrill, flippant, even abusive, and it usually alienates more than it impresses readers. When you raise your voice, the old saying goes, you have lost the argument. The essence of an ethical argument is its voice; an effective arguer speaks or writes in the voice of a wise and reasonable—an ethical—person. Note, for example, the voice or tone of Michele Wucker's essay "Fixing the Borders (Without a Wall)" in Part Three. Illegal immigration is a contentious issue. Emotions can run high when those in favor of amnesty confront those in favor of tighter controls, which often include calls for the construction of a border fence. Wucker opposes a fence and favors overhauling the family preference system and significantly increasing the budget of Citizenship and Immigration Services so its databases can be updated and better managed. But she never rails against those who favor a fence. She makes her case clearly and deliberately. In so doing, she creates the impression that she is a reasonable person and a concerned citizen. Her voice—her ethos—helps to strengthen her argument.

Pathos

Finally, an effective argument evokes some emotion from its readers. Describe the harsh beauty of the Alaskan wilderness and the wildlife threatened by oil exploration, and you help sway your readers to your point of view. Tell the touching story of a lonely widow comforted by a medium who put her in touch with the spirit of her departed husband, and you win your readers' sympathy and, hence, their attention. In classical argument, pathos, as long as it is measured, is an appropriate and effective rhetorical strategy.

For example, in his essay, in Part Two, "Saving the Vancouver Island Marmot," Adam Black describes the physical appearance of the marmot, using an emotional appeal as an argument in support of its survival. "The Vancouver Island marmot," Adam writes, "is blessed with great looks, covered as it is in rich chocolate brown fur broken with patches of white. People tend to react to posters and television images of the marmot the same way they do when an adorable puppy scratches at their feet." Such emotional appeals are common in papers about endangered species. The text is often accompanied by photographs. A photo of a baby polar bear, tentatively jumping off an ice floe into arctic water, or of a baby panda playing with its siblings tug at the heartstrings and strengthen the author's thesis.

● Toulmin: Claim, Support, Warrant

A modern rhetorician, Stephen Toulmin, asserts that a sound argument consists of three parts: the claim, the support, and the warrant. The **claim** is synonymous with the thesis; it is the argument's controlling idea, its main point. Toulmin's system has three types of claim. The claim can be expressed as a fact, as in the following examples:

> Professional hockey players are more prone to concussions than any other professional athletes are.

> Iran's nuclear program is a direct threat to Israel and an indirect threat to peace throughout the Middle East.

Note that these are claims of fact; they need to be proved. The claim may be expressed as a value judgment:

> *Juno* and not *No Country for Old Men* should have won the Academy Award for best picture of 2007.

> Iran under the Shah was a more prosperous and democratic country than it is today.

Or the claim may be a statement of public policy:

> The Republican Party should select a woman to challenge Fred Smith in the race for governor.

> The United States should be more isolationist in its relationships with other nations.

The **support** (or, as it is also known, the grounds) consists of the facts, details, statistics, comparisons, contrasts, causes, effects, emotional appeals, and refutations of opposing arguments that the writer marshals and presents in support of the claim. To support the claim that hockey players are more prone to concussions than other athletes are, the writer needs to provide examples, compare and contrast with other sports the nature of the body contact in hockey, consider the impact of ice over grass or AstroTurf, discuss the uniforms and protective equipment athletes wear, or compile some medical evidence on sports injuries—concussions especially—and individual sports. To provide grounds for the claim that *Juno* should have won the Academy Award for best picture, the writer needs to compare its merits with those of other nominated films, especially *No Country for Old Men,* which was the winner. The writer might try to convince readers that *Juno* is an uplifting comedy among four gloomy tales of serial murder, rapacious greed, and destructive mendacity and, as such, deserves to be singled out. To provide grounds for the claim that the United States should return to an isolationist foreign policy, the writer needs to lay out the foreign policy as it currently is, point out its weaknesses, discuss the advantages gained from isolationism under previous administrations, and speculate on the advantages present-day U.S. society would realize if it were less interventionist. In the Toulmin system, as in classical arguments, the support is the main focus of the essay's body paragraphs.

The **warrant** is an assumption underlying the claim: Head injuries are a concern for professional athletes; Iran is building a nuclear bomb; the Academy Awards should reward the best among those who compete for it; nations should be prosperous and democratic; women have been unfairly underrepresented in races for high political office; current U.S. foreign policy is flawed. Toulmin believed that an effective argument obviously defends its claim but might also have to defend its warrant. The decision depends upon the warrant's level of general acceptability. The warrant stating that certain professional athletes are at risk for head injuries is undeniable and does not need defending. The warrant implying that an Academy Award recognizes the best is shaky, in that some readers might see it as an award for the most popular or as a victory for a film studio's marketing campaign. A writer making this claim needs to include in his or her essay some defense of the warrant that underlies it. The warrant stating that women have been unfairly underrepresented in races for high political office likely needs to be defended as well.

The defense of the warrant is what distinguishes Toulmin's system from the others. Such a defense can cap an already-strong argument and strengthen one that needs additional support.

● Rogerian Argument

Carl Rogers, a contemporary of Toulmin, advocated a different argumentative strategy. Both Toulmin and Aristotle believed that a solid argument addresses the opponent's point of view by showing respect for it, making a fair presentation of its points, and then following it by a firm and direct refutation. Respect for and recognition of the opposition is one part of both Toulmin's approach and the classical argument. But it is the essence of Rogerian argument. By background a humanistic psychologist, Rogers believed that "empathetic listening" is the key to effective argument. Before a writer presents a thesis and before presenting evidence in support of the thesis, he or she must take the time to illustrate the extent to which he or she understands and respects the opposing position. Empathy builds mutual understanding and respect and motivates readers to consider opinions contrary to their own.

A Rogerian argument, then, typically begins by establishing common ground, by indicating the values, beliefs, attitudes, and ideals—insofar as they relate to the issue that forms the subject of the essay—that the writer shares with readers. Next, the writer presents his or her position objectively, in a way that suggests it is a widely shared view, threatening to no one, and worthy of some consideration. And unlike the classical and Toulmin arguments, which typically begin with a thesis, the Rogerian argument typically ends with the thesis. The Rogerian thesis usually implies that the writer has made considerable concessions to the opposition, while expressing hope that the opposition will return the courtesy and consider the writer's point of view.

Keith wanted to argue that the executives of the National Basketball Association should raise the height of the hoop from ten feet to twelve. He began by proclaiming his love for the game of basketball, by insisting his season tickets are among his most valued possessions, by sharing with readers his childhood dreams of playing one day for the Knicks. He told his readers that, because of his love for the traditions of the game, he was skeptical when the three-point play came into being, but that eventually he had to concede it did add an exciting new dimension to the sport. He wanted his readers to see him as a friend and ally, a true fan, a person genuinely concerned about making the game better, not an eccentric recluse whose views could be ignored. He went on to stress how much faster, stronger, and taller the players are today than they were when the game was invented, and he noted that the hoop height has remained standardized at ten feet. Using LexisNexis, Keith found facts and statistics to support his argument that players have become faster, stronger, and taller. He informed his readers that there was a time when few players could slam-dunk or block a shot or execute the perfect alley-oop. Now every player can, and the game is less exciting as a result. Finally, he presented his thesis, but more as a suggestion than as a pronouncement: The league should experiment with the twelve-foot hoop; perhaps teams might play a few preseason games with higher hoops to see how the fans respond. Following the guidelines of a Rogerian argument, Keith tells his readers his idea is worthy of serious consideration, and he offers a nonthreatening suggestion for implementing it, even if only on a temporary, limited basis.

Audience and Purpose in Argument

You have, then, at least three strategies to draw upon as you plan your argumentative academic essay. Which one should you choose? The answer depends, as it usually does in academic writing, on your audience and purpose. Your professor might specify the form your argument is to take. If he or she does not, consider your purpose, the implications of your thesis, and your commitment to it. If you feel strongly about an issue and know you are directing your argument to a neutral audience, you probably should use a classical strategy as you plan your work. If you want to convince your readers, for example, that our borders should be more open, that it should be easier for Mexican citizens to immigrate to the United States, you need to advance a logical argument expressed in the voice of a reasonable but authoritative person. And you want to include the appeal to pathos that the classical mode recommends. Stories about Mexicans living in poverty and dying in their attempts to cross the border illegally will bolster your argument.

If you need to convince your readers that your warrant is valid, choose the Toulmin system. If, for example, you want to convince your readers that English should be declared the official language of the United States, your warrant is that a country runs more efficiently and its citizenry are happier and more productive when there is only one official language. Since there are several liberal democratic countries with more than one official language, this warrant is challengeable, and you should discuss ways bilingual countries are disadvantaged by their language policies.

If you know you have a hostile and defensive audience, one that needs to be won over before it will listen, go with the Rogerian method. If, for example, you want to make the case that phrases such as "under God" should be removed from the Pledge of Allegiance and "In God We Trust" from currency, you are in for a fight, and you will have to assure your readers of your patriotism and your respect for their religious beliefs as you make your case.

Of course, you can also use any combination of the three systems, taking the most useful strategy from each one, as you plan and draft your argument.

Here is an example of a plan for an argumentative essay. The thesis is that the plays attributed to William Shakespeare were actually written by Edward de Vere, seventeenth Earl of Oxford. The warrant—that the authorship of literary works is relevant to reputations and artistic integrity—seems unchallengeable and is not considered. Some readers likely will be hostile to the thesis, so the writer wisely might take a page from Carl Rogers's book and include, in part V of this essay, an expression of empathy and understanding for those readers who think it is sacrilege to cast any doubts upon Shakespeare's reputation.

Title: Alias William Shakespeare: The Case for the de Vere Authorship

Thesis: Overwhelming evidence exists indicating that Edward de Vere is the real author of the great plays and poems attributed to William Shakespeare.

  I.   Author Had a Classical Education and an Insider's Knowledge of the Court
       A. Shakespeare's background and education
       B. de Vere's background and education

 II.   Lord Oxford (de Vere) Artifacts
       A. The Oxford Bible contains annotated and underlined passages found in the plays
       B. The Oxford coat of arms is an English lion shaking a broken spear

III.   Characters in the Plays
       A. Hamlet, Falstaff, Lear, and Prospero have experiences strikingly similar to some of Oxford's own
       B. Polonious as Lord Burghley
       C. Helena as Anne Cecil

 IV.   Sonnets
       A. The story the sonnets tell mirrors Oxford's own life
       B. The characters in the sonnets resemble people he knew

  V.   Refute Opposition
       A. Oxford hid his authorship because it was unseemly for aristocrats to be too involved in the theater
       B. The dating of the plays is uncertain, so the fact that Oxford died in 1604 does not prove he did not write plays allegedly written after his death

Conclusion: The case for Oxford is strong and will grow stronger as more about Oxford's life is discovered.

Note the comprehensiveness of this outline. The author offers four points in support of his thesis. Then he acknowledges and refutes opposing viewpoints in a way that provides him with a fifth point in support of his thesis. Note how direct and unequivocal the thesis is: The author leaves his readers without any doubts about the position his essay will defend. The conclusion promises even more evidence in support as more details about de Vere's life are uncovered.

Conclusion

Planning is an important part of writing a sound academic essay. Do not, however, get locked into a formal, carefully structured plan early in the process of writing your essay. A plan should be fluid and flexible. Early in the writing process, you might feel the need to design a careful, formal plan for your essay. But allow your plan to change as you write your essay. Writing is, among many things, a process of discovery, and you might discover a more effective way of organizing and presenting your thoughts and ideas as you work through successive drafts of your essay. You might have a fresh insight or discover a good research source that contains information that will strengthen your paper. Be willing to alter your plan as you work. If your professor wants you to hand in a plan or outine of your essay with the essay itself, compose that final version of your outline later rather than earlier in the process.

Keep in mind, also, the extent to which the rhetorical mode you are writing in will shape and determine your structure. There are at least two ways to shape a compare/contrast essay and at least three ways to build an effective argument. Choose the structure that will most effectively engage your readers and help you realize your purpose.

WRITING ASSIGNMENT

Select one of the following topics on a current social issue. Or select a current social issue of interest to you, if that topic is not included on the list. Make sure your topic, if you select your own, is not too broad. Note that this assignment calls for a persuasive/argumentative essay.

Find and read carefully two books, two print articles, and two online articles about the topic you have selected. Write an essay of approximately 1,000 words on this topic. Cite correctly at least four of the six sources you have consulted. (At this stage, your instructor might ask only for the plan or outline for this assignment.) See Chapter 8 for information on citing sources correctly.

Submit the plan of your essay along with your finished product. Remember that you likely will begin with a tentative plan but compose the final plan of your essay only after you have finished writing.

- Why _____ has become an endangered species and what we need to do to save it.
- Oil companies should or should not drill for oil in the wilderness of Alaska.
- School vouchers are or are not a good idea.
- Gay/lesbian couples should or should not enjoy all of the same rights heterosexual couples enjoy.
- Capital crimes motivated by racism or homophobia ("hate crimes") should or should not be punished more severely than capital crimes not motivated by racism or homophobia.
- The tactics of some environmental groups are counterproductive.
- We would all be healthier if we didn't eat meat.
- The lyrics of some popular songs need to be censored by the government.
- Mothers with children under five should not work outside of the home.
- English should (should not) be, by law, the official language of the United States.

EXERCISES

1. In a magazine you enjoy reading, find an example of an informative essay that you think is well written. Compose a plan from which the author might have worked. Identify the thesis, the points the author makes to support or develop the thesis, and the points the author uses to develop each main idea.

2. In a magazine you enjoy reading, find an example of an argumentative essay that you think is well written. Determine the argumentative method—classical, Toulmin, Rogerian, or a combination—that the writer uses. Write a two-paragraph assessment of the effectiveness of the argument.

3. Freewrite for ten to fifteen minutes on one of the topics listed for this chapter's writing assignment. Then turn the product of your freewriting into a preliminary outline for an essay.

COLLABORATIVE ACTIVITY

Design an essay topic related to your major or to the discipline you are considering majoring in. Share your topic with others in a group of two or three.

Together develop a preliminary plan for each topic you and your group members have developed.

JOURNAL PROMPT

Explain why you think a sound structure—a definite organizational pattern—is important for good academic writing. What is the relationship between order, structure, and the readability of an academic essay? Do other forms of writing—poems or plays, for example—require the same level of order and structure? Explain your answer.

CHAPTER 5

Write a Draft

In theory, writing the "rough draft" of an essay is a fairly simple process of fleshing out the plan. In reality, it is not simple at all because writers often modify the plan of the essay as they draft. They also edit and revise *while*, not just *after*, they draft. But drafting does have a primary focus, and that focus is the paragraph. By all means, alter your outline and edit and revise as you draft, but focus your attention at this stage of the writing process on composing sound paragraphs.

Write a Clear and Specific Opening

First impressions are important in academic writing. You want to write an introductory paragraph (or paragraphs, if your assignment is a major research paper) that will engage your readers' interest and encourage them to read on, not because they have to but because they want to. You must also clearly establish the topic of your paper in your opening paragraph or paragraphs, so that the context of your thesis is clear. Finally, you must present the thesis, which usually will appear at the end of your introductory paragraph, though it may be implied instead of stated explicitly in a single sentence. Let's look at five examples of introductions to academic essays and then judge, discuss, and analyze the effectiveness of these paragraphs based on the three criteria mentioned in this paragraph:

1. Does it engage the readers' interest?
2. Does it clearly establish the topic?
3. Does it present the thesis?

● Sample Introductory Paragraphs

Sample Introductory Paragraph 1
Progressive, socially responsible people favor recycling as a way of saving natural resources and reducing the strain on landfills. Environmentalists

and city politicians, eager to get elected, exploit this interest in recycling, promising cheaper consumer goods and a cleaner city if recycling programs are implemented. But studies of municipalities that have aggressive recycling programs suggest that recycling is neither cost-effective nor supported by property owners forced to participate in municipal programs. Effective waste management is an essential service, but there are better ways than recycling to handle the tons of waste even a moderately sized city will generate in the course of a week.

Analysis. Introductory paragraph 1 is the opening paragraph for an essay Ethan is writing about effective and ineffective methods of controlling the problems with trash that every city faces. It establishes the essay's topic clearly and effectively and presents the essay's thesis firmly in the last sentence. Does it engage the readers' interest? Perhaps a reader who is already curious about this topic will read on eagerly, but readers without an interest in waste management will not likely be inspired by the paragraph as it now stands to read on. Realizing this as he revised the essay, Ethan decided to open with an anecdote to engage reader interest more effectively:

Our neighbor, Dr. Bringham, a biology professor, has a strong social conscience. He wants to save the whale, ban the internal combustion engine, and recycle every speck of his trash. We were surprised when he led the protests against the building of a recycling plant at the end of our block. "I support recycling," he insisted, "but the noise of the trucks will be annoying, and the smell will ruin the ambience of the neighborhood and probably make our kids sick. And property values will go down." Dr. Bringham's concerns illustrate one reason why recycling programs are doomed to failure: They have only lip-service support among even the most socially conscious citizens. Studies of municipalities that have aggressive recycling programs confirm Dr. Bringham's concerns, suggesting as they do that recycling is neither cost-effective nor supported by property owners forced to participate in municipal programs. Effective waste management is an essential service, but there are better ways than recycling to handle the tons of waste even a moderately sized city will generate in the course of a week.

Sample Introductory Paragraph 2

No composer influenced Mozart's work more than the music of Johann Sebastian Bach. Around 1782, living in Vienna, Mozart, then twenty-five, first heard Bach's music. Immediately he began to blend Bach's style and technique with his own. The result was the birth of a new musical style, which has come to be known as Viennese classical.

Analysis. Introductory paragraph 2 should engage the interest of most readers, since the music of Mozart and Bach has such universal appeal. Maureen, the writer, has also established a clear context for her topic. But what exactly is the essay's thesis? Will she now describe in detail the nature of the influence, tell her readers about the Viennese classical style, or do some combination of both? The paragraph has potential, but it seems somewhat anemic. Another sentence at the end is required to clearly establish the essay's thesis and to provide the reader with a sense of the direction the essay will be taking. Compare the following with the original:

> No music influenced Mozart's work more than the music of Johann Sebastian Bach. Around 1782, living in Vienna, Mozart, then twenty-five, first heard Bach's music. Immediately he began to blend Bach's style and technique with his own. The result was the birth of a new musical style, which has come to be known as Viennese classical. It is characterized by complex melodies and harmonies, which, paradoxically, create a lighter and more joyous impression, evident especially in the sonatas and four move-ment symphonies Mozart composed in the latter part of his career.

Sample Introductory Paragraph 3

The stars in our sky, revealing themselves to us on a clear, dark night, appear randomly scattered. There are large gaps where few stars appear and occa-sional clusters of many stars grouped together. It is as if some divine pres-ence has filled his two hands with many-pointed sparkling rocks and thrown them into the night sky, where they have stuck. In fact, astronomers, some of whom worked 5,000 years ago, have imposed a pattern on our random collection of stars. At first the patterns were based on a form of celestial connect-the-dots, as ancient astronomers drew imaginary lines connecting stars together and concluded that they resembled mythological figures: Leo, Taurus, Orion, and so forth. These astronomers lived in the northern hemi-sphere, so they could not map the stars in the southern sky. They missed, as well, distant stars, glowing faintly, even those in their own hemisphere. Then in 1928, the International Astronomical Union established a more sophisti-cated system, dividing the sky into eighty-eight regions with clearly defined, though invisible, boundaries, much like the boundaries that exist between countries. These eighty-eight celestial counties are called constellations.

Analysis. Introductory paragraph 3 captures the readers' interest in its first few sentences, which are well written and interesting, especially the third sentence with its effective use of metaphor. But soon the paragraph begins to drift. The information it introduces about stars in the southern hemisphere and distant stars might be better placed within the body of the essay. This is a common flaw among student introductory paragraphs: They sometimes contain information that really belongs later in the essay. Moreover, the paragraph seems almost like a complete essay in itself and does not contain an exact thesis. The last sentence suggests that the rest of the essay will elaborate on the definition and description of constellations, but this is a guess on the reader's part. An essay's introduction needs to be clear and explicit. Some of the information in this paragraph should be saved for the essay's body. The following revised paragraph is more focused:

> The stars in our sky, revealing themselves to us on a clear dark night, appear randomly scattered. There are large gaps where few stars appear and occasional clusters of many stars grouped together. It is as if some divine presence has filled his two hands with many-pointed sparkling rocks and thrown them into the night sky, where they have stuck. In fact, astronomers, some of whom worked 5,000 years ago, have imposed a pattern on our random collection of stars. We have today a highly sophisticated map of eighty-eight celestial counties called constellations.

Sample Introductory Paragraph 4

At the time he wrote "Ode to a Nightingale," in the spring of 1819, Keats had been diagnosed with tuberculosis and knew he had not long to live. This news came soon after Keats, who had trained as a physician, had cared for his brother Tom, as he died slowly and painfully of the same fatal illness. In "Ode to a Nightingale," Keats gives voice to his despair. In the poem, he describes his anguish and his suffering; he expresses his desire to escape from his world of pain and sorrow with the help of the nightingale's beautiful song; and he describes the initial success but ultimate failure of his attempt to escape his reality.

Analysis.   Introductory paragraph 4 begins with an anecdote, a story, which is an effective way to engage readers' interest. The writer, Tana, clearly indicates that the essay will be about Keats's poem "Ode to a Nightingale." The paragraph ends with a strong thesis that cues the reader to what will follow in the body of the essay. The thesis is complex; it is a long sentence, about fifty words. Tana might have gone with a more general thesis: In "Ode to a Nightingale," Keats explains how he might try to cope with the despair with which life has surrounded him. A more general thesis, however, might make the introductory paragraph seem rather short and would not provide readers with that sense of direction the longer thesis does.

Sample Introductory Paragraph 5

For centuries, two hundred to be exact, the life of Jesus has been shrouded in mystery. Only one main source documents his birth, though it does so in the most vivid detail. This source skips his childhood and picks up his story only in the last few of the approximately thirty years he lived. It documents his death with the same intensity with which it documents his birth. This source is, of course, the New Testament. The New Testament is gospel (literally) to some, but most biblical historians read, or have read, it skeptically, questioning its historical accuracy. In the last forty years, however, new archaeological discoveries have shed new light on Jesus' life. These new discoveries have, for the most part, confirmed, sometimes dramatically, the New Testament accounts of the life of Christ. Three discoveries in particular suggest that the New Testament authors were much more historians than novelists.

Analysis. Introductory paragraph 5 is a good start for an academic essay. It engages readers by clearly presenting an interesting topic. The paragraph also establishes the necessary historical context for the topic and presents a clear thesis in the last sentence so readers know what to expect from the rest of the essay.

Write Complete Body Paragraphs

● Compose a Topic Sentence

Following your introduction is any number of body paragraphs (depending on the nature of the assignment and the number of words your professor expects) that will elucidate your thesis.

Each body paragraph in your essay should include a topic sentence, which presents the subject of the paragraph. The topic sentence is to the paragraph what the thesis is to the essay as a whole: Just as the other paragraphs within an essay support the thesis, the other sentences within a paragraph support and illuminate the topic sentence.

Where in the body paragraph should you place the topic sentence? It often, of course, is the first sentence. If the first sentence is transitional—that is, if it refers back to the content of the previous paragraph—the topic sentence might be the second one. If the supporting sentences build up to the topic sentence, the topic sentence can also work well at the end of the paragraph, providing a climax. The topic sentence, like a thesis statement, can even be implied from its supporting sentences; however, many professors prefer the clarity that an explicit topic sentence provides to its paragraph.

● Develop Your Topic Sentence

A typical paragraph in the body of an academic essay must be developed in enough detail to satisfy the needs and expectations of its readers. In a long essay, you might have a short paragraph to signal a transition from one main idea to the next; however, most paragraphs in the body of an academic essay will consist of at least four sentences: the topic sentence and at least three others in support of the topic.

One of the most common faults in undergraduate academic essays is an inadequately developed topic sentence, which creates an underdeveloped paragraph. Compare, for example, these two paragraphs:

> It was a vexing celestial mystery. Through a telescope it looked like an ordinary, if faint, star. But it emitted far more ultraviolet radiation and more

radio signals than astronomers had observed coming from ordinary stars. It was, indeed, something new and different, a quasar.

It was a vexing celestial mystery. Through a telescope it looked like an ordinary, if faint, star. But in its wake were red spectral lines of hydrogen, indicating it was hurtling away from the earth at a speed astronomers estimated at 30,000 miles per second, not a behavior any star exhibited. And it emitted far more ultraviolet radiation and more radio signals than astronomers had observed coming from ordinary stars. It was, indeed, something new and different. It was not a star but a quasistar, a quasi-stellar radio source—a quasar.

The paragraphs share an implied topic sentence: Astronomers did not distinguish stars from quasars until they studied differences between them. The first paragraph provides only two points of comparison: the amount of ultraviolet radiation and the intensity of the radio signals. These two alone do not develop the topic sentence adequately. The second paragraph is more effective because it provides a third point of comparison: the quasar's movement indicated by its red tail of hydrogen. The second paragraph also provides a longer concluding sentence that establishes a clearer context for the comparison and a better explanation for the name astronomers decided to use for quasars.

Once you have a strong topic sentence, make certain your body paragraphs are well developed by providing details and examples to support and illuminate your topic sentence. Define key words your readers might not be completely familiar with. Use comparisons and contrasts, descriptions, or any one of the other methods for developing paragraphs discussed in Chapter 2. Relate an anecdote to elucidate your topic sentence if the anecdote is relevant and useful. Do not leave your body paragraphs underdeveloped.

● Maintain Paragraph Unity

Body paragraphs must have unity, which means that all of the sentences within the paragraph must develop, explain, add detail to, or otherwise relate to and elucidate the topic sentence. A body paragraph is typically about one subject specified within the topic sentence. All of the other sentences within a body paragraph must relate to the topic sentence. As you revise, check that all of the sentences in your body paragraphs relate to the topic sentence. Compare, for example, these two paragraphs:

In quantum mechanics the distinction between a wave and a particle is blurred. Physicists have proved that entities such as electrons, which would normally be classified as particles, can behave like waves under certain conditions. Similarly, entities we classify as waves—light being the most obvious example—can manifest the behavior of a particle. Electrons must produce the diffraction of a wave if they are to pass through the narrow slits of atoms. Light must act like a particle if it is to be absorbed by electrons in solids. It is not the composition of the entity itself but the process that entity has to complete that determines its particulate or wavelike nature.

In quantum mechanics the distinction between a wave and a particle is blurred. Physicists have proved that entities such as electrons, which would normally be classified as particles, can behave like waves under certain conditions. Similarly, entities we classify as waves—light being the most obvious example—can manifest the behavior of a particle. Classical or Newtonian physics does not account for quantum mechanics or for relativity developed earlier by Einstein. Relativity describes the physics of very massive and fast entities, while quantum mechanics, which emerged in the 1920s, deals with the physics of microscopic objects. Electrons must produce the diffraction of a wave if they are to pass through the narrow slits of atoms. Light must act like a particle if it is to be absorbed by electrons in solids. It is not the composition of the entity itself that determines its particulate or wavelike nature but the mission the entity has to accomplish.

These paragraphs share the same topic sentence, the first. But note how in the second version, the author drifts away from the topic sentence in the middle of the paragraph when he starts talking about Newtonian physics and relativity. That information belongs somewhere else in the essay, not in a paragraph defining quantum mechanics.

You violate the important principle of paragraph unity if sentences in a body paragraph drift away from the topic. Often these are strong sentences that do not relate to the paragraph's topic but do somehow relate to the essay's thesis and, therefore, can be effectively used in a different body paragraph. Edit out sentences that destroy paragraph unity, or if possible, integrate them into other, more relevant paragraphs.

● Sample Body Paragraphs

Here are five examples of body paragraphs, each followed by an analysis of its strengths and weaknesses.

Sample Body Paragraph 1

But today, intelligence and integrity are not enough. We also expect our politicians, in this age of multimedia, to be charismatic. The word *charisma* is from the Greek word meaning "gift of grace," and, as the "grace" aspect of the definition suggests, the word originally had religious connotations. It maintains some of these connotations, as evident in "charismatic" evangelical sects, who view Christ as the personification of charisma. But its meaning has softened over the years. We do not expect our presidents and prime ministers to be godly, but we do want them to exude self-confidence and a serenity that, in turn, calms us, the people they govern. We expect them to light up a room when they enter it, to command the attention of others by virtue of their physical presence alone. Some insist that Bill Clinton has this presence. Mikhail Gorbachev, Pierre Trudeau, Cleopatra, John F. Kennedy, and Nelson Mandela were charismatic political leaders. Many Americans, and even citizens of other countries, feel that President Obama is among the most charismatic contemporary political leaders.

Analysis. Body paragraph 1 is well done. It has a topic sentence, the second: "We also expect our politicians, in this age of multimedia, to be charismatic." The first sentence is transitional; it refers back to other traits of good politicians discussed in earlier body paragraphs. The topic sentence is well developed in eight supporting sentences through the use of the definition and examples. All of the supporting sentences relate to the topic sentence, giving the paragraph unity.

Sample Body Paragraph 2
Even more baffling is the support for the death penalty voiced by members of the Christian Right. Christians follow the teaching and emulate the actions of Jesus. One of the most famous New Testament stories reveals Jesus as an abolitionist. A group of new Christians brought before Jesus a woman who was convicted of adultery, then a capital crime in the Holy Land. Before they stoned the woman to death, they sought advice from their spiritual leader. As John tells the story (8:3–11), Jesus "lifted himself up and said unto them, 'He that is without sin among you, let him cast the first stone.'" The woman was freed, with Jesus' stern admonition that she "sin no more." As the personification of the compassion and forgiveness that define Christianity, Jesus opposed the death penalty, as must any who profess to follow the Christian faith.

Analysis. Body paragraph 2 is from a persuasive essay in opposition to capital punishment. Its topic sentence, which is not stated but is implicit, is that one argument against the death penalty is that it is anti-Christian. This paragraph is a good example of the use of an anecdote or story to develop a topic sentence, though perhaps the writer, David, could have established the context for the story more clearly. He might have provided more details about the nature of the woman's "crime" and about the nature of capital punishment at that time.

Sample Body Paragraph 3
The real level of social responsibility that corporations need to exercise lies somewhere between the ravings of the Marxists for state control and the "greed is good" mentality of the extreme free marketers. Certainly, U.S. corporations set up shop in third-world countries where they can pay workers a fraction of what they would have to pay U.S. workers and thereby increase their treasured profit margin. Yet the governments of these countries are reluctant to nationalize such companies partly because a poor wage by U.S. standards is often a fair wage by other standards and partly because the governments know they lack the expertise to manage the companies effectively.

Comparatively low wages and the specter of the presence of U.S. capitalism on their sovereign soil are preferable to absolute poverty and the threat of political revolution. Even so, there are U.S. companies that employ children who should be going to school and whom the companies do pay poorly, even by the standards of the countries where they work. Child labor is unconscionable, anathema to developed countries for the past one hundred years. Recently, certain celebrities have been publicly scolded and ridiculed for advertising and even allowing their own names to be placed on clothing made by children who live barely above the poverty level. There are other products besides clothing, which U.S. businesses manufacture in third-world countries to take advantage of the low wages they can pay to children. Nor is there any excuse for substandard working conditions. Adequate pay will not buy loyalty if third-world workers are subject to lead poisoning, work in factories without sufficient sanitation, and labor long hours without breaks.

Analysis. In body paragraph 3, we have two, maybe three body paragraphs crammed into one. The paragraph touches on Marxism, capitalism, nationalism, child labor, and working conditions. The first sentence sounds like a topic sentence for a compare/contrast paragraph, but the writer abandons this topic sentence to touch on celebrities and other manufactured products. The paragraph lacks unity. It needs to be divided into two or three paragraphs, each with its own well-developed topic sentence. Besides the first, two other topic sentences are implicit in this paragraph:

Child labor is, of course, unconscionable under any circumstances, and governments even in the poorest countries must take measures to curtail the exploitation of children.

Celebrities must also take responsibility for the circumstances under which clothing that bears their names is manufactured.

If the writer chooses to write just one paragraph, he needs to edit out the material that doesn't fit.

Sample Body Paragraph 4

Why does Norma Jean decide to leave Leroy? She decides to leave partly because Leroy annoys her. She admits she was happier when he was driving his truck and was away from home much of the time. Because of his injury, he is always at home now, underfoot, smoking marijuana, and dreaming of building a log cabin, in which Norma Jean has little interest. But the real cause of her discontent, the real reason she leaves, has to do with her new-found identity. Norma Jean has grown up. She is a different person from the eighteen-year-old girl who had to get married because she was pregnant. She is working, attending college classes, and even thinking about standing up, at last, to her overbearing mother. Leroy, annoyed, asks his wife if all of this is some "women's lib thing." His retort is meant to be sarcastic, but it contains more truth than he realizes or cares to admit.

Analysis. Body paragraph 4 is from Akira's essay analyzing Bobbie Ann Mason's story "Shiloh." It is a good example of a body paragraph that uses a question as its topic sentence and then uses the other sentences to answer the question. It is also an example of how a body paragraph can build up to a key point. Minor answers to the topic sentence question are presented early in the paragraph, and then the middle sentence begins, "But the real cause. . . ." This is an effective way of highlighting the key information a body paragraph contains.

Sample Body Paragraph 5
The clitellum, a whitish band near the worm's anterior end, forms four to six weeks after birth. It contains both male and female reproductive organs. To mate, two worms join together at the clitellum, their heads pointing in opposite directions. Each worm passes sperm to the other; each stores the sperm in tiny sacs, which evolve into cocoons, tinier than a grain of rice. As the worms back out of the cocoons, they leave behind both eggs and sperm, which unite to form the worm embryo within the cocoon. Anywhere from one to five worm embryos will be in each of the two cocoons. In two to three weeks, the cocoons break open, and the newborns emerge. They are nearly transparent and less than an inch long.

Analysis. Body paragraph 5 is from Roberta's essay about the life cycle of the common earthworm. Its implied topic sentence is "Here is the process worms go through when they mate and reproduce." It describes the process clearly and illustrates good use of detail, as the writer includes such information as the size of the cocoon and the size of the newborn worms.

Write an Explicit Conclusion

A good academic essay needs a clear and strong conclusion. In an essay of fewer than 1,000 words, the conclusion will usually be a single paragraph. In a longer essay or report, the conclusion will be longer in proportion to the length of the essay. A 100-page essay or report might have a 10-page conclusion.

Whatever its length, an effective conclusion must establish a sense of *closure.* The tone and the content of a concluding paragraph or paragraphs must indicate that the essay's purpose has been fulfilled. Readers will recognize such an ending when they read it and feel that nothing else needs to be said about the essay's thesis. A concluding paragraph or paragraphs might also *summarize* the content of the essay's body and will often *reaffirm* the thesis. But above all, the conclusion must give readers the sense that the writer has fulfilled his or her obligations: The writer has said what he or she had promised to say.

Let's look at five examples of concluding paragraphs from academic essays and analyze their effectiveness based upon these criteria for good conclusions.

Sample Concluding Paragraphs

Sample Concluding Paragraph 1

In summary, there is no independent scientific evidence to support any claim by any cosmetics company that one of its "miracle creams" performs anything close to miracles. Studies that cosmetics companies refer to in their advertisements are clearly suspect, conducted as they were by dermatologists employed by those same companies and undertaken without the controls that scientific studies must have to be considered valid. Why do millions of women believe the companies' claims? They believe because they want to think they can recapture their youthful beauty. The billion-dollar U.S. cosmetics industry is a monument to the triumph of vanity and fantasy over science.

Analysis. Concluding paragraph 1's introductory phrase, "In summary," suggests that this is the concluding paragraph of the essay, since summaries are generally included at the end. Some professors are not enthusiastic about concluding paragraphs that begin with *in summary* or *in conclusion,* viewing such phrases as limited and unimaginative. Often such phrases are redundant, since the context makes clear that a summary is being presented and since paragraphs placed at the end of the essay are obviously "in conclusion" paragraphs. The sample paragraph's first sentence also reiterates the essay's thesis, something concluding paragraphs often do. The second sentence reminds readers of key points in the body of the essay, while the third sentence is a question, which is answered in the final two sentences. The question is answered unequivocally and with a blunt tone that indicates the essay is finished.

Sample Concluding Paragraph 2

Eventually, though, Keats would resolve the anguish and torment that comes through so powerfully in "Ode to a Nightingale." He would resign himself to the reality of his illness and accept the fact that his illness meant his life would be so very brief. He would come to learn that the truth cannot be ignored, but that, even though the truth does hurt, it does not have to diminish the beauty of life. As he would learn and write in his next poem, "Ode on a Grecian Urn," "Beauty is truth, truth beauty."

Analysis. Concluding paragraph 2 ends an essay that explains the meaning of Keats's poem "Ode to a Nightingale." It concludes the discussion of the poem and then relates the poem to the next one Keats would write. This technique of hinting at a future concern is common in concluding paragraphs and is used effectively here. The paragraph also ends with a quotation, another common and effective strategy in a concluding paragraph.

Sample Concluding Paragraph 3

With networks, writers can revise and edit work collaboratively much more efficiently than they could by passing hard copy around a room. With spell-checkers, writers can correct a word in a fraction of the time it takes to look a word up in an old-fashioned paper dictionary. With grammar checkers, writers are cued to correct incomplete or rambling sentences. But comput-ers can't think for themselves or develop a weak idea or make style more graceful. The computer makes writing, as it makes so many of the tasks of life, easier, but it needs the guidance of a human mind to make writing more interesting and intelligent.

Analysis. Concluding paragraph 3 is from Jan's essay about the benefits and drawbacks of composing on a computer. It provides a good summary of the points presented in the essay, the points that support computer-based writing and those that express the computer's limitations. In fact, the paragraph is really only summary, though the thesis is implicitly restated, and the last sentence, while still part of the summary, does communicate that sense of closure impor-tant in concluding paragraphs.

Sample Concluding Paragraph 4

The U.S. government should not pressure the Honduran government to shut down its sweatshops, nor should it use sanctions to coerce the Hondurans into enacting child labor laws that would prevent children from working in them. A poor wage is better than no wage. Food, shelter, and clothing trump education in the hierarchy of human needs. But the analysis presented here certainly suggests that the governments of countries whose citizens consume the goods produced in third-world countries could pressure these coun-tries to improve working conditions without provoking the governments of underdeveloped countries into threats of closing down the factories alto-gether. U.S. citizens can continue to exercise their rights to enrich celebrity designers by paying top dollar for clothes made by poor twelve-year-olds earning a dollar a day.

Analysis. Concluding paragraph 4, from Jake's essay about the problem of U.S. clothing manufacturers using underpaid child labor in third-world countries to make their garments, appears to summarize the body of the essay and restate the thesis. Unfortunately, the thesis is ambiguous. The first part of the para-graph suggests that we are benefiting the economy of Honduras by sending its citizens work, even if the workers are young and underpaid by our standards. But the end of the paragraph suggests that we are exploiting third-world chil-dren. Moreover, the first part of the paragraph suggests that the essay focuses on one country, but by the end of the paragraph, it seems as if the essay focuses on underdeveloped countries in general. Academic writing should never be ambiguous. A concluding paragraph especially must reflect specifically the content of the essay it is meant to bring to closure. Jake revised his paragraph as follows:

> As the analysis presented here suggests, the governments of affluent nations and their citizens need to apply gentle pressure on those countries that exploit child labor. No one benefits if poor countries, in response to the threat of sanctions or to other draconian measures, close down clothing factories that provide work for their people. Gentle pressure would include incentives for leaving children in school and for improving the working conditions of the adults—mainly young women—who work in the factories. Given the profit that cheap labor helps them realize, U.S. garment manufacturers and their celebrity spokespeople can well afford to support educational initiatives and better conditions for the many workers in underdeveloped countries who enrich them.

Sample Concluding Paragraph 5
By about 1770, the popularity of the rococo style was fading, even in cities such as Prague, Munich, Dresden, and Vienna, where it had flourished. Trendsetters were beginning to look upon the asymmetrical ornamentation, which was a hallmark of the rococo style, as more ungainly and unbalanced than light-hearted and whimsical. Inevitably, rococo would give way to the symmetry of the neoclassical style, which would dominate European architecture until the end of the century.

Analysis. Concluding paragraph 5, from Tim's brief essay tracing the history of rococo architecture, ends, appropriately, by mentioning the year around which the rococo period began to fade. In an essay organized chronologically, such an ending is appropriate and effective. You might also notice that even though the essay is not about the neoclassical style, which superseded rococo, the paragraph does mention the transition. This technique of ending an essay by hinting at a future trend or development is common and, as long as the essay topic lends itself to the technique, effective.

Conclusion

There is an old adage in writing instruction: Tell them what you're going to tell them, then tell them, and then tell them what you've told them. The adage trivializes the complex process of writing, but it is worth remembering while you plan and draft your essay, because it reinforces the importance of structure and the function of introductory, body, and concluding paragraphs.

Hannah is ready to write a draft of her essay on the effects that our fascination with the lives of celebrities is having on our culture. The paragraph is the foundation of a strong draft, so Hannah's goals, at this stage of the process, are to write an introductory paragraph that presents her topic and her thesis; body paragraphs that are unified and well developed and that integrate information from her sources effectively; and a concluding paragraph that establishes the important sense of closure.

Like many writers, Hannah prints her draft so she can do some revising on a hard-copy version of her paper. While revising, many writers like to have the whole text in front of them so that they can work with longer segments of text than the computer screen gives them. They find that marking up hard copy is a more visceral experience than typing words onto a screen and that, in this way, they can determine more effectively where their essay needs to be better developed, can sense more easily if a paragraph is misplaced, and can ascertain whether they need to communicate their ideas more clearly and cohesively. One of Hannah's composition instructors recommended that she read her essay out loud while she revises, because sometimes the ear hears what the eye fails to see.

Here is the draft of Hannah's essay, along with her handwritten suggestions for revision.

Some Social and Psychological Consequences of Celebrity Worship
~~The Benefits and Drawbacks of Our Celebrity Culture~~

The lifestyles of the rich and famous have always intrigued

ordinary people without vast wealth and fame, but for many
intrigue
people this͵ has become an obsession. On prime-time televi-
most nights of the week,
sion͵ there are at least six programs devoted to keeping America

informed about ~~the activities about~~ the births, deaths, acci-

dents, addictions, convictions, and love lives of movie and

television stars, professional athletes, business moguls, even,

occasionally, politicians. Magazines with the same mandate

~~are numerous~~ fill the racks of drugstores and supermarkets.

~~Online there is....~~ Look online for information about the rich

and the famous and you will be overwhelmed by photographs,

biographies, blogs, and online fan clubs devoted exclusively to

Include sentence about research(?)

worshipping a favorite star.〰Our interest in the lives of celebri-
usually
ties is〰a normal and harmless, even a healthy diversion; but it
can also become an abnormal, even dangerous ~~obsession~~ social
and psychological disorder.

Rebecca Feasy argues that an interest in celebrity culture
is healthy, is, in fact, empowering for women, who are the primary ~~watchers~~ ... consumers of celebrity gossip. A woman who
reads celebrity magazines and wants to dress like the stars
is in control "of her sexuality and social situation" (182).
She has social power because she has taken the initiative
to look beautiful and, as a consequence, to be noticed and
thereby acquire social capital. Lakshmi Chaudhry calls this
"a certain brand of Gen-X feminism that places sexual gratification and independence at the top of the agenda" (22).
Feasy also believes that magazines and TV programs that gossip about celebrity lifestyles provide women with "a valuable
feminine discourse" (189). Women ~~are interested in~~ share
an interest in the dating and the mating patterns of celebrities, in the progress of celebrity marriages, in the welfare of
the children of celebrity couples. They get together to gossip
about their favorite celebrities and, in the process, they share
advice with each other and gain insight into and negotiate
their own personal and family relationships and social identity
(Feasy 190; Halpern 147). 〰*Celebrity relationships are instructive,
even if they might represent bad models of behavior.*

*move this
para-
graph to
draw-
backs
section (?)*

Similarly,
〰Jill Weir questions Feasy's argument about the positive
effects that knowledge of celebrity imperfections can have on
the self esteem of the not-so-famous. To Weir, this interest in

celebrity cellulite and less-than-perfect muscle tone is cruel, vindictive, and mean-spirited. Magazines and websites don't purchase photos of an aging starlet looking far from perfect on vacation in a bikini to heighten the self-esteem of readers. They don't feature close-ups of the haggard faces of yesterday's glamour girls so the huddled masses will smile and relax when they look in the mirror. They do it because mean sells. The appeal, Weir and other social commentators fear, is to the worst part of human nature, and, now that video cameras are in cell phones, anyone can turn into an ethically-challenged paparazzo and sell unflattering images to the media.

Indent

Feasy also argues that stars motivate us to exercise and diet, ~~to look~~ in an attempt to look as good as they do, and that this discipline enhances self esteem. And she notes that more magazines and TV programs focus now on the stars' imperfections—their less-than-perfect skin, ill-advised plastic surgery, and fashion faux pas (185)—and thereby "liberate the reader from feeling inadequate for failing to create her own celebrity body" (187). Sean Redmond argues that we feel better about ourselves when we wear a celebrity's perfume or clothes from the favorite designer to the stars, and that these feelings can be renewed and reinforced ~~in that~~ because we can put on the clothing and perfume again and again. Moreover, the subtext of products endorsed by celebrities is often subversive— you don't need a man to be happy, successful, and free; you can drive a truck or run a company; it's ok to be intimate with someone of a different race—and thereby undermine stereotypes about race and gender roles (40).   *Add Coleman-Bell & Franco on minorities and gay women*

Others social commentators, however, argue ~~that celebrity gossip~~ that engaging in celebrity gossip and using celebrities as role models are anti-feminist activities that, more often than not, diminish self-esteem. Provocative designer clothing and ~~hard~~ fit bodies are as much about a love of male attention, which ~~considers~~ concedes power, as they are about social capital that enhances social power. Feminist authors further point out that women who achieve the greatest fame are those who fall apart and self-destruct, often because of a failed relationship with a man. Naomi Wolf bemoans a culture "increasingly obsessed with showcasing images of glamorous young *delete names (?)* women, [like Britney Spears and Lindsay Lohan,] who are falling apart" (in Chaudhry 24), and she suggests this fascination is anti-feminist in that it reassures the male establishment of the stereotype of the weak and vulnerable woman who needs a man's help if she is to be in control and successful. *Add sentence re: contrast with young male stars*

Moreover, fans can wear the same clothes, eat the same food, and practice the same yoga techniques of their favorite stars, but they don't have access to the air brushes, glamour lenses, makeup artists, personal trainers, and plastic surgeons of the stars, and when they fall short of this physical perfection, even though it is manufactured, they may feel they ~~are a failure~~ have failed. According to one study, nearly sixty percent of women who had cosmetic surgery because they wanted the same feature—lips, breasts, nose—of their favorite celebrity were disappointed with the results (Hecom 38).

Some fans, whose grip on reality is already shaky, imagine they have a personal relationship with the stars, because the stars ~~appear~~ "appear" in their living rooms and bedrooms. Theses fans choose to ignore or are oblivious to the fact that the stars are only there on a television or computer screen. Some of the most fanatic have tried to establish a personal connection with those they are now convinced are friends or, in the extremist of cases, their deity (Halpern 164-65). They are shattered when their access is prevented by very large and menacing security guards. In the worst cases, ~~they lose their admiration for stalk~~ admiration turns to contempt, observing turns to stalking, and the obsessed fan threatens the celebrity with violence, even death.

Move Jill Weir paragraph here

There may be, as well, a broader social cost to celebrity worship. It twists our social and political values and it can divert our attention away from issues that should concern us more. More Americans vote for their favorite American Idol than they do for president, and they are more likely to know the name of the baby of a celebrity couple than the name of their Secretary of State or Speaker of the House. *Insert another example* Ironically, the political leaders we know the best are often those who achieved celebrity status before they were elected, and whose celebrity gave them an unfair advantage while they were campaigning. The greatest social cost of celebrity worship is ~~on the justice is~~ the deleterious effect it has on our justice system. Juries, *seem transfixed* ~~are too impressed~~ by celebrities and seem more likely to acquit those charged with a crime. Despite considerable evidence against them, some famous professional athletes, actors, and pop stars—

delete names (?)   *no names*

[O.J. Simpson, Michael Jackson, <u>and xxxx (guy who waited in car while wife was shot in restaurant</u>)] have been acquitted of crimes as heinous as rape, pedophilia, and murder.

There is nothing wrong with dreaming of possessing the wealth, fame, and good looks celebrities possess, or indulging in the latest water-cooler gossip, or feeling better about ourselves when we discover that a famous person shares our minority status but has still become successful. Problems arise when celebrity worshippers go too far, spending hours in front of their television sets or computer monitors catching up on the latest gossip, or, in worst case scenarios, deluding themselves about the nature of their relationship with someone rich and famous, perhaps to a potentially dangerous extent. *∧Add one more sentence for closure.*

WRITING ASSIGNMENTS

1. Read an article that interests you from a recently published academic journal. Closely examine a section, consisting of about five paragraphs, of the body of the paper. Based upon the characteristics of effective body paragraphs discussed in this chapter, write a 300-word analysis of this passage.

2. Select one of the following topics, and write an introductory paragraph and a concluding paragraph that would work well for that topic. (You may select two topics, one for an introductory paragraph and another for a concluding paragraph, if you prefer.)

   ■ The responsibility of professional athletes as role models
   ■ Classic novels made into movies
   ■ Compare and contrast hamburgers from two different fast-food chains
   ■ Television's best sitcom

EXERCISES

1. Write an opening paragraph for an essay about the characteristics of effective opening paragraphs for an academic essay.

2. Analyze the opening paragraph of an academic essay you have already written, turned in, and have had graded and returned to you. Write a one-paragraph evaluation of the quality of your opening based upon the criteria and the examples discussed in this chapter.

3. In an academic journal or a collection of academic essays related to your major or to a subject you are interested in, find an example of an effective opening. In one paragraph, explain why you think this opening is effective.

4. In an academic journal or a collection of academic essays related to your major or to a subject you are interested in, find an example of an ineffective opening. In one paragraph, explain why you think this opening is ineffective.

5. Correct the violations in paragraph unity contained within the following passage. You may divide the passage into two paragraphs if you wish. You may add to, but not delete from, the information contained within the passage.

    The Castle of Otranto, by Horace Walpole, is another example of a novel of the "mystery and terror school." *The Castle of Otranto* is a Gothic novel. Horace Walpole was born in 1717 and died in 1797. He was a novelist and also something of an art critic and historian. A renaissance man, Walpole was a member of the British Parliament from 1741 to 1767. He followed in his father's footsteps. His father, Robert, was twice prime minister of Great Britain. The main character is Manfred, the Prince of Otranto, who decides to marry Isabella, the daughter of the Marquis of Vincenza, after Otranto's son, who was betrothed to Isabella, dies under mysterious circumstances. Isabella wants no part of Manfred and runs off, her escape aided by the Peasant Theodore. A series of supernatural events follows, culminating in the collapse of the castle. Theodore is declared heir and marries Isabella. The Gothic novel is characterized by horror, terror, the supernatural, murder, and violence. Gothic novels are often set in gloomy, isolated castles. Horace Walpole even built his own imitation Gothic castle in Twickenham.

6. Select one of the following thesis statements. Compose three topic sentences, one for each of three body paragraphs of an essay that would have the thesis you selected. Develop one of the topic sentences into a complete body paragraph.

    - Some professional athletes are not very good role models.
    - Classic novels do not necessarily translate into good movies.
    - The quality of the hamburgers varies widely from one fast-food restaurant to the next.
    - Some television sitcoms have a lot of situation but not much comedy.

7. Compose a concluding paragraph that ends with an effective and relevant quotation.

8. Compose a concluding paragraph that ends by hinting at a future concern related to the essay's topic. See sample concluding paragraphs 2 and 5 in this chapter for examples.

9. Compose a concluding paragraph that includes a relevant question.

COLLABORATIVE ACTIVITY

In small groups, discuss one or several readings from the anthology of readings in Part Two or Three. Discuss the effectiveness of the opening, body, and concluding paragraphs in these articles. Use the criteria for good opening, body, and concluding paragraphs described in this chapter.

JOURNAL PROMPT

Write a summary of the discussion generated in the preceding collaborative activity.

CHAPTER 6

Revise Your Essay

Professional writers regularly pay homage to revision, stressing how essential revision is to the writing process. "I have re-written—often several times—every word I have ever written," says Vladimir Nabakov. "My pencils outlast their erasers." "Half my life," writes novelist John Irving, "is an act of revision." "The beautiful part of writing," notes Robert Cormier, "is that you don't have to get it right the first time, unlike, say, a brain surgeon. You can always do it better, find the exact word, the apt phrase, the leaping simile."

Revision is the process of altering, improving, and clarifying the overall structure of a written text and of reviewing the content of a text to make certain it satisfies the needs and expectations of readers. It is distinct from editing, discussed in the next chapter, which is the process of altering and improving a text, primarily at the sentence level. When revising a work, the writer makes certain the essay or report has a sound overall **structure,** makes certain that the content of the essay or report meets the needs and expectations of his or her readers, and double- and triple-checks for the presence of **cohesive ties** between sentences and paragraphs. During the revising stage of the process, a writer also checks and reconsiders the **style** in which his or her paper is written, checking to make sure the sentence structure is varied and that his or her voice or tone— that attitude to the topic the author conveys to his or her readers—is effective and appropriate.

Structure

In Chapter 4, you learned how to plan and structure an academic essay or report. Specifically, you learned various strategies for organizing an argument and for planning various kinds of expository or informative essays. Expository essays, remember, present information to readers. An expository essay, for example, might describe a process, explain the causes of an important event or natural phenomenon, recount how an important event or natural phenomenon influenced or affected society, present details and examples to illustrate an idea, compare and contrast related entities, or define a complex term or procedure. Often an expository essay will combine any number of these developmental patterns to support its main idea. A persuasive/argumentative essay might also describe a process, present details and examples, give causes and effects, make comparisons and contrasts, or supply definitions to inform readers, but the persuasive essay bears the additional burden of trying to convince readers that the writer's opinion on a controversial issue is valid. For this reason, an important component of the argument is an acknowledgment and refutation of the opposing point of view.

As you revise your work, keep in mind its developmental patterns and the rhetorical expectations those patterns provoke in the minds of readers. If you are writing a compare/contrast essay, for example, check to make sure the essay you are working on is organized using either the common traits or the similarities/differences organizational structure, usually the best choices for comparing and contrasting. If you are presenting an argument, make sure, first, that you have included all of the components of an effective argument: ample evidence in support of your thesis and, if necessary, your warrant; and acknowledgment of, respect for, and refutation of opposing arguments. Make sure, as well, that you have presented these elements in an order that maximizes your chances of winning your readers over to your side. That order is somewhat arbitrary and will depend upon the nature of your argument and upon your readers' level of hostility, skepticism, and cynicism. Proponents of classical argument, remember, recommend you begin with a thesis followed by support, while Rogerians suggest you present evidence leading up to a thesis.

Readers want and expect a clear and logical progression of arguments and ideas. They expect the writer to lead them along competently without getting them lost. A sound structure based upon clear points in support of a thesis and upon ideas and details that clearly elucidate those points in support of the thesis helps readers understand a writer's work. Remember that you likely will not establish that structure, in its entirety, before you draft your essay but will discover an effective structure as you write and revise.

Content

Revise your essay for content. Make sure you have provided enough information in the form of details, examples, comparisons, contrasts, causes, effects, definitions, and anecdotes to fulfill the expectations of your readers. This requires some empathy on your part, an ability to put yourself in your readers' shoes. Don't assume your readers know what you know. You live with a writing assignment for some time, you have researched your topic, and you know a lot about it. Certain points of information might seem obvious to you because you have read about them in several different sources. But this does not mean your readers share your knowledge. Certainly, it is possible to go on too long, but it is generally better to err on the side of providing more information rather than less.

You might have to do additional critical thinking, freewriting, and research as you revise your essay. We tend to conceptualize critical thinking and research as prewriting activities, but to do so limits our chances of success as writers. Good writers often consult new sources during the revising stage in order to generate additional needed content for their essays.

Remember that the single most frequent marginal comment professors make on their students' papers does not concern grammar or spelling or sentence structure. It is some kind of request for additional information, some kind of complaint that the student has not provided enough information to solidify the point or the argument he or she is trying to advance. It is generally a good idea to meet or slightly exceed the word limit your professor has requested. Quality is more important than quantity, but the quantity must be such that your readers understand and appreciate the information you are presenting or the argument you are advancing.

Cohesive Ties

A cohesive tie is a word or a phrase that connects a sentence or a paragraph to the sentence or the paragraph that precedes or follows it. Cohesive ties help readers follow the writer's train of thought. They signal the nature of the relationships between and among sentences and paragraphs and, in so doing, help make writing clear. Cohesive ties include transitional words and phrases, key words that are repeated throughout a paragraph, synonyms that are substitutes for key words, and pronouns that refer to key words. In other words, you can establish cohesion in your writing through transition, repetition, and substitution.

● Transition

A transitional word or phrase defines the nature of the relationship between and among sentences and paragraphs. Transitional words and phrases such as *furthermore, in addition,* and *also* suggest that the sentence containing this word or phrase will add something to a previous sentence, something that will provide further related information. Similarly, transitional words or phrases such as *another, a second,* and *a third* suggest that a new point will be made. Transitional expressions such as *consequently* or *therefore* suggest a cause/effect relationship between two sentences or paragraphs. Transitional words such as *but* and *however* signal a contradiction or a contrast between a sentence and the one that follows. Notice the use of transitional expressions (which appear in boldface) in this passage:

> The human spinal column is an intricate and complex structure. **As a result,** the human back, the lower back especially, is susceptible to trouble. **Indeed,** back problems are one of the most common reasons for a visit to the doctor.
>
> **One** such problem is simple back strain, which typically follows the exercise of muscles that are not used to so much attention. **For example,** back muscles are often put to work for which they are not ready—say, after the first snowfall of the year—and, **consequently,** feel uncommon stress, which leads to mild but still painful inflammation.
>
> **Another,** more serious problem is the so-called slipped disk. **Now,** the disks between each vertebra in the human back are attached to ligaments and cannot literally slip. They can, **however,** prolapse, which means that a portion of the disk may protrude through the fibers of the ligaments.

Examine carefully the transitional words and phrases used in this passage, and note how they improve clarity by establishing the relationship between and among the sentences and between paragraphs. Read the passage without its transitional words, and you will notice the extent to which transitional words and phrases aid clarity.

● Repetition

You can also establish cohesion by repeating a key word or by repeating a particular sentence pattern. Here is a paragraph that repeats a key word to help keep the reader on track:

> The **Sabbath** is a Jewish day of rest and worship. After they were sent into exile, Jews proclaimed their identity, in part by insisting upon the holiness of their **Sabbath** day. Jesus supported the **Sabbath** in principle but was vexed by the number of rules needed to keep the **Sabbath** holy. He refused to honor the **Sabbath** as a day of rest and, as a result, was condemned by the Pharisees.

Here is a paragraph that repeats a sentence pattern to help establish a sense of coherence:

> Unfortunately, all forms of government are imperfect. Left-wing governments are strong on social justice but weak on economic prosperity. Right-wing governments are strong on economic prosperity but weak on social justice. In good economic times, left-wing governments should assume power so that wealth is equitably distributed. In bad economic times, right-wing governments should assume power to work their magic on the economy. Under such a shared system, economic prosperity will lead to social justice.

Notice how the structure of the third sentence in this example mirrors the structure of the sentence that precedes it. Similarly, the fifth sentence mirrors the structure of the fourth. This creates a sense of balance within the paragraph that helps create the sense that the paragraph sticks together, that it is cohesive.

● Substitution

As you learned earlier in this chapter, coherence can be established in a paragraph by repeating a key word. You do not want to repeat a key word too many times in the course of a single paragraph, of course, because such repetition can make your paragraph appear boring and unimaginative. But what you can and should do is substitute the key word with a synonym or pronoun that refers back to the key word. Note the use of substitution for the key word *tourist* to maintain the coherence in the following paragraph:

> Tourists are instantly recognizable by their physical appearance. **They** are usually dressed in baggy shorts and souvenir T-shirts, and **they** usually come armed with camcorders under their arms or hoisted onto their shoulders. These **visitors** also have a way of walking that distinguishes them from the locals. **They** meander quite aimlessly, stopping at every other intersection to gaze up at the street signs or to point their camcorders at buildings, the architectural significance of which usually eludes their hosts. Tourists also tend to have happily vacant facial expressions, in contrast to the grim determination set in the expression of the locals. Still, the locals welcome these **alien invaders,** who can be counted on to boost the local economy.

Style

Academic writing should be clear and straightforward, but there is no reason why it should be dull. An interesting subject makes an interesting essay, but that interest is diminished if the information is conveyed in a dull writing style. A dull writing style is characterized mainly by a series of short, choppy sentences joined together, if at all, by conjunctions such as *and*. A short, simple sentence does not make a dull style. Indeed, a short, simple sentence can be used effectively, especially to emphasize a particular point. What you want to avoid in your writing is a series of short, choppy sentences, which make your writing sound as if it were written by a ten-year-old or by an untalented journalist.

The key to avoiding a passage of dull sentences is to read your essay out loud while you are revising it. If you have written a passage consisting of too many short, dull sentences, you will be able to hear the problem (as will your readers), and you can make the necessary revisions to make your style more pleasing. In a variety of ways, you can vary your sentence structure and thereby improve your writing style. Three common and effective methods are these:

- Use subordination to combine a series of short, choppy sentences together.
- Establish parallelism within a sentence.
- Vary the order of words and phrases in a sentence.

Subordination

You can combine a series of three or four short, choppy sentences into two or even one more interesting and sophisticated sentence by changing some of the sentences into clauses or phrases and adding those clauses or phrases on to one complete sentence. This process is called **subordination.** The writer takes one sentence and changes it into a **phrase** or a **clause** and attaches the phrase or clause to a complete sentence. The phrase or clause thereby becomes "subordinate" to the main clause, the complete sentence.

Let's look at an example. Consider this passage:

> The word *discreet* is an adjective. It means prudent or modest. Here is a sentence that uses the word *discreet* correctly: He was too discreet to reveal her age. The word *discrete* also is an adjective. But spelled this way it means separate or distinct. Here is an example: We are officially part of their department, but we operate as a discrete entity.

This is an informative paragraph, but its pedestrian style has a somnolent effect on the reader and detracts from the interesting information the paragraph contains. A more interesting version of the same paragraph might read like this:

> The word *discreet* is an adjective that means prudent or modest, as in the sentence, He was too discreet to reveal her age. The word *discrete* also is an adjective, but spelled this way, it means separate or distinct, as in the sentence, We are officially part of their department, but we operate as a discrete entity.

This version has a rhythm and flow that signals a more mature writing style and makes the paragraph more authoritative. What accounts for the improvement in the style of this paragraph? The second sentence has been subordinated into a clause, the third sentence has been subordinated into a phrase, and both have been attached (with a comma) to the first sentence. The same process has been repeated with the fourth, fifth, and sixth sentences.

Let's look at one more example. Here is a paragraph written in an uninspired style, consisting, as it does, of a succession of short, choppy sentences:

> William Penn was an English Quaker. His father was a prominent admiral. The British government gave Penn a large tract of land in the new colony of

America. They gave him the land in recognition of his father's naval career. Penn decided to establish a Quaker colony in America. In 1681, Penn and his cousin, William Markham, went to America. They were accompanied by a group of hearty Quaker colonists. They made their way to the junction of the Schuylkill and Delaware Rivers. Here they founded a City of Brotherly Love. This city eventually became Philadelphia. It became the capital of the state named after William Penn.

Here is the same paragraph revised to improve its sentence variety:

William Penn was an English Quaker, the son of a prominent admiral. The British government gave Penn a large tract of land in the new colony of America, in recognition of his father's naval career. Penn decided to establish a Quaker colony in America. In 1681, Penn and his cousin, William Markham, journeyed to America, accompanied by a group of hearty Quaker colonists. They made their way to the junction of the Schuylkill and Delaware Rivers, where they founded a City of Brotherly Love. This city eventually became Philadelphia, the capital of the state named after William Penn.

The first version of the paragraph is not incorrect, but an adult reader likely would find it sophomoric and dull. The revised version is more readable because, through subordination, the choppy sentence structure has been replaced with sentences that have a better sense of rhythm and flow.

● Parallelism

As a term in written composition, **parallelism** describes a sentence within which words, phrases, or clauses complement each other and create a sense of rhythm and balance within the sentence. Effective parallelism can create a graceful and striking sentence. Note the use of parallel structure in this excerpt from Winston Churchill's speech to the House of Commons on October 8, 1940. He was speaking about Great Britain's participation in World War II:

Death and sorrow will be the companions of our journey; hardship our garment; constancy and valor our only shield. We must be united, we must be undaunted, we must be inflexible.

Without parallelism, the passage loses much of its strength:

Death and sorrow will be the companions of our journey. We will also experience much hardship, which we will have to endure. We will have to shield ourselves with constancy and valor. We must be united. We cannot let our enemy frighten us. We must be inflexible.

This version is grammatically correct, but it lacks the passion, concision, and emphasis of the original because Churchill's effective use of parallelism is replaced by short, rather dull sentences.

Here is another example, this time from President Kennedy's inaugural address made on January 20, 1961:

> Let the word go forth from this time and place, to friend and foe alike, that the torch has been passed to a new generation of Americans, born in this century, tempered by war, disciplined by a hard and bitter peace, proud of our ancient heritage, and unwilling to witness or permit the slow undoing of those human rights to which this nation has always been committed, and to which we are committed today at home and around the world.
>
> Let every nation know, whether it wishes us well or ill, that we shall pay any price, bear any burden, meet any hardship, support any friend, oppose any foe, in order to assure the survival and the success of liberty.

Without the parallel structure Kennedy uses so effectively, this passage loses that stirring tone that complements the author's forthright message:

> Let the word go forth from this time and place, to friend and foe alike, that the torch has been passed to a new generation of Americans. These Americans were born in this century, and they have been tempered by war. In addition, they have been disciplined by a hard and bitter peace. They are proud of our ancient heritage and unwilling to witness or permit the slow undoing of those human rights to which this nation has always been committed. We will remain committed to these rights today at home and around the world.
>
> Let every nation know, whether it wishes us well or ill, that we shall pay any price to assure the survival and the success of liberty. Furthermore, we will bear any burden and meet any hardship in the interest of the same cause. Finally, we will support any friend and oppose any foe in order to assure the survival and the success of liberty.

In summary, then, the use of parallel structure can improve a writing style by making it at once more concise and more dramatic.

● Order

Most English sentences are structured so that a subject precedes a verb:

> Their debate was typical. The Democratic candidate promised to increase public spending on education and health care, to win the votes of the soccer moms. The Republican promised to lower taxes, to win the votes of the business community.

You can make your writing style, and hence your message, more interesting if, on occasion, you deviate from the standard "subject followed by a verb" pattern at the beginning of a sentence.

Their debate was typical. To win the votes of the soccer moms, the Democratic candidate promised to increase public spending on education and health care. To win the votes of the business community, the Republican promised to lower taxes.

Such sentences begin with a phrase and so withhold their main points (contained in the independent clause) until the end. The technique is effective because, being at the end, the main clause is stressed. Sentences that delay their main clause are called **periodic sentences.**

The order of words in an English sentence is alterable to a considerable degree. Consider the following sentences:

The tenants refused to pay one more penny of rent until the landlord repaired the plumbing.

Until the landlord repaired the plumbing, the tenants refused to pay one more penny of rent.

One more penny of rent the tenants refused to pay, until the landlord repaired the plumbing.

The tenants refused to pay, until the landlord repaired the plumbing, one more penny of rent.

Which sentence is the most effective? It depends upon the form and shape of the other sentences around it, on the writer's purpose and audience, and on the extent to which the writer wants to emphasize certain information within the sentence. The word order in the third version seems especially unique and emphatic.

If you notice when you are revising your work that the vast majority of your sentences follow the typical subject-verb pattern, consider experimenting with the word order of some of your sentences. There is no "right" way to determine which version of a sentence is the best. It does help to read your work out loud while you revise it. You will be able to hear the rhythm and flow of your sentences and alter them in order to display them to their best advantage.

Hannah has written a draft of her essay about our celebrity culture. Before she began to revise her draft, she printed out a copy, so she could get a good sense of what needed to be done to improve her text as a whole. This is a good strategy because revision often involves major structural changes to the essay. Editing can usually be done directly on the computer screen because editing is usually a sentence-level component of the writing process. And editing is a constant process. Writers edit and proofread while they draft and edit and proofread, again while they revise.

Return for a moment to Hannah's handwritten revisions on pages 84–89. Note the revisions Hannah's handwritten comments recommend:

- She changes her title to "Some Social and Psychological Consequences of Celebrity Worship." While she was refining her thesis statement, at the end of the first paragraph, she included the phrase "social and psychological disorder," and she realized this is the essence of her paper and belongs in the title.
- She decides to add content. Reconsidering content is the most important aspect of the revision process. At this stage, writers realize they may have to delete content, but more often they realize they need to add substance to their paper. Hannah's assignment calls for an essay of approximately 1,500 words. She has about 1,300. As a rule, it is better to exceed slightly the word count the assignment calls for rather than to reduce it. Hannah adds a sentence to the end of her second paragraph because she feels that paragraph needs a better sense of closure. She broadens her paragraph that begins "Feasy also," adding examples that reference minorities and gay women. She adds information to her paragraph that begins "Other social commentators" because she wants to add to the comparison between women and male celebrities. She adds a sentence to the end of her essay to establish a clearer sense of closure.
- She decides to reposition her third paragraph, to place it later in the essay, where it will be more effective and will maintain the structure, which is based upon, first, the benefits of our interest in celebrities and, second, the drawbacks. Paragraph three describes a drawback and needs to be moved. Note that this restructuring is also a typical rhetorical move of the revision process.
- She decides to delete the names of those celebrities whose activities and lifestyles exemplify some of the points she is making. Is this a good idea? The names add specificity to her paper, something composition teachers always say is a good idea. Hannah reasons that the celebrities are so well known, readers will supply the names when they read—and she is not completely comfortable naming names. But this decision might weaken her paper.

Hannah still has to add her list of Works Cited, eliminating from the source list she compiled earlier those sources she does not reference. She also has to make certain her essay—title, page numbers, and spacing— is presented in the correct MLA format.

Here, then, is the final version of Hannah's paper.

Hannah Goldman
Professor Ellis
Cultural Studies 218
18 March 2009

Some Social and Psychological Consequences of Celebrity Worship

The lifestyles of the rich and famous have always intrigued ordinary people   1
without vast wealth and fame, but for many people this intrigue has become an
obsession. On prime-time television almost any night of the week, there are at
least six programs devoted to keeping America informed about the births, deaths,
accidents, addictions, convictions, and love lives of movie and television stars,
professional athletes, business moguls, even, occasionally, politicians. Magazines
with the same mandate fill the racks of drugstores and supermarkets. Look online
for information about the rich and the famous and you will be overwhelmed
by photographs, biographies, blogs, and online fan clubs devoted exclusively
to worshipping a favorite star. Social scientists have been studying America's
fascination with the lives of celebrities and are reaching interesting conclusions.
Our interest in the lives of celebrities is a normal and harmless, even a healthy
diversion; but it can also become an abnormal, even dangerous social and
psychological disorder.

Rebecca Feasy argues that an interest in celebrity culture is healthy, is, in   2
fact, empowering for women, who are the primary consumers of celebrity gossip.
A woman who reads celebrity magazines and wants to dress like the stars is in
control "of her sexuality and social situation" (182). She has social power because
she has taken the initiative to look beautiful and, as a consequence, to be noticed
and thereby acquire social capital. Lakshmi Chaudhry calls this "a certain brand
of Gen-X feminism that places sexual gratification and independence at the top of
the agenda" (22). Feasy also believes that magazines and TV programs that gossip about celebrity lifestyles provide women with "a valuable feminine discourse"
(189). Women share an interest in the dating and the mating patterns of celebrities, in the progress of celebrity marriages, in the welfare of the children of celebrity couples. They get together to gossip about their favorite celebrities, and in
the process, they share advice with each other and gain insight into and negotiate
their own personal and family relationships and social identity (Feasy 190;

Halpern 147). Celebrity relationships are instructive, even if they might represent bad models of behavior.

Feasy also argues that stars motivate us to exercise and diet, in an attempt   3
to look as good as they do, and that this discipline enhances self esteem.
And she notes that more magazines and TV programs focus now on the stars' imperfections—their less-than-perfect skin, ill-advised plastic surgery, and fashion faux pas (185)—and thereby "liberate the reader from feeling inadequate for failing to create her own celebrity body" (187). Sean Redmond argues that we feel better about ourselves when we wear a celebrity's perfume or clothes from the favorite designer to the stars, and that these feelings can be renewed and reinforced because we can put on the clothing and perfume again and again. Moreover, the subtext of products endorsed by celebrities is often subversive—you don't need a man to be happy, successful, and free; you can drive a truck or run a company; it's ok to be intimate with someone of a different race—and thereby undermine stereotypes about race and gender roles (40). Similarly, the self-esteem of people, young people, especially, who do not belong to and may feel alienated from the dominant culture, increases when people who represent that sub-culture become famous. Ramona Coleman-Bell argues that young African American women feel better about their bodies when young black female athletes, who often have powerful but not the currently-favored size two body win endorsements for mainstream companies like McDonalds and Avon (204). Judith Franco makes the same point about lesbian celebrities who validate the identity and desires of young gay women.

Other social commentators, however, argue that engaging in celebrity gossip   4
and using celebrities as role models are anti-feminist activities that, more often than not, diminish self-esteem. Provocative designer clothing and fit bodies are as much about a love of male attention, which concedes power, as they are about social capital that enhances social power. Feminist authors further point out that women who achieve the greatest fame are those who fall apart and self-destruct, often because of a failed relationship with a man. Naomi Wolf bemoans a culture "increasingly obsessed with showcasing images of glamorous young women who are falling apart" (in Chaudhry 24), and she suggests this fascination is anti-feminist in that it reassures the male establishment of the stereotype of the weak and vulnerable woman who needs a man's help if she is to be in control and successful. Young male stars who are sexually indiscreet and behave badly in public

Goldman 3

get by with the boys-will-be-boys defense, while the women are victims of the age-old and sexist double standard: young men can be wild, but a young woman who misbehaves risks her reputation.

Moreover, fans can wear the same clothes, eat the same food, and practice the same yoga techniques of their favorite stars, but they don't have access to the air brushes, glamour lenses, makeup artists, personal trainers, and plastic surgeons of the stars, and when they fall short of this physical perfection, even though it is manufactured, they may feel they have failed. According to one study, nearly sixty percent of women who had cosmetic surgery because they wanted the same feature—lips, breasts, nose—of their favorite celebrity were disappointed with the results (Hecom 38).   5

Some fans, whose grip on reality is already shaky, imagine they have a personal relationship with the stars, because the stars appear in their bedrooms. Theses fans choose to ignore or are oblivious to the fact that the stars are only there on a television or computer screen. Some of the most fanatic have tried to establish a personal connection with those they are now convinced are friends or, in the extremist of cases, their deity (Halpern 164–65). They are shattered when their access is prevented by very large and menacing security guards. In the worst cases, admiration turns to contempt, observing turns to stalking, and the obsessed fan threatens the celebrity with violence, even death.   6

Similarly, Jill Weir questions Feasy's argument about the positive effects that knowledge of celebrity imperfections can have on the self esteem of the not-so-famous. To Weir, this interest in celebrity cellulite and less-than-perfect muscle tone is cruel, vindictive, and mean-spirited. Magazines and websites don't purchase photos of an aging starlet looking far from perfect on vacation in a bikini to heighten the self-esteem of readers. They don't feature close-ups of the haggard faces of yesterday's glamour girls so the huddled masses will smile and relax when they look in the mirror. They do it because mean sells. The appeal, Weir and other social commentators fear, is to the worst part of human nature, and, now that video cameras are in cell phones, anyone can turn into an ethically-challenged paparazzo and sell unflattering images to the media.   7

There may be, as well, a broader social cost to celebrity worship. It twists our social and political values and it can divert our attention away from issues that should concern us more. More Americans vote for their favorite American Idol than they do for president, and they are more likely to know the name of the baby of a celebrity couple than the name of their Secretary of State or Speaker of the House.   8

When *Dancing with the Stars* or other reality shows compete with a presidential debate, the reality show draws many more viewers. Ironically, the political leaders we know the best are often those who achieved celebrity status before they were elected, and whose celebrity gave them an unfair advantage while they were campaigning. The greatest social cost of celebrity worship is the deleterious effect it has on our justice system. Juries seem transfixed by celebrities and seem more likely to acquit those charged with a crime. Despite considerable evidence against them, some famous professional athletes, actors, and pop stars have been acquitted of crimes as heinous as rape, pedophilia, and murder.

There is nothing wrong with dreaming of possessing the wealth, fame, and   9
good looks our heroes possess, or indulging in the latest water-cooler gossip, or feeling better about ourselves when we discover that a famous person shares our minority status but has still become successful. Problems arise when celebrity worshippers go too far, spending hours in front of their television sets or computer monitors catching up on the latest gossip, or, in worst case scenarios, deluding themselves about the nature of their relationship with someone rich and famous, perhaps to a potentially dangerous extent. Experts seem to agree that it is crucial to balance the time we spend as celebrity voyeurs with time spent watching the news, reading a good book, and socializing with our <u>real</u> friends and family.

Works Cited

Chaudhry, Lakshmi. "The Diana/Whore Complex." *The Nation* 27 Aug. 2007: 22–25. Print.

Coleman-Bell, Ramona. "Droppin' It Like It's Hot: The Sporting Body of Serena Williams." *Framing Celebrity: New Directions in Celebrity Culture.* Eds. Sean Redmond and Su Holms. London and New York: Routledge, 2006. 195–206. Print.

Halpern, Jake. *Fame Junkies: The Hidden Truth Behind America's Favorite Addiction.* Boston: Houghton Mifflin, 2007. Print.

Hecom, Dale. "Satisfaction Rates Among Women Undergoing Celebrity Influenced Cosmetic Surgery." *Southwest Journal of Contemporary Culture* 3.3 (2005): n. pag. Web. 9 March 2008.

Feasy, Rebecca. "Get a Famous Body: Star Styles and Celebrity Gossip in *heat* Magazine." *Framing Celebrity: New Directions in Celebrity Culture.* Eds. Sean Redmond and Su Holms. London and New York: Routledge, 2006. 177–194. Print.

Franco, Judith. "Langsters Online: K.D. Lang and the Creation of Internet Fan Communities." *Framing Celebrity: New Directions in Celebrity Culture.* Eds. Sean Redmond and Su Holms. London and New York: Routledge, 2006. 269–284. Print.

Redmond, Sean. "Intimate Fame Everywhere." *Framing Celebrity: New Directions in Celebrity Culture.* Eds. Sean Redmond and Su Holms. London and New York: Routledge, 2006. 27–44. Print.

Weir, Jill. "Why We Are Celebrified." *CultureCow.com* 18 Mar. 2006. 8 March 2008: n. pag. Web.

● Academic Voice

Written discourse reflects the personality and the attitude of the writer, or at least the personality and the attitude the writer chooses to assume for a given assignment. This personality and attitude are known as the writer's **voice** or **tone.** Writers must assume a voice that complements the purpose of their work, the audience for whom it is intended, and the genre in which it is written. A movie reviewer might choose to use a sardonic voice when panning a film. Valedictorians typically assume a solemn, rather formal voice. Your latest e-mail to a friend probably includes slang, inside jokes, and incomplete sentences, establishing a casual, informal, familiar voice.

Our concern here, of course, is with revising your essay to make sure it is written in **academic voice,** which is the persona writers assume when writing an essay for a professor or an article for a professional journal. A good academic voice is formal and authoritative but never too lofty or grandiose. Academic voice is clear and concise. For her first-year writing course, Pauline wrote an essay on avoiding gender-biased language. Read this paragraph from Pauline's essay, paying particular attention to her voice:

> Another controversial way of avoiding the discord caused by the repetition of both the masculine and feminine pronoun is to use only the feminine form—A student at this university will have *her* library privileges suspended if *she* accumulates more than three overdue fines. There are several arguments in support of this usage. The first is that it does solve the problem of the discordant repetition caused by the repeated use of both pronouns. A second argument is that for hundreds of years writers have used the male form exclusively, and now it is time to even things out. Feminists have fought for more than thirty years for linguistic democracy, and it's time their struggle was rewarded. A new millennium is a perfect occasion for progress. A more compelling argument is based upon current usage: the exclusive use of the feminine pronoun has been creeping into the published prose of some professional writers for about a decade and is therefore becoming accepted, if not yet standard, usage (Macher, 1999). Even President Clinton, in his 1998 State of the Union Address, endorsed at least the partial use of the feminine pronoun, when

he read this sentence: "If you know a child from a poor family, tell her not to give up—she can go to college." When a President sanctions such a construction, by using it in a State of the Union Address, its acceptance is endorsed, if not guaranteed.

Note that the tone—the voice—of the passage is calm and measured, even though the writer is making a controversial suggestion. It is written, of course, in Standard English, so the grammar, sentence structure, spelling, and punctuation are correct. The diction and vocabulary are neither too casual nor too grandiose or pompous. There is no slang, which is completely out of place in academic writing. The writer comes across as a thoughtful and intelligent person, and his or her readers will be inclined to trust the accuracy of the information such a writer gives them and to consider his or her argument seriously.

Which point of view to use with the academic voice is a topic of some debate. Some of your professors will <u>not</u> want you to use the first-person pronouns (*I* or *we*) in your essays; others might object to the use of the second person (*you*). They will insist upon an objective point of view, devoid of any personal pronouns. In social science studies, for example, the authors will generally not write, "We received responses from 329 of the 452 school counselors to whom we sent questionnaires," preferring instead the more detached passive voice: "Responses were received from 329 of the 452 school counselors to whom questionnaires were sent." However, look at the "Study 1 Results and Discussion" section of Grossbard et al.'s study, "Are Drinking Games Sports?" in Part Three. These authors consistently use the first-person plural pronoun *we* in reporting their results. Similarly, Hard, Conway, and Moran's "Faculty and College Student Beliefs About the Frequency of Student Academic Misconduct," also in Part Three, is a social science study, yet the authors regularly use first person: "We gathered information"; "We contacted instructors"; "We compared the means." It seems likely that the use of the first-person point of view is more acceptable now in academic writing than it once was.

Point of view depends upon audience and purpose. If you want to establish a sense of familiarity with your readers or to convey a personal touch, the *I* point of view is acceptable. If you are directly instructing your readers, the *you* point of view is effective. If you want to maintain distance from your readers, use an objective point of view.

Academic voice does not require the use of **ostentatious language**, that is, words and phrases that are used not because they are the most appropriate but because they are the most complex and obscure. Writers who use ostentatious language are merely trying to impress their readers with their extensive and sophisticated vocabulary. But readers usually suspect the truth: that the writer has consulted a thesaurus one too many times. Good writers eschew obfuscation with unambiguous linguistic manifestations. Usually a plain and simple style, one that is not pedestrian or dry but clear and straightforward, is most effective in academic writing.

Peer Review

One of the most effective ways to revise your essay is to have a classmate look over your draft and suggest constructively critical ways of improving it. So valuable is this exercise, in fact, that your teacher likely will free up some class time for peer review of drafts, usually done in small groups of three or four. In a peer review session, each writer typically reads his or her essay aloud while other members of the group follow along with their own copy of the draft. When the reading is complete, each group member presents opinions about the strengths and weaknesses of the essay. The writer listens carefully to these opinions, without hostility and in the collegial spirit a good peer conferencing session fosters, and considers making some of the revisions that group members suggest.

To be most effective, peer review of drafts should not be comprehensive; that is, reviewers should not attempt to comment on every aspect of the writing process as it relates to the particular assignment the group is considering. Peer review is most effective when its scope is limited to two or three aspects of the writing process, usually those aspects the instructor wants to stress at the time the peer review is occurring. Peer review is also most effective when that focus is on the global or broad aspects of writing: Are the paragraphs well developed? Does each paragraph relate to the essay's thesis? Is the essay's structure coherent?

But whatever the focus of the peer review session is, it is always a good idea to work with a checklist or a rubric of some kind. A checklist that tries to account for all of the components of good writing would be several pages long and impractical for peer review. An effective checklist isolates certain components of good writing. If, for example, your teacher wants to focus on cultivating an effective style for an academic essay and organizes peer review sessions for this purpose, he or she might distribute a rubric like this:

Week Eight Peer Review: Cultivating an Effective Writing Style
This week we read each other's drafts and focus on the effectiveness of each writer's style. Consider especially these questions:

- Does the writer avoid any prolonged use of short, choppy sentences?
- Is there a sense of rhythm and flow in the writer's essay?
- Is the tone (the voice) of the essay in sync with its audience and purpose?
- Is there variety in the writer's sentence structure?

Remember, this is one possible rubric for one aspect of good writing. There are many other ways a peer review session could be structured. If your teacher wanted to work on paragraph development, sentence grammar, or effective openings, the rubric would be tailored to meet these needs. The key point is that effective peer review sessions do have a specific purpose and structure.

Conclusion

We learned at the beginning of this chapter the difference between revising and editing: Revising changes overall structure and paragraph content; editing changes words and sentences. Many student writers are obsessed with editing—with getting words spelled correctly, commas in the right places, and sentence fragments healed—somewhat at the expense of revising. Students often arrive at college believing that good writing is correct writing. They are half right. Good writing certainly follows the conventions of editing, and in the next chapter, those conventions will be presented in detail. But good writing is more than correct writing. Good writing has a robust form; it is interesting and informative, complete and comprehensive. Make changes—revisions—to the structure, the coherence, and the content of your essays until you are satisfied that your readers will be able to follow your train of thought and will understand what it is you want to tell them.

WRITING ASSIGNMENT

Read an article in an academic journal on a topic of interest to you. Study carefully four sequential paragraphs in the body of the article. Identify the topic sentence of each paragraph. (Remember that the topic sentence might be implied rather than stated explicitly.) Study carefully the author's methods of establishing cohesion within each paragraph and among the four paragraphs.

Write one paragraph in which you describe the methods the writer uses to develop his or her body paragraphs adequately. In another paragraph, describe the author's use of transition, repetition, and substitution as cohesive ties within each paragraph and among the three paragraphs. See the commentary that accompanies the essays in Part Two for examples.

EXERCISES

1. Revise each of the following paragraphs to improve their style. Do not alter the meaning of the paragraphs by adding anything to them or taking anything from them. You may rearrange the order and structure of sentences in ways you think most effective.

   Archimedes was a Greek mathematician. He discovered that the weight of the fluid that was displaced when an object was put in fluid could be used to measure the mass of that object. There is a legend associated with this discovery. Archimedes was in his bath one day. He watched the water rise as he settled into his bath. He shouted "Eureka" and danced into the Athens streets, wearing only his towel.

Chad is a landlocked country in north-central Africa. Chad is slightly smaller than the state of Alaska. Libya is north of Chad. The Sudan is east of Chad. The Central African Empire is south of Chad. Cameroon is also south of Chad. Nigeria is southwest of Chad. Niger is west of Chad. Lake Chad is the largest body of water in Chad. It is in the west. It spills into neighboring Niger and Nigeria. In the north is a desert. It is part of the Sahara Desert.

Mercury is the planet nearest the sun. It is named after the Roman messenger to the gods. Mercury was famous for his speed as a runner. It is an appropriate name for the planet. Mercury whizzes around the sun. It travels at the speed of 30 miles per second. It completes one circuit in 88 days. But it rotates slowly on its axis. It takes 59 days for Mercury to make a single rotation. It spins at the rate of about 6 miles per hour. The Earth spins at the rate of about a thousand miles per hour.

In Egyptian mythology, Ra is the god of the Sun. He is the supreme god in Egyptian mythology. He was the son of Nut. Nut is the goddess of the heavens. Egyptian pharaohs claimed to be descended from Ra. Ra is sometimes represented as a lion. Ra is sometimes represented as a cat. Ra is sometimes represented as a falcon.

When America was founded, the average human life span was 35 years. By 1900, the average life span had increased to 47 years. Today, the average American lives to be 76 years old. An elderly American is defined as one over the age of 65. In 1900, one in twenty-five Americans were over the age of 65. Today, one in eight Americans is over the age of 65. The explosion in the growth of the number of elderly Americans has significant social and political ramifications.

The land that now makes up the state of Wyoming was purchased in 1803. It was a part of the Louisiana Purchase. Great Britain bought land from France in the Louisiana Purchase. In 1846, the United States obtained Wyoming from the British. The takeover was one of the conditions of the Oregon Treaty.

2. Revise the following paragraphs to improve their unity and coherence. Add words and combine sentences together as needed to create a more readable paragraph.

    Achilles fought at the Trojan War. He had magnificent armor. He was killed. An arrow pierced his heel. His heel was the only vulnerable part of his body. His mother, Thetis, knew the war would endanger Achilles' life. She dipped him, when he was a baby, into the River Styx to protect him from injury. She held him by the heel, which did not get covered in water. Odysseus and Ajax fought over Achilles' armor. Odysseus and Ajax were both fearsome warriors. Odysseus killed Ajax. Years later, Odysseus had occasion to visit the land of the dead. Ajax refused to talk to him.

In September 1970, Salvador Allende was elected president of Chile. He was the first politician of a noncommunist country to run as a Marxist-Leninist and be elected in a free vote. He normalized relations with Cuba. He normalized relations with the People's Republic of China. He nationalized American companies. The military despised his policies. Augusto Pinochet was the army chief of staff. In September 1973, he and his junta overthrew Allende and seized power.

For years, astronomers did not know much about the planet Mercury. It is, in our solar system, the planet closest to the sun. The most powerful telescopes could not get a good view of Mercury. There was too much glare from the sun to see Mercury clearly. In the mid-1970s, NASA launched *Mariner 10*. It sent photographs of Mercury back to astronomers on Earth. The photos revealed a mountainous planet. It has cliffs over a mile high and nearly a thousand miles long. It contains a crater over 800 miles in diameter. Its surface is covered by a crust of light silicate rock. It is rich in iron.

COLLABORATIVE ACTIVITY

Exchange the draft of an essay with another student. Make suggestions on ways your partner might revise his or her essay to improve it. Resist the urge, for now, to correct errors in sentence grammar, sentence structure, punctuation, and spelling. Focus on improving the structure, the content, and the cohesion of your partner's paper.

JOURNAL PROMPT

Reflect upon your writing style and the voice you use as a student writer. How would you describe it? What are its strengths? How might you work to improve it?

CHAPTER 7

Edit Your Essay

E diting is the process of correcting and improving the sentences and words within a written text. It is a multifaceted aspect of the composing process that includes checking for good grammar, effective sentence structure, proper punctuation, and clear diction. It is an ongoing process, a task a writer works on while writing and revising his or her essay.

Editing can be one of the most taxing aspects of the writing process. Some grammar and punctuation rules are complex; others are arbitrary. There are editing conventions some professors insist their students adhere to, and they penalize students who violate those conventions. Other professors, when grading, flag but forgive a *who* that should be a *whom*, an *I* that should be a *me*, or a comma that should be a semicolon.

What is the most effective way to edit a written text? Experienced writers usually read their work out loud and base their editing decisions on "what sounds right." This is not a bad strategy, especially for those who, by virtue of their social and cultural background, have had extended exposure to the rules of Standard English. These rules—the patterns of Standard English—become fixed in our minds, and when a convention is violated, we literally hear it: "Me and my brother are coming home for Christmas." "I didn't do too good on my last biology exam." The more reading and writing you do and the more indelibly these language patterns acceptable within the academic community become fixed in your mind, the fewer errors you will make.

Some editing conventions, however, still deceive that sense of "what sounds right." Spoken English is less formal than written English, and sometimes a rendition common in spoken English is transferred to a written text even though the spoken version is grammatically incorrect. It might sound fine to say and hence to write, "My mother can't wait for my brother and I to come home for Thanksgiving," but the *I* is grammatically incorrect and should be changed to *me*—"She can't wait for *me* to come home."

This chapter provides a concise but comprehensive account of editing conventions but focuses on instruction in those editing conventions that most frequently vex student writers. It discusses the rules of **grammar, sentence structure, punctuation,** and **diction** (or word choice) that you need to know to write effective academic essays.

Edit for Grammar

Grammar is the study of the order, the function, and the form of words in sentences and of the rules that govern this order, function, and form. Professors take the rules of English grammar seriously; they do not like to see grammatical errors in the essays they grade, and they are likely to penalize an essay that contains grammatical errors. Grammar and spelling errors diminish the impact of your essay. Readers are not likely to take your ideas seriously if your paper contains grammatical errors. When you revise and edit your academic essays, check your grammar. In particular, check to make certain you meet these requirements:

- Your verbs agree with their subjects.
- Your pronouns clearly refer to the correct nouns.
- The case of your pronouns is correct.
- Your verb tense is correct.

Subject-Verb Agreement

Singular subjects take singular verbs: A poet *paints* with words. Plural subjects take plural verbs: Poets *paint* with words. Usually, subject-verb agreement is that simple. You will write some sentences, however, that will require a moment's thought before you choose the correct verb form.

When Words Intervene Between the Subject and the Verb

If words come between the subject and the verb, be careful not to agree the verb with one of those words. In the sentence "One of my books is out of print," *one* is the subject, which is why the singular verb *is* is used. Compare the following two sentences:

My books <u>are</u> out of print.

One of my books <u>is</u> out of print.

When the Verb Precedes the Subject

You might write a sentence in which the verb precedes its subject. In the following sentence, for example, the verb *are* comes well before the subject *philosophers*:

> There <u>are</u> many more important nineteenth-century philosophers whose work we did not study.

The verb must be the plural *are*, not the singular *is*, because the subject *philosophers* is plural.

When the Subject Is an Indefinite Pronoun

An indefinite pronoun is one that replaces an indefinite or inexact noun. Some examples of indefinite pronouns are *another, anybody, anyone, anything, each, either, every, everybody, everyone, everything, neither, nobody, no one, nothing, somebody, someone, something.* Indefinite pronouns usually require the singular form of the verb:

> Neither of my professors <u>is</u> available on Fridays.

Note that *neither*, not *professors*, is the subject with which the verb *is* must agree.

The indefinite pronouns *both* and *many* are always plural:

> Both of my professors <u>are</u> available on Fridays.

The indefinite pronouns *all, any, more, most, none,* and *some* can take either singular or plural verbs; the choice depends upon the context:

> All of the money <u>is</u> missing, but all of the employees <u>are</u> safe.

When the Noun Following the Verb Is Different in Number from the Subject

Be careful when you have a singular subject followed by a verb followed by a plural noun, as in this sentence:

> The worst part about writing an academic essay <u>is</u> all the grammar rules you need to know.

Because the noun *rules* is plural, you might be tempted to use the plural verb *are* instead of the correct verb *is*, but remember it is the subject the verb must agree with. If you have a plural subject followed by a singular noun, the same condition applies:

> The rules of English grammar <u>are</u> a problem for me.

Do not use the singular noun *is* because it is followed by a singular noun *problem*. The plural verb *are* is required because the subject *rules* is plural.

Collective Noun as Subject

A collective noun is one that identifies a group: *family, team, orchestra, class, audience.* Usually, a collective noun takes a singular verb:

The press <u>is</u> not welcome.

If the collective noun is not acting as a unit but rather is having its individual members emphasized, use the plural form of the verb, as in this sentence:

The press <u>are</u> arguing about who will get the interview.

 Exercise on Subject-Verb Agreement

Circle the correct verb in each sentence.

Neither of these sentences (is, are) correct.

Each of my body paragraphs (contain, contains) a good topic sentence.

Strategies for developing a good body paragraph (is, are) discussed in Chapter 5.

Neither of my science teachers (was, were) willing to help me.

The Barchester Symphony Orchestra (refuse, refuses) to play any contemporary music.

The press (is, are) trying to find out whom Clinton supported in the New Hampshire primary.

The sound of the cannons at the end of the *1812 Overture* always (frighten, frightens) children.

There (is, are) three important primaries later this month.

Neither of Blake's books (was, were) signed out of the library this semester.

Britain's royal family (visit, visits) Commonwealth countries several times each year.

● Pronoun Reference

Pronouns replace nouns. The noun the pronoun replaces is called the **antecedent** of that pronoun. There are three pronoun-antecedent pitfalls to avoid.

First, make certain your pronouns agree in number with their antecedents. In other words, if the antecedent is singular, the pronoun should be singular. Consider these three sentences:

The <u>manager</u> of a Burger World franchise cannot employ members of <u>their</u> immediate family.

The <u>manager</u> of a Burger World franchise cannot employ members of <u>his or her</u> immediate family.

> Managers of Burger World franchises cannot employ members of their immediate families.

The first sentence is grammatically incorrect, because *manager* is a singular noun and *their* is a plural pronoun. *Manager* is the antecedent of *their* but the words don't agree in number. The second sentence is correct, because the *their* has been changed to the singular pronouns *his or her*. The third sentence is correct, because *manager* has been changed to *managers* to match the plural *their*.

Here is another example. Again, the first sentence is incorrect, this time because the noun is singular and the pronoun that replaces it later in the sentence is plural:

> If a soldier is given a command they believe is inappropriate, they can ask for the command to be issued in writing.

> If a soldier is given a command he or she believes is inappropriate, he or she can ask for the command to be issued in writing.

> If soldiers are given commands they believe are inappropriate, they can ask for the commands to be issued in writing.

Some writers and readers will find the repetition of "he or she" in the second version of the sentence jarring; it disrupts the flow of the sentence. Using only one of these pronouns is not grammatically incorrect, but your readers might object to the exclusion, especially of the feminine pronoun.

Remember from the previous discussion of subject-verb agreement that indefinite pronouns such as *anyone, everyone, nobody*, or *somebody* are usually singular. Strictly speaking, this means that if a pronoun has an indefinite pronoun as its antecedent, that pronoun should be singular. However, the use of the plural pronoun in conjunction with an indefinite pronoun is becoming widespread. Strictly speaking, the first of the following sentences is grammatically correct and the second is not, but most readers either will not recognize the error in the second sentence or will not worry enough about it to hold it against the writer.

> Anyone interested in applying for this job should send his or her résumé to the personnel manager.

> Anyone interested in applying for this job should send their résumé to the personnel manager.

Most readers are not going to lose confidence in the work of a writer who uses the plural pronoun *they* when its antecedent is the singular indefinite pronoun *everyone*. If you are writing an academic essay, however, either check with your instructor to see if he or she (not they) will accept the plural, or play it safe and use the singular.

Similarly, the grammar police would insist that this sentence is ungrammatical:

> Everyone complains about the taxes they have to pay, but no one is willing to cut the social programs that benefit them.

They would insist that the sentence be changed to something like this:

> Everyone complains about the taxes he or she has to pay, but no one is willing to cut the social programs that benefit him or her.

Another option is to revise the sentence to reduce the number of pronouns that follow the indefinite pronouns or even eliminate them altogether:

> Everyone complains about paying taxes, but no one is willing to stop receiving taxpayer-funded benefits.

The second pronoun reference pitfall to avoid is the pronoun that seems to refer to more than one antecedent. Consider, for example, this sentence:

> The president hoped to meet the prime minister in Madrid, but fearing an assassination attempt, he did not show up.

The pronoun *he* could refer to either the president or the PM. You would have to revise this sentence to clarify the identity of *he*—change the *he* to either *president* or *prime minister* to correct the ambiguity.

Finally, edit sentences that contain a pronoun that does not appear to have any antecedent at all. Consider this sentence:

> There was a vigorous debate in the House, but Members of Parliament knew the Senate would not agree to it.

The antecedent appears to be *debate,* but this conveys a meaning the writer did not intend. Be specific by changing *it* to *the bill, the resolution,* or *the amendment*—whatever the pronoun is supposed to refer to—and the sentence becomes clear.

When you revise your essays, check all of your pronouns to make certain their antecedents are never ambiguous.

 ## Exercise on Pronoun Reference

Correct the pronoun reference errors in these sentences.

He used the calculator to complete the form, and then he gave it to his roommate.

After Rendell and Fisher debated the issues on television, his approval ratings went up three percentage points.

Diana is overweight and Melissa is not, so she got the part.

Each candidate will have ten minutes to explain their platform.

Not every student at Juan de Fuca College will finish their degree in four years.

The ceremony was held at the tomb of the unknown soldier, who sacrificed their life to preserve the freedom of their countrymen.

A runner who trains five days a week, twice a day, will reach their top level of fitness within two months.

The city decided to renovate the stadium rather than build a new one because they did not want to raise taxes.

As soon as the young girl walked away from her mother and boarded the plane, she began to cry.

● Pronoun Case

There are three types or three **cases** of pronouns: subjective, objective, and possessive. English-language pronouns divide as follows into their three cases:

Subjective	*Objective*	*Possessive*
I	me	my, mine
you	you	your(s)
he	him	his
she	her	her(s)
we	us	our(s)
they	them	their(s)
who	whom	whose
it	it	its

The rules for correct pronoun use are straightforward. Pronouns in the subjective case are used as subjects of verbs:

He was born in 1795.

Pronouns in the objective case are used as objects of verbs:

He met her at a flea market.

or as objects of prepositions:

He knew she was the girl for him.

Pronouns in the possessive case are used to show possession:

He liked <u>her</u> long blond hair, and she liked <u>his</u> red suspenders.

The rules are straightforward, but applying these rules sometimes requires concentration. There are four pronoun pitfalls to avoid.

Pronoun-Noun Combinations

Be careful when you use a noun and a pronoun together; it is easy to make an error. You are unlikely to make an error if the noun-pronoun combination is acting as a subject, as in this sentence:

Dr. Johnson and <u>I</u> met for tea at the Strand.

But remember that you must use the objective case if the pronoun is the object of a verb, even if it is in combination with a noun:

The staff at the Strand expected Dr. Johnson and <u>me</u> to come for tea every Thursday afternoon.

Similarly, you must use the objective case of the pronoun if the pronoun is the object of a preposition, even if the pronoun is used in combination with a noun:

The staff at the Strand wanted to know who was coming with Dr. Johnson and <u>me</u>.

If this use of the objective case of the pronoun sounds wrong to you, eliminate the noun, and you will know immediately that the objective case must be right:

They are expecting <u>me</u>.

They want to know who is coming with <u>me</u>.

Pronouns in a Comparison

When you use a pronoun in a comparison, complete the comparison (in your mind if not in the text), and you will select the correct pronoun. If you write, "She reads poetry more often than me," you are saying, "She reads poetry more than me does," when you obviously mean "more than *I* do." In fact, if you write, "She reads poetry more often than me," you are saying, "She reads poetry more often than she reads me." The grammatically correct form is to write, "She reads poetry more often than I." Imagine the omitted word is included at the end of the sentence, and it will be easier for you to pick the correct pronoun: "She reads poetry more often than I [do]."

Pronouns in comparisons can, indeed, cause confusion. Be careful. If you write, "My mother likes mushrooms more than me," you are saying your mother likes mushrooms more than she likes you. If you mean to say she likes mushrooms more than you like mushrooms, change the *me* to *I*: "My mother likes mushrooms more than I [do]."

Who and Whom

Who is the subjective case of the pronoun, and *whom* is the objective case. *Who*, then, is used as a subject of a verb:

> I know <u>who is coming</u> with you.

Who is the subject of the verb *is coming*. *Whom* is used as the object of a verb:

> Dr. Johnson did not know <u>whom he could trust</u>.

Whom is the object of the verb *could trust*. That verb already has a subject, *he*, so the subjective pronoun *who* cannot be used.

> *Whom* is also used as the object of a preposition:

> I think you know that journalist <u>with whom</u> Dr. Johnson is speaking.

Is it also correct to write the following sentence?

> I think you know that journalist <u>whom</u> Dr. Johnson is speaking <u>with</u>.

To do so puts the preposition at the end of the sentence. Many academics think the rule about never ending a sentence with a preposition is archaic and do not penalize essays that contain such sentences. Some academics, however, still think that ending a sentence with a preposition is a solecism, and they may penalize such a sentence.

Whom used as the object of a verb causes more problems than *whom* used as the object of a preposition. Remember that if the clause needs a subject, *who* is correct; if the clause needs an object, *whom* is correct. Compare these two sentences, both of which are grammatically correct:

> We all know whom you believe.

> We all know who you believe is telling the truth.

Do you see the difference between them? In the first sentence, *whom* is correct because it is the object of the verb *believe*. In the second sentence, *who* is correct because it is the subject of the verb *is telling*.

It's and Its

Its is a possessive pronoun, and *it's* is a contraction for "it is." These two words are often confused, because we indicate possession by adding an apostrophe, so we might reason that *it's* indicates possessive. It does not. No possessive pronoun ever takes an apostrophe. *It's* is only a contraction for *it is*. Never use *it's* as the possessive form of the pronoun *it*. Remember this sentence:

> <u>It's</u> a good movie, though I didn't like <u>its</u> ending.

Exercise on Pronoun Case

Circle the correct pronoun (or pronouns) for each sentence.

They expected my wife and (I, me) to arrive before noon.

The university admitted Raj but not (her, she).

Matt Damon is a much better actor than (he, him).

At the Olympic Games in Athens, my sister bought some wonderful pins for Shauna and (I, me, him, her, us, we).

She says she went to the Olympic Games in Utah with her boyfriend and (they, them).

Most students did not do as well on the third test as (I, me, they, them, us, we).

The Lechuguilla Cave, in Carlsbad Caverns National Park, is famous for (its, it's) beautiful stalagmites and stalactites.

Carl Sagan is one scientist (who, whom) I admire because he writes about science so clearly.

Professor Hickel so traumatized Heather and (I, me) that we have never taken another philosophy course again.

My grandfather was always in better health than (her, she).

Verb Tense and Mood

Verbs express action, and verb forms or **tenses** change to indicate whether that action is taking place in the present, has taken place in the past, or will take place in the future. It is essential that the verb tenses you choose clearly indicate when the action expressed by the verb occurred. Choosing the correct verb is usually quite straightforward, because we rely upon "what sounds right" and upon the logical relationships between actions and their subjects:

> (Was, Were) he alive today, Alexander Graham Bell (would be amazed, is amazed, was amazed) to see how his invention, the telephone, (evolves, has evolved).

We don't need to rely upon sophisticated rules of grammar to select the correct verbs for this sentence:

> Were he alive today, Alexander Graham Bell would be amazed to see how his invention, the telephone, has evolved.

But there are times when verb choice is not a simple matter of "what sounds right." To make certain you edit your writing correctly, you need to learn a few verb tense and mood rules that often cause errors. Be especially careful with the following:

- Past tense of irregular verbs
- Perfect verb forms
- Subjunctive mood

Past Tense of Irregular Verbs

Verbs typically add the suffix *-ed* to indicate past tense:

She attend<u>ed</u> Brown University.

An auxiliary or helping verb establishes the precise tense of the main verb that follows it (*was* hidden; *will* stay). When an auxiliary or helping verb precedes the past tense, the form of the past tense (called the **past participle** when preceded by an auxiliary verb) remains the same:

She <u>has attended</u> Brown University for the past three years.

Irregular verbs, however, indicate tense by changing a vowel:

I <u>gave</u> you my phone number already, and I will not <u>give</u> it to you again.

Complicating matters even further, irregular verbs often have a third form that must be used when such verbs are preceded by an auxiliary or helping verb. In other words, the past participle form of an irregular verb might be different from its past tense form:

I <u>have given</u> you my phone number already. I <u>gave</u> it to you yesterday after class.

It <u>breaks</u> my heart to know he <u>broke</u> your heart because my heart <u>has been broken</u> before.

I <u>see</u> him every day. I <u>saw</u> him just yesterday. I <u>have seen</u> too much of him.

Be careful with irregular verbs. Make sure you use the correct past tense and past participle forms of irregular verbs. If you are not sure if the verb you are using has an irregular past and past participle form, simply look up the verb in the dictionary. In the *Concise Oxford Dictionary*, for example, the entry for the verb *freeze* is followed immediately by its past tense and past participle forms—*froze* and *frozen*.

Perfect Verb Forms

Sentences with more than one verb often require more than one verb tense:

She <u>knows</u> she <u>saw</u> him last Tuesday.

I <u>know</u> you <u>will win</u>.

As is the case with single-verb sentences, time and logic dictate tense, so you usually will not make a tense error:

I <u>know</u> [now, in the present] you <u>will win</u> [at some point in the future].

But be careful using the **perfect form** of the verb, which is the form preceded by the auxiliary verbs *has, had,* or *have.* Consider these two sentences:

She <u>has seen</u> *Gone with the Wind* twenty-seven times.

She <u>saw</u> *Gone with the Wind* twenty-seven times.

A subtle difference in meaning exists between the two sentences. The first sentence, which uses the perfect form of the verb (*has seen*), implies that she might see the film again. The second sentence, which uses the simple past (*saw*), suggests she will not. The perfect verb form indicates such subtle differences in meaning.

Similarly, there is a subtle but important difference between these two sentences:

She was certain she <u>saw</u> him in the audience.

She was certain she <u>had seen</u> him in the audience.

The second sentence implies another related *past* action: He denied he was there, but she was certain she had seen him in the audience. There may be another action associated with the first sentence as well, but not another past action: He denies he was there, but she was certain she saw him in the audience.

Finally, consider the difference in meaning between these two sentences:

She will attend college next fall if she <u>earns</u> enough money.

She will attend college next fall if she <u>has earned</u> enough money.

The first sentence suggests that the earning will take place at a specific time: She will attend college next fall if she earns enough money this summer. The second sentence does not suggest a specific time when the earning will take place: She will attend college next fall if she has earned enough money by then.

When you are revising your academic essays, check your verbs, especially your perfect-tense verbs, to make certain they express your meaning precisely.

Subjunctive Mood

In addition to conveying tense, verbs convey mood. Verb mood describes the attitude a sentence is conveying. A sentence like "Shut the door!" or "Get out of my way!" is expressing an imperative attitude and is said to be in the **imperative mood.** Note that the subject (*you*) is understood, not stated explicitly.

The **subjunctive mood** is used to express a condition contrary to fact, a conjecture, a wish, a recommendation, a demand, or an indirect request. In its present tense, the subjunctive mood is formed by using the uninflected or **infinitive** form of the verb. You normally would write, for example:

She <u>sees</u> a psychiatrist once a month.

But if that sentence is preceded by a demand, its tense changes to indicate subjunctive mood:

Her doctor insisted she <u>see</u> a psychiatrist every month.

In its past tense, the subjunctive mood usually requires the *were* form of the verb *to be*:

If she <u>were</u> the prime minister, she would raise taxes.

However, some professors do not penalize the use of *was* in such sentences. The rule prescribing the use of *were* to indicate the subjunctive mood is less absolute than it once was.

If a verb is not in the imperative or the subjunctive mood, it is in the **indicative** mood. The vast majority of verbs in any given text are in the indicative mood.

 ## Exercise on Verb Tense and Mood

Correct errors in verb tense and mood in the following sentences.

If I was a rich man, I would donate money to my alma mater.

Scientists discovered that certain microorganisms has survived, even after they were frozen for five years.

In March 1999, two adventurers finally succeeded in sailing a hot air balloon around the world on a journey that takes them twenty days.

By the third day of the journey, they realized they have not brought enough drinking water with them.

The state trooper insisted that she drives the rest of the way home.

The flag of Luxembourg, like the French flag, is composing of a red, a white, and a blue stripe, but on the Luxembourg flag the stripes are horizontal, while on the French flag they are vertical.

Since he had chose not to attend, he could hardly criticize her performance.

It was only six o'clock, but it was already obvious they had drank too much.

I let her finish the candy bar because I already brushed my teeth.

It is not likely Martha would have married him if he was a lawyer.

Edit for Sentence Structure

A sentence is a unit of communication that describes at least one act (in the verb) and one agent (the subject) undertaking that action: "Alice is working." Usually, sentences also include phrases and clauses that develop the subject and the verb: "Alice is working on her French essay, which is due tomorrow morning." Because sentences contain a variety of words, phrases, and clauses, sentence structure can become complex and susceptible to error. Before you hand in your essays to your professors, check the structure of each sentence. You likely will lose a mark if a sentence in your essay is incomplete, awkward, improperly punctuated, or ambiguous. Watch especially for common errors in sentence structure that often weaken student writing:

- Sentence fragments
- Run-on sentences
- Misplaced or dangling modifiers
- Faulty parallelism
- Wordiness

● Sentence Fragments

A **sentence fragment** is an incomplete sentence masquerading as a complete one. A sentence must contain a subject and a verb. It is a fragment if one of these elements is missing, as in the following example:

Alice is busy tonight. Working on her French essay.

"Working on her French essay" is not a sentence because it does not contain a subject. To correct this sentence fragment, attach it to the preceding sentence and replace the period with a comma:

Alice is busy tonight, working on her French essay.

A word group can contain a subject and a verb but still be a fragment:

Alice will be working on her French essay all night. Because it is due in her first class tomorrow morning.

The second word group does contain a subject and a verb but is not a complete sentence. It is a sentence fragment because it begins with the word *because*, which is one of those words that introduce subordinate or dependent clauses. A subordinate or dependent clause does contain a subject and a verb but cannot stand alone; it "depends" upon, it is "subordinate" to, a main clause (which is synonymous to a complete sentence). Therefore, the subordinate clause should be a part of the sentence:

Alice will be working on her French essay all night because it is due in her first class tomorrow morning.

It is also acceptable to put the subordinate clause at the beginning of the sentence, though minor alterations should be made to it:

> Because her French essay is due in her first class tomorrow morning, Alice will be working on it all night.

Other words that introduce subordinate or dependent clauses include *after, before, if, since, that, when, which, while, who,* and *whose.* Learn these words, and check to make sure that they appear within a sentence and do not begin a fragment when you use them in your essays. Note that if the preceding sentence had been punctuated like this, it would have a sentence fragment error:

> Learn these words, and check to make sure that they appear within a sentence and do not begin a fragment. When you use them in your essays.

Let's look at one more example. The second sentence in the following pair is a fragment:

> Alice is working on her French essay tonight. The last paper that she needs to hand in to complete the course requirements.

To correct this fragment, make it a complete sentence:

> Alice is working on her French essay tonight. This is the last paper that she needs to hand in to complete the course requirements.

Or attach it to the main clause:

> Tonight Alice is working on her French essay, which is the last paper that she needs to hand in to complete the course requirements.

Note that the word introducing the dependent clause, the word *that,* could be left out because its presence in the sentence is implicit.

Professional writers occasionally use a fragment deliberately, usually for emphasis:

> The prime minister refused to attend the king's funeral. What an insult! To the king's nation as well as to our own.

The last two word groups are fragments but acceptable because they are used deliberately, for emphasis. When writing an academic essay, however, play it safe and avoid fragments altogether.

 ## Exercise on Sentence Fragments

Rewrite the following passages to correct any sentence fragments they contain.

The Berlin Wall was built at the end of World War II. Dividing the eastern part of Berlin into a communist sector and the western part of the city into a capitalist sector.

Americans were at first puzzled and then annoyed. When the Toronto Blue Jays won the World Series.

After World War II, the demand for public education increased dramatically. Mainly as a result of the baby boom.

People suffering from hypothermia need blankets and warm, nonalcoholic liquids. Or else they could become unconscious.

Fewer Americans will be traveling abroad this summer than last summer. Mainly because of the drop in the value of the American dollar.

The hawk and the eagle are both diurnal birds of prey, but the eagle is more common on the West Coast. Where there is an abundance of the small animals that eagles use as their food supply.

The hare has longer ears and legs than the rabbit, so hares can outrun their predators. Instead of burrowing into the ground as rabbits must.

● Run-On Sentences

A **run-on sentence** consists of two complete sentences incorrectly joined together, either by a comma (a **comma splice**) or without any punctuation at all (a **fused sentence**). It is certainly acceptable to join two sentences together to make one, but the merger must be done correctly.

Two complete sentences cannot be separated from each other merely by a comma. (Note that if the comma is missing, this error is referred to as a fused sentence.) Here is a clear example of two separate sentences joined together, incorrectly, by a comma:

Alice is working on her French essay tonight, she can't come to the game.

There are several ways to correct this type of run-on sentence.

You may replace the comma with a period or, if the two sentences are related, with a semicolon. A comma is not considered a strong enough pause to separate two sentences, but a semicolon is.

You may place a coordinate conjunction (*and*, *but*, *or*) before the comma:

Alice is working on her French essay tonight, and she can't come to the game.

You may change one of the sentences into a dependent (subordinate) clause:

Since Alice is working on her French essay tonight, she can't come to the game.

If both subjects refer to the same person, you may add a coordinate conjunction and eliminate the second subject. Note that if you eliminate the second subject, you also dispense with the comma:

> Alice is working on her French essay tonight and can't come to the game.

Note also that this solution is not always a possibility, as the following sentence illustrates:

> Alice is working on her French essay tonight, it is due first period tomorrow.

You would need to correct this run-on sentence using one of the other methods. You could change the comma to a period or a semicolon. Or you could reduce one of the sentences to a subordinate clause:

> Alice is working on her French essay tonight because it is due first period tomorrow.

> Tonight Alice is working on her French essay, which is due first period tomorrow.

Here is one more example. The first sentence is a run-on because it uses only a comma to separate two complete sentences. The sentences following it illustrate ways of correcting the run-on.

> Another common error in sentence structure is the run-on sentence, a run-on sentence consists of two complete sentences joined together by a comma.

> Another common error in sentence structure is the run-on sentence. A run-on sentence consists of two complete sentences joined together by a comma.

> Another common error in sentence structure is the run-on sentence; a run-on sentence consists of two complete sentences joined together by a comma.

> Another common error in sentence structure is the run-on sentence, which consists of two complete sentences joined together by a comma.

> Another common error in sentence structure is the run-on sentence, consisting of two complete sentences joined together by a comma.

Note especially the last method of correction. The second sentence is reduced not to a subordinate clause, as the sentence before it is, but to a phrase introduced by the participle *consisting*. This is another effective method of correcting a run-on sentence.

 ## Exercise on Run-On Sentences

Rewrite the following passages to correct any run-on sentence errors they contain.

The aardvark is a nocturnal mammal about 1.5 meters long, it feeds on termites and ants.

Cats have excellent vision, they can see as well at night as they can during the day.

Leonard Cohen was an influential songwriter, especially during the 1960s, his songs were recorded by artists in several different countries.

A contract is an agreement between two people to allow for the exchange of goods and services, one person provides a product or a service, the other person pays for it.

Newgate Prison was destroyed in the Great Fire of 1666, it was not rebuilt until 1778, it was destroyed by fire again during the Gordon Riots of 1780.

Creon thought Polynices was a traitor and refused to grant him a state funeral, however Polynices's sister Antigone defied Creon and buried her brother with full military honors.

● Misplaced and Dangling Modifiers

Modifiers are words and phrases that describe, clarify, and refine subjects and verbs and other key elements (usually other nouns and verbs) within sentences. You must be careful to place your modifiers within your sentences so that they clearly modify what you intend them to modify.

A **misplaced modifier** is a word or group of words that describes a word in a sentence other than the word it is supposed to describe. In this sentence, for example, "I was able to find two books and several articles in the library that will be useful to me," the phrase "that will be useful to me" is misplaced. It is modifying "library" but is meant to modify "two books and several articles." If the sentence is revised to read, "I was able to find two books and several articles that will be useful to me in the library," we still have a misplaced modifier—in this case, the phrase "in the library." The phrase implies that the books and articles will be useful to me in the library but not necessarily anywhere else. If the phrase "in the library" is placed at the beginning of the sentence, the error is corrected:

> In the library, I was able to find two books and several articles that will be useful to me.

Similarly, if the same phrase is placed after the infinitive *to find*, the error is corrected:

> I was able to find, in the library, two books and several articles that will be useful to me.

Consider a second example:

> The future of the Earth relies almost entirely on the sun, a massive ball of flaming gas 330,000 times as large as the Earth, which is slowly running out of energy.

The last clause modifies *Earth*, but the writer intends it to modify *sun*. A misplaced modifier often indicates that the sentence containing it is too long, and sometimes the best way to correct a misplaced modifier is to compose two shorter sentences:

> The sun is a massive ball of flaming gas 330,000 times as large as the Earth. The future of the Earth relies almost entirely on the sun, which is slowly running out of energy.

A **dangling modifier** is a word or a group of words that is supposed to modify a word in a sentence but that "dangles" because that needed word is missing from the sentence. For example, in the sentence "When writing an essay, the rules for good writing should be kept in mind," the phrase "When writing an essay" dangles at the beginning, in search of a word it can modify. But there is no such word in the sentence. In fact, it sounds as if "the rules" are writing the essay. The sentence needs to be revised to give "When writing an essay" a word it will clearly modify. Here are two possibilities:

> When writing an essay, writers should keep in mind the rules for good writing.

> When you are writing an essay, you should keep the rules for good writing in mind.

Here is another example:

> Looking at present trends in carbon dioxide levels in the air, predictions can be made that levels will drop to 140 parts per million in 500 million years.

Predictions cannot look at present trends. Astronomers can, though. Therefore, the sentence should be revised to mention them:

> Looking at present trends in carbon dioxide levels in the air, astronomers can predict that levels will drop to 140 parts per million in 500 million years.

Misplaced and dangling modifiers make sentences ambiguous. When you are revising your essay, check the placement of your modifiers to make sure they do not make any of your sentences awkward or unclear.

 ### Exercise on Misplaced and Dangling Modifiers

Rewrite the following sentences to correct misplaced and dangling modifiers.

After waiting for over an hour, the concert finally began.

To survive a winter in Winnipeg, warm clothing and patience are essential.

The candidate gave the same speech opposing the bill in every town in the county.

I gave my old copy of the text to my friend with all of the exercises completed.

I thought I might be fired after I refused to pour coffee for the truckers in their own thermoses.

Professor Higgins collected all of the assignments about the civil war on Friday.

Passengers may not take a suitcase onto a plane that won't fit into the overhead compartment.

The bicycle we found at the dump that is missing its handlebars can easily be repaired.

While trying to sneak into the house past curfew, a vase crashed to the floor.

An old man accompanied my wife whom I had never seen before.

Hiking along the West Coast Trail, it is not uncommon to spot a cougar.

● Faulty Parallelism

Faulty parallelism is an error in sentence structure that occurs when words or phrases that should be syntactically equal within a sentence are not. Faulty parallelism adversely affects the balance of a sentence. "He managed to make the team even though he is short, awkward, and weight is a problem for him" lacks parallelism because the phrase "weight is a problem for him" does not balance the adjectives *short* and *awkward*. The sentence comes parallel when the phrase is changed to the adjective *overweight*:

He managed to make the team even though he is short, awkward, and overweight.

Here is another example of faulty parallelism:

The company will either go bankrupt or there was a leveraged buyout possibility that could save it.

"Go bankrupt" does not balance "there was"; "be saved" is a much better match. The following revision establishes a parallel structure and makes the sentence more fluent:

The company will either go bankrupt or be saved by a leveraged buyout.

Exercise on Parallelism

Rewrite the following sentences to improve their parallel structure.

While he was secretary general of the United Nations, Dag Hammarskjold worked tirelessly for peace in the Middle East and the Congo, and the Nobel Prize for peace was awarded to him in 1962.

> Alan is planning to attend the local junior college, Chris is going to the state university, while the decision Jenny has made is to go to work in her mother's business.
>
> By the end of the movie, the main character has become quite unstable, losing his identity and, ultimately, he commits suicide.
>
> Sports psychologists feel that some athletes take steroids not so much because they crave victory but it is from having low self-esteem.
>
> Hydrogen is the lightest of all the elements, but it can be explosive when mixed with air, and bomb making has been one of its uses.

● Wordiness

The structure of some sentences appears shaky because the writer has used more words than necessary to express the ideas the sentence contains. Here is an example of a wordy sentence:

> This essay will explore several different theories that have been developed by paleontologists for attempting to explain why dinosaurs reached the point of becoming extinct.

Read the sentence out loud, and you will hear the wordiness. The first half is not too bad; the second half is a wordy disaster, especially "reached the point of becoming extinct," which could be reduced simply to "became extinct." The sentence is improved when revised as follows:

> This essay will explore several theories paleontologists have developed to explain why dinosaurs became extinct.

Some teachers will find "This essay will explore" unnecessary on the grounds that it is already implied. They might favor an even more concise version of the sentence:

> Paleontologists have developed several theories to explain why dinosaurs became extinct.

Wordiness is a matter of degree, to a certain extent. You want your sentences to be concise but complete.

Here is another example of a wordy sentence:

> In 1916, the disease of polio reached epidemic proportions when 27,363 cases of polio were reported by health care workers in America and more than 7,000 people died of polio as a result in the worst outbreak of polio in the history of the country.

Again, read the sentence out loud, and the need to edit for concision is apparent. "The disease of" is unnecessary; it is not necessary to repeat "polio" three times;

"as a result" is implied. The sentence could be half as long and say the same thing more eloquently:

> In 1916, American health care workers reported 27,363 cases of polio and over 7,000 deaths in the country's worst polio epidemic.

One of the enemies of concision in both of the preceding wordy sentences is **passive voice.** Passive voice is a form of a verb that adds part of the verb *to be* to a past participle: *was thrown, is forbidden, am disappointed, have been developed, were reported.* Passive voice tends to be wordy. "The ball was thrown by my brother" is wordier than "My brother threw the ball." Passive voice is not wrong; indeed, it is useful if the subject of the sentence is indeterminate: "Smoking is forbidden in this building." But passive voice is wordy when a word that should be the sentence's subject is stuck somewhere else, usually as the object in a prepositional phrase. There is nothing wrong with "Three of the goals were scored by defensemen," but it is less concise than writing, "Defensemen scored three of the goals."

 ## Exercise on Wordiness

Rewrite each sentence to make it more clear and concise.

Acid rain is rain that contains too much acid, especially too much acidity, which is found in the nitric acid and the sulphuric acid, which are components of acid rain.

Psychotherapy is not a single method of treating mental illness but a term that encompasses many other types of therapies for treating mental illness using a variety of methods.

A black hole is a star that has such a strong gravitational force that nothing can escape its gravitational pull, including light, which is why a black hole cannot be seen and its existence is speculated upon.

Hundreds of tourists from all over the world enjoying the innovative architecture, the excellent art gallery, and the variety of shops account for the crowds along Robson Street in the Canadian city of Vancouver.

Astronomers can study the outer layers of the sun and its corona when the light from the sun is obscured by the moon during an eclipse when the sun is not too bright to study, and they are eager to do so.

Dixieland jazz originated in the city of New Orleans in the early 1900s and became popular later on when famous people such as F. Scott Fitzgerald, whose glamorous friends and fictional characters danced to it, embraced it.

Thunder follows lightning because thunder is caused by the intense vibrations in the air, which are the by-products of the heat generated by the lightning that then cools rapidly and causes the explosive noise common to thunder.

Edit for Punctuation

Another important aspect of the editing process is the punctuation check. Sentences need to be properly punctuated if they are to be clear and readable. An unpunctuated sentence reads like a puzzle that must be solved before its meaning can be grasped. The sentence "If you can come before it gets too dark" is confusing; it reads, in fact, like a sentence fragment. But the meaning becomes clear when a comma is placed after *can*: "If you can, come before it gets too dark."

When you are revising your writing, check to make sure it is punctuated correctly. Check your use of punctuation marks in the following locations:

- At the end of sentences
- Within sentences
- Within words

● Punctuation at the End of Sentences

At the end of most declarative, informative sentences, you use a period. You may use an exclamation point for extra emphasis, but in an academic essay, do so sparingly. A question mark, of course, comes at the end of a question.

It is acceptable to use a semicolon at the end of a sentence, if the next sentence continues on the same topic:

American Motors manufactures fewer than half a million passenger cars a year; Ford Motors manufactures well over a million.

The American economy faltered in the spring of 2008; lately it has shown signs of a recovery.

A period would be acceptable between these sentences, but the semicolon does emphasize the relationship between them. A comma would not be acceptable. A comma cannot come between two complete sentences unless the comma is followed by a coordinate conjunction.

It is acceptable to use a colon at the end of a sentence if the next sentence explains or clarifies a topic mentioned in the preceding sentence:

He realized, with great sorrow, that there was no other choice: He would have to fight his own brother.

> In the course of the lecture, he explained to us that the city's name derives from the native language: *hono* means "bay," and *lulu* means "sheltered."

A period would be acceptable between these sentences, but the colon does stress the fact that the second sentence embellishes the first.

● Punctuation Within Sentences

Seven punctuation marks can occur within sentences: commas, semicolons, colons, quotation marks, dashes, parentheses, and ellipses. (Remember that semicolons and colons are also used at the ends of sentences. See the examples in the preceding section.)

Commas

Four main rules govern the use of commas in academic writing.

1.   A comma comes before a coordinate conjunction in a compound sentence:

     The topic sentence should contain the main idea of the paragraph, and the other sentences should develop the main idea.

     (Note that this rule is also covered in the "Run-On Sentences" section of this chapter.)

2.   Commas separate a nonrestrictive word, phrase, or clause from the rest of the sentence. A nonrestrictive element is one that is not essential to the meaning of the sentence. It is the opposite of a restricted element, which is essential to the meaning of the sentence. Consider carefully these two sentences:

     Sheehy's *Guide to Reference Books,* which should be at the reference desk of your library, lists sources that you will find useful.

     All of the books that I need to research my essay have been signed out of the library.

     Note that the clause "which should be at the reference desk of your library" is separated from the rest of the sentence by commas. Commas are used because the clause is nonrestrictive, that is, not essential to the meaning of the sentence. The word *which* is used also because the clause is nonrestrictive. To test whether a clause is nonrestrictive, eliminate the clause and see if the sentence still makes sense, which in this case it does:

     Sheehy's *Guide to Reference Books* lists sources that you will find useful.

     Now note the clause "that I need to research my essay" in the second sentence. This clause is not separated from the rest of the sentence by commas. It is a restrictive clause; that is, it is essential to the meaning of the sentence.

The word *that* is used also because the clause is restrictive. To test whether a clause is restrictive, eliminate the clause and see if the sentence still makes sense, which in this case it does not:

All of the books have been signed out of the library.

If you can eliminate a word, phrase, or clause from a sentence without the sentence losing its meaning, then that word, phrase, or clause is nonrestrictive and should be separated from the rest of the sentence by commas. Consider this sentence:

Windsor Castle was damaged by a serious fire.

This sentence is short, simple, and self-contained. Any clauses or phrases added to this sentence would be nonrestrictive and therefore separated from the rest of the sentence by commas. Note carefully the commas in this sentence:

In 1992, Windsor Castle, the queen's house on the banks of the Thames, was damaged by a serious fire.

Transitional and parenthetical words and phrases are almost always nonrestrictive and, therefore, are set off from the rest of the sentence by commas. Note carefully the placement of commas in these sentences. They separate transitional and parenthetical words and phrases from the rest of the sentence:

There is, however, no reason why a new policy cannot be implemented immediately.

Finally, we are considering the implementation of a new policy that should reduce the rate of recidivism.

On the other hand, the current policy has reduced the crime rate in some sections of the city.

That, too, remains to be decided.

There is an exception to the rule that restrictive words, phrases, or clauses are not set off from the rest of the sentence with commas: Even a restrictive word, phrase, or clause usually is followed by a comma if that restrictive element begins the sentence. Compare these two sentences:

Their starting point guard will not be able to play unless her Achilles tendon is better.

Unless her Achilles tendon is better, their starting point guard will not be able to play.

3. Use a comma between coordinate, but not cumulative, adjectives. Coordinate adjectives modify the same noun. In the phrase "a bright, colorful skirt," both adjectives modify the noun *skirt* and are separated from each other by a comma. A cumulative adjective qualifies the adjective that follows it; the second adjective modifies the noun. In the phrase "a black

leather skirt," the adjective *black* qualifies the adjective "leather," which then modifies the noun "skirt." These are cumulative adjectives and are not separated from each other by commas.

An often-used test to determine whether adjectives are coordinate or cumulative is to see if the word *and* can be placed between the adjectives. If it can, the adjectives are coordinate and need a comma between them: "a bright and colorful skirt." If *and* sounds awkward placed between the adjectives, a comma is not required: "She wore a black [not *and*] leather skirt."

4. Use commas to separate words, phrases, or clauses in a series. Note the use of the commas in this sentence:

    In this chapter, we are learning the uses of the period, the comma, the semicolon, the colon, and the dash.

    Commas separate the series of punctuation marks mentioned in the sentence. Note that there is a comma between the words *colon* and *dash*. This comma is optional. Note, as well, the comma after the introductory phrase "In this chapter." It is a nonrestrictive phrase and is therefore set off from the rest of the sentence by the comma.

Semicolons

There are two uses for the semicolon in academic writing.

1. Use a semicolon to separate two complete but related sentences:

    On one side of the street were protesters who wanted the child returned to his father in Cuba; on the other side were protesters who insisted the child be allowed to stay in the country.

    The schools in the senator's district all have access to the Internet; inner-city schools do not have even basic computer equipment.

2. Use a semicolon to separate phrases or clauses in a series when there are commas within those phrases or clauses:

    You want your essay to be well organized; you want your sentences within your paragraphs and your paragraphs within the essay to be logically connected, in other words, to cohere; you want your diction to be accurate and appropriate; you want to avoid errors in grammar, spelling, and punctuation; and you want your prose to be concise.

Colons

Earlier in this chapter, you learned that a colon could come between two sentences if the second sentence explained or clarified the first, for example, "He adhered to the golden rule: Do unto others as you would have others do unto you."

A colon also precedes a word or a phrase that explains or clarifies a sentence:

Fresno is a long way away: 184 miles, to be exact.

Given his personality, he chose an appropriate pseudonym: Joe Average.

Note that the clarifying words or phrases often take the form of a list:

She claimed there were just three qualities she was looking for in a husband: ambition, compassion, and a good sense of humor.

Quotation Marks

In academic writing, quotation marks serve two functions.

1. Quotation marks indicate that you are quoting someone else's spoken or written words.

    "I write slowly," Mullen told one interviewer. "It can take me months to complete a single sonnet."

    In her preface to *Satan's Rainbow*, Mullen responds to criticism that her work is obscure, arguing that her ambiguous syntax is a "deliberate strategy to free readers to interpret my work in ways that mean the most to them."

    Note that if a written quote is more than about three lines in length, it is set off from the rest of the text and does not contain quotation marks (unless the source being quoted also contains them).

    On occasion, you might need to use quotation marks in a context in which other quotation marks already occur. When this happens, revert to single quotation marks to indicate the quote within the quote:

    In her analysis of Keats's sonnet, Foster notes that "the repetition of the adverb 'still' is typical of Keats's style."

2. Quotation marks enclose minor titles. Titles of short stories and poems, for example, are placed within quotation marks:

    My favorite sonnet is "Bright Star" by Keats.

Dashes

In academic writing, the dash is used mainly to enclose a nonrestrictive word group that contains commas:

She eats something from each food group—protein, dairy, fruits and vegetables, and grains—at every meal.

A dash is also used to signal an abrupt change or shift in thought, but a sentence that contains such a shift is rare in academic writing:

> Students can also pay for a database search—if they want to waste their time and money.

Parentheses

Parentheses enclose information of borderline importance to a sentence, in other words, information that a writer decides to include but does not consider vitally important:

> The first volume (in a twelve-volume series) should be published before the end of the month.

Ellipses

The ellipsis mark (a succession of three periods:...) is an important punctuation mark in academic writing, used to indicate that unneeded words have been omitted. The ellipsis comes in handy if you are quoting from a secondary source and want to keep the quote concise and relevant by omitting unnecessary words:

> "Computer viruses are more annoying than harmful, and most hackers cannot do anywhere near the damage... they claim they can."

Use four dots if a period is included in the information you omit or if the remaining material reaches a natural ending point to the sentence:

> Kafka writes poignantly of Gregor's isolation: "Gregor now stationed himself immediately before the living room door, determined to persuade any hesitating visitor to come in.... No one came in, and even the keys were on the other side of the doors."

Punctuation Within Words

There are two punctuation marks that can occur within a word: the apostrophe and the hyphen.

Apostrophes

Apostrophes are used in nouns to indicate ownership. Study carefully the following sentences:

> The professor claimed he had misplaced his student's essay.

> The professor claimed he had misplaced his students' essays.

> For that assignment, the men's essays were not as well written as the women's.

In the first sentence, the apostrophe comes before the *s* because the noun *student* is singular. There is only one student. In the second sentence, the apostrophe comes after the *s* because the noun *students* is plural. The rule, then, is put an apostrophe before the *s* to indicate singular possession and after the *s* to indicate plural possession.

What about the third sentence? *Men* and *women* are plural: Why does the apostrophe come before the *s*? It comes before the *s* because *men* and *women* are nouns that form their plural not by adding an *s* but by changing a vowel: *Man* becomes *men*; *woman* becomes *women*. The apostrophe comes before the *s* in nouns that form their plural by changing a vowel. We write *children's toys*, never *childrens' toys*.

If a noun ends in the letter *s*, there are two options: you may add *'s* to the word, or you may put the apostrophe after the *s* and not add another *s* even if the noun is singular:

I enjoy reading Keats' poetry.

I enjoy reading Keats's poetry.

Choose the version that sounds the best to you.

Apostrophes are also used in contractions such as *don't*, *isn't*, and *weren't*. But note carefully the difference between *it's* and *its*. *It's* is a contraction for "it is." *Its* is a possessive pronoun and never needs an apostrophe because it is already in possessive case. Memorize this sentence to avoid confusing the two:

It's missing one of its pages.

Finally, note the placement of the apostrophe in these sentences:

We are having dinner at Mary and Tom's house.

I wrecked my brother-in-law's car.

Hyphens

Hyphens are used within compound words such as *mother-in-law*, *forty-one*, *one-third*, and *run-on*. Hyphens also are used to join two or more words that modify a noun they precede:

She wore five-inch heels.

Exercise on Punctuation

Punctuate the following sentences correctly.

We planned to serve key lime pie but my brother is allergic to citrus fruit.

Oscar will be fighting an inexperienced opponent and experts are predicting an early knockout.

Your essay should be double spaced and should have one and a half inch margins on both sides of the page.

My uncle who played basketball in college taught me how to dribble behind my back.

She decided to retire early, she could not handle the stress any longer.

Both a coordinate conjunction and a conjunctive adverb link sentences together, a conjunctive adverb is preceded by a semicolon.

The schools in the senators district now have access to the Internet, however inner-city schools are still waiting to get basic computer equipment.

Ellis did not hand in two of his assignments, therefore he did not get a passing grade in his sociology course.

Tia Maria Drambuie Benedictine and Curacao are among the most popular liqueurs and are sold throughout the world.

The tern is a slender gull like bird and with it's long pointed wings and a deeply notched tail it flies with grace energy and strength.

The silver that is mined in Mexico is considered superior to the silver mined in Colorado.

The upper limit of the biosphere the part of earth where life can exist is about 9,000 meters above sea level the lower limit is approximately 3,000 meters beneath the surface of the ocean.

A portion of the play the third scene of the final act to be precise was excluded to meet a two hour time limit.

The anteaters tongue is covered with sticky saliva that allows it to trap ants termites and other insects on which it feeds.

Daves new interest is cybernetics the science that among other things compares brain functions to the function of machines especially computers.

France lost Alsace and Lorraine to Germany in 1871 after a war in which the Germans who were better prepared than the French won nearly every battle.

The greyhound wolfhound and deerhound hunt by sight the bloodhound foxhound and beagle hunt by scent.

Diabetics lack insulin which controls the supply of sugar from the blood to the muscles however with proper insulin injections diabetics can live a normal life.

Film adaptations of novels are usually disappointing but the film version of Kinsellas *Field of Dreams* is better than the book.

Since the beginning of the century the Nobel Prize has been awarded to men and women for outstanding contributions to the following fields physics chemistry medicine literature peace and economics.

As T. S. Eliot writes in Little Gidding one of the poems from his book *Four Quartets* What we call the beginning is often the end. And to make an end is to make a beginning.

Originally the word *tycoon* from the Japanese *taikun* referred to the commander in chief of the Japanese army but now its used often in a derogatory sense to describe a powerful influential businessperson.

The plane will make a ninety minute stop in St. Louis where you are free to disembark for thirty minutes a twenty minute stop in Minneapolis where you may not disembark and a ninety minute stop in Chicago where you may disembark for twenty minutes.

Edit for Diction

The word may be the smallest unit of written communication, but it is no less important than the sentence or the paragraph. "The difference between the right word and the nearly right word," Mark Twain once said, "is the difference between lightning and a lightning bug." When you are editing your writing, you want to check to make certain that the words you have used show respect for your readers and a commitment to your purpose. Check, especially, to make sure your words are appropriate to the context of your essay and convey the meaning you wish to convey as clearly and precisely as possible.

● Context

The words you choose must be appropriate to the context in which you use them. Academic writing is relatively formal, so the **connotation** of your words as well as the **denotation** must be accurate. The denotation of a word is the word's literal, dictionary definition. The connotation refers to the intellectual or emotional associations a word carries with it. Words can have identical denotations. A 6-foot-tall, 130-pound man can be described as *skinny* or *slender*, but he likely would prefer *slender* because the connotations of that word are more positive.

Slang words usually have connotations too informal for academic writing. In this sentence, some verbs would be acceptable in academic writing, and others would not:

> The senator was too (drunk, inebriated, intoxicated, blitzed, bombed, tipsy, trashed, pissed to the gills, wasted, looped, polluted) to debate the bill.

The use of **jargon** also depends upon context. Jargon is language specific to a certain social or professional group. Lawyers, stockbrokers, doctors, professional sports fans, computer programmers, forest rangers, civil servants, and musicians can all speak and write in a language they understand but outsiders do not. Readers can usually identify the social or professional group using the jargon but not the meaning of all of the words and phrases they use. We can figure out, for example, that the writers of the following sentences are a car buff, a basketball fan, and a fashion writer, respectively, but we will have a harder time determining what exactly they are talking about.

> It has side rocker panels, flared wheel wells, and an inline six-cylinder, 2.5-liter, 168-horsepower engine.

> O'Neal took it to the hole for a slam, but Smits was called for three in the paint, so the bucket didn't count.

> By cutting on the bias, she accentuated the drape on the handkerchief hems she will show in next spring's collection.

The use of jargon is not necessarily an error. Its appropriateness depends upon the writer's knowledge of his or her audience. If the writer knows readers will understand the jargon because they are members of the apposite subculture, he or she may use that subculture's jargon. But if the readers are not a part of that subculture, the writer must avoid its jargon and use lay language. Otherwise, he or she runs the risk that readers will not fully understand the text; they may even resent the writer who is making them feel like outsiders.

● Meaning

The meaning of words is hardly absolute. Words have nuances and shades of meaning. Good writers edit their work to make certain they have used words that most accurately convey their intended meaning.

As a rule, choose the specific and concrete word over the vague and abstract one. Concrete and specific words add important shades of meaning to the sentences in which they appear. If a beautiful young woman is sitting on a park bench reading a *book*, we know less about her and see her less clearly than we would if we are told she is reading *Advanced Calculus, The Collected Poems of Emily Dickinson, The Unauthorized Biography of Britney Spears*, or *Das Kapital*. Give a title to the vague and abstract *book*, and the writing becomes more vivid.

For example, compare these two sentences:

Eric was at the bus stop when a car sped past him, hit the puddle, and splashed water over his new suit.

Eric was at the bus stop when a Mercedes sped past him, hit the puddle, and splashed water over his new suit.

Only one word has been changed: *car* has become *Mercedes.* But the effect of the change is considerable. The reader now sees more vividly what the writer is trying to describe. And Eric's anger has an additional cause. A Mercedes driver suggests wealth, which in turn suggests an indifference to poor people waiting for buses. The Mercedes adds insult to the injury. The Mercedes makes a relatively neutral sentence considerably more meaningful.

Your meaning will also be enhanced if you use **euphemisms** sparingly. A euphemism is a word or a phrase that, at best, is deliberately obscure and, at worst, is deliberately deceptive. There are two reasons for using a euphemism.

First, euphemisms are sometimes used to avoid being too blunt or offensive. A teacher might like to write on a report card: "Arthur is loud and obnoxious. He annoys me and the other children. We can't get any work done when he is around, so I often have to kick him out of class." But, unwilling to risk the ire of parents and principals, she more likely will resort to euphemism: "We appreciate Arthur's exuberant personality, though it does interfere sometimes with class work. I encourage Arthur to work independently, which he seems to enjoy."

But second, euphemisms sometimes are used to deflect the truth, to deliberately mislead readers. Management cannot let the plant close, so an accident becomes a "reportable occurrence," which sounds much less threatening. The military can't admit it erred, so civilians killed in the bombing raids are referred to as "collateral damage," which sounds like an unfortunate but inevitable and harmless by-product of war. The government "initiates revenue enhancement programs" so we don't quite realize our taxes are going to go up. This type of euphemism, unlike the first type, does not avoid offending readers. It obfuscates and misleads and should, therefore, be avoided.

In the preceding chapter, you read the final version of Hannah's essay "Some Social and Psychological Consequences of Celebrity Worship." Here is a page from an earlier version of the essay, containing Hannah's handwritten edits.

Note that, like most writers, Hannah had been editing her essay all along, while she drafted and while she revised. Revising and editing are often done simultaneously. Like many writers, though, Hannah printed out a hard copy of her essay so she could see her essay from a different perspective and thereby catch errors she might have missed when reading and editing her essay on the computer screen.

Like revising, editing is an ongoing writing process. Writers don't edit only after they have drafted. They edit while they draft. In fact, most editing changes are made while writers draft and revise. Typically writers compose a few sentences and then edit them immediately as needed; writers tend not to bypass their errors for later correction. The notion that the writing process is sequential—write a draft, then revise the draft, then edit the draft—is a myth.

Even experienced writers need a good handbook when they edit a text. Over 300 rules govern the conventions of Standard English. Not many people know them all. If you are confused about a grammar rule, unsure if a sentence you have written is a fragment, wondering if a comma needs to be inserted at a certain point in your sentence, consult the appropriate section of this book.

Here is a passage from the edited version of Hannah's essay (pages 103–104).

New para

Other social commentators, however, argue that *engaging in* celebrity gossip and using celebrities as role models are anti-feminist activities that, more often than not, diminishes self-esteem. Provocative designer clothing and ~~hard~~ fit bodies are as much about a love of male attention, which *concedes* ~~considers~~ power, as they are about social capital that enhances social power. Feminist authors further point out that women who achieve the greatest fame are those who fall apart and self-destruct, often because of a failed relationship with a man. Naomi Wolf bemoans a culture "increasingly obsessed with showcasing images of glamorous young women, *delete* ~~like Britney Spears and Lindsay Lohan,~~ who are falling apart", *(In Chaudhreg 24)* she suggests this fascination is anti-feminist in *and* that it reassures the male establishment of the stereotype of the weak and vulnerable woman who ~~if she is to be in control and successful~~ needs a man's help if she is to be in control and successful. Young male stars who are sexually indiscreet and behave badly in public get by with the *boys-will-be-boys*

note Hannah corrects faulty parallelism error here.

note Hannah corrects subject-verb agr. error here.

note Hannah corrects run-on sentence error here.

Hannah flags this phrase because she wants to reconsider its use. She will decide to leave it in.

defense, while the women are victims of the age-old and sexist double standard: young men can be wild, but a young woman who misbehaves risks her reputation.

Moreover, fans can wear the same clothes, eat the same food, and practice the same yoga techniques of their favorite stars, but they don't have access to the air brushes, glamour lessons, makeup artists, personal trainers, and plastic surgeons of the stars, and when they fall short of this physical perfection, even *may feel they have failed* though it is manufactured, they ~~are a failure even though it is manufactured~~. According to one study, nearly sixty percent of women who had cosmetic surgery because they wanted the same — *of* feature ~~such as~~ lips, breasts, and nose ~~or~~ their favorite celebrity *(Hecom)* were disappointed with the results.

Note Hannah changed commas to dashes and deleted "such as"

Conclusion

Academic essays must be written in Standard English, in that form of our language used by and expected from those who work in business, government, educational institutions, and other social organizations. In Standard English, words are spelled correctly, commas are in the right places, sentences are complete, verbs agree with their subjects, modifiers don't dangle, pronouns are in the correct case, and verbs use the correct tense. If you edit your essays carefully so that they conform to the rules of Standard English, your work will be clear and forceful, and you will meet the expectations of your readers.

WRITING ASSIGNMENTS

1. Identify a grammatical error that has given you some trouble in the past. (You might look through your old essays to see where your instructors thought you needed some help.) In an essay of 500 to 750 words, describe this error, and discuss strategies writers can use to detect, avoid, and correct it.

2. In an essay of approximately 500 words, compare and contrast the use of the colon and the semicolon.

3. Select a popular magazine that specializes in covering a particular field: sports, fashion, entertainment, computers, interior design, geography, travel, or current affairs. Find several examples of jargon used in an issue of that magazine. Write a brief (200- to 300-word) analysis of the use of jargon, focusing on how it both defines and panders to the magazine's target audience.

EXERCISES

1. Compose a sentence fragment followed by three sentences illustrating three different ways of correcting the fragment.
2. Compose a run-on sentence followed by three sentences illustrating three different ways of correcting the run-on sentence.
3. Compose a sentence rendered comical because it contains a misplaced modifier. Write a corrected version of the sentence as well.
4. Compose five sentences, each of which contains an example of one of the diction errors covered in this chapter:
   - Inappropriate connotation
   - Jargon
   - Vague/abstract language
   - Euphemism

Then write a revised version of each sentence in which you correct the diction errors.

COLLABORATIVE ACTIVITY

In a small group, edit the following text.

Camelot was the most famous castle in the medeeval legends of King Arthur. Where he reigned over Britain before the Saxon conquest. Camelot was the home of the Knights of the Round Table. A group of brilliant statemen and chivalrous warriers. It was from Camelot that a group of these knights set off on a quest for the Holy Grail, the Holy Grail is the cup from which Jesus and his disciples drunk at the Last Supper. It is impossible to determine precisely where Camelot Castle was located. Sir Thomas Malory sets his epic poem Le Morte d'Arthur in Winchester while Wales is where the favored location is for Geoffrey of Monmouth in his History of the Kings of Britain but he can't know for sure where the exact location of the castle is. The best guess are probably in Somerset near Cadbury Castle or it may have been the castle which was excavated in the 1960s and determined to be built during the Iron Age which looks over the Vale of Avalon. Which is close to a river called Cam. According to one of Henry VIIIs historians local people referred to Cadbury Castle as "Camalat," they believed it to be the home of King Arthur. But their are many versions of the legend. There has come to be a sprititual aura around the legend of King Arthur. Followers believe that Camelot was a Utopia. In the USA that period of time when John Kennedy was President is sometimes referred to as Camelot. King Arthur will return some day to rule it again.

JOURNAL PROMPT

Do you think it is important for anyone who wants to live and work in the United States to learn to speak and write Standard English? Explain your answer.

CHAPTER 8

Acknowledge Your Sources

To write a complete and successful academic essay, you need to acquire information from a variety of sources including books, articles in journals and magazines, and the Internet. In Chapter 3, you learned how to research the information you might need to include in an essay. It is essential that you acknowledge these sources accurately and completely. If you do not, you could be charged with **plagiarism.**

Avoiding Plagiarism

Plagiarism is a form of literary misconduct, resulting from a writer's failure to acknowledge sources he or she has used, creating instead the impression that the information the writer has presented is his or her own work, when it is really the work of someone else. In its most blatant form, plagiarism is the use of whole passages of text taken from a source and inserted, without acknowledgment, into another written text, so that it appears as if the "borrowed" material is the original work of the author who has, in fact, stolen the work of another. But plagiarism is not limited to word-for-word copying. It includes, as well, the failure to acknowledge information taken from another source even if you paraphrase that information. Information that is paraphrased or summarized (see Chapter 3) also must be acknowledged. Plagiarism is considered to be a serious offense in the academic community.

In academic writing, sources usually must be cited twice, once in shorthand form within parentheses in the text of the essay and again in a source list at the end of the essay. As a rule, "common knowledge" does not have to be sourced, even if this knowledge was not common to you when you began your essay. For an essay required for his European history class, Basel decided to write about the invasion of the Spanish Armada, during Spain's war against England. When he began his essay, Basel, who was raised in Afghanistan, did not know that

Elizabeth I was Queen of England when the armada sailed in 1588, but a fact such as this would fall into the "common knowledge" realm. However, when he wrote, "The Spanish fleet consisted of about 130 ships carrying about 8,000 sailors," he had to cite his source because this detail would not be commonly known. If you are not certain whether information you are using is common knowledge, it is better to include a citation.

Citing sources accurately and correctly is challenging but important. There are many types of sources—books, journals, newspapers, the Internet, television—and each type has its own citation format. This format is prescribed and must be adhered to precisely. Commas, dates, volume numbers, parentheses all have to be accurate and placed correctly within the citation. Moreover, there is not a single method, agreed upon by all members of the academic community, for citing sources. If you are taking a biology, a history, and a psychology course, you might have to use different citation methods in each course. Rules that govern the location of the date of publication, the use of capital letters, the use of italics or underlining, and indentation differ from one method to the next. Some methods require footnotes for in-text citations, some require endnotes, and some require parenthetical citation. Citing sources is the albatross of the academic life. A student's life would be so much easier if we could all agree upon one method. Unfortunately, this is not likely to happen. Biologists, anthropologists, psychologists, historians, and other scholars tend to think their method is the best and would be reluctant to change.

This chapter presents a thorough explanation of three widely used citation methods: the **MLA method,** developed and prescribed by the Modern Language Association; the **APA method,** developed and prescribed by the American Psychological Association; and the ***Chicago Manual of Style* (CMS) method,** developed and prescribed by the University of Chicago Press. Many of your professors will accept essays with sources acknowledged using one of these three methods. Others will not; they will insist that sources be acknowledged using the method prescribed by the professional organization that governs their own discipline. In this case, you will have to learn to use yet another citation method. Make sure you check with your professors to find out how they expect sources to be acknowledged.

MLA Method of Parenthetical Citation

The Modern Language Association is a professional organization composed primarily of professors of English and other languages. Your English and foreign-language teachers will want you to acknowledge your sources using the MLA method. Some of your other professors probably will accept this method as well. Others will not. Many of those others will ask you to use the APA or the CMS method of citing sources; these methods are explained later in this chapter.

The manuals for writers who use the MLA method are the seventh edition of the *MLA Handbook for Writers of Research Papers* (New York: MLA, 2009) and the third edition of the *MLA Style Manual and Guide to Scholarly Publishing* (New York: MLA, 2008). The information that follows is based upon these books. The MLA method requires two citations for each secondary source. The first is a brief citation enclosed within parentheses in the text of the essay. The second is a complete citation organized alphabetically by the authors' last names in a list of works cited, which appears at the end of the essay.

● Parenthetical Citations Within the Text of the Essay

Direct quotations taken from a secondary source must be acknowledged with a parenthetical citation. To indicate a direct quote from a secondary source, place quotation marks around the words you are quoting, and then put the author's last name and the page number from the secondary source in which the information can be found. Short direct quotes are integrated into the text of the essay and placed between quotation marks, "so a short direct quote properly acknowledged would look like this" (Author 34). Note the quotation marks around our imagined quote from a secondary source, and note that there is not a comma between the author's last name (*Author* in our example) and the page number.

If the author's name is already mentioned in the text, only the page number is placed in parentheses: As Author notes, "only the page number is required" (34).

Long quotes are indented and blocked off from the text of the essay. The distinction between short quotes and long ones is somewhat arbitrary, but quotes of more than about three lines should be set off from the rest of the essay in the manner illustrated here:

> Note that the quotation marks have been eliminated. The indentation indicates that the material is quoted directly from a secondary source. Quotation marks are used only if the original uses quotation marks. Note also that after a short quote comes the parenthetical citation, followed by a period. In the long, indented quote, the period precedes the parenthetical citation. (Author 39)

In addition to direct quotes, you must cite other information taken from a secondary source. The general rule is that if you possessed the information before you began the essay, you do not need to cite it, but if you acquired the information in the course of writing the essay, you do need to cite it. Again, put in parentheses the author's last name and the page number on which the information can be found. You need to include the page number even if you have paraphrased the information.

If you have used two or more works by the same author, you need to provide a shorthand version of the title of the source to distinguish it from other titles by the same author (Author, *Short* 34). Note the use of the comma after the author's name but not between the title and the page number. If the author's name is mentioned in the text, his or her name is not included in the citation: As Author has shown, "citing sources can be frustrating" (*Short* 34).

If your source is written by four or more people, you need only name the first author followed by the Latin words *et al.* (meaning "and others") and, of course, the page number (First et al. 145). Note the period after "al." Again, no commas are used. *Et al.* is also used in place of all but the first author's name if you mention the author's name in the text of the essay: Smith et al. have conducted research suggesting that "students enjoy writing academic essays" (145).

If your source is written by a corporate author, treat the corporate author as you would a single author: According to government sources, ten-year-olds watch an average of four hours of television per day (Royal Commission on Elementary Education 234).

If the author of your source is anonymous, name the title or a shortened version in the parenthetical citation. Underline or *italicize* a book title; put quotation marks around an article title. If you use a shortened version, include the first main word in the title, since it will be alphabetized by title in the list of works cited. If, for example, the title of your source is "Rating the Quality of the Undergraduate Programs of British Universities," your citation could be as short as the word *Rating* ("Rating" 86).

If you quote from a novel, follow the procedure for a single author. You may also include the chapter number to help your readers find the passage in a different edition of the novel from the one you used. If you include the chapter number, put a semicolon between the page number and the chapter number (Austen 79; ch. 6). Usually you do not have to include the author's name, because the context of your discussion will make clear who the author is.

If you quote from a poem, give the line numbers you are quoting instead of the page number on which the quote appears (Wordsworth 34–40). Provide a shortened version of the title if you quote from more than one poem by the same author and if the context has not made clear the author and the title (Wordsworth, "Tintern" 34–40). Note the punctuation.

If you quote from a Shakespearean play or from another play in verse, list the act, scene, and line numbers, separated by periods (4.2.9–11).

If you quote from the Bible, list the chapter and the verse or verses, separated by a period. Include an abbreviated title of the book, if the context does not make it clear (Lev. 12.2–4).

If you quote from a work from an anthology, remember to give the author's name and not the name of the anthology editor in parentheses.

If you quote from an indirect source—a source quoted in one of your sources—include the abbreviation for "quoted in" in your parenthetical citation: Smith notes that "indirect sources must be cited appropriately" (qtd. in Robins 257). Note carefully the way the citation is punctuated.

If you got the same information from more than one source or if you want to underscore the authority of a point by citing more than one source, do so by separating the sources from each other with semicolons: Experts agree that the semicolon can be used between sources (Wilson 34; Martens 68; Pelies 124).

If your source has no page numbers (as many electronic sources do not), you may omit the page numbers or include the paragraph number if the paragraphs are numbered (as they sometimes are in electronic sources): If necessary, "you should cite the paragraph number in place of the page number" (Smith, par. 12). Note the way this citation is punctuated.

● Works Cited List

The in-text parenthetical citations provide readers with minimal information about the sources from which the writer borrowed information or quoted directly. Readers require the complete bibliographical information about the sources in case they want to learn more about the subject of the essay they are reading. This complete information is provided at the end of the essay, in the list of works cited.

The list of works cited contains only those sources actually cited within the essay. For most academic essays, this is all that is required. Some professors, however, might want you to include in your source list not only the sources you actually cited but also sources you read but did not cite specifically within your essay. This list—of all sources you checked whether or not you cited them in your essay—is called Works Consulted. Most academic essays conclude with a Works Cited list.

Following this paragraph is an example of a Works Cited list. Study it carefully. Included on this list are examples of nearly all of the kinds of sources— books, periodicals, electronic—that you might use to gather the research that you need. As you study this list, note the following:

- The title "Works Cited" is centered and appears in roman type. Do not use italics, boldface, or large lettering. Note that one line is left between the title and the first entry.
- The cited works are arranged alphabetically by the author's last name. If the author of the source is anonymous, the source is placed in the list alphabetically by its title. The sources are not numbered.
- The list uses hanging indentation. The first line of each source is not indented, but all subsequent lines are.
- Book, journal, newspaper, and magazine titles are underlined (italicized), but article titles are placed in quotation marks.
- Page numbers are included for articles in journals, newspapers, and magazines and for articles or essays included in an edited anthology or collection of essays.

- Citation of print sources end with the word Print, preceded and followed by a period.
- There is a number between the title of a journal and its year of publication. This number is the volume number. For example, the article by Pratt in the following works cited is from the journal *Profession,* volume number 91. Some journal article citations, such as the one by Pickett in the sample list, have two numbers, separated by a period. The second number is the issue number. There is an important distinction here. Some journals are continuously paginated, which means they are paginated by year and not by issue. If, for example, the first issue for the year 2008 of the journal *Quantum Mechanics Quarterly* began on page 1 and ended on page 159, the next issue for 2008 would begin on page 160. Citations for journals that are continuously paginated (for a full year) include only the volume number. But some journals are paginated by issue—each issue begins on page 1. Citations for journals paginated by issue require the volume number followed by a period followed by the issue number.
- Citations for online sources include both the date the source appeared online and the date the user of the source accessed the source. The second date is essential because the author of the source could go online and change the content of his or her article after the researcher has cited the earlier version. Note that the word Web, preceded and followed by a period, comes before the date of access. MLA does *not* require the source's URL.

Works Cited

Ballenger, Bruce. *Beyond Note Cards: Rethinking the Freshman Research Paper.* Portsmouth, NH: Boynton Cook, 1999. Print.

Bartholomae, David. "Inventing the University." *When a Writer Can't Write: Studies in Writer's Block and Other Composing Possibilities.* Ed. Mike Rose. New York: Guilford, 1985. 134–65. Print.

Council of College Teachers. *Initiation into the Academy.* Chicago: CCT Press, 1998. Print.

Daniels, Christine. "The Decline of English Grammar." *Haverford Daily Times* 9 Feb. 2001: B2+. Print.

Chandler, Sally. "Reflective Discourses in the Classroom: Creating Spaces Where Students Can Change Their Minds." *Feminist Teacher* 15.1 (2004): 16–33. Print.

Collier, Lorna. "Effective Vocabulary Instruction." *Council Chronicle* Mar. 2007. Web. 25 Oct. 2007.

Ede, Lisa, and Andrea Lunsford. "Audience Addressed/Audience Invoked: The Role of Audience in Composition Theory and Pedagogy." *College Composition and Communication* 35 (1984): 155–71. Print.

George, Alice. "Reading Scores on the Rise at Last." *Clarion* Feb. 1999: 18–22. Print.

Haynes, Cynthia. "Inside the Teaching Machine: Actual Feminism and (Virtual) Pedagogy." *Computers, Writing, Rhetoric, and Literature* 2.1 (1996): n. pag. Web. 8 Feb. 2007.

Lanham, Richard. *Revising Prose.* 4th ed. Upper Saddle River, NJ: Pearson Longman, 1999. Print.

Leslie, Peter M. "Education Policy." *Canadian Encyclopedia.* 1988. Print.

Lindemann, Erika. *A Rhetoric for Writing Teachers.* 3rd ed. New York: Oxford University Press, 1995. Print.

Moulthrop, Stuart. "You Say You Want a Revolution? Hypertext and the Laws of Media." *Postmodern Culture* 1.3 (1991): 53 pars. Web. 12 July 2006.

Marsella, Joy, and Thomas L. Hilgers. "Exploring the Potential of Freewriting." *Nothing Begins with N: New Investigations of Freewriting.* Ed. Pat Belanoff, Peter Elbow, and Sheryl I. Fontaine. Carbondale: Southern Illinois UP, 1991. 93–110. Print.

Oxford Essential World Atlas. New York: Oxford UP, 1996. Print.

Pickett, Nell Ann. "Achieving Readability Through Layout." *Teaching English in the Two-Year College* 10.2 (1984): 154–56. Print.

Pratt, Mary Louise. "Arts of the Contact Zone." *Profession* 91 (1991): 33–40. Print.

Rapkin, Angela A. "The Uses of Logic in the College Freshman English Classroom." *Activities to Promote Critical Thinking: Classroom Practices in Teaching English.* Urbana, IL: NCTE, 1986. 130–35. *ERIC.* CD-ROM. SilverPlatter. 1995.

Smith, Charles. Foreword. *A Sourcebook for Writing Teachers.* By Catherine Nobine. Santa Monica: Lantern Press, 1999. viii–xiii. Print.

Sample MLA Works Cited Entries

In this section are examples of MLA Works Cited entries for the kinds of print and electronic sources you will likely reference in your academic essays. The examples are based upon the *MLA Handbook for Writers of Research Papers*, 7th edition and the third edition of the *MLA Style Manual and Guide to Scholarly Publishing.* For additional examples, consult these manuals. You should be able to find these books in your university library and bookstore.

In accordance with the *MLA Handbook*, the following examples are divided into four sections: non-periodical print publications, periodical print publications, web publications, and additional common sources.

Non-Periodical Print Publications

Book by one author

Glawell, Malcolm. *Outliers: The Story of Success.* Boston: Little, Brown, 2008. Print.

If the book has gone into a second or later edition, place the edition number between the title and the place of publication:

White, Edward M. *Teaching and Assessing Writing.* 2nd ed. San Francisco and London: Jossey-Bass, 1994. Print.

Anthology, compilation, or edited book

Jacobus, Lee A., ed. *Literature: An Introduction to Critical Reading.* Compact ed. Upper Saddle River, NJ: Pearson Education, 2002. Print.

Martin, Wolfgang, Maria Gomez, and Edward Johns, eds. *The Effects of Gender on Child Development in Custody Cases.* Oxford: Oxford University Press, 1996. Print.

Later examples in this list show the citation of separate articles from a collection of essays and of literary works from a literature anthology.

Two or more books by the same author

Gladwell, Malcolm. *Blink: The Power of Thinking Without Thinking.* New York: Time Warner, 2005. Print.

---. *The Tipping Point: How Little Things Can Make a Big Difference.* New York: Time Warner, 2000. Print.

Note that three hyphens replace the author's name for the second citation and that the alphabetization is by book title.

Book by two or three authors

Covino, William A., and David A. Jolliffe. *Rhetoric: Concepts, Definitions, Boundaries.* Boston: Allyn and Bacon, 1995. Print.

Marquart, James W., Sheldon Ekland Olson, and Jonathan R. Sorensen. *The Rope, the Chair, and the Needle: Capital Punishment in Texas, 1923–1990.* Austin: U of Texas P, 1994. Print.

Book by more than three authors. If you use a source by three or more authors, you do not have to list all of the authors' names. You need only list the first author's name followed by the Latin abbreviation *et al.*, meaning "and others."

Patterson, Edward J., et al. *Lighting in Miloz Milozovic's Theatrical Productions.* Cambridge: Harvard UP, 1999. Print.

Book by a corporate author

The Modern Language Association of America. *MLA Handbook for Writers of Research Papers.* 7th ed. New York: MLA, 2009. Print.

Work in an anthology

Bricen, Robert. "Leather and Lace." *Fashion in the Sixties*. Ed. Luke M. Walker.
    Vancouver: Ricards, 1997. 134–56. Print.

If you use more than one essay from one anthology, you should cite the entire anthology the way you would an edited book:

Walker, Luke M., ed. *Fashion in the Sixties*. Vancouver: Ricards, 1997. Print.

Then you need only cite the essays by name, article title, editor's last name, and page numbers, for example:

Bricen, Robert. "Leather and Lace." Walker 134–56.

Waller, Kate. "Hippie Threads." Walker 46–59.

Literary work in an anthology

Cohen, Leonard. "Dance Me to the End of Love." *Selected Canadian Poems*. Ed.
    Rosemary Simpson. Toronto: Bluenote, 1995. 56–57. Print.

Work originally published elsewhere and reprinted in an anthology

Flower, Linda. "Cognition, Context, and Theory Building." *College Composition and
    Communication* 40 (1989): 282–311. Rpt. in *Cross Talk in Comp Theory: A Reader*.
    Ed. Victor Villanueva, Jr. Urbana, IL: NCTE, 1997. 701–33. Print.

Article in an encyclopedia or other reference book

Cronin, Blaise. "The ARIST DATA Set." *The Annual Review of Information
    Science & Technology*. Vol. 37. New Jersey: Information Today Inc., 2002. Print.

Leslie, Peter M. "Education Policy." *Canadian Encyclopedia*. 1988. Print.

If the article is anonymous, alphabetize the article by its title:

"Mandarin." *The Encyclopedia Americana*. 2005 ed. Print.

Introduction, preface, foreword, or afterword

Ivins, Molly. Introduction. *Pipe Dreams: Greed, Ego, and the Death of Enron*. By Robert
    Bryce. New York: PublicAffairs, 2002. xv–xvii. Print.

Smith, Charles. Foreword. *A Sourcebook for Writing Teachers*. By Catherine Nobine.
    Santa Monica: Lantern Press, 1999. viii–xiii. Print.

Cross-references. If you need to cite more than one work from an anthology of literary works or a collection of related essays, you need not provide the full bibliographical information for the entire book with each citation. You should provide the full bibliographical information just once, as you do for an edited book. Suppose, for example, that you need to cite three articles from *The Brooklyn Reader.* You need to cite the entire book only once:

Sexton, Andrea Wyatt, and Alice Leccese Powers, eds. *The Brooklyn Reader: Thirty Writers Celebrate America's Favorite Borough.* New York: Harmony, 1994. Print.

The citations for the articles or essays you have used from the book may be shortened, as follows:

McCullers, Carson. "Brooklyn Is My Neighborhood." Sexton and Powers 143–47.

Walcott, Derek. "A Letter from Brooklyn." Sexton and Powers 264–65.

Book by an anonymous author

The Chicago Manual of Style. 15th ed. Chicago: U of Chicago P, 2003. Print.

This book is listed alphabetically by its title, in this case, under *C.*

Edition. Sometimes books, especially those written years ago, are prepared for publication by someone other than the author. Such books have an editor as well as an author, and the editor's name must be included in the citation:

Chaucer, Geoffrey. *The Canterbury Tales: Nine Tales and the General Prologue.* Ed. V. A. Kolve and Glending Olson. New York: Norton, 1989. Print.

Book translated from a foreign language

De Romilly, Jacqueline. *Great Sophists in Periclean Athens.* 1988. Trans. Janet Lloyd. Oxford: Clarendon Press, 1992. Print.

Book published in a second or subsequent edition

Feuer, Jane. *The Hollywood Musical.* 2nd ed. Bloomington: Indiana UP, 1993. Print.

If the title page indicates that the book is a revised edition, use the abbreviation *Rev. ed.* after the title. If the title page indicates that the book is an abridged edition, use the abbreviation *Abr. ed.* after the title.

Multivolume work

Raine, Kathleen, *Blake and Tradition.* Vol. 1. Princeton: Princeton UP, 1968. Print.

If you use all volumes, the entry in the list of works cited appears as follows:

Lauter, Paul, et al., eds. *The Heath Anthology of American Literature.* 5th ed. 5 vols. Lexington, MA: Heath, 2009. Print.

Book in a series

Anderson, Danny, and Jill S. Kuhnheim, eds. *Cultural Studies in the Curriculum: Teaching Latin America.* New York: MLA, Print. Teaching Langs., Lits., and Cultures.

This book is part of a series of books. The series is entitled "Teaching Languages, Literatures, and Cultures." Note that the series title is not italicized (or underlined). The number of the book in the series also is included. The word Print comes *before* the series title.

Republished book

Simpson, Elizabeth. *The Perfection of Hope: A Soul Transformed Through Critical Illness.* 1998. Toronto: Macfarlane Walter & Ross, 1999. Print.

This book came out in hard cover in 1998; a paperback version was then published in 1999.

Pamphlet

Inside Kansas. Wichita: Kansas Visitors Information Bureau, 2006. Print.

Government publication

United States Department of Health and Human Services. *National Evaluation of Welfare-to-Work Strategies: Do Mandatory Welfare-to-Work Programs Affect the Well-Being of Children?* Washington: GPO, 2000. Print.

United States Congressional Senate Committee on Health, Education, Labor, and Pensions. *Stem Cell Research.* Washington: GPO, 2002. Print.

Conference proceedings

Young, Trevor, ed. *Proceedings of the Pacific Northwest Regional Conference on Whole Language Pedagogy,* Seattle, April 9–12, 1999. Tacoma: Howson UP, 2000. Print.

A single paper presented at a conference is cited as follows:

Pader, Emilia. *The Effect of Global Warming on Baffin Island Polar Bears.* Proc. of North Dakota Conference on Climate Change Conf., 8–10 March 2008, U. of North Dakota. Print.

Book without stated publication information or pagination. Some publishers do not provide adequate bibliographical information for the books they publish. They might not list the date of publication, the place of publication, or even number the pages. If you use a source without all the necessary bibliographical information, cite as much as you can, and use the following abbreviations to indicate omissions:

n.p. for no place of publication or for no publisher

n.d. for no date

n. pag. for no pagination

Use brackets if you have provided bibliographical information the publisher has not provided but you have knowledge of.

Malachi, Zvi, ed. *Proceedings of the International Conference on Literary and Linguistic Computing.* [Tel Aviv]: [Fac. of Humanities, Tel Aviv U], n.d. Print.

Dissertation

Cherry, Gilbert. "The Effect on Team Goal Productivity of the Elimination of the Red Line in Ice Hockey." Diss. U of Greenwood, 2008. Print.

If the dissertation is published, underline the title as opposed to enclosing it within quotation marks. If it is published by University Microfilms International, add, after the date of publication, "Ann Arbor:" and the acronym "UMI," followed by the date of microfilm publication, followed by the order number.

Wechsler, Joyce. *Emily Dickinson and Nature's Spiritual Awakening.* Diss. University of Rochester, 2002. Ann Arbor: UMI, 2003. ATT 3023542. Print.

Periodical Print Publications

Article in an academic journal continuously paginated. Continuously paginated means that the pages in the journal are numbered by the year as opposed to by each issue. For example, suppose a journal is published four times a year. The first issue would begin on page 1. Suppose it ended on page 236. The second issue of the year would then begin on page 237. Suppose it ended on page 400. The third issue of the year would begin on page 401. Suppose it ended on page 589. The fourth and final issue of the year would begin on page 590. The first issue published the following year would begin again on page 1.

Horner, Bruce, and John Trimbur. "English Only and U.S. College Composition." *College Composition and Communication* 53 (2002): 594–630. Print.

Russell, David R. "Romantics on Writing: Liberal Culture and the Abolition of Composition Courses." *Rhetoric Review* 6 (1988): 132–48. Print.

Webb, Colleen. "A Complete Classification of Darwinian Extinction in Ecological Interactions." *The American Naturalist* 161 (2003): 181–205. Print.

Article in an academic journal paginated by issue. The only difference in citation between an article in a journal continuously paginated and one in a journal paginated by issue is the inclusion of the issue number in a citation of a paginated-by-issue journal article. Note that a period comes between the volume number and the issue number.

Williams, Linda. "Of Kisses and Ellipses: The Long Adolescence of American Movies."
    Critical Inquiry 32.2 (2006): 288–340. Print.

Abstract in an abstracts journal

Ferguson, Tamara J., and Susan L. Crowley. "Gender Differences in the Organization
    of Guilt and Shame." *Sex Roles* 37 (1997): 19–44. *Psychological Abstracts* 85
    (1998): item 4265. Print.

Newspaper article

Davis, Ann, and Russell Gold. "Surge in Natural-Gas Price Stoked by New Global Trade."
    Wall Street Journal 18 Apr. 2008: A1 + A15. Print.

The letter *A* refers to the section number. The numbers *1* and *15* refer to the page numbers in section A. Use a plus sign to indicate that the article continues later on in the same section.

Note the following also:

- If the city where the newspaper is published is not included in the name of the newspaper, add the name of the city in square brackets, after the name of the paper. You do not have to add the name of the city to nationally published papers such as *USA Today* and the *Wall Street Journal.*
- If an edition is named on the masthead (natl. ed.; late ed.), include this information after the date.
- Abbreviate all months except May, June, and July.

Drury, Cynthia. "How Is Your Congressional Representative Voting?" *Star-Ledger*
    [Newark] 23 Sept. 2003, sec. A1+. Print.
Kiernan, Vincent. "Study Finds Errors in Medical Information Available on the Web."
    Chronicle of Higher Education 12 June 1998: A25. Print.
Trachtenberg, Jeffrey A. "What's in a Movie Soundtrack? Catchy Tunes and Big
    Business." *Wall Street Journal* 1 Apr. 1994, eastern ed.: B1. Print.

Editorial. If you cite an editorial, place the word *Editorial* between the title of the article and the name of the paper.

Reid, Louann. "From the Editor." Editorial. *English Journal* Jan. 2008: 10–11. Print.

Letter to the editor

Gadomski, Kevin. Letter. *Rolling Stone*. 3 Apr. 2008: 8. Print.

Review. If a review is anonymous, begin the citation with "Rev. of" but alpha-betize by title. Include the title of the review, if there is a title, after the author's name.

Rev. of *Romeo and Juliet* by William Shakespeare. Mission Viejo Playhouse, Mission
    Viejo, CA. *The MV Gazette* 14 March 2009: 8. Print.

Mitchell, W. J. T. "The Fog of Abu Ghraib." Rev. of *Standard Operating Procedure,* dir.
    Errol Morris. *Harpers* May 2008: 71. Print.

Updike, John. "No Brakes." Rev. of *Sinclair Lewis: Rebel from Main Street*, by Richard
    Lingeman. *New Yorker* 4 Feb. 2002: 77–80. Print.

Article in a monthly or bimonthly magazine

George, Alice. "Reading Scores on the Rise at Last." *Clarion* Feb. 1999: 18–22. Print.

Kaylin, Lucy. "Johnny in Paradise." *GQ* Aug. 2003: 92–96, 157–58. Print.

Philips, Kevin. "Numbers Racket: Why the Economy Is Worse than We Know." *Harpers*
    May 2008: 43–47. Print.

Article in a weekly magazine

Kidder, Tracy. "The Good Doctor." *New Yorker* 10 July 2000: 40–57. Print.

If the article is anonymous, alphabetize it by title, ignoring articles (*a, an, the*).

Web Publications

Citations for web publications need not only the date the source was published but also the date you accessed the information. This is because the source could be altered after you have accessed it. MLA no longer requires a URL for web publications.

A periodical publication in an online database. As a college or university stu-dent, you will likely do some research by using an online database that your library subscribes to such as Academic Search Premier, LexisNexis, or JSTOR. These databases are invaluable research resources. They contain full texts of articles from scholarly journals, magazines, and newspapers. Study carefully the sample citations below, which illustrate the proper MLA method for citing articles accessed from such databases. Note that both the database and the peri-odical title are italicized. Note that the word Web but not the URL is included in the citations.

Brasfield, Rebecca. "Rereading *Sex and the City:* Exposing the Hegemonic Feminist Narrative." *Journal of Popular Film and Television* 34.2 (2006): 130–138. *Academic Search Premier.* Web. 15 Dec. 2008.

Drake, Laura. "Marmot Returns from the Brink of Extinction." *The Globe and Mail* 13 Aug. 2007:S1–2. *LexisNexis.* Web. 12 Sept. 2007.

McCarthy, Todd. *Casino Royale.* Review of *Casino Royale,* dir. Martin Campbell. *Variety Review Database* Nov. 2006:14–15. *Proquest.* Web. 15 Dec. 2006.

Shin, Su-Jeong Hwnag and Cynthia L. Istook. "The Importance of Understanding the Shape of Diverse Ethnic Female Consumers for Developing Jeans Sizing Systems." *International Journal of Consumer Studies* 31 (2007): 135–143. *Academic Search Premier.* Web. 5 June 2008.

Note that some scholarly journals do not upload a print version of their content to a database such as those referenced above. Some exist only in electronic form. They are cited in a similar manner as the examples above, except they do not include the name of a database. They are also rarely paginated so the abbreviation n. pag. replace page numbers. Here is an example:

Schmidt-Nietro, Jorge R. "The Political Side of Bilingual Education: The Undesirable Becomes Useful." *Arachne@Rutgers* 2.2 (2002): n. pag. Web. 5 June 2008.

A non-periodical publication. "Non-periodical" refers to sources not published on a regular schedule and applies to many books, reference works, newspapers, and magazines. There are three types of non-periodical web publications: works cited only on the web, works cited on the web but with print publication data included, and works cited on the web with publication data for another medium besides print. Here are some examples of each. Study them carefully, noting especially the correct MLA format for online encyclopedias, news networks, magazines, and newspapers.

A work cited only on the web

Behan, Madonna. "Make Nutritious Snacking Choices on the Go." *CNNhealth.com.* Cable News Network, 2 Apr. 2009. Web. 2 Apr. 2009.

Eaves, Morris, Robert Essick, and Joseph Viscomi, eds. *The William Blake Archive.* Lib of Cong., 8 May 2008. Web. 15 May 2008.

"Islam," *Encyclopaedia Britannica Online.* Encyclopaedia Britannica, 2009. Web. 31 Mar. 2009.

Goldberg, Jeffrey. "Netanyahu to Obama: Stop Iran or I Will." Interview with Benjamin Netanyahu. *The Atlantic.com.* 31 Mar. 2009. Web. 2 Apr. 2009.

Keats, John. "Ode on a Grecian Urn." *Poetical Works. Bartleby Project.* Bartleby.com.
  May 1998. Web. 30 Mar. 2009.

Marshall, Barry. Course homepage. *English 2354.* Dept. of English, U. of California.
  Sept. 2008. Web. 10 Sept. 2008.

"Post-Traumatic Stress Tied to Increased Suicide Risk." *U.S. World and News Report.*
  U.S. News and World Report, 2 Mar. 2009. Web. 3 Apr. 2009.

Richman, Alan. "Made (Better) in Japan." *Forked. A Blog.* Men.style.com., Mar. 2008.
  Web. 8 Oct. 2008.

"The Auto Industry Matters, Even on the West Coast." Editorial. *Vancouver Sun.*
  Vancouver Sun, 2 Apr. 2009. Web. 4 April 2009.

"Vampire." *Wikipedia The Free Encyclopedia.* Wikipedia, 2007. Web. 12 Feb. 2007.

A work cited on the web with print publication data. Most books that are available on the web are also available in print, and you should include the print publication information, even if you accessed the book online. To cite a book you accessed online, add to the print version of the citation the name of the database or web site, the word web, and your date of access.

Prince, Jonathan. *The Liberal Spaces of the American University.* New York: Aloysius,
  2007. *American Council of Tertiary Education.* Web. 3 Nov. 2008.

Whitman, Walt. Leaves of Grass. Brooklyn, 1855. *The Walt Whitman Archive.* Web. 6
  Sept. 2005.

A work on the web cited with publication data for another medium besides print. If you have to watch a film or examine fine art as part of your research, you might access your film or painting via the web. You would cite such sources as follows:

It Happened One Night. Dir. Frank Capra. *Turner Classic Movies.* Columbia, 1934. Web.
  13 Aug. 2007.

Picasso, Pablo. *Guernica,* 1937. Google Images. Web. 23 Feb. 2008.

Citing Additional Common Sources
Television or radio program

"Boy, Girl, Boy, Girl." Episode 34. Writ. Jenny Bricks. Dir. Pam Thomas. *Sex and the
  City.* Home Box Office. 25 June 2000. Television.

"Qatar." *The Singular Tourist.* Narr. Heather Jenks. Writ. Heather Jenks. ATV.
  Edmonton. 27 Jan. 2000. Television.

Keillor, Garrison. *A Prairie Home Companion.* With Ledward Ka'apana and Owana
    Salazar. 12 Oct. 2002. Minnesota Public Radio. 18 Oct. 2002. Radio.

Sound recording. You may list first the name of the conductor, the composer,
or the performer. Your choice will depend upon the person you are emphasizing
in your paper.

Boubill, Alain, and Claude-Michel Schonberg. *Miss Saigon.* Perf. Lea Salonga, Claire
    Moore, and Jonathan Pryce. Cond. Martin Koch. Geffen, 1989. CD.

McFerrin, Bobby. "Kalimba Suite." *Beyond Words.* Blue Note, 2002. 21 May 2002. CD.

Film or video recording. There is some leeway in the information you include
for citing a film or a video. Start with the title and include the name of the
director, the distributor, and the year of release. You may add the names of the
star or stars, the writer or writers, and/or the producer if you wish to highlight
their contributions.

Hamlet. By William Shakespeare. Dir. Kenneth Branaugh. Perf. Kenneth Branaugh,
    Kate Winslet. Warner Bros., 1996. Film.

Live performance of a play

The Phantom of the Opera by Andrew Lloyd Webber. Dir. Harold Prince. Orange County
    Performing Arts Center, Costa Mesa, CA. 18 April, 2008. Performance.

Musical score or libretto

Mozart, Wolfgang Amadeus. *The Marriage of Figaro.* 1786. New York: Dorchester, 2002.
    Print.

Interview

Matthews, Christopher. Interview with Don Imus. *Imus in the Morning.* MSNBC, New
    York. 8 May 2003. Television.

If you conducted the interview, begin with the interviewee's name, followed by
the medium (personal, telephone, e-mail), followed by the date.

Advertisement

Tiffany & Co. Advertisement. *Vanity Fair* Jan. 2003: 10–11. Print.

Lecture, speech, address, or reading

Aronson, Molly. Lecture for English 368. City University, Plantsville. 5 Aug. 2002.
    Lecture.

Student Essay: MLA Citation

Edna Bell
Ed B 540
Professor Fizer
December 1, 2006

The Qualities of a Grade A Essay

One of the most important responsibilities of any teacher is to help students   1
achieve academic excellence. One of the most important ways in which teachers
and professors measure academic excellence is by evaluating student writing. It
is essential, then, that teachers help students understand, as precisely and accurately as possible, what the qualities of an outstanding essay are. The qualities of
a B-grade or a C-grade essay are less relevant, in that their value is measured in
relationship to the ideal. A B-grade essay might possess some but not all of the
qualities of the Grade A paper, or it might possess all of the qualities but executed
to a lower standard. A C-grade paper will fall considerably short in all, or almost
all, of the Grade A standards. They are less relevant, as well, because they are not
the standard toward which professors teach or students aspire. Students need to
know the qualities of a Grade A paper and need to know that their grade will be
lower in proportion to the extent that those standards are not met. Most educators
agree that there are, basically, three qualities of outstanding academic writing.

Outstanding academic writing fulfills the purpose of the assignment.   2
Teachers assign essays and reports on a wide variety of topics in a wide variety of genres. A teacher or professor might ask his or her students to write
an argument for or against the war in Iraq, a lab report explaining the results
of an experiment students undertook in their chemistry class, a business plan
or proposal that would help secure a loan to start a fast-food restaurant, an
expository essay explaining Maslow's hierarchy of needs, a literature review of
recent studies on the causes and effects of global warming, a social science
report summarizing and explaining the implications of the responses to a
questionnaire on how students select their college major. An excellent response
to such assignments will understand and achieve the goal—the purpose—of
the assignment. It will not go off topic, incorporate irrelevant information, or
reference unreliable sources.

Bell 1

The purpose of a writing assignment is also fulfilled when the writer   3
conforms to and satisfies the conventions of the genre (Fosen) or rhetorical
mode the assignment requires. A persuasive essay, for example, will usually
require cogent arguments supported by reliable and authoritative evidence and
an acknowledgment and refutation of the opposing point of view (Hacker 497).
A lab report will use a system of headings and subheadings to report clearly
the results of an experiment. A social science report will usually offer support
for a hypothesis, again with a careful and preordained system of headings and
subheadings: Purpose, Method, Participants, Results, Discussion, Limitations. An
excellent expository or informative essay will support its thesis in well-developed
paragraphs that provide the necessary details, facts, examples, definitions. An
essay or report that completely fulfills the purpose of the assignment, sticks to
its topic, and adheres to the requirements of its genre will likely be awarded
higher grades than essays that mistake the purpose of the assignment, go off on
tangents, or adopt a genre inappropriate to the prompt.

The second quality of a Grade A essay, report, or article is that it respects   4
the needs and expectations of its readers or "audience," to use the term many
composition scholars prefer (Lunsford and Straub 179). Writers for newspapers,
magazines, journals, and book publishers have an implied contract with their
readers that they will present certain information, at a certain rhetorical level,
in a certain style. Student academic writing is usually read and assessed by
teachers and professors, who expect students to obey the rules of Standard
English (Blaauw-Hara). They want to see smooth and logical transitions between
and among sentences within a paragraph and paragraphs within the essay or
report as a whole. They don't want to see errors in sentence grammar, sentence
structure, spelling, or punctuation. They want academic voice and academic style.
Academic voice is formal and steady, not ostentatious, not flippant, not sarcastic, while academic style is generally clear and concise, specifically aligned with
the discourse conventions of the discipline. Scientists, for example, writing for
an academic audience typically use a comparatively clear and simple sentence
structure; they will use the language of their discipline, assuming that their
readers share their knowledge of that language. Humanists also will use the
special language—the jargon—of their discipline but typically will favor more
complex sentence structure and often a less formal style.

Bell 2

The third quality of outstanding academic writing is substance. Poll teachers   5
and professors about their grading, and many will say that the most frequent
constructively critical comment they write in the margins of their students' papers
has to do with the development of ideas. Can you provide an example? You need
to define this term; more detail needed here—these are among the comments
that frequently appear on student essays (Lunsford and Straub 173). Paragraphs
in academic essays must be robust. They must not be anemic. Paragraphs must
be developed in enough detail so that the reader understands exactly what point,
idea, argument the writer is trying to express. Body paragraphs in academic
essays are typically around 132 words in length (Soles 74–75). If professors see
a sequence of two or more paragraphs that fall much below the expected length,
they will usually be alert to the fact that the student is not developing his or
her paragraphs in enough detail or that there is a problem with structure and
paragraphs that are too short need to be consolidated.

It is true that there may be some exceptions to the qualities of the Grade A   6
assignment as represented in this paper. For a response journal, teachers might
accept, even encourage some creative violations of the precepts of Standard
English. A teacher might ask for a personal narrative, for example, which will have
a voice and style less formal than an academic argument. There are objections
among some academics to the status of Standard English, on the grounds that
it is the language of a white, largely male, Eurocentric academy and, as such,
discriminates against minority students who don't share the same cultural and
linguistic heritage and experience (Delpit).

While there is truth to these assertions, those who express them remain a   7
minority. Most students want to be successful at school and, ultimately, successful
in the worlds of business, government, or education. Writing excellence is a
prerequisite for success in many of these fields, and writing excellence, a Grade
A paper, is the product of a text that fulfills its purpose, respects its readers, and
values substance.

Works Cited

Blaauw-Hara, M. "Why Our Students Need Instruction in Grammar, and How We Should
    Go About It." *Teaching English in the Two-Year College* 34 (2006): 165–178. Print.
Delpit, Lisa. *Other People's Children: Cultural Conflict in the Classroom.* New York: New
    Press, 2006. Print.

Bell 3

Fosen, Chris. "Genres Made Real: Genre Theory as Pedagogy, Method, and Content." Paper Presented at the Conference on College Composition and Communication, Minnesota, April 2002. Web. 10 Apr. 2002.

Hacker. Diana. *The Bedford Handbook.* 7th ed. Boston: Bedford/St. Martins, 2006. Print.

Lunsford, Ronald F., and Richard Straub. "Twelve Readers Reading: A Survey of Contemporary Teachers' Commenting Strategies." *Key Works on Teacher Response: An Anthology.* Ed. Richard Straub. Portsmouth: Boynton Cook, 2006. 159–189. Print.

Soles, Derek. *The Concise Guide to Teaching Composition.* Upper Saddle River, NJ: Pearson, Prentice Hall, 2007. Print.

APA Method of Parenthetical Citation

Many of your professors will expect you to cite your sources using the APA method, developed and sanctioned by the American Psychological Association. The information in this chapter about using the APA method is based on the fifth edition (2001) of the *Publication Manual of the American Psychological Association.*

Like the MLA system, the APA method has two components: parenthetical citations within the text of the essay and a list of references at the end of the essay. Note, however, that there are significant differences in the format of the two systems. Be careful you do not get the two systems confused.

● Parenthetical Citations Within the Text of the Essay

Direct quotations from a secondary source must be acknowledged with a parenthetical citation. To indicate a direct quote from a secondary source, place quotation marks around the information you are quoting, and then in parentheses put the author's last name, the year the work was published, and the page number from the secondary source on which the information can be found. Short direct quotes are integrated into the text of the essay and placed between quotation marks, "so a short direct quote properly acknowledged would look like this" (Author, 2001, p. 34). Note the quotation marks around our imagined quote from a secondary source, as well as the commas between the author's last name and the year of publication and between the year of publication and the page number. The word *page* is abbreviated as "p." Note how this parenthetical citation differs from an MLA citation.

Long quotes are indented ten spaces and blocked off from the text of the essay. The distinction between short quotes and long ones is somewhat arbitrary, but quotes of more than about three lines should be set off from the rest of the essay in the manner illustrated here:

> Note that the quotation marks have been eliminated. The indentation indicates that the material is quoted directly from a secondary source. Quotation marks are used only if quotation marks are used in the original. Note also that after a short quote comes the parenthetical citation followed by a period. In the long, indented quote, the period precedes the parenthetical citation. (Author, 2007, p. 39)

In addition to direct quotes, you must cite other information taken from a secondary source. The general rule is that if you possessed the information before you began the essay, you do not need to cite it, but if you acquired the information in the course of writing the essay, you do need to cite it. Again, put in parentheses the author's last name and the page number on which the information is found. You need to include the page number even if you have paraphrased the information.

If the author's name is already mentioned in the text, the date follows the author's name, and the page number follows the quote or the borrowed information: As Author (2007) notes, "The date follows the author's name, and the page number follows the quote or borrowed information" (p. 34).

If your source is written by two authors, include both names in the parenthetical citation. Separate the two names with an ampersand (Author & Writer, 2007, p. 57).

If your source is written by three, four, or five people, you need only cite all of the authors the first time you cite the source (Author, Writer, & Artist, 2007, p. 751). Thereafter, you may use only the name of the first author followed by the Latin words *et al.* (meaning "and others") and, of course, the page number (First et al., 2001, p. 145). Note the period after *al.* If a source you use is written by six or more authors, you provide only the last name of the first author followed by *et al.*, even in the first parenthetical citation.

If your source is written by a corporate author, treat the corporate author as you would a single author: According to government sources, ten-year-olds watch an average of four hours of television per day (Royal Commission on Elementary Education, 2007, p. 234). You may shorten the title of the work as long as it remains clear to your readers.

If the author of your source is anonymous, name the title or a shortened version in the parenthetical citation. If you use a shortened version, include the first word in the title (except an article), since it will be alphabetized by title in the references list. If, for example, the title of your source is "Rating the Quality of the Undergraduate Programs of British Universities," your citation could be as short as the word *Rating* ("Rating," 2007, p. 86).

● References List at the End of the Essay

The APA references list, like MLA's list of works cited, contains all of the references you have used in your essay. A sample references list follows this paragraph. Features of the APA references list include the following:

- The list is arranged alphabetically by the authors' last names. If the source is anonymous, it is placed in the list alphabetically by its title.
- Works published by the same author in the same year are differentiated using a small letter after the year, for example 2008a; 2008b. They are then alphabetized by title.
- Authors' first names are not used; only their initials are. (In the MLA method, first names are used.)
- Words in the titles of articles contained within books or journals are not capitalized, except for the first word, the first word of a subtitle, and proper nouns.
- The date of publication follows the author's name.
- Book titles are capitalized the same way article titles are, but book titles are placed in italics or are underlined, while article titles are not.
- Words, other than prepositions, articles, and conjunctions, in journal titles are capitalized, and journal titles are underlined or placed in italics.
- Electronic sources include the online address and the date on which the writer of the essay who is using the online source accessed the source. This date is necessary because authors of online articles can change the content of their articles after a researcher has read and used information from that source.
- There is no period at the end of an entry that ends with a URL.
- If the source has more than one author, the authors' names are separated from each other with commas, including the last of the names, which is preceded by an ampersand (&).
- The volume number is placed between the title of a journal and its year of publication. For example, the article by Macher in the following references list is from the journal *British Journal of Speech and Text Communication,* Volume 22. Note that the volume number is underlined or placed in italics and a comma follows the journal name. Some journal article citations, such as the one by Klimoski, have two numbers, the second enclosed within parentheses. The second number refers to the issue number. There is an important distinction here. Some journals are continuously paginated, which means that they are paginated by year and not by issue. If, for example, the first issue for the year 2008 of the journal *Quantum Mechanics*

Quarterly began on page 1 and ended on page 159, the next issue for the year 2008 would begin on page 160. Citations for journals that are continuously paginated (for a full year) include only the volume number. But some journals are paginated by issue—each issue begins on page 1. Citations for journals paginated by issue require the volume number followed by the issue number in parentheses.

References

Arden, E. (2007). The politically correct writer. *Stringers Quarterly 2.1.* Retrieved March 9, 2007, from http://www/string_quart.bi.camduei/vol2.txt

Burchfield, R. W. (1996). *The new Fowler's modern English usage* (3rd ed.). Oxford: Clarendon Press.

Clinton, W. (1998). State of the union address. (1998, January 27). Retrieved February 24, 1999, from http://www.pub.whitehouse.gov/urires/I2R?pdi://oma.eop.gov.us/1998/01/27/11.text.1

Davidson, T., & Aristos, J. (2007). *The compact English handbook* (3rd ed.). Birmingham: Zevon.

Hacker, D. (1998). *The Bedford handbook* (5th ed., Instr. ann. ed.). Boston: Bedford.

Klimoski, R., & Palmer, S. (1993). The ADA and the hiring process in organizations. *Consulting Psychology Journal: Practice and Research, 45*(2), 10–36.

Macher, Y. (1999). Keeping up with language variation. *British Journal of Speech and Text Communication, 22,* 478–499.

Meyers, M. W. (1990). Current generic pronoun usage: An empirical study. *American Speech, 65,* 228–237.

Schlene, V. J. (1996). *Teaching About Vietnam and the Vietnam War.* (ERIC Clearinghouse for Social Studies/Social Science Education Bloomington, IN). Retrieved July 2, 2006 from http://www.ericdigests.org/19981.vietnam.htm

Taylor, K. R. (2003, November). Bracing for cheating and plagiarism. *Educational Digest* Retrieved November 6, 2006, from http://pqasb.pqarchiver.com/eddigest/results.html

● Sample APA Reference List Entries

Here are examples of the APA style for entries on a references list, illustrating the kinds of print and electronic sources you will likely reference in your academic essays. For additional examples, consult the *Publication Manual of the American Psychological Association*, 5th edition.

In accordance with the APA *Publication Manual,* the following examples are divided into nine sections: periodicals; books, brochures, and book chapters; technical and research reports; proceedings of meetings and symposia; doctoral dissertations and master's theses; unpublished work and publications of limited circulation; reviews; audiovisual media; and electronic media.

Periodicals

Article in an academic journal continuously paginated

Brown, W. S. (2005). The new employment contract and the "at risk" worker. *Journal of Business Ethics, 58,* 195–201.

Article in an academic journal paginated by issue

Miller, L., Chaika, M., & Groppe, L. (1996). Girls' preferences in software design: Insights from a focus group. *Interpersonal Computing and Technology, 4(2),* 27–36.

Newspaper article

Fish, S. (2003, Oct. 3). Grading Congress on tuition. *Chronicle of Higher Education,* pp. C3–4.

Magazine article

Hoffman, B. (2003, June). The logic of suicide terrorism. *Atlantic,* 40–47.

Books, Brochures, and Book Chapters

Book by one author

Lykken, D. T. (1995). *The antisocial personalities.* Hillsdale, NJ: Erlbaum.

Rosenthal, R. (1987). *Meta-analytic procedures for social research* (Rev. ed.). Newbury Park, CA: Sage.

Note that *Rev. ed.* stands for "revised edition." If the book is a revised edition, it will be so indicated on the cover. If the book is a second or subsequent edition, that information also must be included in parentheses, after the title.

Williams, J. D. (2003). *Preparing to teach writing* (3rd ed.). Mahway, NJ: Erlbaum.

Edited book

Kalaidjian, W., Roof, J., & Watt, S. (Eds.). (2004). *Understanding literature: An introduction to reading and writing.* Boston: Houghton Mifflin.

Two or more works by the same author published the same year

Bornstein, R. F. (1993a). *The dependent personality.* New York: Guilford.

Bornstein, R. F. (1993b). Parental representations and psychopathology: A critical review of the empirical literature. In J. Masling & R. Bornstein (Eds.), *Psychoanalytic perspectives on psychopathology* (pp. 1–41). Washington, DC: American Psychological Association.

Book by a corporate author

American Psychiatric Association. (1980). *Diagnostic and statistical manual of mental disorders* (3rd ed.). Washington, DC: Author.

The Concise Oxford Dictionary (5th ed.). (1964). Oxford: UP.

Article in an edited book

Bradburn, N. M. (1983). Response effects. In P. H. Rossi, J. D. Wright, & A. B. Anderson (Eds.), *Handbook of survey research* (pp. 289–328). New York: Academic Press.

Tuchman, B. (2002). The black death. In L. G. Kirszner & S. R. Mandell (Eds.), *The Blair reader* (4th ed.). Upper Saddle River, NJ: Prentice Hall.

Unauthored article in an encyclopedia or other reference book

Neanderthal man. (1994). In C. Cook (Ed.), *Pears cyclopaedia* (Vol. 103, pp. F55–F56). London: Pelham.

Authored article in an encyclopedia or other reference book

Applebaum, E. L. (1998). Ear diseases and hearing disorders. In *The new encyclopaedia Britannica* (Vol. 26, pp. 216–220). Chicago: Encyclopaedia Britannica.

Book translated from a foreign language

Camus, A. (1989). *The stranger* (M. Ward, Trans.). New York: Vintage. (Original work published 1942).

Multivolume work

Baker, R. S., & Sexton, J. (Eds.). (1998–2002). *Aldous Huxley Complete Essays* (Vols. 1–5). Chicago: Ivan Dee.

Government publication

Nebraska Department of Education. (2007). *Statistics and facts about Nebraska schools, 2006–2007*. Lincoln, NE: Author.

Technical and Research Reports

Report available from the U.S. Government Printing Office with government institute as author

Labor Department, Bureau of International Labor Affairs. (2003). Foreign Labor Trends: Switzerland, 2003. (Publication No. FLT 03-10). Washington, DC: U.S. Government Printing Office.

ERIC (Educational Resources Information Center) document
Soles, D. (2001). *Sharing scoring guides* (Report No. CS217406). Bloomington, IN: ERIC Clearinghouse on Reading, English, and Communication. (ERIC Document Reproduction Service No. 450379.)

Proceedings of Meetings and Symposia
Paper presented at a conference

Blair, H., & Sanford, K. (1999, April). *Single-sex classrooms: A place for transformation of policy and practice.* Paper presented at the annual meeting of the American Education Research Association, Montreal, Quebec, Canada.

Paper presented at a symposium

Smith, M. C. (2003, March). Cross-disciplinary teaching and learning: A scholars' program. In S. J. Lu (Chair), *Re-writing the learning environment: Three methods of cross-disciplinary collaboration.* Symposium conducted at the Conference on College Composition and Communication, New York.

Doctoral Dissertations and Master's Theses
Doctoral dissertation abstracted in Dissertation Abstracts International

Willard, S. (2003). Relationship of emotional intelligence and adherence to combination antiretroviral medications by individuals living with HIV disease (Doctoral dissertation, Drexel University, 2003). *Dissertation Abstracts International, 64*, 612.

Master's thesis

Rigby, W. W. (2002). *Collaborative synergy in the work of Richard Rodgers and Oscar Hammerstein.* Unpublished master's thesis. Moore University of the Arts, Redding Village, MA.

Unpublished Works and Publications of Limited Circulation
Unpublished manuscript never submitted for publication

Eisner, F. N., & Bartleby, A. E. (2002). *The effect of profiling miscues on the police investigation of the Washington serial sniper case.* Unpublished manuscript.

Note: If the authors are affiliated with a university, put a comma after *manuscript* followed by the name of the university.

Publication of limited circulation

Dragon benefits. *(2002).* *(Available from Human Resources, Drexel University, 3141 Chestnut Street, Philadelphia, PA, 19103)*

Reviews

Review of a book

Latterell, C. G. (2003). A guide to composition pedagogies. [Review of the book *A guide to composition pedagogies*]. *College Composition and Communication, 54,* 502–505.

Film review

Turan, K. (2006, Nov. 17). Daniel Craig rings true as "Casino Royale" shrewdly remakes 007. [Review of the motion picture *Casino Royale*]. *Los Angeles Times,* pp. C1, C3.

Audiovisual Media

Television or radio program

Cherry, M. (Producer). (2007, Aug. 28). *Desperate Housewives* [Television Broadcast]. Los Angeles: Amer. Broadcasting Corp.

Record, tape cassette, or CD

Mozart, W. A. (1786). Overture to le nozze di Figaro [Conducted by C. M. Giulini]. On *Le nozze di Figaro* [CD]. London: EMI Classics (1990).

Note that the first name listed is that of the song's composer. The first date listed (1786) is the date of composition; use the copyright date if applicable. The last date (1990) is the recording date.

Motion picture

Nayar, D., & Chadha, G. (Producers), & Chadha, G. (Director). (2003). *Bend it like Beckham* [Motion picture]. United Kingdom: Fox Searchlight Pictures.

Electronic Media

Online book

Turoff, M. (1998). *Alternative futures for distance learning: The force and the darkside.* Retrieved October 31, 2002, from http://www.westga.edu/~distance.turoff11.html

Article in an online journal or magazine

Ong, J. S. (2003, Sept./Oct.). From term paper to putsch. *Drexel Online Journal.* Retrieved October 6, 2003, from http://www.drexel.edu/doj/essays/ong_termpaper.asp

Electronic copy of a journal article retrieved from database such as ProQuest or Academic Search Premier

Harley, D. M., & Laughton, I. J. (2002). Historical analysis of photographs of African American victims of vigilante capital punishment in South Carolina during the 1920's and 30's. *Journal of the History of the South, 38,* 12–65. Retrieved November 1, 2002, from AhARTICLES database.

Document available on university program or department website

Wilcox, S. (2002, April). *Prints and drawings.* Retrieved October 6, 2003, from Yale University Center for British Art website: http://www.yale.edu/ycba/collections/index.htm

U.S. government report

United States Bureau of Citizenship and Immigration Services. (2003, September 30). Visa Waiver Program. Retrieved October 6, 2007, from http://www.immigration.gov/graphics/shared/lawenfor/bmgmt/insptct.vwpp.htm

Report from a private organization

Twigg, C. A. The Pew Learning and Technology Program. Pew Charitable Trusts. (1999). *Improving learning and reducing costs: Redesigning large-enrollment courses.* Retrieved October 6, 2003, from http://www.center.rpi.edu/PewSym/mono1.html

Online reference book

Computer use in schools, 1984–1985 and 1997–1998. (1998). In *Information Please Almanac.* San Francisco: Learning Network, Inc. Retrieved September 22, 2002, from http://www.inforplease.com/ipa/A0193911.html

Daily newspaper article

Pear, R. (2006, Jan. 23). Gains reported for children of welfare to work families. *New York Times on the Web.* Retrieved April 19, 2008, from http://www.nytimes.com/2006/01/23/national/23/WELF.html

For additional examples of citing online sources, see the references list in Tersa's essay, which follows.

Student Essay: APA Citation

Is Chocolate Good for You?
A Review of Some Online Sources
Tersa Lyons
University Writing 120
March 1, 2008*

Abstract

Recent studies suggest that, contrary to popular belief, chocolate can be a part of a healthy and nutritious diet. This literature review examines five articles about the health benefits of chocolate. One article questions the results of the studies that claim chocolate contains beneficial minerals and antioxidants and does not recommend chocolate consumption. The other four support the health benefits of chocolate, under the condition that chocolate supplements but does not replace more nutritious fruits and vegetables.

Is Chocolate Good for You?

A Review of Some Online Sources

Chocolate is certainly one of America's favorite indulgences, one about which   1
we often feel guilty because of chocolate's reputation as an unhealthy food, high in calories, high in fat, high in sugar, and too tasty to have any nutritional value. The purpose of this paper is to examine the validity of this assumption by review-ing some of the literature available online about the nutritional benefits or lack thereof of chocolate.

Linda Larsen (2002) asserts that "chocolate, in moderate amounts, can actually   2
be good for you." Chocolate does contain saturated fat, but in the form of stearic acid, which does not raise cholesterol and may thin blood just as aspirin does, reducing the risk of clogged arteries. Chocolate, in fact, might lower cholesterol because, like olive oil, it contains monounsaturated fat, in the form of oleic acid. Chocolate is a source of protein, a typical bar containing three or four grams. It also contains antioxidants in the form of flavonoids, which might reduce the risk of

---

*Note: When using APA style, your title page should include the title of your essay, your name, class, and the date centered on its own page. The running head (your title or an abbreviation of your title) should be included on your title page.

cancer and "other age-related chronic diseases." Chocolate contains the minerals copper, magnesium, and calcium. Contrary to popular belief, chocolate does not cause tooth decay, because it contains tannins, which actually help prevent cavities.

Writing under the auspices of Pennsylvania State University, Mary Alice Gettings 3 (2004) corroborates Larsen's position, confirming that chocolate contains "poly-phenols, the same anti-oxidants that are found in red wine and green tea" and that they "help reduce the formation of plaque in the arteries" (p. 1). She agrees, as well, that the flavonoids in chocolate "decrease platelet stickiness, which reduces blood clotting and, therefore, the chance of having a heart attack" (p. 1). She does, however, refine Larsen's position, pointing out that "dark chocolate, with at least 70% cocoa, is the healthy treat" (p. 1). Milk chocolate is considerably less beneficial. And she cautions against substituting dark chocolate for fresh fruits and vegetables, whose content of antioxidants, fiber, vitamins, and minerals is superior.

In "Chocolate and Prevention of Cardiovascular Disease: A Systematic Review," 4 Eric Ding, Susan Hutfless, and Xin Ding of Harvard's School of Public Health and Saket Girota of the Medical College of Wisconsin (2006) review 136 articles on "experimental, observational, and clinical studies of relations between cocoa, cacao, chocolate, stearic acid, flavonoids... and the risk of cardiovascular disease" (Abstract). The results of their review indicate that "cocoa and chocolate may exert beneficial effects on cardiovascular risk" (Abstract). Their review confirms the connections between the flavonoids in chocolate and heart health. They are less enthusiastic about stearic acid, agreeing that it does not raise cholesterol but expressing concerns about the methodological limitations of the studies on stearic acid they reviewed. They suggest, as well, that most of the studies on the health benefits of chocolate look at short-term effects, and they therefore recommend more studies of the long-term effects of chocolate consumption.

"Chocolate: Food of the Gods," from the *Yale–New Haven Nutrition Advisor* 5 (2005), also confirms the health benefits of chocolate. The author explains why stearic acid does not raise LDL cholesterol, even though it is a saturated fat, noting that "Stearic acid is converted in the liver to oleic acid, a heart-healthy monounsaturated fat" (p. 1). The author cites a 1997 study that suggests chocolate is healthier than butter, which does raise LDL cholesterol. The author also cites a study by Waterhouse that confirms the presence in chocolate of phenols, which help prevent the buildup of plaque in the arteries. Dark chocolate, which contains more cocoa butter, is especially rich in phenols. Chocolate is a rich source of magnesium and phosphorous and has a fraction of the amount of caffeine in coffee. This author does add a cautionary note, claiming, "In some people, chocolate has been associated with kidney stones, headaches, acne, allergies, dental cavities and premenstrual syndrome" (p. 2) and warning against substituting chocolate for fruits and vegetables.

A stronger warning about the nutritional benefits of chocolate comes from   6
Jay Cohen, M.D., in his article "Chocolate: A Health Food?" (2003). He believes that wishful thinking has fooled the media and then the public into reading the studies about the health benefits of chocolate too positively. Some of the studies, he notes, were too small to be significant, and some were funded by the American Cocoa Research Institute, which obviously has a vested interest in good news about chocolate. He cites nutritionists who downplay the significance of the flavonoid content of chocolate. And he cites studies indicating that stearic acid in chocolate, praised by the wishful thinkers, is as deleterious to heart health as saturated fat found in butter. Moreover, chocolate is very high in calories: just three ounces of semisweet chocolate contain 420 calories, almost all of them from fat and sugar.

The edge, though, still goes to those who tout the health benefits of   7
chocolate. A 2006 review of 136 studies of chocolate, prepared by Ding et al., is the most thorough and authoritative of the sources summarized here, given its range and its authors' affiliation with Harvard's School of Public Health. Still, all of the reviews urge <u>moderate</u> consumption of chocolate, note that there is nothing nutritionally unique about chocolate, and advise that chocolate consumption can complement but should never replace fruits and vegetables.

References

Chocolate: Food of the gods (2005, March). *The Yale–New Haven Nutrition Advisor,* Retrieved February 15, 2008, from http://www.ynhh.org/online/nutrition/advisor/chocolate.html

Cohen, J. S. (2003, July-August). Chocolate: A health food? *MedicationSense Underground E-Letter on Medications, Supplements, Nutrition, & Health,* Retrieved February 15, 2008, from http://www.medicationsense.com/articles/july_sept_03/chocolate.html

Ding, E. L., Hutfless, S. M., Ding, X., & Girotra, S. (2006). Chocolate and prevention of cardiovascular disease: A systematic review. *Nutrition & Metabolism,* 3(2). Retrieved February 15, 2008, from http://www.nutitionandmetabolism.com/content/3/1/2

Gettings, M. A. (2004, Spring). Chocolate is good for you! [Electronic version]. *PennState College of Agricultural Sciences Food and Nutrition Notes*, 1–4.

Larsen, L. (2002). Chocolate and nutrition. *Busy Cooks Guide*. Retrieved February 15, 2008, from http://busycooks.about.com/od/holidaycelebrations/a/chocolatenutrit.htm

Chicago Manual of Style Method of Citing Sources

If you are using the MLA or the APA method of citing sources, discussed earlier in this chapter, you will acknowledge your sources first in parentheses and again, at the end of the essay, in a list of works cited (MLA) or references (APA).

But some of your teachers might want you to cite your sources within the text of your essay, using footnotes or endnotes instead of parentheses. If they do, you will need to learn and use the *Chicago Manual of Style* method. The CMS method also offers an in-text citation option, but there are still professors—especially in history, some of the other humanities, and business—who require their students to use footnotes or endnotes, so an explanation of this system follows. The method is explained in full in the fifteenth edition of *The Chicago Manual of Style*, published in 2003 by the University of Chicago Press.

● Footnotes/Endnotes

After you have quoted directly from or paraphrased information from a source, place a number in superscript (that is, above the line) after the quoted or paraphrased information. If you want to add additional information that you don't want in the text of your essay, you may place that information in a footnote or endnote as well. The note numbers are repeated either at the bottom of the page or on a separate page at the end of the essay, and each number is followed by the complete bibliographical information, including page numbers. Notes at the bottom of the page are footnotes; those at the end of the paper are endnotes; either method is acceptable. If you use endnotes, place them on a separate page at the end of the essay but before the bibliography. Use "Notes" as your heading, centered at the top of the page.

Here is an example of a CMS endnote citation:

This alarming trend continues. In the 2004 Presidential election, only 36.4 percent of American citizens eligible to vote actually voted.[1] Such voter apathy, argues Columbian Plains University's Edgar Holman, "indicates a serious disengagement with the political process."[2]

Note that the number follows the punctuation mark, and that there is no space between the punctuation mark and the number. The information in the footnotes or endnotes for the sources cited in this example is formatted as follows:

1. Carl Risterson, "Voter Patterns in Presidential Elections, 1960–2004," *Aegis Quarterly* 2 (2005): 21–54.

2. Edgar Holman, *What America Cares About* (Pittsburgh: Plains Press, 2003), 45.

The first line of the end- or footnote is indented three spaces. The article title is in quotation marks, and the journal title and book title are italicized.

If you use the same source again, you do not have to provide all of the information again in your foot- or endnote. Use the author's last name, followed by a comma, followed by the relevant page number:

5. Risterson, 86.

Note that you do not use an abbreviation (*p.*) for page number.

If you use two different works by the same author and cite one or both of them again in a foot- or endnote, use a shortened version of the title for the second citation:

8. Risterson, *America,* 64.

The Latin abbreviations *ibid.*, *op. cit.*, and *loc. cit.* are not often used now in the CMS method.

Following this paragraph is an example of a brief endnotes page with sources cited using the CMS method. Remember that this page would come after the essay but before the bibliography. As you browse through this list, note the following details:

- The first line of each endnote is indented.
- The authors' names are not reversed and are given in full. (In the bibliography, the author's last name comes first, because the bibliography is organized alphabetically.)
- Book titles are italicized (or underlined), and article titles are in quotation marks.
- Page numbers in endnotes refer to the precise location of the source. (In the bibliography, the range of page numbers is provided.)
- Second references (see format of the second Clinton citation in note 6) require only author's last name and page number.
- The date of access for an Internet citation (see Remington, note 9) follows the URL.

Endnotes

1. Eric J. Hobsbawm, *The Age of Empire, 1875–1914* (New York: Pantheon, 1987), 71.

2. Aileen Kelly, "Dostoevski and the Divided Conscience," *Slavic Review* 47 (Summer 1988): 250.

3. Ilya Omar, *Send Me the Pillow*, 3rd ed. (London: Havington, 2002), 57.

4. Michael T. Clinton, "For Strong Women," in *Home Girls: A Black Feminist Anthology*, ed. Barbara Smith (New York: Kitchen Table, 1983), 325–27.

5. D. D. Cochran, W. Daniel Hale, and Christine P. Hissam, "Personal Space Requirements in Indoor Versus Outdoor Locations," *Journal of Psychology* 117 (1984): 132–33.

6. Clinton, 325.

7. Joan K. Lippinco, "Net Generation Students and Libraries," in *Educating the Net Generation*, eds. Dinana G. Oblinger and James L. Oblinger (Boulder, CO: Educause, 2005). Available online at http://www.educause.edu/educatingthenetgen/. [Accessed April 1, 2008].

8. Paul D. Hightower, "Censorship," in *Contemporary Education* (Terre Haute: Indiana State University, School of Education, Winter 1995), 61, Dialog, ERIC, ED 509251.

9. Elton L. Remington, "The Role of DNA Evidence in the Release of Felons Incarcerated in American State Prisons," *Criminal Justice Quarterly of Hawaii* 34 (2001), http://www.uhawaii.cjqh-34.edu/rem.uh (accessed January 28, 2002).

● Source List at the End of the Essay

At the end of the essay, provide a complete source list, alphabetized by the author's last name or by title if there is no author. The source list is usually referred to as a bibliography. Note that, because all of the bibliographical information is included in the footnotes or endnotes, some journals do not ask their authors to include a bibliography. This is especially true when the essay concludes with a list of endnotes.

Citations in the bibliography are similar to those in complete footnotes, but there are important differences to note. You use the author's first name first in a footnote but his or her last name first in your bibliography, which, remember, is alphabetized. You use paragraph indentation in foot- or endnotes and hanging indentation in bibliographical entries. You place parentheses around the place of publication, the name of the publisher, and the date of publication in a foot- or endnote but not in a bibliographical citation. And you include the page number in the foot- or endnote but not in the bibliographical citation.

Following this paragraph is a bibliography constructed from the sources cited in the previous endnote page. As you study this bibliography, note the following details:

- The bibliography is arranged alphabetically, not numerically.
- Page numbers for books are not included.
- The full range of page numbers for articles from books and journals is included.
- Most of the information within parentheses in endnote citations is not enclosed within parentheses in bibliography citations.

Bibliography

Clinton, Michael T. "For Strong Women." In *Home Girls: A Black Feminist Anthology*, edited by Barbara Smith. New York: Kitchen Table, 1983.

Cochran, D. D., W. Daniel Hale, and Christine P. Hissam. "Personal Space Requirements in Indoor Versus Outdoor Locations." *Journal of Psychology* 117 (1984): 125–46.

Hightower, Paul D. "Censorship." In *Contemporary Education*. Terre Haute: Indiana State University, School of Education, Winter 1995. 61, Dialog, ERIC, ED 509251.

Hobsbawm, Eric J. *The Age of Empire, 1875–1914*. New York: Pantheon, 1987.

Kelly, Aileen. "Dostoevski and the Divided Conscience." *Slavic Review* 47 (Summer 1988): 239–60.

Lippinco, Joan K. "Net Generation Students and Libraries," in *Educating the Net Generation*, edited by Dinana G. Oblinger and James L. Oblinger. Boulder, CO: Educause, 2005. Available online at http://www.educause.edu/educatingthenetgen/. [Accessed April 1, 2008].

Omar, Ilya. *Send Me the Pillow*. 3rd ed. London: Havington, 2002.

Remington, Elton L. "The Role of DNA Evidence in the Release of Felons Incarcerated in American State Prisons." *Criminal Justice Quarterly of Hawaii* 34 (2001). http://www.uhawaii.cjqh-34.edu/rem.uh (accessed January 28, 2002).

● Sample CMS Bibliography Entries

In all of the following examples, the foot- or endnote entry comes first, followed by the bibliographical entry for the same source.

Books

Book by one author

1.   Arthur N. Applebee, *Tradition and Reform in the Teaching of English: A History* (Urbana, IL: NCTE, 1974), 34.

Applebee, Arthur N. *Tradition and Reform in the Teaching of English: A History*. Urbana, IL: NCTE, 1974.

If the book has gone into a second or later edition, place the edition number between the title and the place of publication:

2. Edward M. White, *Teaching and Assessing Writing,* 2nd ed. (San Francisco and London: Jossey-Bass, 1994), 46–47.

White, Edward, M. *Teaching and Assessing Writing.* 2nd ed. San Francisco and London: Jossey-Bass, 1994.

Anthology, a compilation, or an edited book

3. Phillip Lopate, ed., *The Art of the Personal Essay: An Anthology from the Classical Era to the Present* (New York: Anchor-Doubleday, 1994), 89.

Lopate, Phillip, ed. *The Art of the Personal Essay: An Anthology from the Classical Era to the Present.* New York: Anchor-Doubleday, 1994.

4. Wolfgang Martin, Maria Gomez, and Edward Johns, eds., *The Effects of Gender on Child Development in Custody Cases* (Oxford: Oxford University Press, 1996), 34.

Martin, Wolfgang, Maria Gomez, and Edward Johns, eds. *The Effects of Gender on Child Development in Custody Cases.* Oxford: Oxford University Press, 1996.

Later examples give the citation of separate articles from a collection of essays and of literary works from a literature anthology.

Two or more books by the same author

5. R. J. Waller, *The Bridges of Madison County* (New York: Warner, 1992), 39.

6. R. J. Waller, *Slow Waltz in Cedar Bend* (New York: Warner, 1993), 48.

7. Waller, *Bridges,* 76.

8. Waller, *Waltz,* 19.

Waller, R. J. *The Bridges of Madison County.* New York: Warner, 1992.

---. *Slow Waltz in Cedar Bend.* New York: Warner, 1993.

Note that three hyphens replace the author's name for the second citation. The alphabetization is by book title (the "The" in *The Bridges of Madison County* does not count because it's an article).

Book by two or three authors

9. William A. Covino and David R. Jolliffe, *Rhetoric: Concepts, Definitions, Boundaries* (Boston: Allyn and Bacon, 1995), 90.

Covino, William A., and David A. Jolliffe. *Rhetoric: Concepts, Definitions, Boundaries.* Boston: Allyn and Bacon, 1995.

Book by more than three authors

If you use a source by three or more authors, you do not have to list all of the authors' names in a foot- or endnote. You need only list the first author's name followed by *and others* or the equivalent Latin abbreviation, which is *et al.* (You may list all authors if you prefer.) In the bibliography, however, typically all author names are used.

10. John L. Smith and others, *Moving to Las Vegas,* 3rd ed. (East Brunswick, Australia: Barricade Books, 2002), 23.

Smith, John L., Patricia Smith, Theresa A. Mataga, and Lloyd W. Mixdorf. *Moving to Las Vegas,* 3rd ed. East Brunswick, Australia: Barricade Books, 2002.

Book by a corporate author

11. Council of College Teachers, *Initiation into the Academy* (Chicago: CCT Press, 1998), 66.

Council of College Teachers. *Initiation into the Academy.* Chicago: CCT Press, 1998.

Work in an anthology

12. Robert Bricen, "Leather and Lace," in *Fashion in the Sixties,* ed. Luke M. Walker (Vancouver: Ricards, 2005), 134–56.

Bricen, Robert. "Leather and Lace." In *Fashion in the Sixties*, edited by Luke M. Walker, 134–56. Vancouver: Ricards, 2005.

Article in an encyclopedia or other reference book

13. *Encyclopaedia Britannica,* 15th ed., s.v. "Laos."

The page number and volume number are not included; they are not necessary because encyclopedia entries are alphabetized. The entry in the encyclopedia ("Laos" in this example) comes at the end, preceded by the abbreviation *s.v.,* which is Latin for *sub verbo* or "under the word." You do not have to list well-known reference books in your bibliography.

Book by an anonymous author

14. *The Chicago Manual of Style.* 15th ed. (Chicago: University of Chicago Press, 2003), 88.

The Chicago Manual of Style. 15th ed. Chicago: University of Chicago Press, 2003.

This book would be alphabetized in the bibliography by its title.

Book translated from a foreign language

See the subsection on the previous page entitled "Anthology, Compilation, or Edited Book." Use the same format for a translation, except insert the abbreviation *trans.* in place of *ed.*

Book published in a second or subsequent edition

15. Jane Feuer, *The Hollywood Musical*, 2nd ed. (Bloomington: Indiana University Press, 1993), 145–47.

Feuer, Jane. *The Hollywood Musical*. 2nd ed. Bloomington: Indiana University
    Press, 1993.

If the title page indicates that the book is a revised edition, use the abbreviation *Rev. ed.* after the title. If the title page indicates that the book is an abridged edition, use the abbreviation *Abr. ed.* after the title.

Multivolume work

16. Kathleen Raine, *Blake and Tradition* (Princeton, NJ: Princeton University Press, 1968), 1:321.

Raine, Kathleen, *Blake and Tradition*. Vol. 1. Princeton, NJ: Princeton University
    Press, 1968.

If you use all volumes, the bibliography entry would use this format:

Lauter, Paul, ed. *The Heath Anthology of American Literature*. 4th ed. 2 vols. Boston:
    Houghton Mifflin, 2002.

Government publication

17. U.S. Department of State, *The Global 2000 Report to the President: Entering the Twenty-First Century*. 3 vols. (Washington, DC: Government Printing Office, 1981), 3:677.

U.S. Department of State. *The Global 2000 Report to the President: Entering the
    Twenty-First Century*. 3 vols. Washington: Government Printing Office, 1981.

Dissertation

18. Melvin Kinison, "The Influence of Augustan Poets on the Poetry of Samuel Taylor Coleridge" (Ph.D. diss., Howson University, 2006), 29.

Kinison, Melvin. "The Influence of Augustan Poets on the Poetry of Samuel Taylor
    Coleridge." Ph.D. diss. Howson University, 2006.

If the dissertation is published, then underline or italicize the title as opposed to enclosing it within quotation marks. If the dissertation is published commercially in a microform edition, treat the publication details much the way you treat a book's, adding the fiche, frame, and row if available.

Articles

Article in an academic journal continuously paginated. "Continuously paginated" means the pages in the journal are numbered by the year, as opposed to starting at page 1 for each issue.

1. David R. Russell, "Romantics on Writing: Liberal Culture and the Abolition of Composition Courses," *Rhetoric Review* 6 (1988): 141.

Russell, David R. "Romantics on Writing: Liberal Culture and the Abolition of Composition Courses." *Rhetoric Review* 6 (1988): 132–48.

Article in an academic journal paginated by issue

2. Andrea A. Lunsford, "Toward a Mestiza Rhetoric: Gloria Anzaldua on Composition and Postcoloniality," *Journal of Advanced Composition* 18, no. 1 (1998): 22.

Lunsford, Andrea A. "Toward a Mestiza Rhetoric: Gloria Anzaldua on Composition and Postcoloniality." *Journal of Advanced Composition* 18, no. 1 (1998): 1–27.

Newspaper article

3. Rita Henderson, "Zippergate: What the Lewinski Tapes Reveal," *San Francisco Chronicle*, June 18, 1998, sec. B.

Henderson, Rita. "Zippergate: What the Lewinski Tapes Reveal." *San Francisco Chronicle,* June 18, 1998, sec. B15.

Review

4. Bernard Lewis, review of *Autumn of Fury: The Assassination of Anwar Sadat,* by Mohamed Heikal, *New York Review of Books*, May 31, 1984, 26.

Lewis, Bernard. Review of *Autumn of Fury: The Assassination of Anwar Sadat,* by Mohamed Heikal. *New York Review of Books*, May 31, 1984, 25–27.

If the review is anonymous, begin the foot- or endnote citation with "Unsigned review of." In the bibliography, the name of the newspaper or journal stands in for the author and is therefore used to alphabetize the entry.

Article in a magazine

5. Alice George, "Reading Scores on the Rise at Last," *Clarion,* February 1999, 19.

George, Alice. "Reading Scores on the Rise at Last." *Clarion,* February 1999, 18–22.

If you are citing a source from a weekly magazine, you would include the day of the month also.

Electronic Sources

Information service

1. Derek Soles, "Gender Equity and the State of the Union," ERIC Clearinghouse on Reading, English, and Communication, 1999. ERIC Document Number 430 227.

Soles, Derek. "Gender Equity and the State of the Union." ERIC Clearinghouse on Reading, English, and Communication, 1999. ERIC Document Number 430 227.

Online database

2. John Keats, "Bright Star," *Literature Online*, http://lion.chadwyck.co.uk/.

Keats, John. "Bright Star." *Literature Online*. http://lion.chadwyck.co.uk/.

Listserv

3. Allen Renter, "Investing in High-Tech Stocks," posting to WI electronic bulletin board, March 5, 2002, http://WI@investop.com.

Renter, Allen. "Investing in High-Tech Stocks." Posting to WI electronic bulletin board. March 5, 2002. http://WI@investop.com.

Article in an online journal, magazine, or newspaper

4. Cynthia Haynes, "Inside the Teaching Machine: Actual Feminism and (Virtual) Pedagogy," *Computers, Writing, Rhetoric, and Literature* 2, no. 1 (1996), http://www.en.utexas.edu/~cwrl/v2n1/haynes/index.html.

Haynes, Cynthia. "Inside the Teaching Machine: Actual Feminism and (Virtual) Pedagogy." *Computers, Writing, Rhetoric, and Literature* 2, no. 1 (1996). http://www.en.utexas.edu/~cwrl/v2n1/haynes/index.html.

6. L. Gledill, "Drivers Race for Carpool Permits for Hybrids," *San Francisco Chronicle*, 8 August 2005. http://sfgate.com/cgi-bin/article.cgi?file=/c/a/2005/08/20/HYBRID.TMP (accessed April 20, 2008).

Gledill, L. "Drivers Race for Carpool Permits for Hybrids," *San Francisco Chronicle*, 8 August 2005. http://sfgate.com/cgi-bin/article.cgi?file=/c/a/2005/08/20/HYBRID.TMP (accessed April 20, 2008).

Article from a website

7. Renoir Gaither, Plagiarism Detection Services, University of Michigan, Shapiro Undergraduate Library. Available online at http://www.libumich.edu/acadintegrity/instructors/violations/detection.htm (accessed April 20, 2008).

Gaither, Renoir. Plagiarism Detection Services, University of Michigan, Shapiro Undergraduate Library. Available online at http://www.libumich.edu/acadintegrity/instructors/violations/detection.htm (accessed April 20, 2008).

Audiovisual Sources

Film or video recording

1. *Hamlet*, by William Shakespeare, dir. Kenneth Branagh (1996; Burbank, CA: Warner Bros.), videocassette.

Hamlet. By William Shakespeare. Directed by Kenneth Branagh. Burbank, CA: Warner Bros., 1996. Videocassette.

Conclusion

Acknowledging sources is something of a cross students have to bear because there are so many different citation systems and the rules that govern the systems are so exacting. Internet cites, with their long URLs and sometimes questionable content, have exacerbated the challenge. But the effort is worthwhile, because sources carelessly acknowledged or, worse, not acknowledged at all cause problems ranging from lower grades to failing grades, even suspension. Conversely, sources properly acknowledged give academic writing depth and authority, qualities essential to winning the respect and attention of your readers.

WRITING ASSIGNMENTS

1. In an essay of approximately 500 words, define the term *plagiarism*, provide an example, and discuss the procedures writers must follow to avoid a plagiarism charge.

2. In an essay of approximately 1,000 words, compare and contrast any two of the three citation methods covered in this chapter.

EXERCISES

1. Correct any errors you spot in the following examples of MLA-style entries for a list of works cited. (This is not a topical list, so you need not put the entries in alphabetical order.)

Fulwiler, Toby, and Hayakawa. Alan. *The Blair Handbook*. Boston: 1994: Blair-Prentice.

Asman, William, Frederick Lifshitz, Melanie Tate, Claire Buckman, Alice Emyworth, Samuel Klink. *Marriage in Africa*. Second Edition. Toronto: Basic Press. 1999. Find it on the Internet at http:www.ebooksbp/wa/marriageinafrica.htm

S. I. Hayakawa, *Language in Thought and Action*. Fourth edition. New York: Harcourt, 1978.

Trans. Stuart Gilbert. Camus, Albert. *The Stranger*. New York: Random House, 1946.

Art Young and Toby Fulwiler, eds. *Writing Across the Disciplines: Research into Practice*. Odell, Lee. Foreword. Upper Montclair, NJ: Boyton, 1986.

Letter to the *Liberty Sentinel* by Melvin S. Eliot. 20 September 2000: C3.

Different Places, Different Voices. Eds. Janet H. Momsen and Vivian Kinnaird. London: Routledge: 1993. 211–226. Fairbairn-Dunlop, Peggy. "Women and Agriculture in Western Samoa."

Bai, Matt. "Ventura's First Round." *Newsweek* 1999: 30–32. 15 Feb.

Chan, Evans. "Postmodernism and Hong Kong Cinema." *Postmodern Culture Volume 10 Issue 3 year 2000.* Project Muse Website without page numbers. Read it Jan 30, 2007.

Telesford, Frank. "From Each According to His Means." *Synprax* 4.1 (2000). January 2000. www.isotrop.cityscape.edu/pmc/text-only/issue.200/4.1telesford.txt. Internet 10 May 2000.

"Industrial Revolution." Redmond: Microsoft, 1994. *Concise Columbia Encyclopedia. Microsoft Bookshelf.* 1994 edition. CD-ROM.

2. Correct any errors you detect in the following entries from a references list using the APA style. (This is not a topical list, so you need not put the entries in alphabetical order.)

Brunner, C. and David Bennett. Technology and gender: Differences in masculine and feminine views. *NASSP Bulletin, 81*(592), 46–51. 1997.

Kubler-Ross, E. (1969). "On Death and Dying." New York: Macmillan.

Arthur Dedecker. Clinton and Obama Debate in Philadelphia. Germantown Daily News, April 19, 2008. Online version at http://www.germantowndailynews/ clintonandobamadebate/04/19/08/ppr.htm

Mele, A. (1997). Real self-deception. **Behavioural and Brain Sciences, 20,** 91–136. 1997, pp. 91–136.

Fowles, D. "Electrodermal activity and antisocial behaviour: Empirical findings and theoretical issues." In J. C. Roy, W. Boucsein, D. Fowles, & J. Gruzelier (Eds.), Progress in electrodermal research (pp. 223–237). London: Plenum, 1993.

Castellow, W., Chia, R., and Kenneth Wuensch: <u>Paper presented at the meeting of the American Psychological Association, Atlanta, GA.</u> *Physical attractiveness, sex, and cultural differences in juridic decisions.* (1988, August).

Schneider, D. J. (1973*). Implicit personality theory: A review. Psychological Bulletin, 79,* 294–309.

Kongshem, L. (1997, January). [1998, March 10]. Censorware: How well does Internet filtering software protect students? *Electronic School* [Online]. Available: http://www/electronic-school.com/0198fl.html

Feherty, David (2001, August). Get weird with your wedge. *"Golf Magazine," 43, pages* 135–140.

Berton, I. (2001, September 24). An ounce of prevention. [Editorial.] *Meryton Gazette,* p. A11.

Schulman, R. (Ed.). (1998). *The Einstein papers project* [Online]. Boston University.
Available: http://albert.bu.edu [1998, March 10].

3. Correct any errors you spot in the following examples of *Chicago Manual of Style* footnote and bibliography entries. (This is not a topical list, so you need not put the entries in alphabetical or numerical order.)

1. Welty, Eudora. [*One Writer's Beginnings*] (Cambridge: Harvard University Press, 1984), page 44.

Kelly, Alfred H., Winfred A. Harbison, and Herman Belz. (Norton, 1983). "*The American Constitution: Its Origins and Development.*" New York: W. W. Norton, 1983.

1. Milan Kundera, *The Unbearable Lightness of Being*, translated into English by Michael Henry Heim in 1999. (New York: HarperPerennial Library, 1999), 73.

1. Edward, Wyatt; "A High School Without a Home," *New York Times*, 3 December 1999, sec. B1.

Marc Norman and Stoppard, Tom. *Shakespeare in Love* (New York: Miramax Films/ Universal Pictures, 1999), videocassette.

Riordan, William L. *Plunkitt of Tammany Hall.* Edited by Terence J. McDonald. Published in 1994 in Boston by Bedford Books

Darnton, Robert. "The Pursuit of Happiness." *Wilson Quarterly* volume 19, number 4 1995 42–52.

McGann, Jerome J. **"Dante Gabriel Rossetti: A Brief Biography."** *The Complete Writings and Pictures of Dante Gabriel Rossetti: A Hypermedia Research Archive.* 19 March 1997. Available at http://jefferson.village.virginia.edu/rossetti/dgrbio. html [cited from the Internet on 23 March 1997].

1. Elinor Harrison, *The Music of the Night,* second edition Birmingham: Phonemart, 2002

Kidson, Peter. "Architecture and City Planning." In *The Legacy of Greece*, M. I. Finley, New York: Oxford University Press, 1981 pages 376 to 400.

COLLABORATIVE ACTIVITY

Devote one of your peer response sessions to examining only each other's citations of sources in an essay you are currently working on or have recently completed. Check citations within the essay, and check the format of the source list at the end of the essay.

JOURNAL PROMPT

Freewrite on how reader and writer benefit when sources are cited thoroughly and accurately.

Sample Academic Essays

with Instructional Notes and Commentary

To write effective academic essays, you need to learn the components of the process of writing an academic essay: reflect upon your topic, research your topic, plan, draft, revise, and edit. This information is covered in Part One of the text.

Another part of the process of learning to write effective academic essays is to read and reflect upon well-written examples of academic writing. We learn best by doing, but we also learn by studying the techniques of those who have already mastered the skill we are trying to learn and by reflecting upon and trying to imitate their techniques. The aim of this part is to provide you with examples of well-written and informative academic essays, glossed with instructional notes and commentary that will help you understand the process the writers went through to create effective texts and the various methods they used to make their work readable. This knowledge, in turn, will help you to use the same techniques yourself as you plan, draft, revise, and edit your own work.

PART TWO

Abstract   The article begins with an abstract presenting a brief summary of the objectives, participants, methods, results, and conclusions of the study. It is about 135 words long, a typical length for an abstract for a social science report.

Paragraph 1   The authors begin justifying the purpose of their study: more studies of the causes for the decline in the physical and psychological health of college undergraduates are needed so we know how we might improve their health. Note here and throughout the article the use of superscript numbers. The citation method this journal uses is that presented in the *American Medical Association Manual of Style*, 10th edition.

This sample of academic writing is from the *Journal of American College Health,* Volume 56, Number 1, published in 2007.

What Predicts Adjustment Among College Students? A Longitudinal Panel Study

Mary E. Pritchard, PhD; Gregory S. Wilson, PED; Ben Yamnitz, BS

Abstract. Objective: Researchers have previously reported that law students and medical students experience significant distress during their first year. The authors suspected that freshmen undergraduates might experience similar distress in their transition to college. **Participants**: They surveyed 242 undergraduate freshmen at the beginning and end of their first year. **Methods**: The authors asked participants about their physical health, alcohol use and smoking habits, stress levels, perfectionism, self-esteem, coping tactics, optimism, extroversion, and psychological adaptation to college. **Results**: Data replicated the declines reported in law and medical students' psychological and physical health. Negative coping tactics and perfectionism predicted poorer physical health and alcohol use at the end of the year; however, optimism and self-esteem predicted better physical and psychological outcomes. **Conclusion**: Future researchers should investigate steps that college administrators can take to help to alleviate some of these problems, such as offering workshops on stress relief to incoming freshmen.

Keywords: coping, extroversion, optimism, perfectionism, self-esteem

Researchers studying students in post-baccalaureate programs (eg, law students and medical students) have found a decline in psychological and physical health after matriculation.[1–3] Whereas comparisons of law students and the general population show no differences before they begin law school, psychological distress appears soon after law school begins.[3,4] These investigators have found that law student distress is manifested in declines not only in psychological health but physical health as well.[5] Few researchers have examined whether these types of changes occur in undergraduate students. It is not known whether undergraduates undergo similar declines in psychological and physical health as displayed by post-baccalaureate students.

Dr Pritchard *is with Boise State University's Department of Psychology, Idaho.* **Drs Wilson** *and* **Yamnitz** *are with the University of Evansville, Indiana.*

Paragraph 2   The authors note that researchers know that several factors contribute ──────┤
to the successful adjustment to college life, but they don't know for certain the
impact of these factors on health.

Paragraphs 3 through 7   These paragraphs, subtitled respectively Coping Tactics, ──────┤
Self-Esteem, Perfectionism, Optimism, and Extroversion, present the variables
the authors will examine in the context on their study of changes in the physical
and psychological health of undergraduates. Note that each paragraph presents a
brief **literature review**. The "lit review" is a key element of a social science study. It
establishes a historical context for the new study the authors are presenting.

In examining perceptions of the undergraduate experience, it is also 2 unlikely that the college experience would affect all individuals to the same degree. For example, Upcraft and Gardner[6] found that approximately one quarter of incoming freshman do not return to the same institution the following year, with half of these students making the decision to leave in the first 6 weeks. Students who withdraw during first semester often cite emotional reasons for dropping out.[7] Some students are better able to adjust to the undergraduate experience than are others. Such variability in responses to college emphasizes the importance of understanding what factors contribute to negative reactions to the college experience and whether undergraduate students experience similar changes in psychological and physical health as do law students and medical students. Although previous research has suggested several factors that may contribute to the successful adjustment of college students (as we will discuss later), it has not been adequately established whether any of these factors (eg, self-esteem, coping tactics, perfectionism, optimism, and extroversion) play a negative or positive role in positive student health behaviors.

COPING TACTICS

3

Roth et al[8] found that stressful life experiences directly correlate with increased illness, and recent research has shown a dramatic increase in the levels of stress experienced by college students over the past 30 years.[9] In response to these increasing levels of stress, students often engage in negative health behaviors (eg, drinking, smoking). Although certain coping tactics may decrease the impact of stress on psychological[10] and physical outcomes,[11,12] it is unclear whether specific coping styles lead to poorer health outcomes. For example, some researchers[13,14] have reported that problem-focused coping is less likely to produce depressive symptoms, whereas emotion-focused coping correlates with increased depressive symptoms. However, others[15,16] have reported no relation or the opposite pattern.

SELF-ESTEEM

Just as many students engage in negative health behaviors to deal with 4 stress, many students also engage in negative health behaviors to deal with self-esteem issues. Leitschuh and Rawlins[17] found that high self-regard scores and high self-actualizing scores predict better physical health. Researchers[18,19] more recently have found that alcohol abuse was predicted by low self-esteem. Sands et al[19] found that nutritional practices are predicted by level of identity and self-confidence, and Joiner and Tickle[20] found self-esteem to relate to exercise participation in women, but not men. However, Bezjak and Lee[21] found that self-efficacy predicts participation in health-related physical fitness activities regardless of gender.

Paragraph 8 This paragraph is important in that, following the lit review, it presents a clear statement of the study's purpose: to examine how the college experience affects physical and psychological health, focusing especially on coping, self-esteem, perfectionism, optimism, and extroversion.

Paragraph 9 The authors explain the nature of the **design** of their study, an important feature in a social science paper. They present their **hypothesis**, another key aspect of a social science paper. The authors hypothesize that certain coping tactics, high self-esteem, optimism, and extroversion would diminish health problems, while perfectionism would cause a greater decrease in health.

PERFECTIONISM

Researchers[22] have shown that adjustment to college is predicted by person- 5
ality. For example, Rice and Mirzadeh[23] found that depression is predicted
by maladaptive perfectionism. In addition, competitiveness, often thought
to be a component of perfectionism, is also related to depression.[24] Vincent
and Walker[25] found that perfectionism relates to health problems, such as
insomnia.

OPTIMISM

Optimism is another personality factor known to affect health. For example, 6
Kamen and Seligman[26] found that increased optimism correlates with fewer
occurrences of infectious disease, poor health, and early mortality. Many
researchers have found a connection between optimism and specific ill-
nesses, such as heart disease and high blood pressure.[27] However, others
question the link between optimism and mental and physical well-being.[27,28]

EXTROVERSION

A final personality variable that has been connected to health is extrover- 7
sion. Cohen[29] showed that extroverts tend to be happier and thus healthier
than are their introverted counterparts. Other recent studies report that
extroverts tend to be less depressed[30] and experience lower levels of pain.[31]
Schapiro et al,[32] however, found no link between extroversion and health.

In our study, we build on earlier work reporting stress and maladjust- 8
ment caused by law school and medical school.[1–3] First, we examined how
student psychological and physical health changes as a result of the college
experience. Second, we determined what distinguishes students who are
more or less affected by the college experience. In particular, we determined
whether coping propensities, self-esteem, perfectionism, optimism, or
extroversion predicted changes in these outcomes.

The longitudinal panel design of our study enabled us to examine which 9
physical and psychological differences are caused by the college experience
and to determine what individual variables are associated with such changes.
Our study is novel in that we focused on personality factors rather than
demographic variables in predicting maladjustment among college students,
with the intent to pinpoint conditions that could be changed to improve
the college experience and, more broadly, to better understand variables
that predict adjustment to stressful situations. We examined how coping
tactics, self-esteem, perfectionism, optimism, and extroversion may generate
individual differences in adjustment to college. Similar to studies with law
students and medical students,[1–3] we expected that physical and psychological health would decline over the freshman year in undergraduate students.

Paragraph 10   The tenth paragraph begins the Methods section of the report. As in
many social science reports, this section will explain the *procedure* the authors used
to conduct the study, the *participants* in the study, and the *measures* the authors
used to assess the health of the participants. Paragraph 10 explains the procedure.
It tells when the authors collected their data, where the study took place, and how
many students participated.

Paragraph 11   This paragraph elaborates on the profile of the study's participants.
Gender, race, and age are reported. As is typical of this type of study, the authors
had to have the consent of participants and of a special university committee.

Paragraphs 12 through 20   Paragraph 12 begins the Measures subsection of the
Methods section. The Measures subsection will contain nine sub-subsections, one
paragraph allotted to each. The use of headings and subheadings is common in
reports of this nature, but this report uses more than most.

However, we hypothesized that certain coping tactics, having a high self-esteem, being optimistic, and being extroverted would serve as buffers to health problems, whereas being perfectionistic would cause a greater decrease in health.

METHODS

Procedure

We conducted a longitudinal investigation of first-year college students. We collected wave 1 data during orientation week before the start of classes. We believed it was important to collect data before they began classes because starting classes might have had some affect on their health data. We realize that the excitement of orientation week itself might have influenced student's baseline data; however, orientation week was the only forum in which we could reach all incoming freshmen prior to the start of classes. We distributed questionnaires to all 525 first-year students at the University of Evansville with a cover letter explaining the study and that all responses would remain confidential. Wave 1 data provided baseline measures of coping, health, self-esteem, and participation in student organizations and athletics. One month before the end of the second semester, we administered wave 2 questionnaires, with questions similar to those used in wave 1. 10

Participants

Three hundred fifty (67% of the first-year class) students participated in wave 1 (65% women), and 381 (73%) completed wave 2 (60% women). Two hundred forty-two individuals (46%) completed both waves. We used only the data from these 242 students in the analyses; 94.5% were Caucasian, 2.5% were African American, 0.5% were Hispanic, 1.5% were European, and 1% were Native American. Although only 46% of students completed both waves, their demographic breakdown was similar to that of the freshman class. The average student age at wave 1 was 18.02 years ($SD = 1.44$) and at wave 2 was 18.93 years ($SD = 1.30$). Each participant read and completed an informed consent form prior to this study, and we informed them that their responses would be confidential. The University Subcommittee for the Protection of Research Subjects approved procedures for this investigation prior to our initiating the study. 11

Measures

Physical Health

We assessed physical health by asking students how many days during the past month they had experienced any of 21 health symptoms (eg, cold or 12

The authors used a questionnaire to measure each of the nine variables they wanted to assess. To measure some of the variables—stress (paragraph 14), perfectionism (paragraph 15), self-esteem (paragraph 16), coping tactics (paragraph 17), optimism/pessimism (paragraph 18), and psychological adaptation (paragraph 19)—the authors used previously prepared questionnaires, the efficacy of which has been validated. The authors are careful to identify these questionnaires.

flu, shortness of breath).[33] Participants rated whether they had experienced each symptom on a 5-point scale (1 = never, 5 = 15 + days). We summed responses to create a scale score (wave 1 α = .73, wave 2 α = .80). This measure has been used successfully in the past.[3] For information on the development of this survey, see the original authors' article.[33]

Alcohol Use and Smoking

We asked participants to indicate how often they drink (0 = never/rarely, 1 = once a month, 2 = once a week, 3 = 2–3 times a week, 4 = daily or almost daily), how often they drink until intoxication (0 = never/rarely, 1 = once a month, 2 = once a week, 3 = 2–3 times a week, 4 = daily or almost daily), and how much they drink at each drinking occasion (eg, number of drinks, where 1 drink = 12 oz beer, 4 oz wine, 1 oz spirits). This scale has been shown to be reliable and valid.[34,35] We also asked students how many cigarettes they smoke per day.   13

Stress

We assessed 57 stressful events specifically oriented to college students' lives (eg, "struggling to meet your own academic standards") using the Inventory of College Student Recent Life Experiences.[36] Participants were asked to rate to what extent such events have been a part of their lives in the past month on a 4-point scale (1 = not at all part of my life, 4 = very much part of my life; wave 1 α = .85, wave 2 α = .89). This scale has been shown to be reliable and valid.[36]   14

Perfectionism

We assessed perfectionistic tendencies from participants' responses to various questions on their performance levels in activities, such as school, and the influence of the expectations of others (eg, family, teachers, parents: "Only outstanding performance is good enough in my family."). We rated responses on a 6-point scale (1 = never, 6 = always). This measure is a subscale of the Eating Disorders Inventory[37] and demonstrated adequate reliability in this sample (wave 1 α = .78). See the survey authors for validity and reliability information.[37]   15

Self-Esteem

We measured levels of self-esteem using the Rosenberg Self-Esteem Scale,[38] which has been shown to be both valid and reliable. This scale uses a variety of questions assessing personal feelings about oneself as well as positive and negative emotions (eg, "I feel I have a number of good qualities."). Responses were measured on a 4-point scale (1 = strongly agree, 4 = strongly disagree; wave 1 α = .79).   16

Paragraph 21 This is the first paragraph of the Results section of the report. Subtitled "Change over Time in Adjustment Variables," this paragraph simply indicates the statistical procedure—analysis of variance—that the authors used to measure the students' rate of decline.

Paragraph 22 This paragraph indicates that the authors' analysis of variance suggests the validity of the study's hypothesis, in that the ANOVA revealed that health problems did increase.

Coping Tactics

To assess what coping tactics students tend to use, participants reported how [17] they would respond to a stressful event. Participants responded to a subset of items from the Brief COPE,[39] which contains 14 tactics (active coping, planning, positive reframing, acceptance, humor, religion, using emotional support, using instrumental support, self-distraction, denial, venting, substance use, behavioral disengagement, and self-blame), with 2 items per scale. This measure has been tested on a variety of clinical and nonclinical populations,[3,40,41] and the measure has been validated and shown to be reliable on several populations.[39,41]

Optimism/Pessimism

We asked students to respond to the 12-item Life Orientation Test[42] to [18] assess whether they were optimists or pessimists. Responses were rated on a 4-point scale (0 = strongly disagree, 4 = strongly agree; wave 1 α = .75). This scale has been shown to be both valid and reliable.[43]

Psychological Adaptation

To measure psychological adaptation, students responded to a 30-item short [19] version of the Profile of Mood States (POMS),[44] which has been shown to be valid and reliable. The POMS assesses anxiety, tension, depression, anger, vigor, confusion, and fatigue. Responses were measured on a 5-point scale (1 = not at all, 5 = extremely).

Personality

Questions on the Introversion/extraversion scale asked students to [20] choose between 2 adjectives to describe their behavior (eg, introverted vs extraverted).[45] Participants responded by circling a number between 1 and 9, with 1 of the 2 adjectives serving as an endpoint. We then summed responses to create a scale score (wave 1 α = .89). This measure has been shown to be valid and reliable.[46]

RESULTS

Change Over Time in Adjustment Variables

We first tested whether students' physical and psychological states declined [21] over the course of their first year of school using repeated measures analyses of variance (ANOVAs).

Adjustment

Table 1 shows means and standard deviations for outcome variables for [22] each wave. Consistent with our hypotheses, health problems increased during the first year, $F(1, 235) = 9.20, p < .01$. Students did not increase the quantity of alcohol consumed on weekdays, $F(1, 241) < 1$; however,

Table 1   Visual aids such as tables, charts, and graphs are common in social science ⎯⎯⎯⎯|
reports. Such reports typically contain a lot of statistical data. Tables like this one
present a summary of the data and help readers better understand how and why the
authors draw their conclusions and make their recommendations.

Paragraph 23   This paragraph continues the Results section of the report, speculat- ⎯⎯⎯⎯⎯|
ing on the connection between health decline and coping strategies, self-esteem,
and participation in athletics.

TABLE 1
Means (*Ms*) and Standard Deviations (*SDs*) for Changes in Physical and Psychological Health

	Wave 1		Wave 2	
Characteristic	M	SD	M	SD
Health symptoms*	7.27	5.65	8.49	6.07
Quantity of alcohol used on weekdays	.38	1.34	.43	1.47
Quantity of alcohol used on weekends (# drinks)**	1.58	3.06	2.32	3.88
Frequency of alcohol consumption**	.62	.92	.97	1.16
Frequency of alcohol intoxication**	.25	.56	.57	.96
Number of cigarettes smoked a day	.57	2.63	.88	3.61
Stress	1.96	.33	1.93	.34
Negative mood*	76.06	15.04	78.96	15.84

Note: For Frequency of Alcohol Consumption and Intoxication, 0 = never/rarely, 1 = once a month, 2 = once a week, 3 = 2–3 times a week, 4 = daily or almost daily.
*$p < .01$. **$p < .001$.

they did increase the quantity consumed on weekends, $F(1, 233) = 14.53$, $p < .001$. Students also increased their frequency of alcohol consumption over time, $F(1, 233) = 33.25$, $p < .001$, and their frequency of intoxication, $F(1, 223) = 31.40$, $p < .001$. However, cigarette use did not increase over time, $F(1, 228) = 2.33$. Student's stress levels also did not increase over time, $F(1, 243) = 2.26$; however, their negative moods (a combination of anxiety, tension, depression, anger, confusion, fatigue, and lack of vigor) did increase, $F(1, 233) = 7.92$, $p < .01$.

What Predicts Outcomes?

We tested whether propensity to use particular coping strategies, self-esteem, and participation in athletics at wave 1 predicted changes in the aspects of psychological and physical health that changed over time. To evaluate predictive value, we computed partial correlations between each predictor variable and each outcome variable at wave 2, controlling for the outcome at wave 1.

23

Paragraphs 24 through 26   These paragraphs—subtitled Health, Alcohol Consumption, and Negative Mood, respectively—present results of the study as they relate to correlations among perfectionism, alcohol use, coping mechanisms, religious faith, self-esteem, and optimism.

TABLE 2
Partial Correlations Between Physical Health and Predictor Variables at Wave 2 Controlling for Wave 1 Health Status

Variable	Health problems at Wave 2
Coping propensity at wave 1	
Denial	.14*
Criticize yourself	.16*
Learn to live with it	.13*
Self-esteem	−.21**
Perfectionism	.14*
Optimism	−.16*

Note: Coping tactics were rated on a 4-point scale (1 = I wouldn't do this at all, 4 = I would do this a lot). Optimism was rated on a 5-point scale (0 = strongly disagree, 4 = strongly agree). Perfectionism was rated on a 6-point scale (1 = never, 6 = always). Self-esteem was measured on a 4-point scale (1 = strongly agree, 4 = strongly disagree).
$*p < .05.$ $**p < .01.$

Health

Students who reported having more health problems at wave 2 were also more likely to report higher levels of perfectionism, using the coping tactics of saying "this isn't real" (denial), criticizing oneself, and learning to live with it. Students who reported having more health problems were also more likely to report lower levels of self-esteem and optimism (see Table 2). 24

Alcohol Consumption

Students who reported drinking more frequently were less likely to report high levels of perfectionism. Students who reported drinking to intoxication more frequently were also more likely to report using alcohol as a coping mechanism and learning to live with it, but were less likely to report that they coped by finding comfort in religion (see Table 3). 25

Negative Mood

Controlling for negative mood (a combination of anxiety, tension, depression, anger, confusion, fatigue, and lack of vigor) at wave 1, students who reported greater negative moods at wave 2 were also more likely to report that they coped by criticizing themselves, but they were less likely to report high levels of self-esteem and optimism (see Table 4). 26

Tables   This report contains four tables that summarize the results of the study. ———
Tables are very common in social science and science studies, less so in humanities
papers.

Paragraph 27   This paragraph marks the start of the Comment section of the study. ———
(In some studies, this section is called Discussion.) It is a brief recapitulation of the
findings of the study.

TABLE 3
Partial Correlations Between Alcohol Consumption and Predictor Variables at Wave 2 Controlling for Wave 1 Alcohol Consumption

Variable	Alcohol on weekends	Frequency	Intoxication
Coping propensity at wave 1			
Use alcohol to feel better	−.02	.05	.25***
Find comfort in religion	−.09	−.06	−.19**
Learn to live with it	−.08	.05	.15*
Perfectionism	−.08	−.20*	−.07
Extroversion	.03	.16*	.08

Note: Coping tactics were rated on a 4-point scale (1 = I wouldn't do this at all, 4 = I would do this a lot). Perfectionism was rated on a 6-point scale (1 = never, 6 = always). Extroversion was measured on a 9-point scale with 1 of the 2 adjectives (eg, introversion, extroversion) serving as an endpoint. *p<.05. **p<.01. ***p<.001.

TABLE 4
Partial Correlations Between Negative Mood and Predictor Variables at Wave 2 Controlling for Negative Mood at Wave 1

Variable	Negative mood at Wave 2
Coping propensity at wave 1	
Criticize yourself	.19*
Self-esteem	−.34**
Optimism	−.29**

Note: Coping tactics were rated on a 4-point scale (1 = I wouldn't do this at all, 4 = I would do this a lot), as was optimism (0 = strongly disagree, 4 = strongly agree). Self-esteem was measured on a 4-point scale (1 = strongly agree, 4 = strongly disagree). *p<.01. **p<.001.

COMMENT

We are among few researchers who have used a longitudinal panel design to test for changes related to entry into college. Similar to findings with law students[3,4] and medical students,[1,2] our results suggest that for many undergraduate students, the college experience may actually cause physical and psychological distress. These data indicate specific factors that are linked to physical and psychological health.

Paragraph 28   Subtitled "Declines in Physical and Psychological Health and
Attitudes," this paragraph summarizes the list of student health problems more
prevalent at the end than at the beginning of first-year college.

Paragraphs 29 through 34   Subtitled "Predictors and Correlates of Adjustment,"
paragraph 29 introduces an important section on the variables that predict negative
outcomes. These variables—coping styles, self-esteem, perfectionism, optimism,
and extroversion—are considered, respectively, in paragraphs 30 through 34.
Note that only optimism is associated in the study with positive health benefits.
Extroversion was a neutral variable. The others were associated with a decline in
health.

Declines in Physical and Psychological Health and Attitudes

Consistent with earlier studies of law students and medical students, we 28
found that college students' physical and psychological states declined
within a year following matriculation. Physical ailments, quantity of alcohol
consumed on weekends, frequency of drinking, frequency of intoxication,
and negative affect were more prevalent at the end of the first year than they
were at the beginning. Stress levels did not increase over time. This may be
because orientation is a stressful event, being the first taste students have of
college life. If we had been able to survey students prior to orientation, we
likely would have found lower levels of stress than those reported in orientation week.

Predictors and Correlates of Adjustment

We also extend understanding of students' difficulties in college by focusing on 29
what predicts negative outcomes. We investigated several possible explanations.

Coping Styles

Several coping propensities at wave 1 predicted physical and psychological 30
outcome at wave 2. As noted earlier, researchers in previous studies have
offered conflicting results concerning which coping styles are adaptive in
nature. It may be that the adaptive value of particular strategies varies with
situational variables (eg, how much actual control is present). For instance,
saying "this isn't real," criticizing oneself, and learning to live with it predicted poorer health outcomes at wave 2. Using alcohol as a coping mechanism and learning to live with it predicted frequency of alcohol intoxication
at wave 2, whereas finding comfort in religion was negatively related to
frequency of intoxication at wave 2. Criticizing oneself related to negative
mood at wave 2. These findings are consistent with the studies in which
investigators have found a relationship between using emotion-focused
coping styles and negative psychological outcome.[13,14] Researchers should
examine what specific situational or individual variables moderate whether
specific coping tactics are adaptive.

Self-Esteem

Similar to other researchers, we also found that individuals with low 31
self-esteem reported more physical health problems.[17] Unlike previous
research in which investigators[18,19] connected self-esteem to alcohol use, we
did not find any relation between self-esteem and alcohol usage; however,
we did find a relationship between self-esteem and negative moods, with
individuals possessing lower levels of self-esteem reporting more negative
moods.

Paragraphs 35 and 36   These two paragraphs conclude the study. They are subtitled ———
"Limitations and Conclusions." This is an important section in a social science
study. Sometimes they form two different subsections of the report. Researchers
are obligated to point out study limitations so that their findings are used discrimi-
nately in decision making.

The limitations reported here are typical: sample size, the homogeneity of the
participants, and the time the study was conducted. Nevertheless, the researchers
feel they can make some recommendations to university administrators about ways
to reduce health risks to students.

Perfectionism

Similar to Vincent and Walker,[25] we found that individuals who scored high in perfectionism were more likely to report physical health problems; however, perfectionism was negatively related to frequency of drinking. Unlike researchers in previous studies of depression,[23,24] we did not find that perfectionism related to psychological outcomes (mood); however, we examined overall mood and not depression per se. Perhaps perfectionism only relates to certain negative mood aspects, but not all of them.

Optimism

Similar to Kamen and Seligman,[26] we found an inverse relationship between health and optimism.[27] Individuals scoring higher on optimism reported fewer health problems than did those scoring lower on optimism. We also found that optimism was inversely related to psychological health (ie, negative moods). Individuals scoring higher on optimism also reported fewer psychological health problems than did those scoring lower on optimism.

Extroversion

Although we did not find the relationship between extroversion and physical health reported previously,[29,31] we did find that extroverts drank more frequently than their introverted counterparts. Unlike Nakano,[30] we found no relation between psychological health and extroversion; however, Nakano measured only depression, whereas we measured overall psychological health. Investigators in future studies should examine whether extroversion relates to specific aspects of psychological health.

Limitations and Conclusions

There are 3 primary limitations of these data. First, only one half of the first-year class participated in both waves of the research. Although this raises concern about possible biases caused by self-selection, 93% of the students responded to at least 1 of the waves. Second, these data are from a single college. Replication with broader samples would strengthen confidence in the generalizability of these findings. Third, we administered our baseline sample during freshman orientation. Some may argue that orientation is not a true baseline because technically these students are now college students, even though they have not started their college coursework yet. In the future, perhaps researchers should mail the surveys to prospective students during the summer before they begin college or at the end of their senior year of high school.

Similar to investigators[1-3] in previous studies of law students and medical students, we found that undergraduates' physical and psychological health declined over time. We found certain coping tactics, perfectionism,

References   The source list is called References, as used in the APA method for
citing sources, but this article does not use the APA method. Because this essay is
published in a health journal, it uses the American Medical Association style for
citing sources.

The source list is organized numerically, not alphabetically. It has paragraph
rather than hanging indentation. Note the placement of the publication date and
the use of capital letters and italics in each citation. Remember to always check with
your professors to find out which citation method they want you to use.

low optimism, extroversion, and low self-esteem accounted for students' physical and psychological decline. Researchers should investigate steps college administrators can take to help alleviate some of these problems. Regardless, we hope that the information we provided will help university administrators gain some insight into why college results in such a negative experience for some students and what factors may enable students to thrive in this environment. Perhaps administrators could offer workshops for incoming freshmen during orientation week to teach them better strategies for how to cope with the rigors of college and threats to self-esteem. Many colleges have counseling centers that might be able to offer such workshops as required seminars during their orientation week. In addition, many colleges have peer-advising or peer-support groups that would be able to give their fellow students first-hand information on what to expect during their first year of college and how to prepare for and cope with the possible challenges that they might face. Interested colleges could administer preworkshop and postworkshop surveys to evaluate the effectiveness of such interventions. College administrators might also wish to better encourage involvement in student organizations so that students have the opportunities to interact with their fellow freshmen. Findings from previous studies[6,47] have suggested that student involvement can help protect against maladjustment to college life.

NOTE

For comments and further information, address correspondence to Dr Mary Pritchard, Boise State University, Psychology Department, 1910 University Drive, Boise, ID 83725-1715 (e-mail: marypritchard@boisestate.edu).

REFERENCES

1. Bramness JG, Fixdal TC, Vaglum P. Effects of medical school stress on mental health of medical students in early and late clinical curriculum. *Acta Psychiatr Scand.* 1991;84:340–345.
2. Heins M, Fahey SN, Leiden LL. Perceived stress in medical, law, and graduate students. *J Med Educ.* 1984;59:169–179.
3. Pritchard ME, McIntosh DN. What predicts psychological outcomes among law students? A longitudinal panel study. *J Soc Psychol.* 2003;143:727–745.
4. Benjamin GAH, Kaszniak A, Sales B, Shanfield SB. The role of legal education in producing psychological distress among law students and lawyers. *Am Bar Found Res J.* 1986;11:225–252.
5. Beck CJA, Sales BD, Benjamin GAH. Lawyer distress: alcohol-related problems and other psychological concerns among a sample of practicing lawyers. *J Law Health.* 1995;10:1–60.
6. Upcraft ML, Gardner JN. *The Freshman Year Experience.* San Francisco, CA: Jossey-Bass Publishers; 1989.
7. Rickinson B, Rutherford D. Increasing undergraduate student retention rates. *Br J Guid Counc.* 1995;23:161–172.
8. Roth DL, Wiebe DJ, Fillingim RB, Shay KA. Life events fitness hardiness and health: a simultaneous analysis of proposed stress-resistance effects. *J Pers Soc Psychol.* 1989;57:136–142.

9. Sax LJ. Health trends among college freshman. *J Am Coll Health.* 1997;45:252–262.
10. Pearlin LI, Schooler C. The structure of coping. *J Health Soc Behav.* 1978;19:2–21.
11. Feeney JA. Adult attachment coping style and health locus of control as predictors of health behavior. *Aust J Psychol.* 1995;47:171–177.
12. James K. Worker social identity and health-related costs for organizations: a comparative study between ethnic groups. *J Occup Health Psychol.* 1997;2:108–117.
13. Kolenc KM, Hartley DL, Murdock NL. The relationship of mild depression to stress and coping. *J Ment Health Couns.* 1990;12:76–92.
14. Lapp WM, Collins RL. Relative/proportional scoring of the Ways of Coping checklist: is it advantageous or artifactual? *Multivariate Behav Res.* 1993;28:483–512.
15. Arthur N. The effects of stress depression and anxiety on postsecondary students' coping strategies. *J Coll Stud Dev.* 1998;39:11–22.
16. Cobiella CW, Mabe PA, Forehand RL. A comparison of two stress-reduction treatments for mothers of neonates hospitalized in a neonatal intensive care unit. *Child Health Care.* 1990;19:93–100.
17. Leitschuh GA, Rawlins ME. Personal orientation inventory correlated with physical health. *Psychol Rep.* 1991;69:687–690.
18. Pullen L. The relationships among alcohol abuse in college students and selected psychological/demographic variables. *J Alcohol Drug Educ.* 1994;40:36–50.
19. Sands T, Archer J, Puelo S. Prevention of health-risk behaviors in college students: evaluating seven variables. *J Coll Stud Dev.* 1998;39:331–342.
20. Joiner TE, Tickle JJ. Exercise and depressive and anxious symptoms: what is the nature of their interrelations? *J Occup Rehabil.* 1998;8:191–198.
21. Bezjak JE, Lee JW. Relationship of self-efficacy and locus of control constructs in predicting college students' physical fitness behaviors. *Percept Mot Skills.* 1990;71:499–508.
22. Halamandaris KF, Power KG. Individual differences dysfunctional attitudes and social support: a study of the psychosocial adjustment to university life of home students. *Pers Individ Differ.* 1997;22:93–104.
23. Rice KG, Mirzadeh SA. Perfectionism attachment and adjustment. *J Couns Psychol.* 2000;47:238–250.
24. Northam S, Bluen SD. Differential correlates of components of Type A behavior. *S Afr J Psychol.* 1994;24:131–137.
25. Vincent NK, Walker JR. Perfectionism and chronic insomnia. *J Psychol Res.* 2000;49:349–354.
26. Kamen LP, Seligman ME. Explanatory style and health. *Curr Psychol Rev.* 1987;6:207–218.
27. Miller MC. The benefits of positive psychology. *Harv Ment Health Lett.* 2002;18:6–7.
28. Held BS. The tyranny of the positive attitude in America: observation and speculation. *J Clin Psychol.* 2002;58:965–992.
29. Cohen M. Happiness and humor: a medical perspective. *Aust Fam Physician.* 2001;30:17–19, 53–55.
30. Nakano K. Personality hassles and psychological and physical well-being. *Jpn J Psychol.* 1993;64:123–127.
31. Taenzer P, Melzack R, Jeans ME. Influence of psychological factors on postoperative pain mood and analgesic requirements. *Pain.* 1986;24:331–342.
32. Schapiro IR, Ross-Petersen L, Saelan H, Garde K, Olsen JH, Johansen C. Extroversion and neuroticism and the associated risk of cancer: a Danish cohort study. *Am J Epidemiol.* 2001;153:757–763.
33. Reifman A, Biernat M, Lang EL. Stress social support and health in married professional women with small children. *Psychol Women Q.* 1991;15:431–445.
34. Cooper ML, Russell M, Skinner JB, Windle M. Development and validation of a 3-dimensional measure of drinking motives. *Psychol Assess.* 1992;4:123–132
35. Stewart SH, Zeitlin SB, Samoluk SB. Examination of a three-dimensional drinking motives questionnaire in a young adult university sample. *Behav Res Ther.* 1996;34:61–71.

36. Kohn PM, Lafreniere K, Gurevhich M. The inventory of college student's recent life experiences: a decontaminated hassles scale for a special population. *J Behav Med*. 1990;13:619–630.

37. Garner DM, Olmstead MP, Polivy J. Development and validation of a multidimensional eating disorder inventory for anorexia nervosa and bulimia. *Int J Eat Disord*. 1983;2:15–34.

38. Rosenberg M. *Society and the Adolescent Self-Image*. Princeton, NJ: Princeton University Press; 1965.

39. Carver CS. You want to measure coping, but your protocol's too long: consider the brief COPE. *Int J Behav Med*. 1997;4:92–100.

40. Greenhouse WJ, Meyer B, Johnson SL. Coping and medication adherence in bipolar disorder. *J Affect Disord*. 2000;59: 237–241.

41. Perczek R, Carver CS, Price AA, Pozo-Kaderman C. Coping, mood, and aspects of personality in Spanish translation and evidence of convergence with English versions. *J Pers Assess*. 2000;74: 63–87.

42. Scheier MF, Carver CS, Bridges MW. Distinguishing optimism from neuroticism (and trait anxiety self-mastery and self-esteem): a re-evaluation of the Life Orientation Test. *J Pers Soc Psychol*. 1994;67:1063–1078.

43. Hatchett GT, Park HL. Relationships among optimism, coping styles, psychopathology, and counseling outcome. *Pers Individ Dif*. 2004;36:1775–1769.

44. McNair DM, Lorr M, Droppleman LF. *Manual for the Profile of Mood State*. San Diego, CA: Educational and Industrial Testing Service; 1981.

45. Goldberg L. The development of markers for the Big Five factor structure. *Psychol Assess*. 1992;4:26–42.

46. Smith DR, Snell WE Jr. Goldberg's bipolar measure of the Big-Five personality dimensions: reliability and validity. *Eur J Pers*. 1996;10:283–299.

47. Cooper DL, Healy MA, Simpson J. Student development through involvement: specific changes over time. *J Coll Stud Dev*. 1994;35:98–102.

Paragraph 1   The differences between a humanities and a social science article are
immediately evident in the first paragraph. Actually, they are evident even before
the first paragraph, in that a humanities article usually has no abstract. In addition, this piece lacks subtitles, which is common in a humanities essay but rare in
one written for the sciences or social sciences. Also note the use of the first person *I*, which begins in the second sentence and continues throughout the article.
That pronoun signals the use, at least in part, of the narrative mode, which is not
unusual in a humanities paper but is rare in other disciplines. The essay's thesis is
stated clearly in the last sentence of this paragraph.

Paragraph 2   This paragraph presents the essay's literature review. Of course, there
are reams of studies on Dickinson's religious themes, so the author limits his lit
review to those studies especially relevant to his thesis.
    Note the MLA format of the parenthetical citations.

This essay about interpreting poetry appeared in the Fall 2006 issue of *Cross Currents*, a humanities journal.

Meeting her Maker: Emily Dickinson's God
Jay Ladin

It's common for secular academics to assume that religious belief—   1
adherence to any religious system or ideology—is fundamentally at odds
with the open-minded, exploratory enterprise of critical interpretation. That
was certainly my assumption two autumns ago, when, as a new member
of the English Department of the women's college of an Orthodox Jewish
university, I led a seminar-style exploration of Emily Dickinson's poems
about God. The question of Dickinson's religious beliefs—what, if any,
beliefs she held and what, if anything, her poems reveal of them—has long
been a subject of debate among Dickinson scholars. As I expected, the question was of great interest to my students, who had grown up practicing a
modern Orthodox form of Judaism. What I did not expect was that these
young women, who knew little about poetry, less about Dickinson, and
nothing about Christianity or its nineteenth-century New England manifestations, would see so clearly through the tangle of Dickinson's contradictory portrayals of God and the equally contradictory conclusions scholars
have drawn from them. I had assumed that the intellectual habits promoted
by traditional religious belief and humanistic inquiry are inherently at
odds, that while humanism encourages the exploration of complexity and
contradiction, traditional belief encourages the opposite—simplification,
homogenization, retreat from the messiness of existence into the comfort
of tautological projection. But rather than inhibiting their ability to engage
with Dickinson's challenging texts, my students' lifelong immersion in
Orthodox Judaism helped them recognize dynamics at work in Dickinson's
poems about God that my secular approach had obscured.

One of the nice things about teaching is the way it transforms vexing   2
scholarly uncertainties into signs of professorial sophistication. Rather than
feeling anxious that I didn't know the answers to the questions I was raising, I felt quite pleased to introduce the subject of Dickinson's religious
beliefs by informing my class that scholars had been utterly unable to agree
on them. For example, while Dorothy Oberhaus has argued that Dickinson
wrote "in the poetic tradition of Christian devotion," Richard Wilbur

With affectionate thanks to my students in English 1100, Fall 2003: Ofelia Behar, Kim Chiert,
Nisa Davidovics, Ariela Fuchs, Yona Glass, Amit Kattan, Shani Kirschenbaum, Batsheva Merlis,
Lauren Pietruszka, and Alex Weiser.

Paragraph 3   Note the author's use of metaphor—"the humanistic equivalent of Original Sin," "Moebius-strip-like syntax." Again, such rhetorical flourishes are embraced by humanists but generally shunned by scientists. Academic style varies from one discipline to the next.

and many others since have seen Dickinson's poems as expressions of an idiosyncratic, home-made relation to religious belief—what Wilbur calls "a precarious convergence between her inner experience and her religious inheritance" (Farr 105, 54). Other readers, focusing on Dickinson's most iconoclastic texts, see Dickinson as radically challenging Christianity and indeed all religious belief. This extraordinary range of opinions as to what Dickinson believed—and the abundance of textual evidence to support each of them—has prompted many scholars to adopt what we might call an agnostic attitude toward Dickinson's beliefs. As Denis Donoghue put it, "of her religious faith virtually anything may be said. She may be represented as an agnostic, a heretic, a skeptic, a Christian" (quoted in Yezzi 20). Wary that my students might simplify Dickinson's beliefs by filtering her contradictions through the lens of their own faith, I presented Donoghue-style agnosticism as the only intellectually responsible position possible—that is, the only position that confronted the entire range of beliefs presented in Dickinson's poems. To demonstrate Dickinson's irresolvable religious contradictions, I started my students off with poems that present completely incommensurate representations of God: the amputated absentee of "Those – dying then"; the withholding parent of the poem that begins "Of Course – I prayed – / And did God Care?"; the outgrown childhood God of "I prayed, at first, a little Girl"; the faceless, dematerialized "Infinitude" of "My period had come for Prayer"; the Disneyesque savior of vermin addressed in the poem that begins "Papa above! / Regard a Mouse / O'erpowered by the Cat!" No one, I assured them, could infer a coherent idea of God from this blizzard of conflicting evidence.

My students dutifully jotted down my words, relieved no doubt that I was excusing them from at least one measure of responsibility for understanding a poet they found so difficult. Having saved them from the humanistic equivalent of Original Sin—belief in absolute interpretation—I set my students to working their way through the poems line by line. They chose to begin with "Of Course – I prayed":

3

> Of Course – I prayed –
> And did God Care?
> He cared as much as on the Air
> A Bird – had stamped her foot –
> And cried "Give Me" –
> My Reason – Life –
> I had not had – but for Yourself –
> 'Twere better Charity
> To leave me in the Atom's Tomb –
> Merry, and Nought, and gay, and numb –
> Than this smart Misery.

Paragraphs 4 through 6   These paragraphs describe how the author's students responded to one of the Emily Dickinson poems he assigned and how their reading of the poem changed his own. Note the effective blending of the narrative and persuasive modes here. This is primarily a persuasive essay with a clear persuasive thesis: religious devotion can expand, not restrict how poems about faith can be interpreted. The article's narrative edge helps make the argument interesting and accessible.

At first we focused on grammar rather than theology. My students were baffled by the radical shifts in tone and perspective in the long sentence—or is it a sentence?—that begins "He cared as much as on the Air" and either concludes with "'Give Me,'" or with "Life." Or, since "My Reason – Life" can be read both as the end of the thought ("'Give Me' – / My Reason – Life") that begins the poem or the beginning of the thought that ends the poem, perhaps the sentence never really concludes at all. They were fascinated to discover that Dickinson uses this Moebius-strip-like syntax—an inelegant version of the technique Cristanne Miller calls "syntactical doubling"—to seamlessly shift from the melodramatic rage of the opening lines to the John Donne-like intellectual complaint of the last.

Once my students recognized that the poem represented two distinct   4
attitudes, they began to find it easier to understand. Having themselves wrestled with God as both an inconsistent source of blessings and as the ultimate guarantor of the meaning of their lives, they found the opening lines' rage at God's refusal to respond to prayer quite familiar. For them, these lines were dramatizing a childish, egocentric relation to God, in which God is seen purely as a function of one's own needs. The end of the poem, they saw, was a more adult, intellectualized version of the same relationship. Though they weren't sure of the speaker's sincerity in stating that she would rather have been left in "the Atom's Tomb" as uncreated matter, they understood that God's unresponsiveness had provoked the speaker to question the value of consciousness.

Having identified both parts of the poems as forms of rage at God for   5
failing to respond to prayer, my students found themselves back at the question of syntax. What, they wondered, was the relationship between these very different attitudes toward God? Why did Dickinson fudge the syntactical boundaries that would normally enable us to clearly distinguish them? Though they still couldn't figure out the sentence, they began to see that the defective syntax embodied a deeper problem: the difficulty, for the speaker and for anyone engaged in a serious practice of prayer, of separating the psychological from the theological. That is, the blurred syntax reflects the difficulty of distinguishing between subjective rage at a God who fails to personally respond to prayer, and the objective questions, such as the nature of God or the value of human existence, that Divine non-responsiveness raises. Perhaps, they speculated, the defective syntax was Dickinson's way of emphasizing the underlying similarity of these two very different theological tantrums.

I had guided my students through the syntactical issues raised by the   6
poem, but to my astonishment, my students' discussion of its content had changed my own reading of the poem. Before our discussion, I read

Paragraphs 7 through 10 These paragraphs describe the author's students'
responses to another Emily Dickinson poem he assigned. Note the casual voice of
the first sentence of the eighth paragraph, which an editor of a science or social science journal would likely question.

"Of Course – I prayed" as a deliberately incoherent critique of God. Now I saw it as a trenchant critique of an "immature" relation to God and prayer whose symptoms could range from childish rage to Metaphysical wit to a profound rejection of human existence.

I was both delighted by my students' ability to connect Dickinson's work to their personal experiences, and startled by the effectiveness of that connection. Rather than oversimphfying the complexities of the text, reading Dickinson through the lens of their religious experience had made my students more effective, subtler readers than they would have been had they adopted the humanist framework I offered them.

A fluke, I told myself. My students had transformed my reading of "Of Course – I Prayed," but my overall sense of Dickinson's indeterminate religious belief—a claim based not on individual poems, but on her work as a whole—was still unchallenged. Thus, it was not without a certain eagerness that I turned discussion to "Those – dying then," a poem whose "Nietzschean post-Christianity," as David Yezzi puts it, would demonstrate the essential instability of Dickinson's religious beliefs:

> Those – dying then,
> Knew where they went –
> They went to God's Right Hand –
> That Hand is amputated now
> And God cannot be found.
>
> The abdication of Belief
> Makes the Behavior small –
> Better an ignis fatuus
> Than no illume at all.

After the syntactical mishmash of "Of Course – I prayed," my students had little difficulty fleshing out the compressed spiritual history presented in the first stanza. "Those ... then," they saw, referred to an earher time, when belief in God and the afterlife was far more firmly and generally established. They also recognized the epistemological shadings in the stanza's phrasing—that is, that rather than making a statement about the actual organization of life, death and eternity, the statement that "Those dying then / Knew" they were headed to "God's Right Hand" was describing "Their" beliefs. With this understanding, it was easy for my students to see through the shock of the imagery of the amputated "Right Hand" to the deeper shock of moving from a description of beliefs (what "They" used to believe) to a statement of ontological fact (what God is now). They saw that, like the defective syntax in "Of Course – I prayed," this shock raises but does not answer the question of the relation between human belief and the nature of reality—whether the decay of human belief in some way led to God's

Paragraph 11   This paragraph is transitional. Having discussed his students'
responses to the two Dickinson poems, the author now moves to talk more generally about how these responses altered his own interpretations.

amputated "abdication," or, conversely, whether "Those – dying then" were simply shielded by their belief from the harsh realities the last lines of the stanza assert.

This of course was the very sort of "Nietzschean post-Christian"   8 perspective I wanted my students to glean from the poem, and I rather smugly pointed out that the vision of God this stanza presented was utterly unlike the God about whom the frustrated speaker of "Of Course – I prayed" complains. While the speaker of the first poem blames God for failure to respond, the second poem's image of God's amputated hand suggests a deity who is powerless to respond. Obviously, I concluded, the poems represent different theological universes—and demonstrate the inconsistency of Dickinson's beliefs.

Here, however, my students balked. Both poems, they argued, represent   9 different takes on the same fundamental problem: the difficulty of establishing a relationship with God. One student startled me by pointing out that the statement "That Hand is amputated now" presents God's existence as ontological fact rather than simply a matter of belief. While the statement can certainly be read figuratively, as a metaphor for Divine ineffectuality in the face of modernity, it also presents a vividly physical image of God—an image that emphasizes rather than undercuts the sense of God's existence. They also challenged my claim that the poem's second stanza represents a Wallace Stevens-type assertion that humans need "supreme fictions" such as belief in God, even when we know they are fictions. Rather, they argued, the leap from "God cannot be found" to "The abdication of belief" suggests that God's absence may be a sign of human dereliction of duty (the peculiar verb "abdication" implicitly equates human "Belief" with royal obligation). Just because God "cannot be found," they said, doesn't mean that God is not there; after all, Jews have wrestled for millennia with the question of how human beings should respond to the "hiddenness" of God at times of personal and collective suffering. From their perspective, the second stanza laments not the absence of God but human acceptance of God's absence.

Though I insisted on the ambiguous relation between the stanzas,   10 I could not escape the sense that my students were right: even here, at her most apparently nihilistic, Dickinson's poetry evinced a passionate engagement with God, an engagement that affirmed God's existence and importance even as it fretted or raged over God's inaccessibility.

My students had opened my eyes to the superabundance of evidence   11 of Dickinson's relationship to God—evidence so strong that it appears to rule out the idea that Dickinson was an "agnostic" or a "skeptic." Though Dickinson wrote deeply skeptical poems, as my students demonstrated with regard to "Those – dying then," even these poems can be understood

Paragraph 12   Here the author is more specific about just how his students changed ————
his views, noting that it is not God's existence but the nature of God's relationship
with the human world, the "human condition," that is at question.

Paragraphs 13 and 14   Here the author expands the purview of his article to include ————
some of Emily Dickinson's letters. He finds in these letters the same multiple identities his students helped him find in the religious poems. The letters and the God
poems are similar in that they never seem to satisfy the poet's needs.

as reflecting a tumultuous but clearly ongoing relationship to God. Robert Frost, who wrote some of the bleakest verses ever penned in English, claimed he had a lover's quarrel with life. My students convinced me that the same could be said of Dickinson and God. Like Frost's quarrel with life, Dickinson's quarrel with God reflects the full panoply of human disaffection. But though Dickinson's God rarely seems to make her happy, she never breaks off the affair, never rejects the idea that, however incompatible we may be, human and Divine are made for each other.

Once I accepted my students' contention that Dickinson's belief in God   12 was neither contradictory nor inconsistent, I also found myself agreeing that the nature of Dickinson's relationship to God was not, as I had insisted, "indeterminate." The relation to God my students found in Dickinson's poems is both simpler and more complex than most critical accounts suggest. Rather than contradictory religious beliefs, they recognized in her rhetoric and imagery a core assumption of God's existence—an assumption that underwrites and gives rise to a range of challenges and pleas. For them, what is at stake in Dickinson's religious poems is not God's existence, but God's accessibility, responsiveness, accountability, comprehensibility, and concern for the human condition.

From my students' perspective, the baffling array of religious attitudes   13 Dickinson portrays in her poems reflect a clear, coherent and—to young women born along the fault-line between traditional religious belief and American modernity—quite familiar spiritual struggle. As a longtime ponderer of Dickinson's highly theatrical poses, I realized that I found her relationship to God familiar in a different way. Dickinson adopts a similar variety of moods and roles in her letters. For example, in her famous correspondence with Thomas Wentworth Higginson, Dickinson shuttles from flirt to adoring "scholar," condescending epigrammatist to eyelash-batting naif. As in so many of the relationships she carried on via written language, Dickinson ceaselessly reinvented herself and her relationship to God. The list of Dickinson's theological poses is nearly as long as the list of her God-related poems: the lisping child of "I never felt at Home – Below" who anticipates wanting to run away from "Paradise" because "it's Sunday – all the time – / And Recess – never comes"; the beset but endearing rodent of "Papa above!"; the ontological adventurer of "My Period had come – for Prayer," who travels "Vast Prairies of Air" in an effort to face the ultimately faceless "Infinitude"; the sardonic skeptic of the poem that begins "It's easy to invent a Life / God does it – every Day." As in her letters, in her poems about God, Dickinson—or her alter egos—wheels from dominance to submission, from childish directness to arch sophistication, from loneliness to love.

Paragraph 15   In this paragraph, the author connects his comments on the poems
and letters to Dickinson's infamous reclusiveness. She wants neither God nor her
correspondents to be "too present." Note how the author smoothly integrates
quotes from Dickinson's poems into his own texts, an effective rhetorical strategy
when explicating literature.

Paragraph 16   In his concluding paragraph, the author attempts to explain why his
students interpreted Dickinson as they did, noting that their religious frame of
reference did not inhibit but expanded their appreciation of the poet's work. They
were confident in the validity of their interpretation because of the religious framework within which they live. The author began committed to the indeterminacy
of interpretation and ends less so. Note the clever and effective metaphor, "post-
modernist vanilla of indeterminacy," which is another example of the type
of writing humanists value but scientists tend to eschew.

In fact, the more closely one compares Dickinson's poems about God   14
to her letters to acquaintances, the more typical of Dickinson her relationship with God seems. Both the poems and letters express an insatiable need
for a level of response Dickinson's addressees rarely seem to supply. And in
both poems and letters, whatever posture Dickinson adopts in her protean
playacting, as my students noted, the focus, the drama, centers ultimately on
her rather than her addressee, who recedes, despite the speaker's rhetorical
grasping, into a life beyond her ken.

Perhaps that recession was the point of Dickinson's posturing. Though   15
God and the others she engaged so passionately through her words
always seem to fail her, their very distance secured the integrity of the self
Dickinson kept so closely guarded. Many of Dickinson's religious poems
dramatize her fear that God, unlike her human correspondents, would
prove too present, too perceptive, too insistent to evade. The childish
speaker of "I never felt at Home – Below," for example, worries that God,
"a Telescope // Perennial beholds us." This nightmarish (for the reclusive
Dickinson, at least) vision of an All-Seeing God obsessed with eyeing any
soul foolish enough to attempt to hide itself rises to a pitch of post-Puritan
paranoia in "Of Consciousness, her awful mate," which envisions a God as
inescapable as consciousness itself, whose "Eyes" are "triple Lenses" that
"burn" through any attempt at anonymity.

My students readily grasped Dickinson's rage at God's silence or   16
absence; such feelings are common aspects of religious engagement. But as
religious people focused on seeking rather than evading God, and as young
women focused more on finding life partners than on maintaining personal boundaries, they found it difficult to understand Dickinson's horror
of God's "triple lenses." A lifelong relationship involves endless negotia-
tions over intrusiveness and distance, power and impotence, but even during the most difficult periods, there are moments when a couple's eyes will
meet, and each will recognize the other and the difficult bond they share.
For Dickinson and God, this moment seems to have come when both
found themselves stranded face to face between Earth and Heaven, Eternity
and Time:

> It was too late for Man –
> But early, yet, for God –
> Creation – impotent to help –
> But Prayer – remained – Our Side –
>
> How excellent the Heaven –
> When Earth – cannot be had –
> How hospitable – then – the face
> Of our Old Neighbor – God –

Works Cited   Writing for a humanities journal, the author acknowledges his sources ———
using the MLA method. This essay was written before 2009, when MLA revised
its citation method. The new MLA citation rules are explained in Chapter 8.
Remember that "Works Cited" is to MLA as a references list is to APA, and
"Works Consulted" is to MLA as a bibliography is to APA.

My students' readings of Dickinson's relationship to her "Old neighbor – God" do not constitute a conclusive account of her religious thought. But they do expose the fallacy of assumptions about the inherent intellectual limitations of religious belief. Rather than preventing my students from engaging with complexity, their beliefs helped them discern complexities I had sought to bland into the all-embracing, post-modernist vanilla of indeterminacy. For my students, as for Dickinson, religious belief is not a static answer but a lifelong pursuit of the most difficult existential questions, a pursuit that makes them supremely sensitive to the nuances and contradictions of the human effort to engage with that which is beyond us.

WORKS CITED

Dickinson, Emily. *The Complete Poems of Emily Dickinson*. Ed. Thomas H.Johnson. NY: Little, Brown, 1960.

Farr, Judith. *Emily Dickinson: A Collection of Critical Essays*. NY: Prentice Hall, 1995.

Yezzi, David. "Straying Close to Home: Author/Poet Emily Dickinson's Religious Beliefs and Spirituality." *Commonweal* 125, Issue 17 (Oct. 9.1998): 20–21.

Format   This essay by student Adam Black is in MLA format. Note the spacing and
the placement of the student's name, course number, professor's name, and date.
Note that the title is centered but not in bold and not underlined. Note that the
running header consists of the author's last name and the page number. Compare
this format with that of an APA student essay, pages 178–181.

Paragraph 1   Adam introduces his topic and presents his thesis, the last sentence of
the paragraph. The thesis indicates that this will be an expository essay (here is what
is being done to save the marmot) but that it will have an argumentative subtext
(the marmot should be saved). Such a blending of rhetorical modes is more the rule
than the exception.

Paragraph 2   Here is the first point in support of Adam's thesis. One thing being
done to save the marmot is the captive breeding program. Note that the paragraph
is developed and cites sources.

Paragraph 3   Here is the second point in support of his thesis. One challenge to the
marmot's survival is its predators, and that challenge is being met. Note the clear
transition into this paragraph and the transitions between sentences within the
paragraph.

This essay was written by a student for a freshman composition class.

Adam Black

English 101

Professor Giamatti

20 September 2007

Saving the Vancouver Island Marmot

The Vancouver Island marmot is a furry brown and white animal, a member of   1
the squirrel family. Adults weigh about six kilograms, the size of a large house
cat. Once abundant in central and southern Vancouver Island, the marmot has
become an endangered species. In the 1990s, the death rate of Vancouver Island
marmots exceeded the birth rate, and the species was in serious danger of becoming extinct. The logging industry adversely impacted much of the marmot's
natural habitat; abundant wolves, cougars, and golden eagles preyed upon scarce
Vancouver Island marmots; disease and cold weather also took a toll. By the
mid-1990s, there were fewer than forty Vancouver Island marmots (Drake S1).
Fortunately, British Columbia's Ministry of Environment, the logging industry, and
the general public became aware of the problem and began to support an aggressive program to save *Marmota vancouverensis* from extinction.

At the heart of this program are efforts, funded by government, the general   2
public, and the logging industry, to breed marmots in captivity and then reintroduce them into their native habitat. Zoos and conservation centers in Calgary,
Langley, Toronto, and Mount Washington on Vancouver Island have been breeding marmots in captivity now for about twenty years. They hope they can breed
enough animals and then reintroduce them to their native habitat, where they
will thrive. Success has been slow but steady. By 2004, the marmot population
was about 130; by 2007, it stood at 255 (Drake S1). Most of the animals remain
in captivity, but eighty-one have been released into the wild, and forty-two have
survived.

Still, major challenges remain, if the Vancouver Island marmot is to be saved.   3
One such challenge is predation. The marmot is a food source to wolves, cougars,
and golden eagles, all of which live and hunt on Vancouver Island. According to
Bryant and Page, predators accounted for 83% of known Marmot deaths (674). The
deer population, the major food source for marmot predators, has declined on the
island, and the wolf and cougar population has increased (Bryant and Page 680),

Paragraph 4   Here is the third point in support of Adam's thesis. Another challenge ———
that needs to be met if the marmot is to survive is that money has to be raised.
Adam explains how this challenge is being met.

Paragraph 5   Here Adam makes an interesting rhetorical move. He introduces ———
another challenge to the marmot's survival: convincing those who think it is the
natural order that species die out. In the process, he is acknowledging the opposing
argument, as an effective argument should. Note that he places this paragraph in
the middle of his essay. His other choice would be to place it closer to the beginning. It would be a mistake to place this paragraph nearer the end. You don't want
to leave your reader with a point that refutes your thesis.

Paragraph 6   Here the author returns to arguments in support of his thesis. The ———
argument in this paragraph focuses on the good looks of the Vancouver Island
marmot, which wins it support from the public. Note the detail in this paragraph,
supported, as needed, with reference to information from sources.

Paragraph 7   Here the author discusses research being done that will help scientists ———
learn about the nutritional requirements and breeding habits of the marmot. This
is the fifth point Adam makes to fulfill the purpose of his essay, which is to describe
what is being done to save the marmot.

making the marmots more vulnerable than ever. Biologists are now in the awkward position of having to recommend that some species—wolves, cougars, and maybe even eagles—be culled to save another (Markels 7).

Another challenge is funding. It costs millions of dollars to breed the marmots 4 in captivity and implant radio transmitters in them when they are released into the wild, so biologists can track their progress. At the present time, the Marmot Recovery Foundation is adequately, if not generously funded. The provincial and federal governments provide funding, assisted by grants from forest companies Weyerhaeuser and TimberWest (O'Neill 53) and donations from the public. But it will likely cost another fifteen million dollars to achieve the dream of reestablishing a viable marmot population that can survive indefinitely in the wild. There is no guarantee that the governments will continue the funding, especially given public pressures to increase funding for health care and education. Nor is it certain that the forest companies will continue to provide funds to atone for their clear-cutting practices which contributed to the decline in the marmot population.

A third problem is one that might be termed Darwinian. There are some politi- 5 cians and even biologists who argue that species extinction is part of a normal course of natural selection and survival of the fittest. Many species, they argue, have become extinct and humankind is no worse off as a result. Perhaps we should not fool with Mother Nature. Sometimes one species dies off so others have a better chance to survive and thrive (O'Neill 53). Maybe we should just simply let nature take its course, the argument goes, and let the marmots die off in the wild, if that is their evolutionary destiny.

Will *Marmota vancouverensis* survive? There is reason to be optimistic. The 6 Vancouver Island marmot is blessed with great looks, covered as it is in rich chocolate brown fur broken with patches of white. People tend to react to posters and television images of the marmot the same way they do when an adorable puppy scratches at their feet. Largely for this reason, there is considerable public support for the marmot's survival. The most ardent supporters have organized an adopt-a-marmot program, which urges members of the public to donate ten dollars a month to the cause. This program raises almost half a million dollars a year (Markels 5). It is likely, as well, that the government and the logging industry will continue to provide funding.

Another cause for optimism is the work being done at the captive breeding 7 sites. Biologists and veterinarians are learning more about the nutritional requirements of marmots to maximize the health of those reared in captivity. They are

Paragraph 8   Adam concludes his essay with a reasoned assessment of the evidence
he has presented. Clearly, he wants the marmot to survive, but he does not sugar-
coat its chances. He notes that its chances for surviving in captivity remain strong,
but that its chances of surviving in the wild will require continued vigilance and
commitment. Note how his concluding paragraph reaffirms his thesis and establishes a sense of closure.

Works Cited   This essay uses MLA format, so it ends with a Works Cited list. Note
the good mix of sources Adam has used: two journal articles, one magazine article,
an online newspaper, and an online magazine. Note that this essay was written earlier than 2009, before MLA revised its citation system. The revised system is covered
in Chapter 8.

studying mating behavior so they can establish conditions within which mating is most likely to occur. And they are learning more about the genetic makeup of the marmot to determine, among other things, if it is best to breed one genetically advantaged male with several females. At the present time, marmots are breeding more successfully in captivity than they are in the wild (Bryant).

There seems to be little doubt that the Vancouver Island marmots will con-   8
tinue to breed and thrive in captivity. Establishing a viable wild community remains a much more vexing problem, requiring, as it does, millions of dollars, the controversial practice of reducing the number of predators, and the continued energy and support of those who champion the marmots' survival.

Works Cited

Bryant, Andrew A. "Reproductive Rates of Wild and Captive Vancouver Island Marmots (*Marmota vancouverensis*)." *Canadian Journal of Zoology* 83 (2005): 664–673.

Bryant, Andrew A., and Rick E. Page. "Timing and Causes of Mortality in the Endangered Vancouver Island Marmot (*Marmota vancouverensis*)." *Canadian Journal of Zoology* 83 (2005): 674–682.

Drake, Laura. "Marmot Returns from the Brink of Extinction." *The Globe and Mail* 13 Aug. 2007: S1-2. *LexisNexis*. Soka University of America Library, Aliso Viejo, CA. 01 Sept. 2007 <www.lexisnexis.com>.

Markels, Alex. "Last Stand." *Audubon* May 2004. 01 Sept. 2007 <http://magazine.audubon.org/features0405/endangered-species.html>.

O'Neill, Terry. "Warm, Fuzzy, and Very Expensive." *The Report* 8 Oct. 2001: 52–53.

Abstract   The abstract summarizes the content of the article. Note that it is very brief ————
yet manages to touch on the most important points the authors present.

Paragraphs 1 through 3   The first three paragraphs make up the paper's ———————
introduction.

The first paragraph notes that the growth in U.S. labor productivity is stronger
than that of Europe while weaker than that of India and China.

The second paragraph defines the essay's key term, *labor productivity growth*.
Clear definitions are an important component, especially of persuasive essays. The
second paragraph goes on to introduce another important concern: the fear that
China's and India's strong productivity growth will harm the American economy.

The third paragraph sets out the content of the paper and presents the paper's
thesis: the high productivity growth in other countries will have both positive and
negative effects on the U.S. economy.

The article's introduction establishes its rhetorical mode—argument—and
presents its thesis clearly.

This essay appeared in *Current Issues in Economics and Finance*, Volume 13, Number 8, published in September 2007.

Is the United States Losing Its Productivity Advantage?
Mary Amiti and Kevin Stiroh

Strikingly high rates of labor productivity growth in China, India, and other emerging economies have prompted concerns that U.S. workers and firms are losing ground to their competitors in world markets. A closer look at the evidence, however, suggests that rapid foreign productivity growth will bring gains as well as losses to the U.S. economy. Some import-competing firms may be compelled to restructure or leave the market, but consumers will benefit from lower import prices and more import varieties, and U.S. exporters may gain access to cheaper intermediate products from abroad.

Since 1995, the United States has experienced a period of strong labor pro-   1
ductivity growth, with GDP per employee advancing at a rate of 2.0 percent a year. While this rate easily exceeds the 1.0 percent average growth rate seen in the euro area, it falls markedly short of labor productivity growth in emerging markets, which has averaged more than 4.0 percent across developing Asia and Eastern Europe.[1] China and India, two large emerging economies of particular interest, have seen spectacular growth rates of 6.4 and 4.4 percent per year, respectively.

Labor productivity growth—the ability to produce more output per   2
hour worked—is almost universally viewed as a positive development for an economy. When productivity growth is strong, an economy becomes wealthier, living standards rise, and short-run inflationary pressures may be tempered. Many observers of the rapid rise of China and India, however, express fear that strong productivity growth in foreign countries will harm the U.S. economy, displacing workers and making it more difficult for U.S. producers to compete in a global marketplace.

In this edition of *Current Issues*, we look more closely at differences in   3
productivity growth across countries and examine how strong produc-
tivity growth abroad may affect the U.S. economy. We consider the reasons for the euro area's weak productivity growth and the emerging market

[1]All data on output per employee are from the Groningen Growth and Development Centre and predate the July 2007 revisions to the U.S. National Income and Product Accounts. The estimate of U.S. productivity growth cited here is somewhat lower than the headline numbers produced by the U.S. Bureau of Labor Statistics (BLS). The difference reflects the Groningen Centre's use of a broader measure of output—full-economy GDP as opposed to nonfarm business output in the BLS data. Unless explicitly stated otherwise, productivity refers to labor productivity.

Paragraphs 4 through 9   These paragraphs form a section of the essay, under the
title "Productivity Trends in the United States and Developed Economies."

Paragraph 4 compares growth in the American economy with growth in the
Japanese and European economies in the 1960s and 1970s, noting that those economies outperformed America's.

Paragraph 5 notes that the trend was reversed in the 1990s, due mainly to
American leadership in information technology.

economies' robust performance. We then turn our attention to the potential channels through which foreign productivity growth can affect U.S. workers, producers, and consumers. Our review of the evidence suggests that rapid growth of productivity abroad will have mixed effects on the U.S. economy, bringing gains to some groups and losses to others. Consumers, for example, may benefit from lower import prices and a greater variety of imports, while U.S. firms that compete with firms in emerging economies may be forced to restructure or exit the market. In the concluding section, we discuss some of the implications of our analysis.

PRODUCTIVITY TRENDS IN THE UNITED STATES AND DEVELOPED ECONOMIES

We begin with a long-term perspective and compare trend productivity growth in the United States, fifteen European Union economies (EU-15), and Japan over the last forty-five years (see box).[2] In the 1960s and 1970s, trend productivity growth rates in Japan and the EU-15 were much higher than those in the United States. The contrast was especially sharp in the 1960s: while Japan's productivity grew more than 8 percent per year and the EU-15 saw annual growth rates above 5 percent, the United States experienced growth rates of less than 3 percent (Chart 1).

This picture has changed recently, however, with a dramatic reversal in the mid-1990s as the United States experienced a sharp rise in productivity growth while the EU-15 in particular entered a period of slowing growth. The resurgence of U.S. productivity growth since 1995 has been traced to the impact of information technology (IT) through two primary channels. Firms that produce IT have benefited from fundamental technological progress that has allowed them to develop more powerful IT products at lower prices. This advance is measured as rapid productivity growth in the relatively small *IT-producing* sector of the U.S. economy. Firms in other industries have made massive investments in IT and incorporated the latest technology in their production processes—developments that have improved labor productivity in the *IT-using* sectors. These IT-related productivity gains have been facilitated by competitive product markets, flexible labor markets, and the ability of firms to adapt quickly to changing economic conditions.[3]

4

5

---

[2]Our trend estimates are made via a Hodrick-Prescott filter (smoothing parameter of 100), using annual data from the Groningen Growth and Development Centre. Productivity here is defined as GDP per hour worked. This approach follows van Ark and Fosler (2007) and Gómez-Salvador et al. (2006).

[3]See Jorgenson, Ho, and Stiroh (2007) for a review of the literature on the U.S. productivity resurgence and the role of IT, and Baily (2002) for a discussion of deregulation, increased competitiveness, and other structural changes that have contributed to stronger productivity growth in the United States.

Chart 1   Chart 1, "Trend Labor Productivity Growth," provides clear visual proof of ———— the changes in productivity among the three economies—American, Japanese, and European—that the authors compare. The source of the chart is cited right below the chart itself, and below that is a note defining the key term *labor productivity*.

Paragraph 6 explains why productivity growth in Europe and Japan is slowing. Note that the topic sentence, the first, is in the form of a question, which the rest of the paragraph answers. This is a commonly used and effective rhetorical strategy. In some papers, the thesis statement is in the form of a question that the entire text responds to. Note also how transitional words such as "One key reason," "First," and "Second" establish cohesion within this paragraph.

Paragraph 7 continues to answer the question posited in the first sentence of paragraph 6. The opening phrase "A second reason" refers back to that question.

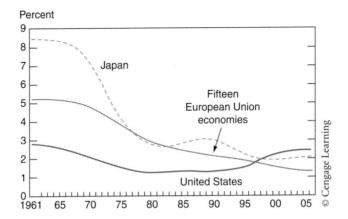

CHART 1
Trend Labor Productivity Growth

Source: The Conference Board and Groningen Growth and Development Centre, Total Economy Database, January 2007, <http://www.ggdc.net>.

Notes: Labor productivity is defined as real GDP per hour worked. Trend estimates are based on a Hodrick-Prescott filter with a smoothing parameter of 100.

Why is productivity growth in Europe and Japan slowing? One key rea- 6
son is that these countries are nearing the end of a "catch-up" phase, after
largely closing the technological gap with the United States, the country
whose production efficiency defines the world's technology frontier.
Economic theory predicts that economies very far from the frontier with
low productivity levels will experience relatively strong productivity growth
for two reasons. First, when levels of capital per worker are low, capital is
relatively productive, so it has a high marginal product and makes a substantial contribution to labor productivity growth. Second, firms have
the ability to imitate the latest technologies and production processes to
which they are exposed through foreign direct investment or collaborative
ventures. As economies approach the frontier and productivity levels rise,
however, the marginal product of capital falls, imitation becomes harder,
and achieving relatively fast productivity growth rates proves increasingly
difficult.[4] This progression toward the technology frontier helps explain why
productivity growth in the 1990s in Europe and Japan was much slower
relative to the United States than it was during the 1960s.

A second reason for slower productivity growth in Europe is that the 7
labor and product market frictions that characterize many European

---

[4]Economists refer to this phenomenon as "convergence"; there is a large literature on other
factors that may contribute to or hinder the catch-up process.

Paragraph 8 introduces another reason why productivity growth in Europe has lagged behind America's. The last sentence summarizes not only this paragraph's content but the content of preceding paragraphs as well. Note how clearly and carefully this section of the report—indeed, the report as a whole—is organized.

In paragraph 9, the authors present one more example of America's productivity growth compared with Europe's. The paragraph is a summary of a 2007 study that illustrates how growth in the service industry in America has superseded that of Europe and goes on to explain why this is so. Note that this paper does not have a separate literature review section, as some business and social science papers do. Instead, relevant studies are reviewed in this paper in the context of the argument the authors are making at the time.

Paragraphs 10 through 15   These paragraphs form a section of the essay, under the title "Productivity Trends in the United States and Emerging Markets." Note that this paper combines the compare/contrast and the persuasive rhetorical modes. The authors are comparing and contrasting productivity in the United States with productivity in European and emerging markets. At the same time, they are arguing that the growth in emerging markets has both benefits and drawbacks for the American consumer.

Paragraph 10 begins with the words "We now compare," signaling a main shift in focus. The authors identify the other countries whose productivity they will compare with America's.

economies may have become more binding. In a recent report on European policy reforms, the Organisation for Economic Co-operation and Development (OECD 2006) highlighted a number of these frictions: barriers to entry in product markets and other regulations that inhibit competition, administrative burdens on new business formation, widespread public ownership, restricted foreign direct investment, limited financing structures for research and development, weak protection of intellectual property, excess regulation of the financial sector, and agricultural supports.

While these types of labor and product rigidities have long been a feature   8
of many European economies, recent research summarized by Aghion and Howitt (2006) suggests that it is the interaction between an economy's place in the catch-up process, its use of new technologies, and the flexibility of its markets that determines how fast its productivity will grow relative to the frontier. At low levels of productivity, the positive catch-up effects dominate, and countries may grow fast relative to the frontier. Closer to the frontier, however, market rigidities become more of a constraint, reducing the economy's ability to innovate, make technological advances, and reallocate resources efficiently. In sum, market rigidities and institutional factors are more of a detriment to productivity growth for those countries that have achieved relatively high levels of productivity and are near the technological frontier.

There is considerable evidence, for example, that European economies   9
have been less able to benefit from the information technology revolution since the mid-1990s. For example, one recent study (Inklaar, Timmer, and van Ark 2007) compares the growth rate of total factor productivity (TFP), a common measure of the overall efficiency of production (see box), in the service industries of major European economies and the United States. The performance of service industries in this respect is particularly revealing because they are intensive users of IT and, in the United States, have played a key role in the recent resurgence of productivity growth.[5] The study shows a stark divergence in TFP growth in the service industries of these countries, with slow growth in European services and much faster growth in the United States. The authors find no single factor, such as product market regulation, that would explain this divergence, but suggest that the difference in performance is linked to organizational structure, management, and workplace practices.

PRODUCTIVITY TRENDS IN THE UNITED STATES AND EMERGING MARKETS

We now compare U.S. productivity growth with productivity growth in several   10
large emerging markets—Brazil, China, India, Indonesia, Mexico, Russia, and South Korea. We chose these economies because they were the largest in terms

[5]See Bosworth and Triplett (2007).

Charts and Highlight Box   In its original form, this article contains three charts and one highlight box. Charts, graphs, tables, and boxes are common in business articles. They lend visual support to the points the authors are making and help readers understand the context and the content of the article. They also add authority to business writing.

Chart 1, Trend Labor Productivity Growth, is included in this text. Note that it provides clear visual proof of the changes in productivity among the three economies—American, Japanese, and European—that the authors compare. Note that the source of the chart is listed right below the chart itself and below that is a note defining the key term "labor productivity."

In paragraph 11, the authors offer one reason why growth in some emerging economies has been so high.

In paragraph 12, they admit that explaining why productivity growth in some countries is higher than in others is an inexact science.

Comparing Productivity Across Countries

International comparisons of productivity growth are notoriously difficult to make because of differences in the way countries construct official measures of output, the need to convert currencies into common units, and the paucity of detailed labor market data, particularly for developing countries. Given the critical importance of productivity in understanding economic growth across countries, however, economists spend considerable resources developing productivity estimates that are as comparable as possible.

In our analysis, we rely primarily on data constructed jointly by the Conference Board and the Groningen Growth and Development Centre.[a] The data provide comparable measures of labor productivity for a wide range of countries that produce virtually all of world output. The underlying sources for the data are country national accounts, surveys, and labor market indicators.[b]

Our primary measure of productivity is labor productivity, defined as output per hour worked. Output is measured as real GDP, converted into 1990 U.S. dollars using the Gheary-Khamis purchasing power parities to adjust for differences in relative prices. Because comparable data on hours worked do not exist for all countries, however, we also use output per total employment as a measure of labor productivity when examining a broader range

of market size in 2006. Our measure of productivity growth is growth in GDP per employee for the 1995–2005 period.[6] China experienced spectacular productivity growth of 6.4 percent, while South Korea, Russia, and India saw growth rates above 3.0 percent per year. These rates are all considerably faster than the 2.0 percent growth rate in the United States over the same period. Nevertheless, not all emerging markets outpaced U.S. growth rates; Indonesia, Brazil, and Mexico showed slower growth.

Given the importance of an economy's place in the catch-up process, it is not surprising that some of these emerging market economies are experiencing strong productivity growth, because they are still at the beginning of their catch-up phase and have ample high-return investment opportunities and scope for technological advance. Indeed, these countries lag far behind the United States in productivity levels. For example, GDP per worker in China was only 15 percent of that in the United States in 2005. In the same year, South Korea posted the highest productivity level of any of the emerging countries in the sample, but its GDP per worker was just 58 percent of the U.S. level.

Because the factors that determine productivity growth interact in complex ways, it is not possible to isolate any one factor that leads some emerging markets to grow rapidly while others lag behind. For example, although Brazil has undergone major episodes of

11

12

---

[6]Because we do not have data on total hours worked in these countries, we use total employment to construct the labor productivity estimates.

In paragraph 13, they announce their intention to focus on productivity growth in two economies—those of China and India—that have shown impressive growth.

Paragraph 14 belongs to China. Note how the authors support their topic sentence. They give three reasons why growth in labor productivity in China has been so high.

Paragraph 15 belongs to India. The authors note that outsourcing has spurred growth in the Indian economy.

(Continued)

of emerging market economies. Labor productivity reflects all of the factors that allow a worker to produce more output, including access to more or better capital and improved technology.

A second productivity concept, also used in our analysis, is total factor productivity, defined as output per all units of input. Total factor productivity growth is often viewed as a measure of efficiency gains or technological progress and reflects the ability to produce more output from the same set of inputs. The production process is complicated, however, and measured total factor productivity growth also includes the impact of any measurement error or omitted inputs such as intangible capital.

[a]The Conference Board and Groningen Growth and Development Centre, Total Economy Database, January 2007, <http://www.ggdc.net>.
[b]Methodological details and information on the sources are available from the Groningen Centre's website, <http://www.ggdc.net>.

trade liberalization, which often spurs productivity growth, it has more rigid labor markets than China and some other countries in the sample—a feature that may have prevented it from reallocating resources to more efficient uses (Aquino Menezes Filho and Muendler 2007).

Nonetheless, it is useful to review 13 what is known about the sources of productivity growth in China and India, two of the largest and most discussed countries. While the data for these countries are far from perfect, Bosworth and Collins (2007) have investigated these factors and concluded that both capital accumulation and increased efficiency played an important role in the recent strength of productivity growth.

The authors' estimates for China 14 suggest that about half of its growth in labor productivity over the last decade can be traced to capital deepening (rapid investment that provides more physical capital to workers) and half to increased efficiency in the use of inputs (measured as TFP growth). Government policies have helped increase productivity growth in China where, for example, many industries have been privatized (OECD 2005). In addition, trade has been liberalized with China's entry into the World Trade Organization in 2001, rules on inflows of foreign direct investment have been relaxed, and labor mobility out of agriculture and into industry has risen as restrictions have been lifted.

For India, Bosworth and Collins estimate that total factor productivity 15 has accounted for roughly 60 percent of the country's aggregate labor productivity growth—an experience similar to that of China. Many observers, however, have focused on India's service industry, particularly that part of the industry related to outsourcing technology and support services, and there are substantial differences with China. Bosworth and Collins estimate that TFP growth in service industries averaged 3.9 percent for 1993–2004 in India—a far higher growth rate than the 0.9 percent rate for China. In the primary

Paragraphs 16 through 26   These paragraphs form a section of the essay called
"Foreign Productivity Growth and the U.S. Economy." This section contains
four subsections—Consumers, Exporters, Import-Competing Firms, and Labor.
Organizational structures like this one are more common in business and social
science articles than they are in humanities articles.

Paragraph 16 begins with a question that applies to this entire section. Then the
authors begin to provide general answers to the question.

Paragraph 17 continues to answer the question, as the transitional phrase
"In addition" suggests. The issue of outsourcing, touched on in paragraph 15, is
explained in more detail here.

In paragraph 18, the authors announce that they will discuss in more detail the
effects on the American economy of foreign productivity growth. In other words,
they introduce this section's four subsections.

sectors (agriculture, forestry, and fishing) and in manufacturing, however, both labor productivity growth and TFP growth were weaker in India than in China.[7] Despite differences in the sectors where the booms in efficiency are taking place, both India and China are experiencing much faster productivity growth than the United States.

FOREIGN PRODUCTIVITY GROWTH AND THE U.S. ECONOMY

How does strong productivity growth abroad affect the U.S. economy?   16
In general, rapid foreign productivity growth, by reducing the price of foreign goods, has the direct effect of increasing the competition faced by U.S. producers at home and abroad and benefiting U.S. consumers. Of course, increased foreign competition could equally result from a reduction in international trade costs stemming from, say, lower U.S. import tariffs or lower shipping costs. However, U.S. tariffs have been low for the last couple of decades, so reductions in trade costs are unlikely to be the source of increased foreign competition over this period.

In addition to its direct effects, strong foreign productivity growth may   17
have indirect effects on the U.S economy by hastening the adoption of new technologies by U.S. firms and encouraging the creation of global production networks—outcomes that may increase U.S. productivity. For example, U.S. firms are purchasing an increasing share of intermediate material and services inputs from abroad, a practice that is commonly referred to as international outsourcing. As firms relocate the relatively inefficient stages of their production processes to countries where those stages can be carried out more cheaply, they are better positioned to expand their domestic output in stages where they have a comparative advantage, and thus they increase their productivity. Furthermore, the productivity of the remaining workers is also likely to improve because the imports of new services may enable firms to restructure their operations and activities (Amiti and Wei 2006).

Below, we discuss in more detail the individual channels through   18
which foreign productivity growth can potentially affect the U.S. economy. Throughout the discussion, we highlight the complex linkages between these channels and various parts of the economy. After reviewing the evidence, we conclude that it is not particularly useful to think about foreign productivity growth as having a single impact on the U.S. economy as a whole. Rather, one should consider the impact from a number of perspectives—those of the consumer, worker, and firm, for example—all of which can be affected in different ways and through different mechanisms.

---

[7]India did enjoy high productivity growth in its manufacturing sector—a fact that has been partly attributed to the country's trade reforms in the early 1990s. Tariffs, for example, fell from an average of 80 percent in 1990 to 37 percent in 2001 (Topalova 2004).

Paragraphs 19 and 20 discuss how consumers will be affected by strong productivity growth abroad. Paragraph 19 references lower prices, and 20, greater variety.

Paragraph 21 discusses the effects on U.S. exporters. Note the structure of this paragraph. It begins by citing benefits to exporters. Then, just past the paragraph's halfway point, the word "however" signals a shift to negative effects—the erosion in market share caused by increased competition.

Consumers

U.S. consumers should gain from strong productivity growth abroad   19
primarily through lower import prices.[8] For example, prices for imported
goods from the newly industrialized countries (NICs) of Asia—a group that
includes Hong Kong, Singapore, South Korea, and Taiwan—fell 2.4 percent
per year from 1993 to 2006, compared with a 0.3 percent rise in price for
total non-oil imports into the United States.[9] Although this evidence is
consistent with foreign productivity gains being passed through to lower
prices, to date there is no rigorous evidence establishing this link.[10]

There could also be gains to consumers arising from more product varieties.   20
The number of different products imported into the United States increased
by 40 percent in the 1990s, with China accounting for 6 percent of this growth
(Broda and Weinstein 2006).[11] Finally, Schott (2004) shows that countries with
higher GDP per capita tend to produce higher quality goods, another boon for
U.S. consumers. All of these effects are positive developments for U.S. consumers,
who now enjoy access to a broader range of consumer goods at lower prices.

Exporters

The net impact of strong foreign productivity gains on U.S. exporters is less   21
clear. U.S. exporters are likely to benefit as fast productivity growth raises
incomes abroad and increases demand for U.S. exports. For example, the
share of exports to China from the United States increased from 2 percent
in 1995 to 5.5 percent in 2005.[12] U.S. exporters can also benefit from access
to relatively cheap intermediate inputs that are produced abroad—semi-
conductors being a notable example. Strong productivity growth abroad,
however, also has the potential to erode the market share of U.S. exporters
in foreign countries as they are faced with increased competition. Given the
relatively low productivity levels of emerging markets and the small overlap
between the products of U.S. exporters and those of emerging market firms,
however, it seems unlikely that this latter effect would dominate.

---

[8]If the foreign productivity gains occur in industries where the United States imports,
consumers will directly benefit from lower prices; however, if the productivity gains occur in
industries where the United States exports, there will be no effect on U.S. consumer prices unless
the gains are strong enough to induce the United States to begin importing those goods.

[9]The Bureau of Labor Statistics began constructing import price indexes by country of origin
in 1993 (see <http://www.bls.gov/mxp/>). Data on imports from China are available beginning in
2003 and show price trends similar to those for the Asian NICs.

[10]Some or all of the foreign productivity growth may be retained as profits or passed on to
workers in the form of higher wages. This dynamic is the subject of ongoing research. Of course,
lower import prices may arise from factors other than increased productivity growth.

[11]A new variety is generally defined as a product that is being imported from a particular
foreign country for the first time. While widely used, this measure may overstate product variety if
the United States begins to import identical products from many countries.

[12]The data are from the U.S. Bureau of the Census, Foreign Trade Division.

Paragraph 22 covers the effects on import-competing firms, as its heading indicates. The cheaper imports threaten the future of businesses that market the same product.

In paragraph 23, the authors cite a study that supports the contention presented in the previous paragraph.

In paragraph 24, the authors cite literature indicating that plants will be more likely to close if their products are the same as products made at lower cost in other countries. The authors use precise facts and figures from these studies to support their topic sentence.

Paragraph 25 is the first of two in the subsection discussing labor. Facts and figures from a government study indicate bad news for American workers in firms that compete with foreign firms making the same product.

Import-Competing Firms

Gains in foreign productivity relative to U.S. productivity should improve   22
the ability of foreign firms to produce at lower prices and to compete inter-
nationally. Such an outcome would directly affect the U.S. firms whose
products are in competition with imports from foreign countries. These
import-competing firms will either have to become more efficient or be
forced out of the market.

Bernard, Jensen, and Schott (2006) show that U.S. manufacturing indus-   23
tries that face more low-wage competition (defined as imports from countries
with less than 5 percent of U.S. GDP per capita) have incurred the largest
employment losses over the last three decades. In these industries, including
leather, textiles, and apparel, each 10 percentage point increase in import share
for low-wage countries is associated with a 1.3 percent fall in employment
growth for a U.S. plant. In contrast, industries that do not face direct competition from low-wage countries, such as instruments and plastics, have experienced employment growth over this period. If these low-wage countries are
also experiencing relatively strong productivity growth, then one would expect
the import-competing industries in the United States to feel the biggest impact.

Increased competition from low-wage countries also leads to more plant   24
closures in the import-competing industries. According to Bernard, Jensen, and
Schott (2004, 2006), the probability of a plant shutting down increases by 13
percent with a 10 percentage point increase in low-wage competition. Not all of
these plants disappear, however; some change their product mix to make goods
that are not in direct competition with imports from low-wage countries.

Labor

Strong foreign productivity growth has heterogeneous effects on U.S.   25
workers. Drawing on a displaced worker survey by the Bureau of Labor
Statistics for the 1984–2000 period,[13] Kletzer (2001) finds that 37 percent of
displaced workers in import-competing industries were not reemployed at
the time of the survey and 25 percent took longer than six months to find
new employment.[14] Even among those able to find new employment, however, the effects varied widely—average earnings were 13 percent lower than
in the original job, with 40 percent of the reemployed respondents showing
income declines and 23 percent showing income gains.

[13]See <http://stats.bls.gov/news.release/disp.nr0.htm>.

[14]In each survey, adults (twenty years and older) were asked if they had lost a job in the preceding three to five years because of a plant closing, an employer going out of business, or a layoff
from which they were not recalled. (Note that individuals were only surveyed once.) In Kletzer, all
workers displaced from a high-import-competing industry were treated as if they had lost their jobs
because of increased imports from low-wage countries, although they could have lost their jobs for
other reasons, such as automation. We are unaware of any evidence on whether the subsequent
employment and earnings experience of displaced workers varies with the reason for their job loss.

Paragraph 26 explains how outsourcing—a recurring topic in this article—is affecting American labor. It increases the wages of skilled workers but eliminates jobs for unskilled workers.

Paragraphs 27 through 29   These paragraphs form the conclusion to this article. One function of a conclusion is to summarize the content of the paper; paragraph 27 does this efficiently and effectively.

Sometimes a conclusion will speculate on the broader implications of the article's findings, and paragraph 28 begins to do this. Here the authors talk about the possible effects of import tariffs, which may be imposed to help American firms compete, on other segments of the economy.

Paragraph 29 continues to speculate on the broader implications of the article's content. Soon, the authors hypothesize, the emerging economies of China and India might manufacture more products that compete with goods made by U.S. companies. But the article ends on an upbeat note: Such competition will spur American companies to continue being innovative.

With heightened foreign competition, incentives to outsource produc-   26
tion and pressure to adopt new technologies increase. These developments
have also had large impacts on labor markets by shifting demand away from
unskilled workers toward skilled workers. Feenstra and Hanson (1999)
found that 25 percent of the increase in the wages of skilled relative to
unskilled workers can be explained by outsourcing and 30 percent by the
growing use of high-tech capital.[15] Outsourcing, by increasing productivity,
also increased the real wage of skilled workers by 1 to 2 percent per year
during the 1990s while having no significant effect for unskilled workers.

CONCLUSION

Productivity growth is the engine of economic growth, and the rapid gains   27
in many foreign countries, particularly large emerging economies such as
China and India, will produce significant benefits for these countries. In the
United States, however, strong foreign productivity growth will likely have
mixed effects, with some winners and some losers. Consumers are likely to
gain from lower import prices and more varieties of imports, for example,
while U.S. firms and workers in direct competition with emerging economies
are likely to experience potentially painful disruptions and reallocations.

These diverse effects of strong foreign productivity growth raise   28
important policy questions. Whenever a particular portion of the economy
disproportionately bears the adverse impact of heightened competition, a
common reaction is to call for increased support and protectionism for that
particular sector. While the disruptions and losses brought about by foreign
competition are real, policymakers should consider the full range of costs
and benefits when evaluating such proposals. For example, levying import
tariffs on inputs such as paper or steel can help U.S. producers that compete
in those markets, but will hurt the U.S. producers that use these goods in
making other products, as well as U.S. consumers who are effectively denied
the benefits of lower cost products.

Another key issue concerns the outlook for the United States as it con-   29
tinues to face increased competitive pressures from large emerging economies. Although China's GDP per worker grew at a spectacular rate over the
last decade, its level of productivity remains low, only 15 percent of that in
the United States. Moreover, the set of goods that China exports are quite
different from those produced in developed countries,[16] suggesting that

---

[15]Of course, firms also adopt new technologies for reasons other than strong productivity
growth abroad.

[16]Schott (forthcoming) shows that the products exported by China are more like those
exported from other Asian countries than those produced by the OECD nations and other
developed countries.

Footnotes and References   This article contains sixteen footnotes and twenty references. The article presents an argument on a controversial topic, and its notes and references add authority to the argument.

This article uses the Chicago Manual of Style method for footnotes and references.

direct competition from China has been limited to a subset of industries. Nevertheless, as China and other emerging market economies continue to grow, such differences with the United States are likely to diminish. In that event, strong competitive pressures from abroad will prompt U.S. firms to develop new and more advanced production techniques that will further push out the world technology frontier.

REFERENCES

Aghion, Philippe, and Peter Howitt. 2006. "Appropriate Growth Policy: A Unifying Framework," Joseph Schumpeter Lecture. *Journal of the European Economic Association* 4, no. 2–3 (April–May): 269–314. Papers and Proceedings of the 20th Annual Congress of the European Economic Association.

Amiti, Mary, and Shang-Jin Wei. 2006. "Service Offshoring and Productivity: Evidence from the United States." NBER Working Paper no. 11926, January.

Aquino Menezes Filho, Naércio, and Marc Muendler. 2007."Labor Reallocation in Response to Trade Reform." Unpublished paper.

Baily, Martin N. 2002. "The New Economy: Post Mortem or Second Wind?" *Journal of Economic Perspectives* 16, no. 2 (spring): 3–22.

Bernard, Andrew B., J. Bradford Jensen, and Peter K. Schott. 2004. "Facing the Dragon: Prospects for U.S. Manufactures in the Coming Decade." Unpublished paper, May.

———. 2006. "Survival of the Fit: Exposure to Low-Wage Countries and the (Uneven) Growth of U.S. Manufacturing Plants." *Journal of International Economics* 68, no. 1 (January): 219–37.

Bosworth, Barry, and Susan M. Collins. 2007. "Accounting for Growth: Comparing China and India." NBER Working Paper no. 12943, February.

Bosworth, Barry, and Jack E. Triplett. 2007."The Early 21st Century Productivity Expansion Is Still in Services." *International Productivity Monitor*, no. 14 (spring): 3–19.

Broda, Christian, and David Weinstein. 2006."Globalization and the Gains from Variety." *Quarterly Journal of Economics* 121, no. 2 (May): 541–85.

Feenstra, Robert C., and Gordon H. Hanson. 1999."The Impact of Outsourcing and High-Technology Capital on Wages: Estimates for the United States, 1979–1990." *Quarterly Journal of Economics* 114, no. 3 (August): 907–40.

Gómez-Salvador, Ramón, Alberto Musso, Marc Stocker, and Jarkko Turunen. 2006."Labor Productivity Developments in the EuroArea." European Central Bank Occasional Paper Series, no. 53, October.

Inklaar, Robert, Marcel P. Timmer, and Bart van Ark. 2007. "The End of Convergence: Market Services Productivity in Europe." Unpublished paper, University of Groningen, March.

Jorgenson, Dale W., Mun S. Ho, and Kevin J. Stiroh. 2007."A Retrospective Look at the U.S. Productivity Growth Resurgence." Federal Reserve Bank of New York *Staff Reports*, no. 277, February.

Kletzer, Lori G. 2001. *Job Loss from Imports: Measuring the Costs*. Washington, D.C.: Peterson Institute for International Economics.

Organisation for Economic Co-operation and Development (OECD). 2005. *Economic Surveys: China, 2005*, vol. 2005/13, September.

———. 2006. *Economic Policy Reforms: Going for Growth, 2006*. Paris.

Schott, Peter. 2004. "Across-Product versus Within-Product Specialization in International Trade." *Quarterly Journal of Economics* 119, no. 2 (May): 647–78.

———. Forthcoming. "The Relative Sophistication of Chinese Exports." *Economic Policy*.

Topalova, Petia. 2004."Trade Liberalization and Firm Productivity: The Case of India." IMF Working Paper no. WP/04/28, February.

van Ark, Bart, and Gail Fosler. 2007. "Is ICT's Contribution to Productivity Growth Peaking?" Conference Board Executive Action Series, no. 224, January.

Abstract   This is a social science essay, using APA format, so it begins with an abstract, summarizing the findings of the study. At about 110 words, this abstract is typical of the length of abstracts in social science papers.

Paragraphs 1 through 15   The first fifteen paragraphs form the article's literature review. Taking up about half the study, the lit review is longer in this article than in similar social science studies.

The first paragraph comments on the very long history of tattooing.

The second paragraph talks about the history of piercing, which is not mentioned in the title but is referenced in the first sentence of the abstract. The authors connect tattooing and body piercing as types of body art but note that tattooing is more frequently studied.

This article is from *College Student Journal*, Volume 41, Issue 4, Part B (December 2007).

Getting Inked: Tattoos and College Students

Laura Manuel, Metropolitan State College, and
Eugene P. Sheehan, University of Northern Colorado

This study explores whether college students with tattoos or piercings demonstrate extreme personalities and behaviors. Participants were 46 men and 164 women (mean = 20.0 years). Questions assessed participants' attitudes toward tattooing, presence of a tattoo, and participation in risk taking behaviors. Participants completed the Personality Research Form (PRF) Form E (Jackson, 1984). Those with tattoos scored higher in autonomy (mean = 9.96) than those without tattoos (mean = 5.55). Women with tattoos scored higher on impulsivity (p = .04). Men with piercings were significantly higher on exhibitionism (p = .02) and sentience (p = .04), and significantly lower on harm avoidance (p = .05). Women with piercings were significantly higher on social recognition (p = .04). Those with and without tattoos reported similar attitudes toward tattoos and levels of risk taking behavior.

Tattooing had a long history even prior to the discovery of a tattooed man [1] embedded in ice, a find that suggested the practice occurred circa 3300 B.C. (Rademackers & Schoenthal, 1992). Prior to that discovery, it was thought that tattooing was primarily an ancient Egyptian practice dating from circa 2000 B.C. (Nadler, 1983). Tattooing was brought to the New World in 1769 by sailors returning from voyages to the South Pacific (Post, 1968; Sanders, 1991). Although the association with sailors has never completely dissipated (Armstrong, Murphy, Sallee & Watson, 2000; Mallon & Russell, 1999; Sanders, 1991; Yamamoto, Seeman, & Boyd, 1963), the practice of tattooing became more widespread and occasionally socially acceptable in the Western world after that time (Sanders, 1991). Tattooing enjoyed a brief period of popularity in the late 19th Century in England, and in the United States in the 1920s (Sanders, 1991). It later began to be relegated to the socially marginal (Armstrong, 1991; Fox, 1976; Post, 1968; Sanders, 1991).

Piercing has almost as long a history as tattooing, having been practiced [2] by Egyptian pharaohs, Mayans, and Roman centurions (Armstrong, 1996). Body piercing is sometimes studied along with tattooing, partly because people with tattoos often have piercings (Buhrich, 1983; Frederick & Bradley, 2000). Piercing, particularly in adolescents, is usually done in tattoo parlors (Armstrong, 1996) or is self-inflicted (Martin, 1997). For women, ear piercing has come to be viewed as a mainstream practice

The third paragraph notes the connection between tattoos and deviant behavior, an important theme in this study. Note how thoroughly sourced this paragraph and the preceding two are. In the first sentence alone, the authors cite eleven sources, an unusually high number. In the list of references, forty-six sources are cited.

Paragraph 4 continues to cite many sources noting the correlation between tattooing and deviant behavior.

but piercing eyebrows, nose, cheeks, or other areas appears to symbolize one's disaffection from society, much like tattooing (Sanders, 1988). Body piercing other than the earlobe has been associated with the gay subculture (Buhrich, 1983). Researchers in one recent study found that the younger individuals begin piercing the more likely they are to exhibit antisocial tendencies (Frederick & Bradley, 2000). However, piercing is generally regarded as less extreme than tattooing because removing the body jewelry will ordinarily cause the pierced hole to heal (Armstrong, 1996). This may explain why this practice of body alteration has been only briefly mentioned in the literature and rarely studied in its own right.

Tattoos have been empirically associated with several deviant behaviors   3 (Braithwaite, Stephens, Bowman, Milton, & Braithwaite, 1998; Buhrich, 1983; Ceniceros, 1998; Drews, Allison, & Probst, 2000; Raspa & Cusack, 1990; Verberne, 1969) and criminality (Fox, 1976; Mallon & Russell, 1999; Post, 1968; Taylor, 1970; Yamamoto et al., 1963). Research on tattoos has documented a strong relationship between people with tattoos and antisocial personalities (Post, 1968; Raspa & Cusack, 1990; Taylor, 1968) or actual criminal conduct (Fox, 1976; Measey, 1972; Roc, Howell, & Payne, 1974; Taylor, 1968; Taylor, 1970). For example, studies have documented that more heavily tattooed Naval detainees were more likely to have a previous naval or civilian offense (Measey, 1972). Taylor (1968) found that among delinquent girls incarcerated in juvenile facilities, the more heavily tattooed were more aggressive, uncooperative, and unstable in addition to being more criminal in their attitude and behavior. Female prison inmates with tattoos were more likely to have been in all four types of institutions— juvenile halls, reformatories, jails, and prisons (Fox, 1976).

In a later study, Taylor (1970) attempted to obtain a control group to   4 match his incarcerated girls, 55% of whom were tattooed, but failed because "there was only 1 tattooed woman non-offender available of any age" (p. 88). Tattooed women prisoners had more violent and aggressive offenses in addition to more prior convictions (Taylor, 1970). While in prison, women with tattoos were more frequently charged with violation of prison rules, with fighting, and with insubordination (Fox, 1976). In research involving college student respondents, males with tattoos were more likely to report having been arrested and females with tattoos were more likely to report shoplifting (Drews et al., 2000). Tattooed people have been found to be more likely to engage in substance abuse (Braithwaite et al., 1998; Ceniceros, 1998; Drews et al., 2000; Dhossche, Snell, & Larder, 1999; Raspa and Cusack, 1990) and risk taking behaviors (Armstrong, 1991; Ceniceros, 1998; Grief, Hewitt, & Armstrong, 1999). In a study of people who played Russian roulette, there was a strong correlation between this form of risk taking and the kind and quantity of the person's tattoos and body piercings

Paragraph 5 notes the connection between tattooing and homosexuality. Note how the studies the authors cite are sometimes contradictory. Contradictory findings in studies with similar hypotheses are not unusual in the social sciences.

Again, in paragraph 6, contradictory studies of the correlation between tattooing and certain sexual proclivities are cited.

Paragraph 7 links tattooing with mental illness.

Paragraph 8 summarizes a study that speculates on the possibility of a link between tattooing and suicide.

(Ceniceros, 1998). As the severity of the tattoos and piercings increased, all forms of violent behavior increased (Ceniceros, 1998).

Prior studies have reported strong associations between tattoos and 5 homosexual orientation for both males (Buhrich, 1983), and females (Fox, 1976; Taylor, 1970). However, Grief et al. (1999) reported that 87% of their tattooed college student respondents claimed a heterosexual orientation; less than 1% reported a homosexual preference. Grief et al.'s study consisted of college students from 18 universities, 69% of the participants were 18–22 years old. In that study, 24% of the respondents with tattoos reported having 6 to 10 sexual partners and 26% reported having more than 11 partners. In the National Health and Social Life Survey (NHSLS) 15% of the participants 18–24 had 5 to 10 sex partners and 11% had more than 10 since age 18 (Michael, Gagnon, Laumann, & Kolata, 1994). Although the two studies are obviously not directly comparable, it would appear that tattooed respondents in the Grief study were above national averages for the number of sexual partners.

A less stable heterosexual adjustment has also been found in several 6 studies (Taylor, 1968; Yamamoto et al., 1963). Grief et al. (1999) found that 12% of college respondents reported engaging in bisexual activity. Buhrich (1983) also found a strong association between tattooing and sexual sado-machism, bondage, or fetishism. However, in a recent study of young adults who were mostly college students, only 3% of tattooers or piercers reported engaging in sadomasochistic activities (Frederick & Bradley, 2000).

The association of tattoos with mental illness has been frequently inves- 7 tigated. Tattooing has been empirically associated with personality disorders (Armstrong, 1991; Caplan, Komaroni, & Rhodes, 1996; Ceniceros, 1998; Measey, 1972; Post, 1968) and psychopathic personality (McKerracher & Watson, 1969; Yamamoto et al., 1963). In Measey's (1972) study of Royal Navy detainees, the correlation with personality disorder increased in significance with the number of tattoos possessed; 48% of those with no tattoos had a personality disorder whereas the percentage increased to 58% for those with 1 to 4 tattoos and up to 82% for those with more than 16 tattoos. Raspa and Cusack (1990) found the association between personality disorders and tattoos so clear that they state "finding a tattoo on physical examination should alert the physician to the possibility of an underlying psychiatric condition" (p. 1481).

One recent study linked the practice of tattooing and suicide (Dhossche 8 et al., 1999). Suicides and accidental deaths were matched in a 3-year case-control study and it was found that 57% of the young suicides were tattooed compared to 29% of the accidental deaths. The researchers con-cluded that tattoos may be possible markers for lethality from both suicide and accidental death due to the correlations with substance abuse and personality dysfunction (Dhossche et al., 1999).

Paragraph 9 links tattooing to a predilection for nonconformity.

Paragraph 10 marks a slight shift in focus. After reviewing substantial literature indicating a connection between tattooing and various antisocial behaviors, the authors note that tattooing is gaining popularity.

Paragraph 11 confirms again that tattoos are common among criminals and patients in mental institutions but notes, as well, that military personnel and professional basketball players are much more likely than members of the general public to be tattooed.

Paragraph 12 notes the rise in tattooing among women.

Paragraph 13 cites national surveys that suggest tattooing is most prevalent among 15–25 year olds. After going back and forth between information that suggests a connection between tattooing and various forms of nonconformity and information that suggests tattooing is or is becoming more mainstream, the authors, in paragraph 14, begin to approach the purpose of their study. Has the tattoo culture changed? Is it becoming more mainstream?

The literature review finished, paragraph 15 brings the reader to the purpose of the study, expressed as questions that the data the authors have gathered will answer: Are today's college students with tattoos and piercings likelier than their counterparts without tattoos and piercings to be more extreme in their personalities and behavior?

Sanders (1988) has described tattoos as "marks of dissaffliation"   9
with society which become "voluntary stigma" for the bearers, marking
their owners as being apart from the mainstream culture. People obtaining tattoos are usually aware of this attribute of tattoos and often state
that they obtained the tattoo in order to feel unique (Armstrong, 1991;
Sanders, 1988; DeMello, 1995; Phelan & Hunt, 1998), mark their independence (Armstrong, 1991; Sanders, 1991), or as a sign of special affiliation
(Armstrong et al., 2000; Measey, 1972; Phelan & Hunt, 1998).

Although tattoos remain negatively regarded by the public (Armstrong,   10
1991; Armstrong et al., 2000; Hawkins & Popplestone, 1964) and are pro-
scribed by most mainstream religions (Post, 1968; Raspa & Cusack, 1990;
Taylor, 1968), it is clear that the popularity of obtaining a tattoo, known as
'getting inked' (Mason, 1991), is rising again (Houghton Durkin, & Carroll
1995; Inch & Huws, 1993; Mallon & Russell, 1999; Mason, 1991). The city
council of New York was recently persuaded to lift a 37-year ban on tattoo
parlors within the city (Kennedy, 1997). Tattoo parlors are the fifth largest
growth business in the United States (Armsrong & Fell, 2000; Vail, 1999). It
was estimated that there were about 300 tattoo parlors in the United States
in the early 1970s compared to about 4,000 in 1991 (Mason, 1991).

The practice remains common among servicemen (Armstrong et al.,   11
2000; Mallon & Russell, 1999), so common, in fact, that the Marine Corp
was forced to codify rules on what tattoos recruits may have ("Taboo
Tattoos" 1996). Tattooing is also clearly more popular among certain
groups, such as the National Basketball Association. Thirty-five percent of
the members have tatoos (Ewey, 1998; Mallon & Russell, 1999). Additionally,
it is generally agreed that the practice of tattooing is more widespread among
prison populations (Fox, 1976, DiFrancesco, 1990; Houghton, Durkin,
Parry, Turbett, & Odgers, 1996; Mallon & Russell, 1999; Taylor, 1968) and
people in mental health institutions (Raspa & Cusak, 1990).

Perhaps the population with the most dramatic increase in tatooing   12
is that of women (Armstrong, 1991; DeMello, 1995; Inch & Huws, 1993;
Nadler, 1983; Sanders, 1991). In the past 20 years, the number of women
getting tattooed has quadrupled (Nadler, 1983). It is estimated that 40–50%
of the clients in tattoo parlors are women (Armstrong, 1991; Sanders, 1991).

Estimates for the prevalence of tattooing itself have varied from a low   13
of 3% in a random national survey conducted in 1990 (Armstrong & Fell,
2000) to 25% of people 15–25 years old (Armstrong et al., 2000). The
Alliance of Professional Tattooists estimates that 15–20% of teenagers are
tattooed (Braithwaite et al., 1998). Nationwide estimates vary from 7 million
people to 20 million people with tattoos (Grief et al., 1999; Martin, Dogen,
Colin, Annin, & Gegax 1995).

Paragraphs 16 through 19   Paragraphs 16 through 19 form the "Method" section of————
the report.

Paragraph 16 is the "Participants" subsection of the "Method" section. The affiliation of the participants is simply indicated as "a western university." Such anonymity is typical of a social science report, though the specific university can sometimes be identified if the author's employer is identified.

Paragraph 17 is the first of two in the "Measures" subsection. The authors indicate that they created a questionnaire to find out the information they needed to undertake their study. Questionnaires are widely used in social science studies, and they must be carefully designed. Sometimes the authors will include their questionnaire as an appendix to their report, but these authors do not.

Paragraph 18 indicates that the researchers also used a questionnaire—the Personality Research Form—designed by a psychological testing agency. The authors describe the questionnaire carefully to establish its validity and reliability.

Paragraph 19 constitutes the brief "Procedure" subsection of the "Method" section. It tells us who filled out the questionnaires and how, if at all, they were rewarded for their participation.

Some researchers argue that the trend in tattooing and piercing indi-   14
cates a shift in fashion and a break with body art's exclusive association
with lower class people and deviant activities (DeMello, 1995; Ewey, 1998;
Martin, 1997). In this argument, the concept that tattoos or piercings are a
form of self-mutilation or a way of expressing a negative attitude is rejected
(Frederick & Bradley, 2000; Martin, 1997). However, little evidence has been
presented to demonstrate that the association between tattooing and various
negative behaviors or personality disorders was unjustified in the past or has
changed in the current culture.

In this study, we asked two research questions. Research question #1:   15
Are college students who have tattoos more extreme in their personalities
and behavior? Research question #2: Are college students with piercings
more extreme in their personalities and behaviors?

METHOD
Participants

Participants in the present study were 210 men and women ranging in age   16
from 17 to 37 with a mean age of 20.0 years. Within the total group, there
were 46 men and 164 women participants. Participants were all recruited
from psychology classes at a western university.

Measures

A set of 12 questions was created to assess the participants' attitudes toward   17
tattooing. An additional 16 questions were asked of those who reported
having a tattoo to determine their attitudes toward their own tattoos, the
kind of tattoo they had, where it was located on the body, and how old they
were when they obtained the tattoo. Participants were also asked to report
on body piercings, specifically where they were pierced and how old they
were when they modified their body. Seven questions were asked about
various behaviors such as driving above the speed limit, smoking marijuana,
drinking too much alcohol, engaging in unprotected sex, and shoplifting.
Participants were also asked to provide background information about their
age, sex, academic major, career plans, race/ethnicity, marital status, and the
population size of their hometown.

Participants were then asked to fill in the Personality Research Form   18
(PRF)-Form E (Jackson, 1984). This personality inventory has 352 true-false
items. The PRF-E has a reading level of 6th grade (Schinka & Borum, 1994)
and was not challenging for any of the student participants. The norms for
PRF-E were obtained from college samples and therefore this instrument
was considered appropriate for this particular sample (Jackson, 1987).

Paragraphs 20 through 23   These paragraphs make up the "Results" section of the report.

In paragraph 20, we learn how many of the participants had tattoos and piercings.

In paragraph 21, we learn that tattooed participants were more autonomous and impulsive than their nontattooed counterparts.

In paragraph 22, we learn that college men with piercings were significantly more exhibitionistic, sentient (meaning aesthetic, sensitive, and open to experience), and risk-taking than their unpierced counterparts, while women were higher on social recognition.

Paragraph 23 suggests there was no correlation between being tattooed and the types of behavior measured.

Note that the authors do not summarize their results in a table or graph, as we might expect in a social science study.

Note the short length of these paragraphs. They are blunt and to the point, as paragraphs in social science studies often are.

Paragraphs 24 through 32   These paragraphs form the "Discussion" section of the report. Typically, this section will speculate on the significance of the results of the study.

Paragraph 24 notes that the study replicates the results of other studies in finding that tattooed individuals tend to be rebellious and nonconformist.

Paragraph 25 also notes that this study replicates the correlation between tattooing and impulsivity found in other studies.

The PRF-E measures the following personality traits: abasement, achievement, affiliation, aggression, autonomy, change, cognitive structure, defendence, dominance, endurance, exhibition, harm avoidance, impulsivity, nurturance, order, play, sentience, social recognition, succorance, understanding, and desirability. The instrument also has a scale for infrequency to detect implausible responses.

Procedure

Surveys were administered to the students in all levels of psychology courses 19
at a Western university. The participants were given course credit for their participation. Participants were given a debriefing sheet when they turned in their completed forms to the primary researcher.

RESULTS

Of the total sample of 210 people, 67 participants had tattoos (32%) and 20
135 (64%) had piercings. Of the 46 men in the study, 30% reported having obtained a tattoo. Of the 164 women in the study, 53 (32%) reported having tattoos. Most of the women (75%) reported some piercing, primarily ear piercing. Only twelve men reported piercing.

Men and women with tattoos were both higher in autonomy on the 21
PRF-E with a mean score of 6.96 (SD = 3.44) compared to their non-tattooed peers' mean score of 5.55 (SD = 2.93). When the sexes were viewed separately, the correlation remained for both sexes (men r = .38, p = .008; women r = .17, p = .03). Women with tattoos also scored higher on the PRF-E on impulsivity (r = .16, p = .04).

Men who had pierced their bodies were significantly higher on exhibi- 22
tionism (r = .34, p = .02) and sentience (r = .31, p = .04). They were significantly lower on harm avoidance (r = −.30, p = .05). Women with piercings, however, were significantly higher on social recognition (r = .16, p = .04).

Both tattooed and non-tattooed students reported similar attitudes 23
toward tattoos, agreeing that they are mainstream and that lots of people have tattoos these days. In addition, there were no differences between the groups on any of the seven behavioral questions (e.g., "I drink too much," "I engage in unprotected sex").

DISCUSSION

A high scorer on autonomy on the PRF-E is defined as a person who "tries 24
to break away from restraints, confinement, or restrictions of any kind ... may be rebellious when faced with restraints" (Jackson, 1984, p. 6). The defining trait adjectives also describe the person as "unmanageable, free, self-reliant, independent, autonomous, rebellious, unconstrained, individualistic, ungovernable, self-determined, non-conforming, uncompliant,

Paragraph 26 indicates that the participants in this study tended not to regret getting tattooed, as older tattooed people tend to.

Paragraph 27 notes that only two of the twenty-one personality variables the researchers measured showed significance for tattooed students.

Paragraph 28 is interesting. It indicates strong personality differences across gender for body piercings. Pierced women scored high on social recognition, while pierced men scored high in exhibitionism, sentience, and risk taking.

Paragraph 29 tells us where female college students are most often tattooed.

undominated, resistant, lone-wolf" (Jackson, 1984, p.6). The findings in this study would seem to concur with previous studies that found people with tattoos willing to be regarded as outside mainstream society (e.g., Sanders, 1988, 1991) and therefore are not surprising.

Previous studies have also noted the correlation between impulsivity and   25
tattooing so this finding also supports prior research. Two additional questions related to impulsivity were asked of people who had obtained tattoos: whether they intended to obtain another tattoo and whether they regretted the one(s) they already had. The mean for the former question was 2.5, indicating the midpoint between agreeing and disagreeing. For most people, one tattooing experience may be enough.

In this study, people with tattoos averaged 3.5 on the question about   26
regret (between disagree 3 and strongly disagree 4) indicating they do not yet regret getting a tattoo. Regret is a frequent experience among older people with tattoos (Martin et al., 1995). It is possible that the reason that these participants do not regret their decision to tattoo is partly due to the fact that people in this study obtained their first tattoo at an average age of 18.2 years and were an average age of 19.8 at the time of the study. It may be a few years yet before any "tattoers' remorse" becomes evident.

Given that there are 21 personality scales on the PRF-E and only two   27
personality variables with significant differences between those with and without tattoos, these results support the recent finding that in some populations, tattooing may be more normal than abnormal (Frederick & Bradley, 2000). There were few differences in the groups.

In addition it seems reasonable that reasons for piercing may be very   28
different by gender. Women may pierce their ears or other body parts in order to be normative, although this may be considered attention-seeking behavior in men. Female participants scored high on social recognition that is described as "approval seeking, proper, and well-behaved" (Jackson, 1984, p. 7). This finding would be in keeping with someone who goes along with normative behavior, which ear piercing clearly is for females. On the other hand, male piercers scored high in exhibitionism, described as being "dramatic, ostentatious, and showy," and sentience, described as being "aesthetic, sensitive, and open to experience" (Jackson, 1984, p.7). In addition, male piercers scored lower on harm avoidance, described as someone who is not pain avoidant, does not avoid risks, and is not self-protecting.

As with previous studies, this study also found that women tended to   29
place their tattoos on "private skin." Fully 48% of the women with tattoos chose the lower back as the first location for a tattoo. In their initial tattooing, only six chose the relatively public area of the upper arm and seven selected the ankle (25%).

Paragraph 30 continues, telling us the location of additional tattoos on college women. Note that paragraphs 29 and 30 could be combined to form a single paragraph, since their content is closely related. But the authors maintain their short-paragraph style, confining one point to one paragraph.

Paragraph 31 tells us where male college students most often get tattooed. Note again the gender difference here. Women prefer "private skin" as tattoo locations, while men's tattoos are more likely to be visible.

Paragraph 32 offers a concise conclusion to the study. In some social science reports there is a separate "Conclusions" subsection, but this one is succinct and to the point.

References   References are cited using the APA method.

Of the 17 women reporting a second tattoo, eight (47%) of them also   30
reported tattoos in relatively private areas (upper or lower back, chest,
torso). Only five women reported obtaining a third tattoo (80% on private
skin) and only one woman obtained a fourth (on private skin).

For men, upper arms (4) or upper backs (5) were the most popular   31
locations for a first tattoo. Only 5 men reported having second tattoos and
these were again located in the upper arm or upper back. Two men had a
third tattoo choosing the upper arm and chest for those tattoos. No men
reported having a fourth tattoo.

In conclusion, the results of this study concur with most studies in   32
finding that people choosing to tattoo are different on some personality
variables. However, in this college population the differences were not as
extreme as they have been in previous studies involving less normative
people (e.g., incarcerated people, suicides, and mental health facilities).

AUTHOR NOTE

Correspondence concerning this paper should be addressed to the second
author: Dr. Eugene P. Sheehan, College of Education, Box 106, University of
Northern Colorado, Greeley, CO 80639.

REFERENCES

Armstrong, M. (1991). Career oriented women with tattoos. *Image-The Journal of Nursing Scholarship, 23*(4), 215–220.

Armstrong, M. (1995). Adolescent tattooing: Educating vs. pontificating. *Pediatric Nursing, 21*(6), 561.

Armstrong, M. (1996). You pierced your what? *Pediatric Nursing, 22*(3), 236–238.

Armstrong, M., & Fell, P. (2000). Body art: Regulatory issues and the NEHA body art model code. *Journal of Environmental Health, 62*(19), 25.

Armstrong, M. L., Murphy, K. P., Sallee, A., & Watson, M. (2000). Tattooed army soldiers: Examining the incidence, behavior, risk. *Military Medicine, 165*(2), 135–141.

Armstrong, M., Murphy, K. P., Sallee, A., & Watson, A. (2000). Tattooed army soliders: examining the incidence, behavior, risk. *Military Medicine, 165*(2), 135–141.

Braithwaite, R., Stephens, T., Bowman, N., Milton, M., & Braithwaite, K. (1998). Tattooing and body piercing. *Corrections Today, 60*(2), 120–121, 178.

Buhrich, N. (1983). The association of erotic piercing with homosexuality, sadistic bondage, fetishism, and tattoos. *Archives of Sexual Behavior, 12*(2), 167–171.

Caplan, R., Komaromi, J., & Rhodes, M. (1996). Obsessive-compulsive disorder and tattooing and bizarre sexual practice. *British Journal of Psychiatry, 168*(3), 379–380.

Ceniceros, S. (1998). Tattooing, body piercing, and Russian roulette. *Journal of Nervous and Mental Disease, 186*(8), 503–504.

DeMello, M. (1995). Not just for bikers anymore: Popular representation of American tattooing. *Journal of Popular Culture, 29*(3), 37–52.

Dhossche, D., Snell, K. S., & Larder, S. (2000). A case-control study of tattoos in young suicide victims as a possible marker of risk. *Journal of Affective Disorders, 59*(2), 165–168.

DiFrancesco, C. (1990). "Dermal body language" among prison inmates: The multiple unprofessional tattoo. *Unpublished Doctoral Dissertation*, University of Mississippi.

Drews, D., Allison, C., & Probst, J. (2000). Behavior and self concept differences in tattooed and nontattooed college students. *Psychological Reports, 86,* 475–481.

Ewey, M. (1998, July 1). Who has a tattoo and where? *Ebony,* 76.

Fox, J. (1976). Self-imposed stigmata: A study among female inmates. *Unpublished Doctoral Dissertation,* State University of New York at Albany.

Frederick, C. M., & Bradley, K. A. (2000). A different kind of normal? Psychological and motivational characteristics of young adult tattooers and body piercers. *North American Journal of Psychology, 2*(2), 379–392.

Grief, J., Hewitt, W., & Armstrong, M. (1999). Tattooing and body piercing. *Clincial Nursing Research, 8*(4), 368–385.

Hawkins, R., & Popplestone, J. (1964). The tattoo as exoskeletal defense. *Perceptual and Motor Skills, 19,* 500.

Houghton, S., Durkin, K., & Carroll, A. (1995). Children's and adolescents' awareness of the physical and mental health risks associated with tattooing: A focus group study. *Adolescence, 30*(120), 971–988.

Houghton, S., Durkin, K., Parry, E., Turbett, Y., & Odgers, P. (1996). Amateur tattooing practices and beliefs among high school adolescents. *Journal of Adolescent Health, 19,* 420–425.

Inch, H., & Huws, R. (1993). Tattooed female psychiatric patients. *British Journal of Psychiatry, 162,* 128.

Jackson, D. (1984). *Personality Research Form Manual.* Port Huron, MI. Research Psychologists Press, Inc.

Kennedy, R. (1997, February 26). City council gives tattooing its mark of approval. *The New York Times,* pp. B1, B5.

McKerracher, D. W., & Watson, R. A. (1969). Tattoo marks and behavior disorder. *British Journal of Criminology, 9,* 167–171.

Mallon, W. K., & Russell, M. (1999). Clinical and forensic significance of tattoos. *Topics in Emergency Medicine, 21,* 21–29.

Martin, A. (1997). On teenagers and tattoos. *Journal of American Academy of Child Psychiatry, 36*(6), 860–861.

Martin, R., Dogen, H., Colin, M., Annin, P., & Gegax, T. T. (1995, February 6). Turning in the badges of rebellion: Tattooing hits the morning after. *Newsweek,* 46.

Mason, M. (1991, January 7). Every picture tells a story from sailor to sales representative: Tattoos go mainstream. *Newsweek,* 117.

Measey, L.G. (1972). The psychiatric and social relevance of tattoos in Royal Navy detainees. *British Journal of Criminology, 19*(2), 182–186.

Michael, R.T., Gagnon, J.H., Laumann, E.O., & Kolata, G. (1994). *Sex in America: A definitive survey.* Boston: Little, Brown & Co.

Nadler, S. (1983). Why more women are being tattooed. *Glamour,* 196–198.

Phelan, M. P., & Hunt, S. (1998). Prison gang members' tattoos as identity work: The visual communication of moral careers. *Symbolic Interaction, 21*(3), 277–298.

Post, R. S. (1968). The relationship of tattoos to personality disorders. *Journal of Criminal Law, Criminology, and Police Science, 59*(4), 516–524.

Rademaekers, W., & Schoenthal, R. (1992, October 26). The Iceman's secrets. *Time, 140*(17), 62–67.

Raspa, R. F., & Cusack, J. (1990). Psychiatric implications of tattoos. *American Family Physician, 41,* 1481–1486.

Roc, A., Howell, R., & Payne, J. R. (1974). Comparison of prison inmates with and without juvenile records. *Psychological Reports, 34,* 1315–1319.

Sanders, C. (1988). Becoming and being tattooed. *Journal of Contemporary Ethnography, 16*(4), 395–432.

Sanders, C. (1991). Memorial decoration: Women, tattooing, and the meanings of body alteration. *Michigan Quarterly Review, 30,* 146–157.

Schinka, J., & Borum, R. (1994). Readability of normal personality inventories. *Journal of Personnel Assessment, 6*(1), 95–101.

Taboo Tattoos (1996, April 8). *Time,* 18.

Taylor, A.J.W. (1968). A search among Borstal girls for the psychological and social significance of their tattoos. *British Journal of Criminology, 8,* 171–185.

Taylor, A.J.W. (1970). Tattooing among male and female offenders of different ages in different types of institutions. *Genetic Psychology Monographs, 81,* 81–119.

Vail, D.A. (1999). Tattoos are like potato chips … you can't have just one: The process of becoming and being a collector. *Deviant Behavior 20,* 253–273.

Verberne, J.P. (1969). The personality traits of tattooed adolescent offenders. *British Journal of Criminology, 9,* 172–175.

Yamamoto, J., Seeman, W., & Boyd, L. (1963). The tattooed man. *Journal of Nervous and Mental Disease, 136,* 365.

An Anthology of Academic Writing

Eight additional examples of good academic writing are presented here in Part Three. Collectively, they illustrate that academic writing is a diverse and extensive genre. The style, diction, jargon, and citation method vary from one essay to the next. But as diverse and extensive as the academic genre is, good essays still share several basic characteristics. They are *informative*. The authors present interesting ideas and present them in enough *detail* so that readers can understand the information and arguments. They are *clear*. The specialized language of the discipline within which the writer is writing might send general readers to the dictionary a few more times than they would like, but once readers have those definitions, they can read the text quite easily. And good essays have *energy*. Varied sentence structure provides rhythm and flow to maintain readers' attention and interest.

Following each reading is a set of questions for study and discussion, designed to help you understand why the essay is a good example of the kind of writing your professors value. Your professors will not expect you to produce comparable work, of course, but to do your best to approach in content and style the sophistication exemplified by these models. Following the questions for study and discussion is a journal prompt to encourage you to explore further the issues raised in each paper and the ways in which the writers express themselves.

Reading Actively and Critically

To read academic writing in a way that will help you learn to write academic essays, and in order to discuss articulately and respond in writing to academic discourse, you need to develop some active and critical reading skills. Critical reading is considerably more demanding than the casual reading you do while you relax with your favorite magazine or a popular novel. It demands more attention and concentration. You read your magazines and best-sellers first for pleasure and second for intellectual stimulation; academic writing you read first for intellectual stimulation and second for pleasure. It is wise to cultivate a strategy for reading academic writing, a strategy for reading critically.

Begin by reflecting on what you already know about the topic of the book or article. Reading experts talk about the benefits of "activating prior knowledge as a prereading strategy." What they mean is that if you take some time before you read to reflect on what you already know about the topic, you will enhance your understanding. Many experts in reading comprehension support the notion of *schema theory*, which asserts that the human mind is a schema, composed of a highly intricate series of elaborately connected bites of information. The schema is constantly being reconstituted and reorganized as we accept and process new bites of information. If we activate the appropriate schema by reflecting on the topic before we begin to read a difficult text, our understanding of that text will be enhanced.

Suppose, for example, you are taking a geology course and have to read a paper about how gold deposits form beneath the Earth's surface. Before you read, reflect on what you already know about gold, the other minerals within which gold might be embedded, and the formation of other metals and minerals beneath the Earth's surface. By activating your "gold" schema, your "mining" schema, and your "geology" schema, you prime your mind for the new information it is about to receive, meaning it will receive and process the new information more efficiently. When you start reading complicated material—for example, descriptions about how magma heats groundwater and forces that water into the Earth's surface, where it triggers intricate chemical processes that produce gold, or explanations about how gold-bearing solutions are expelled from magma as it cools—you will better understand the author's meaning and intentions.

Next, browse through the book or article, trying to get the general drift and overall structure of the discussion. This should give you a good, if preliminary, understanding of the article's main ideas. If you are reading the article as part of the research you are doing for a paper, this skim-through will also help you decide whether the article is worth a detailed study or whether it will give you the kind of information you need to make your own assignment stronger. Some journal articles include a synopsis or an abstract right below the title; either of these will help you understand the essence of the article before you begin to read it in detail. If you are reading a book, pay special attention, at this stage, to its table of contents; read the table of contents carefully, and you will get a good sense of whether the book will be useful to you.

You are ready now for a detailed, active, and critical reading. This is a hand-eye activity because to read actively and critically means to highlight important passages, annotate the margins of the text (if the book is yours and not borrowed from the library or your teacher), or take notes summarizing and paraphrasing key points. If you take notes, it is a good idea to put the book or article aside after you have studied it and then paraphrase and condense those notes. The knowledge really becomes your own if you reconstitute it in this way, though, of course, you still must acknowledge the source with a citation.

If you know you will need the information contained within this book or article for an academic essay you are working on, and if you already have at least a rough draft of your essay, read the book or the article as you revise your essay. Alternate your attention between your draft and the source, revising your draft in the context of what you are reading. This is an efficient, time-saving strategy. You must read closely and critically to understand how this knowledge can be integrated into your essay, and you must accommodate your essay to this new knowledge and information. In other words, you read and revise almost simultaneously, thereby abridging the demanding process of composing a research paper.

You need, as well, a strategy to evaluate the authority of the text you are reading. If the book or article is on your reading list or was, in some other way, recommended by your professor and if the work is written by a reputable author and published by a reputable firm or in a reputable journal, you can be confident that the information is authoritative (though you still want to read it with a critical eye). If you found the book or article in the library or downloaded it from the Internet, it is especially important that you activate some critical reading strategies as you read. An effective way of reading critically is to read slowly and deliberately, pausing at appropriate places to consider and take notes on these questions:

- What is the thesis, and does the thesis address a relevant and important issue?
- Does the author offer ample support for the thesis, and is the support on topic—does it elucidate the thesis?
- Are the thesis and the support the author offers logical? (See pages 61–62 for information on logical fallacies.)
- Does the author cite sources, and are these sources valid and reliable?
- Is the voice, the tone, of the essay strong and confident? Does the author convey the sense that he or she is committed to the topic and sure of his or her position?

If you can give positive answers to these questions, you can be confident that the information contained within the book or article is authoritative, and you can use this information as your own academic essay takes shape.

Try to use these active and critical reading strategies as you read the essays that follow. And consider the questions that follow each essay; discuss the questions with classmates, or compose a written response for your journal. It's true that academic articles are not usually followed by questions designed to help you understand the content of the article. But by responding to the questions at the end of the articles anthologized here, you will further develop your active and critical reading skills and will begin to acquire an understanding of what is important in academic writing, an understanding that will carry over as you read independently.

Visuals in Academic Writing

Many academic essays and reports, especially those in business, the sciences, and the social sciences, include figures, charts, graphs, tables, and photographs. You will get a clearer understanding of the content of these essays and reports if you learn how to read and process the visuals they contain—a set of skills now commonly known as visual literacy.

You have learned from this text that good writing fulfills a purpose, connects with its readers, and has substance. Good visuals do the same. A good way to interpret and understand a visual, then, is to assess the extent to which it meets these three criteria.

Examine, for example, the visuals in Valerie Wee's "Resurrecting and Updating the Teen Slasher: The Case of *Scream*" (pp. 358–380). Under the title is a face of what appears to be an attractive young woman, white against a black background. The face is "slashed" into two, drawing the reader into the text of the essay and telegraphing its theme in that the illustration is white with fear and slashed into two. Excerpts from the paper in highlight boxes come with the frightening emaciated-looking, skull-like mask that the killer in the films wore. How much this adds to the impact of Wee's essay.

Now look at the visuals from Molé's "9/11 Conspiracy Theories" (pp. 381–399). Notice how well they fulfill the purpose of visuals: helping the author confirm his thesis, draw the reader into his argument, and add depth to his point of view. Figure 2, for example, dramatically underscores the contention that the World Trade Center's South Tower did not fall straight down, as it would have if it had imploded. Similarly, Figure 3, the photograph of the airplane debris on the lawn of the Pentagon debunks the conspiracy theorists' contention that a missile or bomb damaged the Pentagon.

Finally, look at the visuals from Mote and Kaser's essay "The Shrinking Glaciers of Kilimanjaro: Can Global Warming Be Blamed?" (pp. 412–426). Notice how clearly Figure 1, with its photographs from 1928 and 2000, underscores the authors' intent to show that the Kilimanjaro glaciers are, indeed, shrinking. Figure 4, scientists' tents at the base of the glacier and scientists working on the glacier's ridge, does more than a written description could to communicate to readers the glacier's overwhelming size. Figure 5, of a scientist walking over the Kibo ice cap's penitentes, adds striking substance to the authors' contention that solar radiation more than global warming is affecting the Kilimanjaro glaciers. Examine these visuals in the context of the paper's purpose, the authors' determination to connect meaningfully with their readers, and their goal of producing an essay of real substance, and you will understand the extent to which visuals, properly appreciated, can assist comprehension.

Disciplines: Education; Sociology

Citation Method: Modified APA

Rhetorical Mode: Exposition; Argument

This article is from the *Journal of Studies on Alcohol and Drugs*, dated January 2007. It follows the APA method for source citation.

Are Drinking Games Sports? College Athlete Participation in Drinking Games and Alcohol-Related Problems*

Joel Grossbard, M.S.,[†] Irene Markman Geisner, PH.C., Clayton Neighbors, PH.D., Jason R. Kilmer, PH.D.,[†] and Mary E. Larimer, PH.D.

Department of Psychiatry and Behavioral Sciences, University of Washington, Seattle, Washington

Abstract. Objective: Studies indicate greater heavy episodic drinking and related consequences for college student-athletes compared with nonathletes. Surprisingly, little research has examined college athletes' participation in drinking games, a context associated with excessive alcohol consumption and negative alcohol-related consequences in college students. Method: We examined how drinking game participation contributes to alcohol consumption and alcohol-related consequences among college-level intramural and intercollegiate athletes compared with nonathletes in two independent samples. Study 1 consisted of 1,395 randomly selected students (61% women) at a West Coast college campus, including 335 students who reported intramural athletic participation. Study 2 consisted of 6,055 randomly selected college students (63% women) from three college campuses, including 1,439 intramural athletes and 317 intercollegiate athletes. Results: Results of Study 1 indicated that intramural athletes consumed significantly more drinks per week, had significantly higher typical and peak blood alcohol concentration levels, and reported more negative consequences than nonathletes. Drinking game participation mediated the relationship between intramural athlete status and measures of consumption and consequences. Results of Study 2, including both intramural and intercollegiate athletes, were consistent with those of

Received: March 2, 2006. Revision: July 20, 2006.

*This research was supported in part by National Institute on Alcohol Abuse and Alcoholism grants T32AA07455 and 5U01AA14742 awarded to Mary E. Larimer and 5R01AA01259 awarded to Rob Turissi.

[†]Correspondence should be sent to Joel Grossbard at the Department of Psychology, University of Washington, Box 351525, Seattle, WA 98195 or via email at: joelg13@u.washington.edu. Jason R. Kilmer is with The Evergreen State College, Olympia, WA, and Saint Martin's University, Lacey, WA.

Study 1, revealing drinking game participation as a mediator of the relationships between athlete status and alcohol consumption and consequences. Conclusions: Drinking games represent contexts for college athletes to engage in heavy episodic drinking, and participation in drinking games mediates the relationship between alcohol consumption and negative consequences in athletes. Interventions targeted at college athletes should consider the impact of drinking game participation. (*J. Stud. Alcohol Drugs* 68: 97–105, 2007)

National studies of college samples indicate greater heavy episodic drinking in athletes than nonathletes (Leichliter et al., 1998; Nelson and Wechsler, 2001; Wechsler et al., 1997; Wilson et al., 2004). Excessive alcohol consumption and higher blood alcohol concentrations (BACs) in college students are associated with physical, psychological, interpersonal, and academic problems (e.g., Borsari et al., 2003; Hingson et al., 2002; Latimer et al., 2004; Wechsler et al., 1994), and research demonstrates greater alcohol-related negative consequences in athletes than nonathletes (Leichliter et al., 1998; Nelson and Wechsler, 2001; Wechsler et al., 1997; Wilson et al., 2004). A factor that has received little research attention is college athletes' participation in drinking games. 1

Drinking games promote social drinking environments, and excessive alcohol consumption is encouraged by players (e.g., Borsari, 2004). There are hundreds of different drinking games involving competitions and games requiring the demonstration of both cognitive and physical skills, and estimates of college student drinking game participation in the past month range from 47% to 62% (Borsari, 2004; Borsari et al., 2003). College students are drawn to drinking games because the games promote social interaction and group cohesion, and students' motives for drinking games include playing to get drunk, get others drunk, meet new people, and compete against others. However, given that drinking games promote heavy drinking during short periods, players are at risk for experiencing interpersonal consequences, including arguments, fights, and physical consequences (e.g., vomiting, hangovers). 2

Several factors suggest college athletes are likely to play drinking games, making them susceptible to heavy drinking and negative consequences. Many drinking games require participants to perform motor tasks (e.g., "Quarters"), and performance is enhanced with good hand-eye coordination. Many games are "team oriented" (e.g., "Beer Pong") and typically include winners, losers, and spectators (Borsari, 2004). Athletes may be drawn to drinking games to engage in "sport or game-oriented" competitions and demonstrate their skills in a social context. Additionally, research on personality factors and motives for playing 3 drinking games provides evidence for athletes' involvement. Johnson and Sheets (2004) found that motives for drinking game participation associated with "competition and thrills" were also associated with greater alcohol consumption and negative consequences for college students than other motives. They suggested that playing drinking games for competition and thrills may be related to sensation seeking, a personality trait shown to be positively associated with greater frequency of drinking game participation (Johnson and Cropsey, 2000) as well as athletes' tendency to engage in risky behaviors, including physical fights and having more sexual partners (Nattiv and Puffer, 1991).

Surprisingly, little research has investigated college athletes' participation   4
in drinking games; however, one study has examined female intercollegiate athletes' participation in drinking games (Zamboanga et al., 2005). The authors found a positive relationship between drinking game participation and alcohol-related problems, but given that there was not a nonathlete group in the study, no comparisons between athletes and nonathletes were possible. In addition, participants were exclusively women; therefore, results may not generalize to male athletes. Research on gender differences in drinking game participation indicates men report greater frequency of drinking game involvement than women. However, women drink more during drinking games than in other contexts, a finding not evident in men (Johnson and Sheets, 2004; Nagoshi et al., 1994). Thus, athletic participation and gender are important to consider when investigating alcohol use and consequences in the context of drinking games.

The major objective of the current investigation was to examine   5
drinking game participation as a mediator between athlete status and alcohol consumption and consequences. In light of research indicating greater consumption and consequences associated with drinking games, and our hypothesis that athletes participate in drinking games more frequently than nonathletes, an examination of drinking game involvement as a mediator seemed plausible. To examine potential differences between levels of athletic participation and drinking game participation, alcohol consumption, and consequences, we examined two separate samples of athletes, including intramural and intercollegiate athletes. Previous research suggests that the level of collegiate athletic involvement is positively associated with alcohol consumption. Hildebrand and colleagues (2001) found that a greater proportion of students classified as "heavy drinkers" were collegiate athletes, and the lowest percentage of those classified as "heavy drinkers" were students not involved in athletics in high school or college. We predicted intercollegiate athletes would report the highest alcohol use and consequences, and nonathletes would report less use and consequences than both intercollegiate and intramural athletes.

STUDY 1 METHOD

Participants and procedures

Participants included 1,395 first-year college students at a large West Coast   6
campus. Participants responded to letters sent to a random sample of 3,000
students (50% women) identified by the registrar, inviting them to complete
a screening assessment for an intervention study. A higher percentage of
women responded and completed the assessment. The sample consisted of
837 women (60%) and 558 men. Participants had a mean (SD) age of 18.4
(0.55) years. The majority of the sample was white (61%), with Asian (24%),
Hispanic/Latino (4%), black (1%), American Indian/ Alaskan Native (1%),
and others/multiracial (9%) composing the rest of the sample. Participants
completed informed consent and assessments online via a secure Web server
and were paid $10 for completing the assessments.

Measures

The assessment battery included a number of measures related to college   7
student drinking and took 30–60 minutes to complete. Measures relevant to
the current study are described here.

Alcohol consumption. Alcohol consumption was measured by items from   8
the Quantity-Frequency and Peak Alcohol Use Index (QF; Marlatt et al.,
1995) and the Daily Drinking Questionnaire (DDQ; Collins et al., 1985).
The QF is a self-report scale assessing typical weekend drinking quantity and
hours spent drinking (typical consumption) in the past month. To assess
peak consumption, participants were asked to report the single greatest
amount of alcohol consumed and hours of consumption in the past month.
Number of hours spent drinking and self-reported weight were used to calcu-
late participants' typical BAC and peak BAC in the past month (Dimeff et al.,
1999); the formula for men and women differed based on mean water body
weight percentage (men = 58%; women = 49%). The QF has been shown to
be reliable when assessing college student drinking rates (Larimer et al., 2001).

The DDQ assesses participants' average number of drinks consumed on   9
each day of the week in the previous 3 months. Reported daily consumption
rates were summed to obtain participants' weekly total consumption. Previous
research has demonstrated that the DDQ is highly correlated with other measures of self-reported alcohol consumption (Latimer et al., 2004). For both
the QF and DDQ, a drink was defined as 12 oz of beer (8 oz of Canadian beer,
malt liquor, or ice beers, or 10 oz of microbrew), 10 oz of wine cooler, 4 oz of
wine, or 1 cocktail with 1 oz of 100-proof liquor or 1.25 oz of 80-proof liquor.

Alcohol-related negative consequences. Alcohol-related negative conse-   10
quences were assessed using the Rutgers Alcohol Problem Index (RAPI;
White and Labouvie, 1989). The original RAPI measures the occurrence

of 23 items that reflect the impact alcohol use has had on health and social functioning in the previous 3 months. In this study, two items assessing driving after drinking were added. Sample items include "neglected your responsibilities" and "caused shame and embarrassment to someone." Internal consistency of the RAPI in Study 1 was $\alpha = .89$.

Drinking game participation. Drinking game participation was assessed 11 by a question from the Young Adult Alcohol Problem Severity Test (YAAPST; Hurlbut and Sher, 1992), a measure of alcohol-related consequences specific to college students. Participants were asked, "Have you participated in drinking contests or drinking games (e.g., 'quarters', chugging contests, 'progressive' parties)?" Response options included, "No, never," "Yes, but not in the past year," and then 1 time, 2 times, 3 times, 4–6 times, 7–11 times, 12–20 times, 21–39 times, or 40 or more times in the past year, and values ranged from "0" (No, never) to "9" (40 or more times).

Demographics. Information collected included age, gender, racial/ethnic 12 identity, height, and weight. Athlete status was assessed by two questions. To assess intercollegiate athletic participation, participants were asked, "Are you a collegiate athlete playing for your university?", and to assess intramural athletic participation, participants were asked, "Do you participate in intramural sports?" Response options included "Yes" or "No," and participants who responded "Yes" to both questions were coded as intercollegiate athletes.

Statistical analyses: Tests for mediation. We were interested in examin- 13 ing drinking game participation as a potential mediator of the relation between athlete status and alcohol consumption and related consequences. Mediation was evaluated based on the approach of Baron and Kenny (1986). In this case, evidence of mediation requires (1) significant relationships between athlete status and consumption and consequences; (2) a significant relationship between athlete status and drinking game participation; (3) significant relationships between drinking game participation and consumption and consequences, controlling for athlete status; and (4) the relationships between athlete status and consumption and consequences are no longer significant or are substantially reduced when controlling for drinking game participation. The magnitude of the reductions of the final criteria can be evaluated with a z distributed Sobel (1982) test.

STUDY 1 RESULTS AND DISCUSSION

Although we had hoped to examine both intramural and intercollegiate ath- 14 letes, preliminary analysis of the sample ($N = 1,395$) revealed a small number ($n = 35$) of intercollegiate athletes. Thus, we did not include them in our analyses. Of the 1,360 remaining study participants, 335 (25%) indicated intramural athletic participation. Table 1 presents a comparison of drinking

TABLE 1
Drinking and consequences in nonathletes and intramural athletes

Variable	Nonathletes (n = 1,025)	Intramural athletes (n = 335)
Drinking game participation	2.04 (2.73)	3.33* (2.94)
Total drinks per week	4.35 (7.32)	7.18* (8.81)
Typical BAC, g/dl	.04 (.07)	.05* (.08)
Peak BAC, g/dl	.09 (.10)	.12* (.10)
Negative consequences, RAPI score	5.87 (4.54)	7.75* (5.14)

Notes: Drinking game participation is based on the following values from the Young Adult Alcohol Problem Severity Test: 0 = never; 1 = yes but not in the past year; 2 = 1 time in the past year; 3 = 2 times in the past year; 4 = 3 times in the past year; 5 = 4–6 times in the past year; 6 = 7–11 times in the past year; 7 = 12–20 times in the past year; 8 = 21–39 times in the past year; 9 = 40 or more times in the past year. BAC = blood alcohol concentration; RAPI = Rutgers Alcohol Problem Index.
*$p < .05$; all intramural athlete scores are significantly greater than nonathlete scores.

game participation, alcohol consumption, and alcohol-related consequences between intramural athletes and nonathletes. In addition, the percentage of intramural athletes who indicated they were members of a fraternity or sorority was 30%, compared with only 12% of the nonathletes. Thus, to examine whether fraternity/sorority status affected our results, we repeated all analyses controlling for fraternity/sorority status.

All analyses used the general linear model, with gender and intramural   15
athletic participation as dichotomous variables and alcohol consumption, consequences, and drinking game participation as continuous variables. The first three of the criteria indicating drinking games as a mediator between intramural athlete status and consumption and consequences are evident from the following results.

Weekly alcohol consumption

We first examined weekly alcohol consumption during the past 3 months   16
as a function of intramural athlete status and gender. Results revealed main effects for intramural athletes ($F = 26.92$, 1/1,346 df, $p < .001$; $d = 0.28$), with intramural athletes drinking more than nonathletes, and for gender ($F = 5.47$, 1/1,346 df, $p < .05$; $d = 0.13$), with men drinking more than women. The Intramural Athlete×Gender interaction was also significant ($F = 4.15$, 1/1,345 df, $p < .05$; $d = 0.11$), and post hoc contrasts revealed that male intramural athletes drank significantly more than female intramural athletes ($p < .01$), although no significant gender differences were found for nonathletes.

Typical and peak BAC

We next looked at typical BAC as a function of intramural athlete status   17
and gender. Results revealed main effects for intramural athletes ($F = 14.11$,
1/1,344 df, $p<.001$; $d = 0.20$), with intramural athletes reporting higher
typical BACs than nonathletes, and for gender ($F = 11.09$, 1/1,344 df,
$p = .001$; $d = 0.18$), with women reporting higher typical BACs than men.
The Intramural Athlete×Gender interaction was not significant ($F = 1.12$,
1/1,343 df, $p = $ NS; $d = 0.06$).

Similar results were found for peak BAC, with main effects revealed for   18
intramural athletes ($F = 24.32$, 1/1,346 df, $p<.001$; $d = 0.27$), with intramural athletes having higher peak BACs than nonathletes, and for gender
($F = 8.13$, 1/1,346 df, $p<.01$; $d = 0.16$), with women having higher peak
BACs than men. The Intramural Athlete×Gender interaction was not
significant ($F = 1.17$, 1/1,345 df, $p = $ NS; $d = 0.06$).

Alcohol-related consequences

For alcohol-related problems (RAPI total score) as a function of intramural   19
athlete status and gender, results indicated a main effect for intramural athletes ($F = 7.23$, 1/801 df, $p = .007$; $d = 0.19$), with intramural athletes reporting more consequences than nonathletes, whereas gender ($F = 0.38$, 1/801
df, $p = $ NS; $d = 0.04$) and the Intramural Athlete×Gender interaction
($F = 0.08$, 1/800 df, $p = $ NS; $d = 0.02$) were not significant.

Drinking game participation

Analysis of the responses measuring drinking game participation on the   20
YAAPST indicated that 47% of the sample participated in drinking games at
least once in the past year.

Relationship to intramural athlete status. We examined drinking game   21
participation as a function of intramural athlete status and gender, and
results revealed a main effect for intramural athletes ($F = 53.60$, 1/1,337 df,
$p<.001$; $d = 0.40$) but not for gender ($F = 0.72$, 1/1,337 df, $p = $ NS; $d = 0.05$).
The Intramural Athlete×Gender interaction was not significant ($F = 1.20$,
1/1,336 df, $p = $ NS; $d = 0.06$).

Relationship to consumption and consequences. Drinking games were sig-   22
nificantly related (all p's $<.001$) to all outcomes, including total drinks per week
($F = 1328.28$, 1/1,339 df, $p<.001$; $d = 1.99$), typical BAC ($F = 440.46$, 1/1,334 df,
$p<.001$; $d = 1.15$), peak BAC ($F = 1212.80$, 1/1,336 df, $p<.001$; $d = 1.91$), and
alcohol-related consequences ($F = 396.40$, 1/801 df, $p<.001$; $d = 1.41$).

As the final step in evaluating mediation, when adding drinking game   23
participation to the model, in addition to intramural athlete status and gender, intramural athlete status was no longer significant for any of the alcohol-
use variables, including total weekly consumption ($F = 0.00$, 1/1,336 df,

$p =$ ns; $d = 0.00$), typical BAC ($F = 0.05$, $1/1,332$ df, $p =$ ns; $d = .01$), and peak BAC ($F = 0.01$, $1/1,334$ df, $p =$ ns; $d = 0.01$). Likewise, for alcohol-related consequences, intramural athlete status was no longer significant when adding drinking game participation into the model ($F = 0.18$, $1/798$ dr, $p =$ ns, $d = 0.03$). Sobel (1982) tests confirmed the magnitudes of the reductions were significant for all drinking outcomes (z's ranged from 6.87 to 7.18, all p's $< .001$). Thus, drinking game participation mediated the relationship between intramural athlete status and all alcohol consumption and consequence measures.

Overall, results indicated significantly greater weekly consumption,   24
typical and peak BACs, and negative consequences in intramural athletes compared with nonathletes. Intramural athletes also reported significantly more drinking game participation than nonathletes. Examination of the interaction for weekly drinking between gender and intramural athlete status revealed greater weekly consumption for male intramural athletes compared with female intramural athletes, yet this difference was not apparent in nonathletes. Thus, intramural athletic participation had a greater impact on weekly consumption in male intramural athletes than in female intramural athletes, although this was a small effect. Drinking game participation accounted for the significant relationship between intramural athlete status and all measures of consumption and consequences. These results strongly suggest drinking game participation as a risk factor for excessive alcohol consumption and negative consequences in college students participating in intramural athletics.

STUDY 2 METHOD
Participants and procedures

Study 2 consisted of secondary data analyses from a randomly selected   25
sample of 6,055 college students enrolled in a longitudinal study at three West Coast colleges. The sample consisted of 3,829 women (63%) and 2,226 men. Participants had a mean age of 21.2 (4.6). The majority of the sample was white (75%), with Asian (15%), Hispanic/ Latino (2%), black (1%), American Indian/Alaskan Native (1%), and others/multiracial (6%) comprising the rest of the sample. Letters were initially sent to participants providing information about the study and instructions for completing informed consent and assessments online via a secure Web server. Participants were paid $10 for completing the assessments.

Measures and statistical analyses

The same measures and statistical analyses used in Study 1 for assessing   26
alcohol consumption, consequences, drinking game participation, and

demographics were used in Study 2. In terms of reliability, the internal consistency for consequences assessed by the RAPI in Study 2 was $\alpha = .91$.

STUDY 2 RESULTS AND DISCUSSION

Of the 6,055 study participants, 1,439 (24%) indicated that they participated 27 in intramural athletics, and 317 (5%) participated in intercollegiate athletics. Table 2 presents levels of drinking game participation, alcohol consumption, and alcohol-related consequences in athletes (both intramural and intercollegiate athletes) and nonathletes. Preliminary analysis of the sample also revealed that 11% of the intramural athletes and 6% of the intercollegiate athletes were members of the fraternity/sorority system at their campuses, compared with 6% of the nonathletes. As in Study 1, we repeated all analyses controlling for fraternity/sorority status.

We were again interested in examining drinking game participation as a 28 potential mediator of athlete status and its impact on drinking and related problems. All analyses used the general linear model, and athletic participation was dummy-coded for intramural athletic participation, intercollegiate athletic participation, and no athletic participation. The first three mediation criteria were evident as described in the following analyses.

TABLE 2
Drinking and consequences in nonathletes, intramural athletes, and intercollegiate athletes

Variable	Nonathletes (n = 4,299)	Intramural athletes (n = 1,439)	Intercollegiate athletes (n = 317)
Drinking game participation	2.12 (2.56)	3.28* (2.92)	3.14* (2.86)
Total drinks per week	4.63 (7.27)	7.20* (9.99)	6.49* (9.44)
Typical BAC, g/dl	.05 (.08)	.06* (.08)	.06* (.10)
Peak BAC, g/dl	.10 (.11)	.14* (.11)	.14* (.11)
Negative consequences, RAPI score	3.88 (6.94)	4.87* (7.30)	5.32* (7.97)

Notes: Drinking game participation is based on the following values from the Young Adult Alcohol Problem Severity Test: 0 = never; 1 = yes but not in the past year; 2 = 1 time in the past year; 3 = 2 times in the past year; 4 = 3 times in the past year; 5 = 4–6 times in the past year; 6 = 7–11 times in the past year; 7 = 12–20 times in the past year; 8 = 21–39 times in the past year; 9 = 40 or more times in the past year. BAC = blood alcohol concentration; RAPI = Rutgers Alcohol Problem Index.
*$p < .05$ (all intramural and intercollegiate athlete scores are significantly greater than nonathlete scores); all intramural and intercollegiate athlete scores are not significantly different ($p > .05$).

Weekly alcohol consumption

The analysis of weekly alcohol consumption as a function of athletic
participation and gender revealed main effects for athletes ($F = 37.16$,
2/5836 df, $p < .001$; $d = 0.16$), with nonathletes drinking less than both types
of athletes, and for gender ($F = 145.51$, 1/5,836 df, $p < .001$; $d = 0.32$), with
men drinking more than women. The Athlete×Gender interaction was
significant ($F = 23.02$, 2/5,834 df, $p < .001$; $d = 0.13$). Post hoc contrasts were
conducted and revealed female intramural athletes drank more than female
nonathletes ($p = .03$), but no other significant differences were found for
women based on athlete status. Male intramural and intercollegiate athletes
drank significantly more than male nonathletes ($p < .001$), but surprisingly,
no significant differences were found between male intramural and intercollegiate athletes.

29

Typical and peak BAC

For typical BAC, results revealed main effects for athletes ($F = 28.69$,
2/5,390 df, $p < .001$; $d = 0.15$), again with nonathletes having lower BACs,
and for gender ($F = 5.67$, 1/5,390 df, $p < .05$; $d = 0.06$), with women having
greater typical BACs than men. The Athlete×Gender interaction was not
significant ($F = 2.28$, 2/5,388 df, $p = $ NS; $d = 0.04$).

30

Similar results were found for peak BAC, with main effects for athletes
($F = 40.29$, 2/5,432 df, $p < .001$; $d = 0.17$), with nonathletes reporting lower
peak BACs than both athlete groups, and for gender ($F = 41.32$, 1/5,432 df,
$p < .001$; $d = 0.17$), with men reporting higher peak BACs than women. The
Athlete×Gender interaction was significant ($F = 5.30$, 2/5,430 df, $p < .01$;
$d = 0.06$). Post hoc contrasts were conducted and revealed that female intramural and intercollegiate athletes both had significantly higher peak BACs
than female nonathletes ($p < .001$), but no other significant differences were
found in women based on athlete status. Male nonathletes and intramural
athletes had significantly higher peak BACs than their female counterparts
($p < .01$ for both), although no significant differences were found between
male and female intercollegiate athletes.

31

Alcohol-related consequences

The examination of alcohol-related problems as a function of athlete status
and gender revealed main effects for athletes ($F = 9.53$, 2/5,943 dr, $p < .001$;
$d = 0.08$), with nonathletes reporting fewer consequences than both types of
athletes, and for gender ($F = 30.42$, 1/5,943 df, $p < .001$; $d = 0.14$), with men
reporting more consequences than women. The Athlete×Gender interaction
was significant ($F = 2.92$, 2/5,941 dr, $p = .05$; $d = 0.04$). Post hoc contrasts were
conducted and revealed no significant differences in women based on athlete
status. Male intramural and intercollegiate athletes reported significantly more

32

consequences than male nonathletes ($p<.001$), although no significant differences were found between male intramural and intercollegiate athletes.

Drinking game participation

Analysis of drinking game participation in the YAAPST indicated 49% of   33
the sample participated in drinking games at least once in the past year.

Relationship to athlete status. We examined drinking game participation   34
as a function of athlete status and gender, and results revealed a main effect
for athletes ($F = 96.31$, 2/5,502 df, $p<.001$; $d = 0.26$), with nonathletes reporting less drinking game involvement than either of the athlete groups, but not
for gender ($F = 0.17$, 1/5,502 df, $p = $ NS; $d = 0.01$). The Athlete×Gender interaction was not significant ($F = 0.94$, 2/5,500 df, $p = $ NS; $d = .03$).

Relationship to consumption and consequences. Drinking games were sig-   35
nificantly related to all alcohol use variables (all p's $<.001$), including total
drinks per week ($F = 2465.28$, 1/5,350 df, $p<.001$; $d = 1.36$), typical BAC
($F = 1391.29$, 1/5,366 df, $p<.001$; $d = 1.02$), and peak BAC ($F = 2452.71$,
1/5,407 df, $p<.001$; $d = 1.35$) as well as the alcohol-related consequences as
measured by the RAPI ($F = 1467.94$, 1/5,476 df, $p<.001$; $d = 1.04$).

As the final step, when adding drinking game participation as a predic-   36
tor, in addition to athlete status and gender, athlete status was no longer
significant for any consumption measures, including total weekly consumption ($F = 1.66$, 2/5,347 df, $p = $ NS; $d = 0.04$), typical BAC ($F = 1.39$, 2/5,363
df, $p = $ NS; $d = 0.03$), and peak BAC ($F = 1.67$, 2/5,404 df, $p = $ NS; $d = 0.04$).
Sobel (1982) tests confirmed that the magnitudes of reductions were significant for all drinking outcomes (z's ranged from 9.48 to 9.62, all p's $<.001$).
Mediation analyses for negative consequences revealed athlete status as a
significant predictor, even with drinking games included in the model, but
the effect was reduced, suggesting partial mediation. The Sobel test confirmed the significance of the reduction ($z = 9.50$, $p<.01$).

Consistent with our hypotheses, intramural and intercollegiate   37
athletes reported greater levels of consumption and consequences than
nonathletes. Drinking game participation was positively associated with all
consumption and consequence variables, and both intramural and intercollegiate athletes reported greater drinking game participation than nonathletes. Contrary to expectations, intramural and intercollegiate athletes
did not differ significantly on measures of consumption and consequences.
Examination of the interactions between athlete status and gender revealed
that intramural and intercollegiate athletic participation for men, but
not women, was associated with greater consumption and consequences.
Female intramural athletes reported significantly greater consumption than
female nonathletes, although no other significant differences were evident
for women on the basis of athlete status. For intramural and intercollegiate

athletes, drinking game participation accounted for the higher levels of alcohol consumption as compared with nonathletes. Alcohol-related consequences were still predicted by athlete status, although the effect was reduced when drinking game participation was added to the model.

GENERAL DISCUSSION

The results of these studies indicated greater alcohol consumption, drinking game participation, and negative alcohol-related consequences in both intercollegiate and intramural athletes compared with nonathletes. The mediating effects found for drinking game participation on consumption and consequences in athletes suggest the importance of examining drinking games as a risk factor for heavy drinking and alcohol-related problems. Surprisingly, intramural and intercollegiate athletes in Study 2 did not differ significantly on levels of alcohol consumption and consequences, suggesting that interventions targeted at college athletes may need to focus on both intramural and intercollegiate athletes.   38

One factor previously found to be associated with athletic participation and heavy alcohol consumption in college is membership and residence in fraternities and sororities (Larimer et al., 2004; Wechsler et al., 1997). The results of the current study remained relatively consistent when we controlled for fraternity/sorority status in both Study 1 and Study 2, although for weekly alcohol consumption, the interactions between athlete status and gender were not significant in both Study 1 and Study 2 when we controlled for fraternity/sorority status. It should also be noted that two of the three campuses included in Study 2 did not have a fraternity/sorority system, and when these campuses were examined separately, the analyses produced the same results as our findings including the campus with a fraternity/sorority system. Thus, it appears that although intramural athletes may be overrepresented in fraternities and sororities, drinking games still significantly contribute to athlete drinking patterns, whether or not these athletes are members of the fraternity/sorority system.   39

It is possible that athletic participation before college exposes students to social environments associated with excessive drinking and may predispose individuals to becoming involved in the fraternity/sorority system in college. These students may play either intercollegiate or intramural athletics in college and may seek stimulating social opportunities, including drinking games. Although high school athletic status was not assessed in this study, it is possible that athlete involvement and drinking game participation in high school may socialize incoming college students to such "risky" drinking behaviors.   40

Consistent with previous research, results indicated greater consumption and consequences in male athletes than all other groups based on athlete status and gender (Wechsler et al., 1997). Yet, previous research examining   41 college athlete drinking patterns have not typically examined estimated BAC as an outcome measure. Contrary to expectations, male intercollegiate athletes in Study 2 did not have significantly higher estimated peak BACs than female intercollegiate athletes. Overall, women in both Study 1 and Study 2 had higher estimated typical BACs than men, and higher estimated peak BACs in Study 1. Although greater drinking frequency and consumption are typically found in college men, BACs for both typical and peak drinking occasions have been shown to be similar in men and women, or even higher in women (Lo and Globetti, 1995), highlighting the importance of considering body weight and duration of consumption. Worthy of note, women have been shown to underreport their weight on self-report measures (Betz et al., 1994), possibly resulting in their higher estimated BACs on self-report measures compared with men. Further work is needed to elucidate the relations between athlete status and gender on alcohol consumption measures.

Although this investigation provides a preliminary framework for examining college athlete drinking game involvement, there are several limitations to consider. Methodologically, drinking game participation was assessed by one question on the YAAPST, and participants were not asked whether alcohol consumption and consequences were directly related to drinking games. Participants were asked to recall their drinking game involvement within the past year, and the assessments of consumption and consequences were within the last 3 months. Yet, we suspect somewhat consistent student drinking patterns during this period, given previous research indicating a relatively stable pattern of average alcohol consumption and frequency of drinking across a 1-year period (Marlatt et al., 1998). However, longitudinal research focusing on college athlete drinking patterns from high school through college is warranted. 42

The use of self-report measures is an additional limitation of this research, as students may not accurately report alcohol-related information. Confidentiality of participants' responses was assured, and previous research suggests that self-report of drinking behavior is generally accurate (Babor et al., 2000; Chermack et al., 1998; Darke, 1998). Additionally, the demographics of the samples were not identical, specifically in terms of age and race/ethnicity. Study 1 participants were all first-year students attending the same university, and Study 2 consisted of students from three different campuses and across all years in school. Future research examining athlete involvement in drinking games with consideration of age and race/ethnicity as potential moderators is warranted. 43

Another limitation is that "athlete" was defined as a participant in intramural or intercollegiate athletics. It is possible that some intramural activities may not warrant athlete status and that, in turn, there could be differences within the intramural category. In the current study, we did 44 not examine whether the actual sport the student participated in was associated with differences in alcohol consumption and consequences. Future research could examine differences in drinking game involvement across sports. Further, no information was collected about the season during which athletic involvement occurs. This could have had an impact on drinking data, as research suggests athletes may drink less during their competitive season than during the off-season (e.g., Bower and Martin, 1999; Martin, 1998).

Despite these limitations, this research adds significantly to the literature   45 on college athlete drinking and drinking games and suggests that athletes drink more than nonathletes, at least in part because they participate more frequently in drinking games. It is also possible that athletes participate in drinking games more because they drink more. The cross-sectional data reported here cannot distinguish between these factors, and future research should address the temporal relationship of these variables to elucidate college athlete drinking patterns. Nevertheless, it is clear that drinking games are an important piece of the puzzle in considering drinking behavior among college athletes.

REFERENCES

Babor, T.F., Steinberg, K., Anton, R., and Del Boca, F. Talk is cheap: Measuring drinking outcomes in clinical trials. J. Stud. Alcohol 61: 55–63, 2000.

Baron, R.M. and Kenny, D.A. The moderator-mediator variable distinction in social psychological research: Conceptual, strategic, and statistical considerations. J. Pers. Social Psychol. 51:1173–1182, 1986.

Betz, N.E., Mintz, L., and Speakmon, G. Gender differences in the accuracy of self-reported weight. Sex Roles 30: 543–552, 1994.

Borsari, B. Drinking games in the college environment: A review. J. Alcohol Drug Educ. 48 (2): 29–51, 2004.

Borsari, B., Bergen-Cico, D., and Carey, K.B. Self-reported drinking-game participation of incoming college students. J. Amer. Coll. Hlth 51: 149–154, 2003.

Bower, B.L. and Martin, M. African American female basketball players: An examination of alcohol and drug behaviors. J. Amer. Coll. Hlth 48: 129–133, 1999.

Chermack, S.T., Singer, K., and Beresford, T.P. Screening for alcoholism among medical inpatients: How important is corroboration of patient self-report? Alcsm Clin. Exp. Res. 22: 1393–1398, 1998.

Collins, R.L., Parks, G.A., and Marlatt, G.A. Social determinants of alcohol consumption: The effects of social interaction and model status on the self-administration of alcohol. J. Cons. Clin. Psychol. 53: 189–200, 1985.

Darke, S. Self-report among injecting drug users: A review. Drug Alcohol Depend. 51: 253–263, 1998.

Dimeff, L.A., Baer, J.S., Kivlahan, D.R., and Marlatt, G.A. Brief Alcohol Screening and Intervention for College Students (BASICS): A Harm Reduction Approach, New York: Guilford Press, 1999.

Hildebrand, K.M., Johnson, D.J., and Bogle, K. Comparison of patterns of alcohol use between high school and college athletes and non-athletes. Coll. Student J. 35: 358–365, 2001.

Hingson, R.W., Heeren, T., Zakocs, R.C., Kopstein, A., and Wechsler, H. Magnitude of alcohol-related mortality and morbidity among U.S. college students ages 18–24. J. Stud. Alcohol 63: 136–144, 2002.

Hurlbut, S.C. and Sher, K.J. Assessing alcohol problems in college students. J. Amer. Coll. Hlth 41: 49–58, 1992.

Johnson, T.J. and Cropsey, K.L. Sensation seeking and drinking game participation in heavy-drinking college students. Addict. Behav. 25: 109–116, 2000.

Johnson, T.J. and Sheets, V.L. Measuring college students' motives for playing drinking games. Psychol. Addict. Behav. 18: 91–99, 2004.

Larimer, M.E., Turner, A.P., Anderson, B.K., Fader, J.S., Kilmer, J.R., Palmer, R.S., and Cronce, J.M. Evaluating a brief alcohol intervention with fraternities. J. Stud. Alcohol 62: 370–380, 2001.

Larimer, M.E., Turner, A.P., Mallett, K.A., and Geisner, I.M. Predicting drinking behavior and alcohol-related problems among fraternity and sorority members: Examining the role of descriptive and injunctive norms. Psychol. Addict. Behav. 18: 203–212, 2004.

Leichliter, J.S., Meilman, P.W., Presley, C.A., and Cashin, J.R. Alcohol use and related consequences among students with varying levels of involvement with college athletics. J. Amer. Coll. Hlth 46: 257–262, 1998.

Lo, C.C. and Globetti, G. Are males actually heavier drinkers than females? Addiction 90: 1547–1550, 1995.

Marlatt, G.A., Baer, J.S., Kivlahan, D.R., Dimeff, L.A., Larimer, M.E., Quigley, L.A., Somers, J.M., and Williams, E. Screening and brief intervention for high-risk college student drinkers: Results from a 2-year follow-up assessment. J. Cons. Clin. Psychol. 66: 604–615, 1998.

Marlatt, G.A., Baer, J.S., and Larimer, M. Preventing alcohol abuse in college students: A harm-reduction approach. In: Boyd, G.M., Howard, J., and Zucker, R.A. (Eds.) Alcohol Problems Among Adolescents: Current Directions in Prevention Research, Mahwah, NJ: Lawrence Erlbaum, 1995, pp. 147–172.

Martin, M. The use of alcohol among NCAA Division 1 female college basketball, softball, and volleyball athletes. J. Athl. Train. 33: 163–167, 1998.

Nagoshi, C.T., Wood, M.D., Cote, C.C., and Abbit, S.M. College drinking game participation within the context of other predictors of alcohol use and problems. Psychol. Addict. Behav. 8: 203–213, 1994.

Nattiv, A. and Puffer, J.C. Lifestyles and health risks of collegiate athletes. J. Faro. Pract. 33: 585–590, 1991.

Nelson, T.F. and Wechsler, H. Alcohol and college athletes. Med. Sci. Sports Exerc. 33: 43–47, 2001.

Sobel, M.E. Asymptotic confidence intervals for indirect effects in structural equation models. In: Leinhardt, S. (Ed.) Sociological Methodology, Washington DC: American Sociological Association, 1982, pp. 290–312.

Wechsler, H., Davenport, A.E., Dowdall, G.W., Grossman, S.J., and Zanakos, S.I. Binge drinking, tobacco, and illicit drug use and involvement in college athletics. A survey of students at 140 American colleges. J. Amer. Coll. Hlth 45: 195–200, 1997.

Wechsler, H., Davenport, A., Dowdall, G., Moeykens, B., and Castillo, S. Health and behavioral consequences of binge drinking in college. A national survey of students at 140 campuses. JAMA 272: 1672–1677, 1994.

White, H.R. and Labouvie, E.W. Towards the assessment of adolescent problem drinking. J. Stud. Alcohol 50: 30–37, 1989.

Wilson, G.S., Pritchard, M.E., and Schaffer, J. Athletic status and drinking behavior in college students: The influence of gender and coping styles. J. Amer. Coll. Hlth 52: 269–273, 2004.

Zamboanga, B.L., Bean, J.L., Pietras, A.C., and Pabon, L.C. Subjective evaluations of alcohol expectancies and their relevance to drinking game involvement in female college students. J. Adolesc. Hlth 37: 77–80, 2005.

QUESTIONS FOR COMPREHENSION, STUDY, AND DISCUSSION

1. What was the major objective of this study?

2. What prediction did the authors make about the outcome of their study?

3. Why could the authors not, in Study 1, analyze data collected from intercollegiate athletes?

4. What variable—in addition to gender and participation in drinking games—did the researchers add to their study?

5. What do the researchers mean by the phrase "negative alcohol-related consequences"?

6. The authors conclude, "Women in both Study 1 and Study 2 had higher estimated typical BACs [blood alcohol concentrations] than men and higher estimated peak BACs in Study 1." Why is this the case?

7. What do the authors admit are three limitations to the validity of this study?

8. Why, according to this study, do college athletes drink more than nonathletes?

9. Are you surprised by the results of this study? Explain your answer.

10. What does this study suggest about the relationship between membership in a fraternity or sorority and drinking habits?

JOURNAL PROMPT

Does the study reported here suggest that drinking games should be banned from college campuses? Explain your answer.

Discipline: Higher Education
Citation Method: APA
Rhetorical Mode: Exposition; Argument

This article is from the *Journal of Higher Education*, Volume 7, Number 66, dated November/December 2006. It follows the APA method for source citation.

Faculty and College Student Beliefs about the Frequency of Student Academic Misconduct

Stephen F. Hard, James M. Conway, and Antonia C. Moran

Student academic misconduct, such as cheating and plagiarism, has increased 1
in recent decades (McCabe, Trevifio, & Butterfield, 2001) and is an important concern in higher education. Meanwhile, it has been reported that faculty members often do little to prevent misconduct or to challenge students who engage in it (Keith-Spiegel, Tabachnik, Whitley, & Washburn, 1998; Schneider, 1999). Reducing misconduct requires understanding the factors influencing the behaviors of each of the two parties most closely involved: the students, whose behavior determines whether and how often misconduct occurs, and the faculty, whose behavior can potentially deter misconduct. (Institutional policy is another important factor, but is not the subject of the present study.)

The present study concerns the prediction of behavior by both students 2
(i.e., committing misconduct) and faculty (i.e., attempting to prevent and to challenge misconduct). We believe an important (and understudied, at least for faculty) behavioral predictor is beliefs about the prevalence of student academic misconduct. These beliefs concern descriptive norms (Cialdini, Reno, & Kallgren, 1990), which concern what members of a group actually do. Cialdini et al. distinguished these norms from injunctive or prescriptive norms, which refer to the moral rules of one's peers or of some other social group. The effects of beliefs about descriptive norms on students' own behavior have been studied, for example, regarding college student peer alcohol use (Perkins, 2002) and academic misconduct (McCabe et al., 2001). These effects have also been applied to a group of which one is not a member (i.e., faculty beliefs about the frequency of student misconduct,

This work was undertaken as part of a Strategic Planning Grant on Academic Integrity from Central Connecticut State University.

Stephen F. Hard is Instructor in Psychology at Briarwood College. James M. Conway is Associate Professor of Psychology at Central Connecticut State University. Antonia C. Moran is Associate Professor of Political Science at Central Connecticut State University.

The Journal of Higher Education, Vol. 77, No. 6 (November/December 2006) Copyright © 2006 by The Ohio State University

Koljatic & Silva, 2002). As we argue below, we believe student beliefs about the behavior of their peers (peer descriptive norms) can influence misconduct, while faculty beliefs about student academic misconduct can influence efforts to prevent and challenge the misconduct. Before making those arguments, we give a brief description of academic misconduct.

STUDENT ACADEMIC MISCONDUCT

Using our university's code of conduct, we define academic misconduct as   3

> providing or receiving assistance in a manner not authorized by the instructor in the creation of work to be submitted for academic evaluation including papers, projects and examinations (cheating); and presenting, as one's own, the ideas or words of another person or persons for academic evaluation without proper acknowledgement (plagiarism).

We recognize that misconduct can vary along a number of dimensions.   4
One dimension is the type of work submitted, with the major categories being examinations and written work (e.g., papers). Another dimension is whether the misconduct is planned in advance or spontaneous. A third dimension is whether a student is providing or receiving assistance. These distinctions may be important to the extent that students' and/or faculty members' beliefs and attitudes differ. For example, Lim and See (2001) found evidence that students considered examination cheating more serious than plagiarism. It is also possible that students and/or faculty members perceive planned misconduct as more serious than spontaneous misconduct. We will therefore consider these distinctions later.

STUDENT BELIEFS ABOUT PEER BEHAVIOR

There is a large theoretical and empirical literature indicating that expec-   5
tations and beliefs about peers' behavior (i.e., peer descriptive norms) influence individual behavioral choices. Social norms theory says that people tend to maintain behavior consistent with peer descriptive norms, and that overestimating the frequency that one's peers engage in a behavior can lead to increases in that behavior (e.g., overestimating peer alcohol use can increase students' drinking, Berkowitz, 2003; Perkins, 2002). According to Berkowitz (2003) and Perkins (2002), college students often overestimate peer descriptive norms for alcohol use, and interventions intended to correct these mistaken beliefs have shown evidence of success in reducing drinking (though Smith, 2004, has challenged the supportive evidence).

If these findings hold for academic misconduct as well as for alcohol   6
use, then student beliefs concerning peer descriptive norms of student academic misconduct are an important research topic. In fact, Whitley (1998) reviewed 16 studies and concluded that overall, there was a strong

association between beliefs about the frequency of peer academic misconduct and a student's own misconduct. This finding is consistent with beliefs about alcohol use and with the idea that overestimating peers' misconduct can increase a student's own misconduct. The accuracy of students' beliefs about peer descriptive norms has received less attention, and results have not been consistent. Two studies showed evidence of *under*estimation of peer misconduct, one involving undergraduates (Jordan, 2001) and the other involving graduate students (Wajda-Johnston, Handal, Brawer, & Fabricatore, 2001). A third study, by Koljatic and Silva (2002), found that undergraduates *over*estimated peers' misconduct. The discrepancy between the two undergraduate studies may be explained by the different types of universities involved (a small, private U.S. liberal arts college for Jordan, 2001, and a Latin American Catholic university for Koljatic & Silva, 2002). We studied beliefs about the frequency of student academic misconduct in a medium-sized state university in the northeastern U.S., and we had two goals:

Research goal #1: Replicate the positive relationship between student beliefs about the academic misconduct of their peers and students' reports of their own misconduct.

Research goal #2: Assess the accuracy of students' beliefs about the academic misconduct of their peers.

FACULTY BELIEFS ABOUT THE DESCRIPTIVE NORMS OF STUDENT ACADEMIC MISCONDUCT

There is little theoretical or empirical literature bearing directly on faculty beliefs about the frequency of student misconduct. Social norms theory is not relevant here—the key issue is the effect of faculty beliefs and expectations about students on behavior toward those students. However, there is a literature demonstrating an effect of expectations on behavior toward others. Research on the Pygmalion effect has demonstrated that bogus expectations of teachers for students influenced teachers' behavior, and the teachers' behavior influenced students' achievement (Harris & Rosenthal, 1985; Rosenthal & Jacobsen, 1968). Similar effects have been shown in other contexts such as supervisor-subordinate, client-therapist, and nurse-patient relationships (White & Locke, 2000). There is also evidence that managers with different assumptions about human nature (and therefore different expectations) treat employees differently (Neuliep, 1987).

While these findings do not directly address the effect of faculty beliefs about student academic misconduct descriptive norms on faculty behavior toward students regarding academic misconduct, they do show that expectations for a group of which one is not a member can influence behavior toward that group. We expected to find evidence of such an effect in our study. Specifically, we believe higher faculty beliefs about the frequency of student academic misconduct lead to two important types of behavior. One type of behavior is efforts to prevent misconduct (e.g., designing assignments that make it difficult to use unapproved sources). Faculty members who believe misconduct is more frequent should be more motivated to take preventive action. The second type of faculty behavior is challenging students about suspected misconduct. This is a crucial behavior because failing to challenge misconduct may send the message that a student can get away with it, but our anecdotal experience is that challenging students is a difficult, unpleasant task that faculty members would often prefer to avoid. We believe that faculty members with higher beliefs about the prevalence of student academic misconduct will be more likely to be motivated to challenge students (as well as to be more vigilant in detection efforts). To summarize, while we know of no existing evidence on the correlates of faculty beliefs about the frequency of student academic misconduct, we expect those beliefs to predict both prevention efforts and efforts to challenge misconduct.

If we are correct about faculty beliefs predicting efforts to prevent   9
misconduct and to challenge suspected students, an interesting possibility about the accuracy of faculty beliefs is raised. Unlike the desirability of lowering student beliefs about the frequency of the academic misconduct of their peers, it may be useful for faculty to have *higher* beliefs. Higher beliefs should be useful in encouraging efforts to prevent and challenge misconduct. In two studies looking at faculty beliefs, one showed that faculty were fairly accurate in estimating undergraduate students' actual reports of misconduct (Koljatic & Silva, 2002), while the other found that faculty estimates *under*estimated graduate student misconduct (Wajda-Johnston et al., 2001). It is worth noting that in both studies, faculty beliefs were lower than student beliefs were.

In addition to the overall levels of accuracy, we should consider vari-   10
ability among faculty members. Wajda-Johnston et al. (2001) reported that faculty members varied substantially in their estimates, and we suspect the same is true for Koljatic and Silva (2002). This means that even if the average of faculty estimates is accurate, there will be a considerable number of underestimators. These faculty members are of particular interest because if beliefs predict efforts to deal with misconduct, the underestimators may be doing relatively little about the problem.

We had several research goals regarding faculty beliefs about the fre-   11
quency of student academic misconduct:

Research goal #3: Test the hypothesis that faculty beliefs about the frequency of student academic misconduct will be positively associated with efforts to prevent misconduct.

Research goal #4: Test the hypothesis that faculty beliefs about the frequency of student academic misconduct will be positively associated with efforts to challenge students suspected of misconduct.

Research goal #5: Test the hypothesis that faculty beliefs about the frequency of student academic misconduct will be lower, and more accurate, than student beliefs.

Research goal #6: Examine efforts by faculty who underestimate a given misconduct behavior to challenge students on that behavior.

SUMMARY

The present study focused on investigating student and faculty beliefs 12
about the descriptive norms of student academic misconduct as predictors of (a) student misconduct and (b) faculty efforts to prevent and challenge misconduct. We also investigated the accuracy of student and faculty descriptive norm beliefs as estimates of actual student academic misconduct rates. We would like to draw attention especially to our focus on faculty beliefs regarding the frequency of student academic misconduct. There has been much less research on faculty beliefs than on student beliefs. We add to a small literature comparing the accuracy of student and faculty beliefs concerning the frequency of student academic misconduct. To our knowledge, we are the first researchers to study the behavioral correlates of faculty beliefs about levels of student academic misconduct (with a particular focus on faculty underestimators of student misconduct).

METHOD
Background

The present research was undertaken at a medium-sized public university 13
in the northeastern U.S. as part of an initiative to reduce student academic misconduct. We gathered information on undergraduate student and faculty beliefs about the frequency of various student academic misconduct behaviors for dissemination to the university community. Student data were gathered in the spring of 2002 and the spring of 2003, and faculty data were gathered in the spring of 2003. Independent-samples *t* tests comparing 2002 and 2003 student data indicated no significant differences on total scores for self-reported misconduct or beliefs about the misconduct of the students' peers (despite some dissemination of the information in between the administrations), so the two years' data were analyzed together.

Participants

Students. In the spring of 2002, 166 undergraduate students (representing 14
1.7% of the undergraduate population of 9,551) completed the student survey. Another 255 undergraduate students completed the survey in the spring

of 2003, representing 2.6% of the total undergraduate population of 9,794 at that time. The total student sample size was 421. Of the 400 who reported their gender, 45.75% were male and 54.25% were female; these percentages are very close to the student population, which included about 49% males and 51% females. The only other demographic information asked of the students was their age; the mean was 20.9 years. Students under 18 years of age were excluded from our study.

Faculty. Out of a total faculty population of 848 (including both full-   15
time and part-time faculty), 157 members of the faculty responded to the faculty survey, providing a response rate of 18.5%. This response rate is not high and raises the possibility of selection bias in our sample. Some evidence of representativeness is provided by the demographic similar-ity of our sample and the population. Of 144 faculty respondents who reported gender, 86 (59.7%) were male and 58 (40.3%) were female; these percentages are almost identical to those for the faculty population. There were 75 who reported teaching full-time and 74 who reported teaching part-time; the percentages are very close to the faculty population, which included 47% full-time and 53% part-time faculty members. Among those who reported the length of time they taught at the university, 39% reported teaching for 5 years or less; 21% reported teaching 5–10 years; 16% 10–15 years; 7% 15–20 years; and 17% reported teaching more than 20 years. We did not have access to population data for years of teaching, so we cannot make a comparison. Most of the faculty respondents (82%) reported teaching in the School of Arts and Sciences; this is somewhat higher than the population value of 65% in the fall of 2004. Percentages for other schools were 8% for the School of Education and Professional Studies (population value of 16%), 8% for the School of Business (popu-lation value of 11%), and 3% for the School of Technology (population value of 8%).

Survey Instruments

Two surveys were developed as part of the research project, one for   16
students and one for faculty. The main part of each survey was a list of 16 misconduct behaviors adapted from examples in the university's mis-conduct policy. Because respondents may disagree on what constitutes cheating or plagiarism, we described the behaviors devoid of any moral or ethical judgment (see Table 1 for the actual behaviors). One adaptation we made was to distinguish between planned and unplanned misconduct; for some behaviors, we included separate items for planned and unplanned instances. We also included some items about students' resistance to misconduct when they had the opportunity, but those items are not reported here.

Student survey. For each of the 16 behaviors, students were asked   17
two questions. The first question was intended to gather students' actual
self-reports of misconduct: "How frequently have **YOU** engaged in each
behavior?" The second question was intended to measure students' beliefs
about the academic misconduct of their peers: "How frequently do you
believe other [university] students typically engage in each behavior?"
A 5-point Likert-type scale was used, including the following response
options: 1 = Never, 2 = Seldom (once or twice), 3 = Occasionally (several
times), 4 = Often (5 to 10 times), and 5 = Very Often (more than 10 times).
Students were also asked how much they knew about the university policy
on academic misconduct (they responded on a 5-point Likert-type scale
ranging from 1 = Nothing to 5 = A lot). There was also a checklist asking students to report the sources of their information on the university's
academic misconduct policy (a course syllabus, a course instructor, the
university webpage, other students, The Learning Center, and some other
source). The student survey concluded by requesting respondents' age and
gender.

Faculty survey. Faculty respondents were asked for two responses about   18
each of the 16 behaviors. The first response concerned their beliefs about
student academic misconduct. The description of the behavior was followed
by the question "I believe the typical [university] student has done this,"
followed by the same response scale used for the student survey. The second
response concerned the extent to which faculty members had challenged
students. Phrased thus, "I have accused specific students of engaging in this
behavior," it was followed by response options: 1 = Never, 2 = Once in my
career, 3 = Every few years, 4 = Once or twice a year, 5 = More often. As on
the student survey, there were also questions regarding students declining to
cheat or plagiarize when they had the opportunity (again, these results are
not reported here). Faculty were also asked for their knowledge of the university's Academic Misconduct Policy (they responded on a 5-point Likert-
like scale ranging from 1 = Nothing to 5 = A lot). Next, they were asked what
strategies they used to deter academic misconduct (e.g., provide information
on university policy, design assignments that make it difficult to use unapproved sources). The demographic variables included length of time teaching at the university, part-time or full-time status, gender, and the school in
which the instructor taught.

Survey Procedures

Student survey. We contacted instructors from a selection of general educa-   19
tion courses by telephone or email and asked for 15 minutes at the end of
class for the administration of the survey. We focused on general education
courses because the students represent a cross-section of undergraduates

at the university. Instructors in a variety of disciplines including mathematics, geography, psychology, and political science agreed to allow data collection. The survey was administered by a graduate research assistant after the course instructor had left, so that no faculty member was nearby when students were responding. Students were told that their participation was entirely voluntary, and that they could leave at any time before or after beginning the survey. Students were assured that their responses would be completely anonymous. Students were not offered any remuneration for their participation, although in a few instances students received extra credit for their involvement in the project. Very few students declined to participate.

Faculty survey. All full-time and part-time members of the faculty were contacted by email and invited to participate in the survey. The email provided a link to the Academic Integrity Web site homepage, where faculty members could access the survey online. Access to the online survey was restricted to faculty members by requiring them to enter their University ID and password. Faculty identities were not stored in the database containing faculty responses. Confidentiality of all responses was assured. All faculty members were provided with the option of contacting the project coordinator to obtain a paper copy of the survey. In addition, because many of the university's part-time faculty members do not reliably use their university email accounts, paper surveys with cover letters were sent to all part-time faculty members via interdepartmental mail. Eighty-nine responses (56.7%) were received via the Web survey and 68 (43.3%) were received on paper. Almost all the paper surveys were from part-time instructors.

Data Aggregation

For some of our research goals, we analyzed individual behaviors (e.g., looking at the accuracy of student and faculty student academic misconduct descriptive norm beliefs), while for others we aggregated responses across behaviors (e.g., to test the hypothesis that student beliefs about levels of peer academic misconduct predicted student misconduct). Here we describe how we aggregated data.

For student self-reported misconduct, we simply took each student's mean response (on the 5-point scale) across the 16 behaviors as their total misconduct score. If a student failed to respond to more than two behaviors (i.e., left more than two blank), we did not compute that student's total score and the student was excluded from all relevant analyses. Of the 421 respondents, 18 had their total misconduct scores excluded for this reason. Additionally, we computed subscores for different types of misconduct. These types included exam cheating and plagiarism; planned misconduct and unplanned misconduct; and receiving unauthorized assistance and giving unauthorized assistance.

For the student academic misconduct descriptive norm beliefs of   23
both students and faculty, we created total scores in the same way as for self-reported misconduct. We excluded 25 students' peer descriptive norms belief scores and 12 faculty members' student descriptive norms belief scores due to more than two missing responses. We also aggregated faculty challenging responses in the same way, and excluded 17 cases due to missing responses.

Finally, we created summary scores on students' number of sources of   24
misconduct information (the number of sources the student checked) and faculty members' number of prevention strategies used (the number of strategies checked).

RESULTS

Frequency of Misconduct

Table 1 provides information on students' reports of their own actual mis-   25
conduct on the 16 behaviors. These results are reported in two ways; first, the percentage of students who said they have ever done the behavior is given, followed by the mean on the 1–5 scale. The percentages ranged from a low of 8.0% for "Improperly acquired or distributed examinations" to a high of 65.2% for "Worked with another student on material to be submitted for academic evaluation when the instructor had not authorized working together." The average percentage across behaviors was 32.2%. While these percentages are substantial, the means on the 1–5 scale indicated that students typically were not habitual offenders. Only one behavior had a mean higher than 2 (a 2 on the response scale represented having done the behavior once or twice). Moreover, across all 16 behaviors, the mean scores averaged 1.49. On the other hand, results not shown in Table 1 indicated that 90.1% of students admitted engaging in at least one misconduct behavior at least once. These results as a whole indicate that the large majority of students have engaged in misconduct, but for most students it is a very rare occurrence.

Student Beliefs about the Academic Misconduct of Their Peers (Research Goals 1 and 2)

Research goal #1: Replicate the positive relationship between student beliefs about the academic misconduct of their peers and students' reports of their own misconduct.

We used the aggregated belief and self-reported misconduct vari-   26
ables, and tested for the relationship two ways. First, we used a Pearson

correlation coefficient, and then we used multiple regression to control for other variables. In the regression analysis, the outcome variable was self-reports of misconduct; the main predictor variable was peer academic misconduct descriptive norms beliefs; and the control variables included self-reported knowledge of the academic misconduct policy (found by Jordan, 2001, to be a predictor of cheating), the number of sources from which the student had received information about the policy (we suspected students with more information would be less likely to cheat), age (McCabe et al., 2001, reviewed evidence that younger students tend to cheat more), gender (male = 0; female = 1) (according to McCabe et al., 2001, some studies have shown that males cheated more than females), and year in which the data were collected (in case there was any change).

The correlation matrix for all variables is shown in Table 2. Consistent with previous research, there was a significant ($p < .05$) correlation between beliefs regarding peer academic misconduct and self-reported misconduct, $r = .35$. The regression analysis (see Table 3) also showed a significant relationship when we controlled for the other variables. One further finding from the regression analysis was the negative regression coefficient for gender, indicating that males reported more misconduct than did females. Both the correlational and regression results replicated previous research.

27

To see whether our results depended on the type of misconduct, we conducted six additional analyses. Each one used one of our six misconduct subscores as the outcome variable, the corresponding descriptive norms belief subscore as a predictor, and all additional predictors included in the overall analysis. These analyses showed results virtually identical to those from the overall analyses (the same predictors showed significant regression coefficients).

28

Research goal #2: Assess the accuracy of students' beliefs about the academic misconduct of their peers.

Table 1 provides mean beliefs for each of the 16 behaviors, and these belief results can be directly compared with means for actual self-reported misconduct, which are also provided in Table 1. For every one of the 16 behaviors, beliefs were higher than actual misconduct. We compared the means using dependent-samples *t* tests, and every one was statistically significant ($p < .05$). (As a check, we also conducted non-parametric comparisons using the Wilcoxon Signed-Ranks test, and again all 16 behaviors showed significant differences.) These results provide strong evidence that student academic misconduct peer descriptive norms beliefs overestimated the actual occurrence of misconduct.

29

TABLE 1
Means and Frequencies for Student Misconduct, Student Peer Descriptive Norms Beliefs, Faculty Descriptive Norms Beliefs, and Faculty Accusations

Misconduct Behavior	% Students reporting at least once	Student Mean Behavior[a]	Student Mean Descriptive Norms Belief[a]	Faculty Mean Descriptive Norms Belief[a]	Faculty Mean Accusation[b]	% Faculty Accusing at least once
1. Planned in advance and then copied from another person's paper or received unauthorized aid from another person during an examination.	26.9	1.38 (0.75)	2.88 (0.91)	2.03 (0.74)	1.95 (1.03)	53
2. Did not plan to, but did copy from another person's paper or received unauthorized aid from another person during an examination.	39.4	1.50 (0.71)	3.02 (0.98)	2.29 (0.67)	2.02 (1.13)	51
3. Planned to and then used unauthorized materials or devices during an examination or any other form of academic evaluation and grading; for example, used signals, notes, books, or calculators during an examination when the instructor has not approved their use.	29.9	1.44 (0.79)	2.88 (1.00)	1.88 (0.70)	1.58 (0.95)	32.2

(Continued)

TABLE 1
(Continued)

Misconduct Behavior	% Students reporting at least once	Student Mean Behavior[a]	Student Mean Descriptive Norms Belief[a]	Faculty Mean Descriptive Norms Belief[a]	Faculty Mean Accusation[b]	% Faculty Accusing at least once
4. Did not plan to, but did use unauthorized materials or devices during an examination or any other form of academic evaluation and grading.	28.5	1.37 (0.67)	2.66 (0.85)	1.87 (0.76)	1.58 (1.02)	28.5
5. Planned to and then allowed another person to copy from your paper during an examination.	35.7	1.55 (0.88)	2.79 (1.00)	1.95 (0.70)	1.62 (0.91)	35.9
6. Realized during an exam that another student wanted to copy from your paper, and allowed that student to copy (or did not prevent the student from copying).	46.6	1.73 (0.95)	2.78 (0.98)	2.00 (0.69)	1.55 (0.94)	30.3
7. Improperly acquired or distributed examinations; for example, stealing examinations before the test period or taking a copy of an examination from a testing room without the permission of the instructor.	8	1.13 (0.53)	2.14 (0.90)	1.54 (0.70)	1.17 (0.53)	11.1

8.	Submitted another's material as one's own for academic evaluation.	12.3	1.17 (0.51)	2.54 (1.00)	2.40 (0.98)	2.50 (1.30)	70.5
9.	Prepared work for another student to submit for academic evaluation.	18.8	1.25 (0.58)	2.45 (0.92)	2.02 (0.81)	1.59 (0.98)	31
10.	Worked with another student on material to be submitted for academic evaluation when the instructor had not authorized working together.	65.2	2.11 (1.03)	3.13 (1.05)	2.62 (0.91)	2.01 (1.12)	52.1
11.	Submitted the same work, or substantially similar work, in more than one course without prior consent of the evaluating instructor(s).	42.9	1.70 (0.99)	2.89 (1.08)	2.36 (0.80)	1.75 (1.03)	41
12.	Used unauthorized materials or fabricated data in an academic exercise; for example, falsifying data in a research paper or laboratory activity.	35.1	1.52 (0.86)	2.67 (1.02)	1.98 (0.84)	1.47 (0.94)	23.7
13.	Copied sentences, phrases, paragraphs, tables, figures or data directly or in slightly modified form from a book, article, or other academic source without using quotation marks or giving proper acknowledgment to the original author or source.	60.6	1.98 (1.00)	3.17 (1.09)	3.31 (1.07)	3.04 (1.52)	70.3

(Continued)

TABLE 1
(Continued)

Misconduct Behavior	% Students reporting at least once	Student Mean Behavior[a]	Student Mean Descriptive Norms Belief[a]	Faculty Mean Descriptive Norms Belief[a]	Faculty Mean Accusation[b]	% Faculty Accusing at least once
14. Copied information from Internet websites and submitted it as your own work.	39.4	1.60 (0.90)	3.04 (1.05)	3.01 (1.14)	2.76 (1.57)	62.7
15. Bought papers for the purpose of turning them in as your own work.	8.2	1.15 (0.59)	2.55 (1.00)	1.86 (0.82)	1.34 (0.78)	18.9
16. Sold or lent papers so another student could turn them in as his or her own work.	18	1.25 (0.63)	2.64 (1.00)	1.94 (0.83)	1.23 (0.67)	13.8

[a]Response scale for self-reported misconduct and peer descriptive norms beliefs: 1: Never; 2: Seldom (once or twice); 3: Occasionally (several times); 4: Often (5 to 10 times); 5: Very Often (more than 10 times).

[b]Response scale for faculty accusations: 1: Never; 2: Once in my career; 3: Every few years; 4: Once or twice a year; 5: More often.

Note: Because of the different scale used, comparisons between faculty mean accusation and student mean behavior, student mean perception, and faculty mean perception are not viable.

TABLE 2
Correlations for Student Variables

Variable	1.	2.	3.	4.	5.	6.
1. Misconduct	1					
2. Descriptive Norms Beliefs	0.35*	1				
3. Knowledge of Policy	−0.05	0.09	1			
4. # of sources of information	0.07	0.10	0.35*	1		
5. Age	−0.06	−0.11*	0.02	−0.01	1	
6. Gender (1 = M, 2 = F)	−0.19*	0.11*	0.22*	0.03	−0.09	1
7. Year	0.09	0.09	0.07	0.06	−0.10	−0.00

Note: N = 373
*$p < 0.05$

TABLE 3
Results for Regression Predicting Student Misconduct

Predictor	Unstandardized Coefficient	95% Confidence Interval	Standardized Coefficient	Significance
Descriptive Norms Beliefs	0.25	0.18 to 0.31	0.37	*
Knowledge of Policy	−0.02	−0.07 to 0.02	−0.05	n.s.
# of sources of information	0.02	−0.02 to 0.06	0.05	n.s.
Age	−0.003	−0.02 to 0.01	−0.03	n.s.
Gender	−0.22	−0.31 to −0.13	−0.23	*
Year	0.05	−0.04 to 0.15	0.06	n.s.

Note: $R^2 = 0.18$.
*$p < 0.05$.

Faculty Beliefs about Student Academic Misconduct (Research Goals 3–6)

Research goal #3: Test the hypothesis that faculty beliefs about the frequency of student academic misconduct will be positively associated with efforts to prevent misconduct.

We tested this hypothesis using multiple regression. The outcome variable was prevention efforts, and the main predictor was beliefs about the

30

frequency of misconduct. Control variables included self-rated knowledge of the misconduct policy, the four dummy variables representing years of service at the university, full-time versus part-time status (coded 1 and 2, respectively), and gender (coded 1 for male and 2 for female). The correlation matrix for all these variables appears in Table 4, and regression results appear in Table 5. As we hypothesized, beliefs about the frequency of misconduct had a significant ($p < .05$) regression coefficient with a standardized coefficient of .30. Knowledge of the policy also had a significant regression weight, with the same standardized coefficient of .30. The variable indicating full-time versus part-time faculty status was also a significant predictor, with a standardized coefficient of $-.24$, indicating more prevention efforts by full-time faculty. The R^2 was .32.

We conducted six additional regression analyses using descriptive   31
norms belief subscores as predictors. These analyses each showed the descriptive norms beliefs variable, knowledge of the policy, and full-time versus part-time status to be the only significant predictors, as in the overall analysis.

> *Research goal #4: Test the hypothesis that faculty beliefs about the frequency of student academic misconduct will be positively associated with efforts to challenge students suspected of misconduct.*

We conducted another multiple regression analysis to test this hypothesis.   32
The outcome variable was challenging misconduct, and the predictors were the same as for prevention efforts. Correlations of challenging misconduct appear in Table 4, and regression results are in Table 6. There was a significant regression coefficient for descriptive norms beliefs only; the standardized coefficient was .49. The R^2 was .32.

Additional regression analyses using descriptive norms belief subscores   33
as predictors showed results very similar to the overall results. The only difference was that for some of the subscore analyses, knowledge of the policy was a significant predictor in addition to the descriptive norms beliefs variable.

It is important to note that, overall, faculty reports of challenging   34
students were quite low—the mean response across all 16 behaviors was 1.82. A response of 1 meant "Never" while a 2 meant "Once in my career." This indicates that faculty members have very rarely challenged students suspected of misconduct. This is consistent with previous reports (Keith-Spiegel et al., 1998; Schneider, 1999) and means that most misconduct is going undetected or unchallenged. We believe this is a serious matter that needs to be investigated further. Research goal #6 (below) focuses on this issue.

TABLE 4
Correlation Matrix for Faculty Variables

	1.	2.	3.	4.	5.	6.	7.	8.	9.
1. Prevention Efforts	1.00								
2. Challenging Students	0.43*	1.00							
3. Descriptive Norms Beliefs	0.35*	0.53*	1.00						
4. Knowledge of Policy	0.40*	0.21*	0.17*	1.00					
5. Full-time/Part-time	−0.30*	−0.13	0.01	−0.20*	1.00				
6. Gender	0.11	0.06	0.02	−0.04	0.01	1.00			
7. Years-of-service Dummy Variable 1	−0.09	−0.18*	−0.24*	−0.10	0.06	−0.16	1.00		
8. Years-of-service Dummy Variable 2	0.07	0.10	0.19*	0.02	−0.01	0.16	−0.39*	1.00	
9. Years-of-service Dummy Variable 3	0.00	0.00	−0.03	0.04	0.02	0.19*	−0.34*	−0.24*	1.00
10. Years-of-service Dummy Variable 4	−0.11	−0.09	−0.04	−0.01	0.08	0.06	−0.21*	−0.15	−0.13

Note: N = 135, except for 'Challenging Students', for which N = 129.
*$p < 0.05$

TABLE 5
Results for Regression Predicting Faculty Prevention Efforts

Predictor	Unstandardized Coefficient	95% Confidence Interval	Standardized Coefficient	Significance
Descriptive Norms Beliefs	1.07	0.52 to 1.62	0.30	*
Knowledge of Policy	0.57	0.29 to 0.86	0.30	*
Full-time/Part-time	−0.92	−1.51 to −.34	−0.24	*
Gender	0.57	−0.04 to 1.18	0.14	n.s.
Yrs-of-Service 1	−0.01	−0.86 to 0.83	−.004	n.s.
Yrs-of-Service 2	−0.22	−1.15 to 0.70	−0.05	n.s.
Yrs-of-Service 3	−0.26	−1.25 to 0.73	−0.05	n.s.
Yrs-of-Service 4	−0.76	−2.02 to 0.50	−0.10	n.s.

Note: R^2 = .32.
*$p < 0.05$.

TABLE 6
Results for Regression Predicting Faculty Efforts to Challenge Student Misconduct

Predictor	Unstandardized Coefficient	95% Confidence Interval	Standardized Coefficient	Significance
Descriptive Norms Beliefs	0.56	0.38 to 0.74	0.49	*
Knowledge of Policy	0.07	−0.02 to 0.17	0.12	n.s.
Full-time/Part-time	−0.12	−0.32 to 0.08	−0.10	n.s.
Gender	0.06	−0.14 to 0.26	0.05	n.s.
Yrs-of-Service 1	−0.17	−0.45 to 0.11	−0.13	n.s.
Yrs-of-Service 2	−0.13	−0.44 to 0.18	−0.09	n.s.
Yrs-of-Service 3	−0.12	−0.45 to 0.20	−0.07	n.s.
Yrs-of-Service 4	−0.26	−0.68 to 0.15	−0.11	n.s.

Note: $R^2 = 0.32$.
*$p < 0.05$.

Research goal #5: Test the hypothesis that faculty beliefs about the frequency of student academic misconduct will be lower, and more accurate, than student beliefs.

Table 1 provides mean faculty descriptive norms beliefs for each of the 16 behaviors, and these belief results can be directly compared with means for (a) students' peer descriptive norms beliefs and (b) students' actual self-reported misconduct, which is also included in Table 1. Faculty belief means were lower than student belief means for all behaviors except "Copied sentences, phrases, paragraphs, tables, figures or data directly or in slightly modified form from a book, article, or other academic source without using quotation marks or giving proper acknowledgment to the original author or source," for which the faculty mean was higher. Independent-samples *t* tests showed significant differences on 14 of the 16 behaviors. The only behaviors for which the differences were nonsignificant were "Submitted another's material as one's own for academic evaluation" and "Copied sentences, phrases, paragraphs, tables, figures or data directly or in slightly modified form from a book, article, or other academic source without using quotation marks or giving proper acknowledgment to the original author or source." In general, our hypothesis was confirmed: Faculty beliefs about the frequency of student academic misconduct were lower than those of students, and therefore they were more accurate in that they were significantly closer to student self-reports of academic misconduct. 35

Although faculty beliefs about the frequency of student academic misconduct were more accurate than those of students, we conducted independent-samples *t* tests to see if faculty beliefs were significantly higher than students' self-reports. In all cases, faculty overestimated the actual occurrence of misconduct; the differences were all significant, $p < .05$ (nonparametric Mann-Whitney *U* tests confirmed all 16 significant differences). Therefore, while faculty beliefs were more accurate than were student beliefs, faculty as a group still overestimated student misconduct. 36

Research goal #6: Examine efforts by faculty who underestimate a given misconduct behavior to challenge students on that behavior.

As we noted earlier, failure to challenge misconduct is a frequent problem. We wanted to know if it is a particular problem for faculty who underestimate the frequency of misconduct. To address this goal, we defined underestimators, one behavior at a time, as faculty whose response to a particular behavior fell below the mean of students' actual self-reports of engaging in that behavior. Most behaviors had student self-reported means between 37

1 and 2, so underestimators were generally the faculty who chose 1, the lowest response option. Because none of the mean self-reports was a whole number, it was impossible to be "accurate" in the strict sense, so all faculty not classified as underestimators were actually overestimators (even though in some cases these overestimators were as accurate as it was possible to be). We divided faculty into these two categories for each behavior. For each behavior, we report (separately for under- and overestimators) in Table 7 the efforts to challenge students on the behavior. Specifically, we report the percentage of faculty members in each category who said they never challenged a student on that behavior.

For each of the 16 behaviors, more than half the underestimators   38
reported *never* having challenged a student on that behavior. The mean percentage across all 16 behaviors was 87%. The comparable mean for overestimators was 54%. Even the overestimators apparently rarely challenge students on misconduct, but this is true in the extreme for underestimators.

TABLE 7
Comparing Faculty Underestimators with Others on Challenging Misconduct

Behavior (#s from Table 1)	Percent Who Never Challenged a Student	
	Underestimators	*Overestimators*
1	66% (23 of 35)	41% (46 of 112)
2	85% (11 of 13)	46% (61 of 134)
3	88% (37 of 42)	60% (62 of 104)
4	94% (45 of 48)	60% (57 of 95)
5	84% (32 of 38)	58% (61 of 105)
6	90% (26 of 29)	64% (71 of 111)
7	96% (76 of 79)	79% (49 of 62)
8	72% (18 of 25)	23% (27 of 117)
9	93% (37 of 40)	59% (61 of 103)
10	57% (35 of 61)	41% (34 of 83)
11	88% (14 of 16)	55% (68 of 124)
12	100% (41 of 41)	66% (62 of 94)
13	100% (4 of 4)	28% (39 of 142)
14	83% (10 of 12)	33% (44 of 135)
15	96% (48 of 50)	74% (67 of 91)
16	98% (45 of 46)	80% (77 of 96)

DISCUSSION

We found that faculty beliefs about the frequency of student academic mis-   39
conduct were positively related to two important faculty behaviors: prevention efforts and efforts to challenge students suspected of misconduct. To
our knowledge, faculty descriptive norms beliefs about student misconduct
have not been related to faculty behavior in previous research. Faculty
beliefs were lower than student beliefs, indicating that faculty considered
misconduct less common, and this finding is consistent with two prior studies (Koljatic & Silva, 2002; Wajda-Johnston et al., 2001). However, faculty
in the current study still overestimated the actual frequency of misconduct;
in previous studies, Koljatic and Silva (2002) found that on average faculty
were quite accurate, while Wajda-Johnston et al. found that faculty underes-
timated misconduct.

Our data on student descriptive norms beliefs about peer misconduct   40
replicated previous findings that beliefs are related to actual misconduct
(Whitley, 1998) and showed that students considerably overestimated the
frequency of peers' misconduct (in fact, most students reported very rarely
engaging in misconduct). The overestimation by undergraduate students is
consistent with Koljatic and Silva (2002) but inconsistent with Jordan (2001).

Our findings demonstrate the importance of beliefs about the frequency   41
of student academic misconduct for both faculty and students. We believe
the most important of our results are those showing faculty descriptive
norms beliefs to predict efforts to prevent and challenge misconduct. These
behaviors are crucial, though others have noted that faculty members often
seem hesitant to make strong efforts to head off and deal with misconduct
(Keith-Spiegel et al., 1998; Schneider, 1999). Our research sheds light on
one possible factor that may influence faculty behavior. It is plausible that
believing misconduct very rarely occurs would lead faculty members to de-
emphasize prevention efforts and efforts to identify and confront offenders.
In fact, our results showed that faculty members who underestimate the frequency of misconduct *very* rarely take action to challenge students' misconduct. It is highly likely that at least some students in these faculty members'
classes engage in misconduct and "get away with it." In fact, and this is just
speculation, it may even be that the lack of prevention efforts has the effect
of encouraging students and therefore increasing the amount of misconduct
for faculty members who underestimate the problem. In any case, we believe
it is important for students to understand that faculty members take misconduct seriously, and that means faculty members need to send that message to students through prevention and detection efforts.

We suggest that one way to increase the number of faculty members   42
actively working against misconduct is to make faculty more aware of the

scope of misconduct. Campuses may wish to measure and disseminate accurate information concerning the frequency of student academic misconduct to the faculty. This brings up an interesting difference between interventions regarding faculty versus student descriptive norms beliefs. Social norming interventions for alcohol use focus on *reducing* student beliefs about the frequency of peers' behavior (Berkowitz, 2003), but possibly faculty interventions need in some cases to *increase* beliefs regarding academic misconduct so that faculty members do not underestimate the problem. We would caution that the presentation of this type of information should be done carefully. Our findings indicate that most students only rarely engaged in misconduct, so it would be wrong to imply that the typical student at our university cheats a lot. But even with misconduct at low levels per student in any given semester, it is very likely that a faculty member will have at least one instance of misconduct in at least one class each term.

Another finding regarding faculty deserves mention. Greater knowledge 43 of the misconduct policy had significant positive correlations with prevention efforts and with more challenging of misconduct (see Table 4). Multiple regression results showed a significant regression coefficient for predicting prevention but not challenging. These findings suggest that it may be useful for colleges and universities to promote their policies to make sure faculty are familiar with them. Future research on faculty behavior should evaluate the effects of providing accurate information and increasing awareness of misconduct policies.

The importance for students of peer descriptive norms has long been 44 known (Berkowitz, 2003), so the overestimation by students of peers' misconduct behavior has important implications. It may well lead to higher levels of misconduct than would occur if students had beliefs that are more accurate. Possibly social norming interventions, intended to give students information about peer behavior that is more accurate, could be useful in reducing misconduct.

One interesting question is why students have been found to overes- 45 timate peer descriptive norms in some research (Koljatic & Silva, 2002, as well as the current study), while other research has found underestimation (Jordan, 2001). We suspect the degree of over- or underestimation at a college or university is influenced by many local factors such as the nature of the student population, faculty behavior, and campus policies (e.g., whether the campus has an honor code and stresses its importance). Another question is why student beliefs about the frequency of student academic misconduct have consistently been found to be higher than faculty beliefs. Students certainly have opportunities to discuss misconduct issues with each other (e.g., gossiping about cheating by friends or classmates; hearing other students brag about cheating), whereas students are unlikely to share that information with faculty. Students should therefore find it easier than faculty members to call to mind examples of misconduct. This easy availability can lead to overestimation, as noted by Tversky and Kahneman (1974). On the other hand, news reports of high levels of cheating are certainly available to faculty, so it would not be surprising for faculty to have similarly high estimates. It may be that the information available to students is more influential, leading to higher estimates than for faculty.

Future research can explore what factors determine beliefs about misconduct for both students and faculty members. In the previous paragraph, we suggested that beliefs might be increased by exposure to particular instances of cheating (e.g., finding out that some acquaintances just cheated may raise a student's perception of the typical behavior). It is possible that a student's peer group is an important factor. Some groups of students may actually have higher rates of misconduct (e.g., McCabe & Treviño, 1997, found higher rates for fraternity and sorority members), and students in those groups may therefore have higher beliefs. Future research should explore this and other factors, such as year in school and personality variables. 46

We think it is important to reiterate our finding about the frequency of student misconduct. Previous evidence suggests high rates of cheating (e.g., McCabe et al., 2001; Michaels & Miethe, 1989), and our own data could be interpreted as supporting that same conclusion: Slightly more than 90% of our sample reported engaging in misconduct. However, our conclusion is actually that misconduct was rare for the typical student in our sample. This conclusion reflects the frequency of misconduct. While most students admit to having engaged in at least one misconduct behavior at least one time, most students report having done so very infrequently. Looking at the data this way leads to a different conclusion from examination of overall misconduct rates. 47

We should mention some limitations of the current study. First, like other studies investigating descriptive norms beliefs about student academic misconduct, our research is correlational rather than experimental. Because of the type of research design, we cannot be sure about the nature of cause-and-effect. For example, while we suggested that greater knowledge of the misconduct policy might have increased prevention efforts, it might actually be that those more concerned about preventing misconduct took the time to learn more about the policy. 48

A second limitation is that our study took place at a single university. This means that care needs to be exercised in generalizing these results until our findings are replicated in other settings (which we recommend as a topic for future research). 49

A third limitation concerns differences between academic disciplines.   50
Disciplines differ substantially in a variety of ways such as mechanisms for
dealing with deviance (misconduct) (Braxton & Hargen, 1996). This might
be reflected in faculty members' greater or lesser attentiveness to student
misconduct and also in students' misconduct behavior. It would be ideal to
look for differences among disciplines in both faculty and student data; we
were not able to do that, but we recommend it as a topic for future research.

While we believe our study has made an important contribution to the   51
knowledge base on student misconduct, particularly regarding the importance of faculty descriptive norms beliefs, we reiterate our call for future
research. Important questions remain regarding the source of descriptive
norms beliefs by both faculty members and students, as well as why students' beliefs tend to differ from those of faculty. We also call for research
to see whether descriptive norms beliefs and/or the relationships we found
differ by academic discipline. Another important question is how to increase
faculty efforts at prevention and enforcement. Perhaps the most important
question is how to change beliefs about the frequency of student academic
misconduct to reflect the actual levels. There is evidence that "social norms"
campaigns providing accurate descriptive norms information about student
alcohol use can reduce alcohol consumption, and campaigns regarding misconduct might have a similar effect.

REFERENCES

Berkowitz, A. D. (2003). *The social norms approach: Theory, research and annotated bibliography.* Retrieved June 12, 2004, from http://www.edc.org/hec/socialnorms/theory.html

Braxton, J. M., & Hargen, L. L. (1996). Variations among academic disciplines: Analytical frame-works and research. In J. C. Smart (Ed.), *Higher education: A handbook of theory and research* (Vol. 11, pp. 1–46). NY: Agathon Press.

Cialdini, R. B., Reno, R. R., & Kallgren, C. A. (1990). A focus theory of normative conduct: Recycling the concept of norms to reduce littering in public places. *Journal of Personality and Social Psychology, 58,* 1015–1026.

Harris, M. J., & Rosenthal, R. (1985). Mediation of interpersonal expectancy effects: 31 Meta-analyses. *Psychological Bulletin, 97,* 363–386.

Jordan, A. E. (2001). College student cheating: The role of motivation, perceived norms, attitudes, and knowledge of institutional policy. *Ethics & Behavior, 11,* 233–247.

Keith-Spiegel, P., Tabachnik, B. G., Whitley, B. E., Jr., & Washburn, J. (1998). Why professors ignore cheating: Opinions of a national sample of psychology instructors. *Ethics & Behavior, 8,* 215–227.

Koljatic, M., & Silva, M. (2002). Comparison of students' and faculty's perceptions of occurrence of dishonest academic behaviors. *Psychological Reports, 90,* 883–888.

Lim, V. K. G., & See, S. K. B. (2001). Attitudes toward, and intentions to report, academic cheat-ing among students in Singapore. *Ethics & Behavior, 11,* 261–274.

McCabe, D. L., & Treviño, L. K. (1997). Individual and contextual influences on academic dis-honesty: A multicampus investigation. *Research in Higher Education, 38,* 379–396.

McCabe, D. L., Treviño, L. K., & Butterfield, K. D. (2001). Cheating in academic institutions: A decade of research. *Ethics & Behavior, 11*(3), 219–232.

Michaels, J. W., & Miethe, T. D. (1989). Applying theories of deviance to academic cheating. *Social Science Quarterly, 70*, 870–885.

Neuliep, J. W. (1987). The influence of Theory X and Theory Y management styles on the selection of compliance-gaining strategies. *Communication Research Reports, 4*(1), 14–19.

Perkins, H. W. (2002). Social norms and the prevention of alcohol use in collegiate contexts. *Journal of Studies on Alcohol, Supplement 14*, 164–172.

Rosenthal, R., & Jacobson, L. (1968). Pygmalion in the classroom: Teacher expectation and pupils' intellectual development. New York: Holt, Rinehart, & Winston.

Schneider, A. (1999). Why professors don't do more to stop students who cheat. *Chronicle of Higher Education, 45*(20), A8–A10.

Smith, B. H. (2004). A randomized study of a peer-led, small group social norming intervention designed to reduce drinking among college students. *Journal of Alcohol & Drug Education, 47*(3), 67–75.

Tversky, A., & Kahneman, D. (1974). Judgment under uncertainty: Heuristics and biases. *Science, 185*, 1124–1131.

Wajda-Johnston, V. A., Handal, P. J., Brawer, P. A., & Fabricatore, A. N. (2001). Academic dishonesty at the graduate level. *Ethics & Behavior, 11*, 287–305.

White, S. S., & Locke, E. A. (2000). Problems with the Pygmalion effect and some proposed solutions. *Leadership Quarterly, 11*, 389–415.

Whitley, B. E., Jr. (1998). Factors associated with cheating among college students. *Research in Higher Education, 39*, 235–274.

QUESTIONS FOR COMPREHENSION, STUDY, AND DISCUSSION

1. What is the difference between descriptive norms and prescriptive norms?

2. Why would it be misleading to suggest that this study indicates that 90.1 percent of students admitted to academic misconduct?

3. The authors of this study hoped to show a relationship between a student's own academic misconduct and that student's beliefs about the misconduct of other students. To what extent did the authors succeed?

4. What did the authors find out about the accuracy of students' beliefs about the misconduct of their peers?

5. What did the authors find out about the relationship between faculty beliefs about the frequency of student misconduct and faculty efforts to *prevent* misconduct?

6. What did the authors find out about the relationship between faculty beliefs about the frequency of student misconduct and faculty efforts to *challenge* misconduct?

7. What did the authors find out about the differences between faculty beliefs about the frequency of student academic misconduct and students' beliefs?

8. What did the authors find out about faculty willingness to challenge student academic misconduct?

9. What recommendations do the authors make for reducing academic misconduct?

10. What do the authors admit are three limitations of their study?

JOURNAL PROMPT

Do you think plagiarism is a problem at your college? What do you think needs to be done to curtail this problem?

Academic Disciplines: Popular Culture; Sociology

Citation Method: APA

Rhetorical Modes: Exposition; Persuasion

This article is from the *Journal of Sex Research*, Volume 44, Number 2 (2007). It follows the APA method for source citation.

From Sex to Sexuality: Exposing the Heterosexual Script on Primetime Network Television

Janna L. Kim

California State University, Fullerton

C. Lynn Sorsoli, Katherine Collins, Bonnie A. Zylbergold, Deborah Schooler, and Deborah L. Tolman

San Francisco State University

Although it is widely recognized that sexual content pervades television, research rarely examines how television's sexual messages are gendered and occur in a relational context. This study describes the development and implementation of a new coding scheme to evaluate sexual content from a feminist perspective. Merging scripting theory (Simon & Gagnon, 1986) with the theory of compulsory heterosexuality (Rich, 1980), we explicate a heteronormative and dominant sexual script, the Heterosexual Script, and assessed its presence in the 25 primetime television programs viewed most frequently by adolescents. Our codes captured depictions of boys/men and girls/women thinking, feeling, and behaving in relational and sexual encounters in ways that sustain power inequalities between men and women. Male characters most frequently enacted the Heterosexual Script by actively and aggressively pursuing sex. Less frequently but still at high rates were depictions of female characters willingly objectifying themselves and being judged by their sexual conduct.

Recent broadcasts of sexually provocative images during primetime hours   1
have contributed to widespread concern about the pervasiveness of sex on mainstream entertainment television. One public opinion poll indicated over 60% of parents are "very concerned" about the amount of sexual

This study was supported by Grant No. R01 HD 38393-01 awarded to the final author by the National Institute of Child Health and Development. All authors wish to thank L. Monique Ward for consultation, and Meredith Everson and Andres Nunez for research assistance.

Correspondence should be addressed to Janna L. Kim, Department of Child and Adolescent Studies, California State University, Fullerton. P.O. Box 6868, Fullerton, CA 92834. E-mail: jkim@fullerton.edu

content their children see (Kaiser Family Foundation, 2004). Television portrayals of sexuality have been evaluated for decades in content analyses. These systematic analyses of television's sexual content provide an empirical backdrop for parents' concerns. Whereas initial studies often counted the number of discrete and observable sexual acts appearing on television, contemporary researchers approach this topic with greater sophistication and sensitivity (Sorsoli, Ward, & Tolman, in press).

The large-scale longitudinal content analysis conducted by the Kaiser   2
Family Foundation is the most comprehensive and recent example (Kunkel et al., 1999, 2005). Kunkel and his colleagues operationalized sexual content as "any depiction of sexual activity, sexually suggestive behavior, or talk about sexuality or sexual activity" (2005, p. 14), which accounts for different types of sexual dialogue and a wide variety of sexual behaviors, ranging from kissing and physical flirting to depicted sexual intercourse. Kunkel's group and others have confirmed that verbal and visual references to sexual activity are numerous (Lowry & Shidler, 1993; Lowry & Towles, 1989; Ward, 1995), especially in programming that is viewed by adolescents (Cope-Farrar & Kunkel, 2002), and that rates of sexual content have increased dramatically over time (Kunkel et al., 2003, 2005). The context of sexual behavior has also been assessed in terms of whether sex is portrayed as a recreational or relational activity (Ward, 1995), whether sexual partners are married or not (Kunkel, Cope, & Biely, 1999; Lowry & Shidler, 1993), and how frequently references to sexual risk or responsibility (e.g., contraception, pregnancy, sexually transmitted infections) are made (Kunkel et al., 2005; Lowry & Shidler, 1993).

Which facet of television's sexual content is highlighted is largely guided   3
by the theoretical orientation of the researchers. Previous studies are often anchored in cultivation or social learning theories. The former posits that repeated exposure to sexually oriented content on television cultivates analogous attitudes towards sex through a gradual and cumulative process (Gerbner, Gross, Morgan, & Signorielli, 1994). This theoretical perspective provides justification for studies that evaluate how often and what types of sex appear on television, since the more sex viewers see on television, the higher their sexual expectations are for people in the real world. Social learning theory (Bandura, 1977) states that television is a source of observational learning; viewers model the behaviors they see being rewarded, avoid the behaviors that are punished, and are drawn to characters who they perceive as likeable or similar to them. From this perspective, the most salient dimensions of television's sexual content include the immediate context in which sexual activity occurs, the consequences of sexual behavior, and the characteristics of individuals who are sexually active (e.g., marital status, nudity, age, gender).

Few studies have used scripting theory to address the meaning and   4
significance of sexual content on television, and even fewer have adopted

a feminist perspective to evaluate television's portrayals of heterosexuality and heterosexual romantic relationships more specifically. Scripting theory posits that sexuality is learned from culturally available "sexual scripts" that define what counts as sex, how to recognize sexual situations, and what to do in relational and sexual encounters (Gagnon & Simon, 1973; Simon & Gagnon, 1986). Scripting theory necessarily broadens the conceptualization of sexuality to encompass both its social dimensions and the relational contexts in which sexuality emerges (e.g., within romantic relationships, dating, or courtship). Ward's (1995) content analysis of 12 primetime television programs is one of the few exceptions that has focused on television's portrayals of gender and heterosexuality in tandem. Her study sheds light on several gendered sexual themes portrayed on television, including traditional beliefs that men value women primarily for their appearance, that men actively seek sexual activity, and that women use their bodies and looks to attract wealthy and handsome men.

In this article, we combine scripting theory with feminist theory that builds on and extends Ward's previous work and yields a new approach to evaluating sexual content portrayed on television. In the feminist theory of compulsory heterosexuality, Adrienne Rich (1980) argues that, rather than being "natural," heterosexual relationships are the only sanctioned social arrangement that constitutes "appropriate" or "normal" relational and sexual behavior for boys/men and girls/women. In this study, we identify the Heterosexual Script[1] as the blueprint for societally sanctioned romantic and sexual encounters and interactions (Hyde & Oliver, 1995). Reflecting dimensions of compulsory heterosexuality outlined by Rich, the Heterosexual Script entitles boys/men to prioritize their own sexual desire, to act on their sexual needs, to perceive their hormones to be "out of control," and to promise power and status to women in return for sex. Shoring up this "cultural story" (Tolman, 2002, 2006) about boys'/men's sexuality is the notion that girls/women must manage boys'/men's sexual needs in order to gain some share of their privilege. Thus, the Heterosexual Script compels girls/women to deny or devalue their own sexual desire, to seek to please boys/men, to "wish and wait" to be chosen, and to trade their own sexuality as a commodity.

5

---

[1]Several scholars have referred to a "Heterosexual Script" before, primarily in terms of how heterosexual sex gets accomplished (McCormick, 1994) or the turn-taking sequence of behaviors that take place in a sexual situation. For example, Rosotsky and Travis (2000) describe a traditional sexual script as the script that deems heterosexual intercourse as the only sexual behavior with any significance (see also McCormick, 1994, 1987; O'Sullivan & Byers, 1993). Our conception is that relational and sexual thoughts, feelings, beliefs, and behaviors are scripted at the cultural level (Simon & Gagnon, 1986), which extends beyond just the sequencing of sexual behaviors.

This feminist spin on scripting theory is particularly relevant when   6
investigating television use, since television literally presents scripts of
male and female characters coupling and uncoupling in relational and
sexual contexts. The Heterosexual Script would be what Simon & Gagnon
(1986) identify as a "cultural level" script. Although they argue that there
are interpersonal and intrapsychic variations when cultural level scripts
are enacted by actual people, we suggest that televised enactments of the
Heterosexual Script are the most reified and least variable versions of the
cultural-level script and that they have pervasive normalizing and regulatory functions. We posit not only that the Heterosexual Script is a form of
sexual content that saturates television programs targeting teens, but also
that this approach to evaluating sexual content on television is especially
relevant for studying adolescents' television viewing. Indeed, adolescents
who are engaging in their first relational and sexual experiences may seek
such scripts that orient them to how boys/men and girls/women think, feel,
and behave in relationships until they develop a body of experiences of
their own.

We depart from others who have described heterosexual scripts (e.g.,   7
Frith & Kitzinger, 2001; Oliver & Hyde, 1993; O'Sullivan and Byers, 1993,
Ward, 1995) in arguing that rather than two separate scripts for girls/
women and boys/men, there is one integrated script comprised of (a) one
"part" for how girls/women think, feel, and behave in romantic and sexual
encounters and (b) another "part" for how men think, feel, and behave in
romantic and sexual encounters. Like two voices engaging in dialogue, these
complementary "parts" comprise a single, integrated script, working in tandem to produce "culturally intelligible" (Butler, 1993, p. 46) heterosexual
interactions and relationships (e.g., the story that "real men pursue sex" and
that "good girls set sexual limits").

The purpose of this study was twofold. Our first objective was to describe   8
in detail the development of a new system for coding sexual content that
would illuminate the presence of the Heterosexual Script on television.
Our goal was to establish a coherent and credible set of codes reflecting elements of this script that could be applied reliably to television programming
though a rigorous coding procedure. Our second objective was to implement
this coding system using a sample of primetime network television programs popular among adolescent viewers. Here our goal was to assess how
frequently the Heterosexual Script was enacted in two narrative television
program genres, sitcoms and dramas, popular with teens. By systematically
assessing the gendered meanings of television's sexual content, which are
parsimoniously captured by the Heterosexual Script, this study represents
the first step in our attempt to evaluate the relationship between adolescents'
television consumption and their sexuality development in a new way.

METHOD

Code Development

Deductive and Inductive Development of the Heterosexual Script Codebook

We developed our categorical coding system to capture the ways in which   9
specific elements of the Heterosexual Script were invoked, enacted, followed or triggered on network programming popular among an adolescent
audience. Coding for the Heterosexual Script required disaggregating the
"blue print" and looking for discrete messages about the gendered and
powerful/less ways in which men and women negotiate romantic and sexual
encounters.

To ensure that our codes were firmly grounded in our theoretical frame-   10
work, the first step in this process was primarily deductive. Drawing heavily from themes initially identified by Ward (1995) in her work identifying
sexual roles on television, our research team generated a list of ideas about
how the Heterosexual Script is enacted in the dominant (white, middle
class) North American culture. Sorting these items into sets of complementary codes about how boys/men and girls/women think, feel, and behave in
romantic and sexual relationships (Tolman, 2006) served as a useful organizational tool. Situated in positions of power, men enact the Heterosexual
Script by actively pursuing sexual relationships, treating women as sexual
objects, experiencing their sexual feelings as uncontrollable, being demanding in sexual situations, rejecting homosexual feelings or behavior, appro-
priating female sexual desire (Diamond, 2005; Zylbergold, 2005), and
avoiding commitment and emotional attachment with women (Tolman
& Higgins, 1996; Check & Malamuth, 1985; Korman & Leslie, 1982; Reiss,
1960; Connell, 1987). Situated in positions of subordination, women enact
the Heterosexual Script by acting sexually passive, setting sexual limits,
using their bodies and looks to attract men, seeking stability and emotional
involvement from male partners, appearing sexually chaste, and not having or prioritizing their sexual desire (Tolman, 1996, 2002; McCormick,
Brannigan, & LaPlante, 1984; McCormick, 1979; Clark & Hatfield, 1989).

Next, a subset of our research team spent two months watching televi-   11
sion together with this initial list of codes in mind. At this primarily induc-
tive phase, the goal was to assess whether our preliminary coding scheme
adequately captured how male and female characters actually invoked the
Heterosexual Script on television programs. For this task, we used a selection of programs that were similar to (but not overlapping with) the programs recorded in our sample. Each episode was co-viewed and paused
repeatedly for coders to discuss whether an interaction warranted the application of one or more codes and why. Codes were elaborated and refined as

a result of these discussions. For example, early on, we came across a portrayal of a man expressing uncertainty about his ability to satisfy his female partner sexually. Although this depiction of male vulnerability initially seemed counter to the Heterosexual Script, we eventually deemed that his preoccupation with his sexual performance reaffirmed the scripted notion that sexual prowess is an important component of boys'/men's masculinity.

The research team determined that the codebook had matured sufficiently when it reached a point of saturation—that is, the point at which we deemed all television content relevant to the script was captured by our codes and all elements of the Heterosexual Script were represented in the codebook, which occurred after approximately 20 sessions. The procedure was then altered slightly; each coder began watching and coding programs independently, meeting periodically to review how reliably they applied the codes. The codebook was further refined based on coders talking through their disagreements and developing consensus, as is standard practice for feminist methodology. This process continued for approximately 20 additional sessions.

Description of Specific Codes

In total, our final coding scheme includes eight complementary codes reflecting four specific elements of the Heterosexual Script: the sexual double standard, courtship strategies, attitudes toward commitment, and homophobia.

The first set of complementary codes reflects the sexual double standard. *Sex as Masculinity* (SM) positions sexuality as a defining component of masculinity and encompasses notions that men are sexual initiators who are preoccupied with sex and who will go to great lengths to have intercourse. It includes the idea that men are supposed to sexually objectify women and value them primarily for their physical attractiveness. Comments about phallus size or references to men's fears about being unable to perform sexually also reflect this idea that it is important for men to actively exhibit their sexual prowess. The complementary *Good Girls* (GG) describes women as sexual gate-keepers, and accordingly, holds several contradictory ideas in tension. It encompasses notions that women are passive partners in sexual relationships who do not expect, demand, or prioritize their own sexual pleasure, but who do partake in sexual activities to fulfill the sexual needs of their male partners under acceptable conditions (i.e., to keep a relationship). This code also incorporates the belief that women are responsible for setting sexual limits, for thwarting men's sexual advances, and for dealing with the negative sexual consequences of sexual activity (e.g., pregnancy, feeling used). The use of words that link a woman's sexual history to her value as a person (i.e., slut, tramp, skanky, loose, jezebel, bimbo) warrants a Good Girls code.

The second set of complementary codes reflects strategies used by   15
women and men to attract, court, and impress their actual or potential
relational and sexual partners. *Masculine Courting Strategies* (MCS) describe
the active and powerful ways in which men attract and/or court a female
partner. They encompass notions that men are protectors and providers in
romantic relationships, that they assert their power in the courting ritual by
buying gifts or showing off their physical strength, and that they are responsible for making the first move in dating relationships.[2] Portrayals of women
being attracted to men who exhibit wealth, power, or physical strength also
warrant this code. *Feminine Courting Strategies* (FCS) state that women wait
to be asked out by men rather than asking them out directly. They describe
the passive and indirect ways in which women attract or court a male partner, such as by dressing provocatively, touching themselves suggestively,
using playful innuendo, ego-stroking, or pretending to be in need of assistance. Central to this code is the notion that women objectify themselves
(Frederickson & Roberts, 1997) and exploit their bodies to attain power in
romantic relationships.

The third set of complementary codes reflects attitudes toward com-   16
mitment in relationships. *Masculine Commitment* (MC) states that men
actively avoid commitment, marriage, monogamy, or taking their romantic
relationships "to the next level." It states that men do not take part in relationship maintenance (e.g., resolving a fight, spending time together) and
try to evade becoming emotionally involved with their female partners. The
MC code also describes men as prioritizing sex and other activities or people
(e.g., career, friends) over their romantic relationships. Accordingly, depictions of men cheating on their girlfriends or wives warrant the MC code, as
do comments that either mock or pity monogamous men for having lost
their freedom, power, or masculinity. In contrast, *Feminine Commitment*
(FC) encompasses ideas about women prioritizing their romantic relationships, making sacrifices for the sake of their partners (e.g., giving up a
career, spending less time with friends), seeking or asking for more commitment, monogamy, or marriage, and needing a boyfriend or a husband to
feel like their lives are complete.

The final set of complementary codes refers to same-sex attraction   17
and homophobia. *Male-Oriented Homophobia* (MOH) states that men
must avoid behaving in a manner that could be construed as homosexual.
Accordingly, men who are "caught" in such situations express discomfort
or embarrassment. Jokes that hinge upon the audience's understanding

---

[2]Accordingly, a depiction of a man asking a woman out on a date warranted the MCS code;
however, a depiction of a man initiating a passionate kiss with a woman received the SM code
instead.

that a male character is being ridiculed for behaving in a manner deemed homosexual warrant the MOH code. Jokes that rely on transgressions of gender roles are not coded if no explicit ties are made to a character's sexual orientation. For example, a boy who dresses in girl's clothing receives the MOH code only if it is clear that the other characteres believe his choice of apparel reflects his sexual orientation. *Appropriation of Female Homosexuality* (AFH) is the complementary code to MOH. It describes homoeroticism between female characters as arousing or as a "turn-on" to men.

Implementation of the Heterosexual Script Codebook

Selection of Television Programs

In 2001, we surveyed 273 eighth grade, 144 ninth grade, and 430 tenth   18
grade students (aged 12–17 years) as part of a larger, longitudinal study examining the impact of television consumption on adolescent sexual behavior. Students were from two diverse public school districts in the Northeastern United States. Approximately 54% of the sample was female, 58% was White, 20% was Latino, and 40% received free or reduced fee lunch. Students completed paper and pencil questionnaires assessing their television viewing habits, including their viewing frequency of 50 primetime programs that were popular among teen audiences, according to Nielsen ratings, industry publications (e.g., *Entertainment Weekly*), and extensive pilot testing. The list included situation comedies and serial dramas from network television (ABC, NBC, CBS, WB, UPN). Participants indicated how frequently they viewed each program on a 5-point scale (*never/not this season, a few times a month, once a week, a couple of times a week, almost daily*).

Based on students' viewing frequencies, we selected the top 25 programs   19
in the 2001–2002 season that participants reported watching regularly (i.e., at least a few times per month). As presented in Table 1, the final list included 16 half-hour sitcoms and 9-hour-long serial dramas. Three episodes of each program were videotaped over a four-month period and were then transferred to digital format. The inclusion of three episodes per program is standard practice in television content analyses (Kunkel et al., 2005; Ward, 1995). In total, this approach yielded a data base that included 51 hours of programming to be analyzed.

Coding Procedure

Following the analysis strategy of Ward (1995), our main unit of analysis   20
was the interaction. An interaction is defined as a segment in which one set of characters are together at one place and at one time. The entrance or exit of an additional character into a scene indicated the beginning of a new interaction, as did an interruption by time or location (e.g., a flashback) or by commercial break. In our sample, a 30-minute sitcom typically consisted

TABLE 1
Adolescents' 25 Most Popular Primetime Network Programs in the 2001–2002 Television Season

Sitcoms	Dramas
Dharma and Greg	7th Heaven
Everybody Loves Raymond	Angel
Family Guy	Boston Public
Friends	Buffy the Vampire Slayer
Futurama	Charmed
Grounded for Life	Dark Angel
Just Shoot Me	Dawson's Creek
Malcolm in the Middle	ER
Nikki	Gilmore Girls
Sabrina	
The Drew Carey Show	
The Hughleys	
The Simpsons	
Titus	
Will and Grace	

of about 35 interactions, while an hour-long drama usually consisted of about 48 interactions. This strategy departs from Kunkel et al.'s (1999, 2005) practice of coding programs at the scene and program levels. We utilized this approach in order to maximize variability in subsequent analyses that would test associations between adolescents' viewing sexual content and their sexual attitudes and behaviors. In an interaction, the Heterosexual Script could be enacted through either dialogue (e.g., a GG code was applied when a woman said no to a man's sexual advance) or behavior (e.g., a GG code was applied when a woman used her hands to push a man away after he made a sexual advance). Although multiple codes could be applied to a single interaction (e.g., both SM and GG), each specific code could only be recorded once per interaction.

The credibility of our codes and the integrity of our analysis rested on   21 our ability to establish a rigorous coding procedure and satisfactory inter-rater reliability. During training, each episode was independently coded by two researchers at three levels. Inter-rater reliability was assessed for each level using percent agreement. Specifically, we assessed coders' (1) agreement on segmenting episodes into individual interactions, (2) agreement on whether one or more Heterosexual Script codes were present in an interaction, and (3) agreement on which specific codes were to be applied to the interaction. Once a pre-determined threshold of 75% agreement was met at all three levels on a pilot set of programs, coders commenced independently unitizing and coding the episodes in the sample. First, one coder would watch an episode and record all of the codes for that episode. Due to the nuanced and sometimes contradictory nature of the Heterosexual Script codes, whenever a code was applied, this first coder would include a brief description of the specific content that warranted its application. Next, the second coder watched the same episode, verifying the first coder's decisions. When disagreements were apparent, the two coders met to discuss the discrepancies and assign a final code. In some cases, a third researcher familiar with the coding scheme was consulted to make the final decision.

RESULTS

Overall Level of Scriptedness

In the 51 hours of television programming recorded for this study, the Heterosexual Script was enacted 662 times. To ease interpretation of the amount of scriptedness in our sample, we calculated the mean number of codes applied to each program across the three episodes. To facilitate comparisons between 30-minute sitcoms and 60-minute dramas, we doubled the values for sitcoms so that our analyses would reflect how many times an adolescent would be exposed to the Heterosexual Script per hour of programming. In the 2001–2002 season, all 25 of the primetime television programs most popular among adolescents contained some element of the Heterosexual Script. However, as presented in Figure 1, there was considerable variability across individual programs, ranging from 3 references per hour in the medical drama, *ER*, to over 30 references per hour for the sitcoms, *Dharma and Greg* and *Futurama*. On average, adolescents who watched these primetime television programs encountered 15.53 references to the Heterosexual Script per hour. 22

We explored variability in different types of programs by conducting a series of independent-samples t-tests based on the program's genre. Sitcoms invoked the Heterosexual Script more often per hour than did dramas, $t(23) = -3.30$, $p < .01$. Indeed, prior to weighting the programs for length, the average 30-minute sitcom contained as many references to the Heterosexual Script ($M = 9.7$) as an hour-long drama ($M = 8.9$). Whereas the programs invoking the Heterosexual Script most often were all sitcoms, with the exception of *Will and Grace*, the programs invoking the Heterosexual Script least often were all dramas. 23

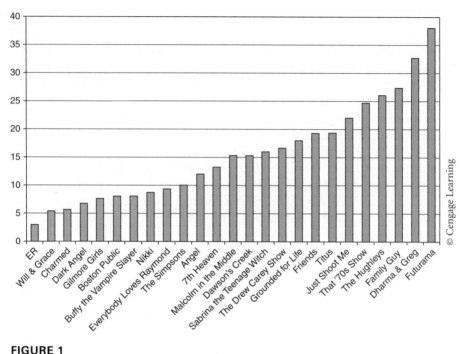

FIGURE 1
Average number of references to the heterosexual script appearing per hour by program name.

Prevalence of Specific Elements of the Heterosexual Script

We assessed the frequency with which specific elements of the Heterosexual   24
Script were invoked in the sample per hour. As summarized in Table 2,
results from a within-samples *t*-test indicated that masculine elements of the
script were enacted more frequently than feminine elements, $t(24) = 4.42$,
$p < .001$; however, further analyses comparing each complementary set
of codes revealed that this finding was attributable to the overwhelming
prevalence of Sex as Masculinity in our sample. In the following section, we
provide specific examples of how the Heterosexual Script was enacted in our
sample according to the relative order of prevalence by code.

Sex as Masculinity

By far, the Heterosexual Script was enacted most frequently by depictions   25
of sexuality being a defining component of men's masculinity, comprising 45.15% of the total number of references identified in our analyses.
The programs most saturated in SM messages were sitcoms featuring

TABLE 2
Frequency of Specific Scripted Messages per Hour Overall and by Genre

	Min	Max	M overall	SD	M sitcom	SD	M drama	SD	t	Cohen's d
Sex as Masculinity	3.00	18.67	7.01	4.59	9.25	1.83	3.04	1.83	-3.87**	1.78
Good Girls	0.00	4.67	1.79	1.50	2.25	0.68	0.96	0.68	-2.43*	1.11
Masculine Courtship Strategies	0.00	6.00	1.37	1.92	1.71	0.76	0.78	0.76	-1.39	0.64
Feminine Courtship Strategies	0.00	10.00	2.08	3.35	2.54	0.81	1.26	0.81	-1.39	0.53
Masculine Commitment	0.00	8.00	1.31	2.10	1.29	1.93	1.33	1.93	0.05	-0.02
Feminine Commitment	0.00	7.33	1.24	1.89	1.21	2.01	1.30	2.01	0.11	0.05
Male-Oriented Homophobia	0.00	4.00	0.51	1.11	0.75	0.15	0.07	0.15	-1.80	0.86
Appropriation of Female Homosexuality	0.00	1.33	0.23	0.48	0.29	0.33	0.11	0.33	-0.99	0.44

$*p < .05; **p < .01.$

male characters in leading roles, each containing between 10 and 20 SM messages per hour. Only one program, *Will and Grace*, contained no references to SM. Because this code hinged on men's sexual interest in women, its absence on *Will and Grace*, which features two gay male leads, is not entirely surprising. Sitcoms contained significantly more SM references per hour than did dramas.

Men are preoccupied with women's bodies. Boys and men unabashedly   26
ogled female characters, openly judged women by their physical appearance, and treated women as sexual objects. In one sitcom, a man drives past a group of women, exclaiming, "Damn! Look at that! Those are some heavy-set honeys!" (*Just Shoot Me*). In another sitcom, a group of teenage boys fantasize about their large-busted neighbor. A daydream montage ensues with the camera focused squarely on the woman's breasts as she runs and bounces in a variety of activities (*That '70s Show*). Comments about women's bodies were not limited to sitcoms, nor were they solely initiated by male characters. In one drama, a young woman and man are perusing an ancient book filled with graphic pictures of demons. Pointing at a demon that has six breasts, the woman states matter-of-factly, "Any man's gonna love that" (*Angel*).

Men are constantly consumed by sexual thoughts, fantasies, and urges.   27
In the sitcom, *Dharma and Greg*, the husband is repeatedly distracted by sexual fantasies he is having of his new female co-worker. As his wife tries to engage him in conversation, Greg imagines the new lawyer in the corner of the room, dressed in a tight black skirt and unbuttoned blouse, touching herself and opening and closing her legs suggestively. In another sitcom, a teenage boy is less than enthusiastic about attending a special fishing trip his father has planned for them. As they fish, the boy fantasizes about a naked mermaid who beckons him to join her in the water (*Malcolm in the Middle*). The centrality of sexuality in male characters' lives was prominent, regardless of age, race, or family role. In one sitcom, an elderly father insists that there was never a need to have a sex talk with his sons because "You don't need to tell a bee where to find the honey" (*Everybody Loves Raymond*). In another sitcom, a mother yells at her pre-teen son to "Get out of that bathroom! I threw *those* magazines away!" a comment that causes the father to react with alarm (*The Hughleys*).

Men talk openly about their sexual desires and experiences. A slew of male   28
characters congregate in the workplace to talk about their new attractive office-mate. Watching her drink a cup of coffee, one man says to the others, "I wish I was that coffee mug 'cause then her lips would be all over me" (*Just Shoot Me*). Men also praised each other for their sexual conquests. On an animated sitcom that spoofs a popular children's cartoon, one smurf congratulates another smurf for "smurfing" Smurfette in a clear sexual allusion

(*The Family Guy*). In turn, boys/men expressed pride over accumulating sexual experience with girls/women, such as a teenage boy who flaunts a hickey on his neck to his envious brother and friend (*Malcolm in the Middle*).

Men are sexual initiators. Men actively attempted to engage women   29
in sexual activity and sometimes using devious or forceful means to do so. In a sitcom, a husband whispers into his wife's ear, "Come on. Let's go upstairs and lock ourselves in one of the bedrooms" (*The Hughleys*), and in a drama, a man draws a woman closer to him, asking, "Do you want me to make love to you?" (*Angel*). On *Buffy the Vampire Slayer*, a male character's attempt to initiate sex is less overt, at least initially. The heroine wakes up next to a male vampire she had slept with the night before. Obviously upset by her actions, she hurriedly puts her clothes on, prompting the vampire to say, "I just don't see why you have to run off so quick. I thought we could ... you know ... ," raising his eyebrows suggestively (*Buffy the Vampire Slayer*). When Buffy rejects this sexual overture, the vampire physically grabs her and pulls her onto his lap, touching her under her skirt as she struggles and squirms in protest. Although this interaction eventually ends with Buffy consenting to the activity, portrayals of men kissing, groping, grabbing, and touching women in unwelcomed ways were not uncommon in our sample. On sitcoms, men's uninvited sexual overtures were portrayed as light-hearted, playful, and, for the most part, free of negative consequences. A teenage boy goes to the supermarket and grabs an older woman's buttocks as she leans over into the freezer (*That '70s Show*). Although the woman initially acts upset, it becomes clear that she is flattered by the boy's attention.

Feminine Courtship Strategies

The second most prevalent code in this sample focused on feminine court-   30
ship strategies, accounting for 13.39% of the total number of scripts identified in our analyses. Although sitcoms depicted more FCS scripts than did dramas per hour, this difference was not significant.

Women can/do/should objectify themselves. Exploiting their bodies and   31
looks was portrayed as an important, if not necessary, way for women to attract male suitors. While fishing, a group of teenage boys spot a boat full of bikini-clad teenage girls who pose flirtatiously for them. One girl unties her girlfriend's bikini top, which she clutches to her chest while giggling (*Malcolm in the Middle*). In another sitcom, a woman poses in several sexually suggestive Yoga positions, intending to incite jealousy in her ex-boyfriend (*The Drew Carey Show*). In a drama, two women are shopping at an upscale boutique for outfits to wear on their double date. One woman advises the other to find a dress "that will make Angel [her male love interest] crazy" (*Angel*).

Women are valued primarily for their physical appearance. Female char-   32
acters were frequently reminded that their physical appearance was more
important than their intelligence, personality, and other attributes. When a
college student wonders why her professor invited her to an academic meeting at his house, her roommate says in an exasperated tone, "Please! Because
you're hot!" The roommate proceeds to dig through the woman's closet to
find an enticing outfit for her to wear (*Dawson's Creek*). While preparing
for their "coming out" at a debutante ball, a group of teenage girls are told,
"Everyone must be beautiful and ready to go by 7:30!" As one debutante
deliberates over which shade of lipstick to wear, she warns another, "The
two minutes you are standing on those stairs tonight will determine your
social status for the rest of your life" (*Gilmore Girls*).

Women use passive and alluring strategies to win men's affection. In a drama,   33
a woman smiles coyly at two men from across the bar, prompting them to ask
her to dance (*Buffy the Vampire Slayer*). In a sitcom, a woman flirts with the
bodyguard of teenage rap star, Li'l Romeo. Rubbing his arm suggestively, she
smiles and says, "You must be Big Romeo" (*The Hughleys*). The heroine of an
action-based drama plays dumb to gain access to a male Mafioso clan. On a
dinner date, she asks sweetly, "So you're into waste management. Is that like
garbage men? … There's like, so much trash on the streets." The men are
charmed by her sweet and innocuous behavior (*Dark Angel*).

Good Girls

The Good Girls code was the third most prevalent in our sample, repre-   34
senting 11.50% of all codes we identified. Sitcoms contained significantly
more GG references per hour than did dramas.

Women are judged by their sexual conduct. On *Buffy the Vampire Slayer*,   35
Buffy refuses to talk to her on-again, off-again love interest, Spike, about
the fact that they had kissed in a previous episode. Spike sneers, "Don't
get all prim and proper on me. I know what kind of girl you really are."
On *Friends*, Rachel's father learns that she is pregnant with Ross's child.
To dodge her father's accusations that his "first grandchild is going to be
a bastard," Rachel tells her father that Ross will not marry her because she
is "damaged goods." The GG code was also frequently applied to passing
comments made about certain women being "whores," "sluts," "tarts,"
"hoochies," "hos," "concubines," or "tramps." A woman's clothing, or
often, the lack thereof, also provided clues to her virtue as a person. In a
sitcom, a teenage couple is leafing through a stack of pictures at a photo
shop labeling certain girls as "whorey" (*That '70s Show*). In a time-twisting
encounter on a drama, a female character is visited by herself as an elderly
woman. The woman chides her younger self, saying, "No one will take you
seriously until you stop dressing like a tramp!" (*Charmed*).

Women set sexual limits. Women were sometimes portrayed actively 36
rejecting men's sexual advances. In a sitcom, a man whispers something into
a woman's ear, which the audience assumes is a request for a sexual favor.
The woman responds by smacking him across the face and storming away
in a huff (*Dharma and Greg*). On a drama, a young woman at a dance club
informs her two male dancing partners that she wants to "sit this one out."
One man grabs her arm and insists, "Uh-uh, you can't work us up like that
and just … ," causing her female friend to interject firmly, "Hey, I think
she said no!" (*Buffy the Vampire Slayer*) On sitcoms, wives' repeated efforts
to curb their husbands' requests for sex was the source of humor. In more
than one episode, husbands attempted to initiate sex with their wives in the
presence of their young children. Outraged, one wife stops her husband,
exclaiming, "For God's sakes! Stewie is right here!" (*The Family Guy*).

On dramas, female characters expressed more ambivalence toward set- 37
ting sexual limits. In *Buffy the Vampire Slayer*, Buffy repeatedly expresses
regret over her sexual involvement with the vampire, Spike. When Spike
wants to talk about a kiss they shared in a previous episode, she shouts,
"I will never kiss you Spike! Never touch you *ever. Ever* again!" (*Buffy the
Vampire Slayer*). Later, Spike pulls Buffy onto his lap and reaches under
her skirt as she cries, "Stop!" and "No!" before returning his fervent kisses.
In another supernatural-themed drama, a woman and man are invaded by
ghostly spirits, causing them to kiss passionately. When they regain control
over their true identities, the woman stops the sexual encounter, asking
incredulously, "Did I actually just ask you to undress me?" (*Angel*).

Masculine Courtship Strategies

Masculine Courtship Strategies were the fourth most prevalent code applied to 38
the sample, comprising 8.84% of all codes identified in our analyses. Sitcoms
and dramas did not differ in the amount of MCS they conveyed per hour.

Men use active and powerful strategies to win women's affection. The 39
MCS code was most frequently applied when male suitors took part in the
courting ritual by asking women out, lavishing them with gifts, or impress-
ing them with their physical strength, intelligence, or wealth. Men were
open and assertive about their romantic interest in women. At a dance
club, two young men approach two women to ask if they would like to
dance (*Buffy the Vampire Slayer*). In another drama, a man strategizes
about how he will ask his female love interest on a date, telling his friend,
"I'll make my move when I feel the iron is hot" (*Dark Angel*). Men on sitcoms also actively courted women, but were often less adept at the task. On
Friends, a male suitor asks Phoebe "if you are the sort of person who eats
lunch?" When she replies that she is, he pauses awkwardly and asks if she
would like to eat lunch with him.

Men are valued for their strength, wealth, and power. In a sitcom,   40
a woman taunts her male co-worker who is noticeably shorter in stature.
She wonders out loud about why they never dated, then makes the scathing
remark that it is because he is "poor and tiny" (*Just Shoot Me*). Two men
discuss their chances of dating an attractive female friend. One man says to
the other, "Good luck, my friend, I've seen better men try and fail," to which
his friend replies, "But did they have a 50-foot yacht to lure her with?"
(*Dawson's Creek*). Women were also impressed by men's heroic gestures.
In an action-based drama, a man saves his fiancée from impending death,
causing her to embrace him and swoon, "You're … my hero!" (*Charmed*).

Masculine Commitment and Feminine Commitment

The Masculine Commitment and Feminine Commitment codes were   41
equally frequent in network television, representing 8.41% and 7.98% of
the total scripts identified in our analyses, respectively. Sitcoms and dramas did not differ in the amount of Commitment codes they portrayed
per hour. Indeed, the programs that were most saturated (e.g., *Dawson's
Creek, Seventh Heaven, Futurama, Sabrina*) and least saturated (e.g., *Will
and Grace, ER, Nikki, Buffy the Vampire Slayer*) by these codes represented
both genres.

Men want/need independence. Women want/need relationships. Whereas   42
men actively avoided commitment and craved "space" from their partners, women sought greater stability and emotional intimacy. A couple on
a sitcom is thick in the midst of a marital dispute. While playing scrabble,
the husband spells out the word "suffocate" in attempt to indicate that he
needs more breathing room in the relationship (*Malcolm in the Middle*). In
a family-oriented drama, two teenage brothers list the drawbacks of being in
a committed relationship, describing a male friend as "in love and … miser-
able!" One brother declares, "I don't know why they [his sisters] even want
to find a serious relationship. I know I don't. No sir, not me! I am happy!
Single!" (*7th Heaven*). In the same episode, their two teenage sisters discuss
how much they miss their ex-boyfriends. A younger sister responds to their
laments, saying, "You should get up, get out and find yourselves some new
boyfriends … Someone new and exciting to love … Someone who holds
a promise for a real future. Isn't that what we all want?" (*7th Heaven*). In
an animated sitcom, a male robot and female computer are dating. The
male robot is also visibly uncomfortable with the computer's suggestion to
"merge programs," a clear allusion to marriage.

Women need boyfriends or husbands. Female characters without boy-   43
friends or husbands were made to feel deficient. A teenage boy asks his
inexperienced sister, "What kind of gifts have boys gotten for you, Meg?,"
causing Meg to cry hysterically and run out of the room (*The Family Guy*).

A middle-aged woman introduces her new boyfriend to her parents. The parents welcome him gladly, saying, "Thank you Lord for sending him into Christine's life to prove that her divorce did not turn her into a lesbian." Her mother adds "She hasn't has a date in eight years!" (*The Drew Carey Show*), indicating that a woman's love life is a public affair.

Men prefer sexual fulfillment over emotional intimacy. At a bachelor party, 44 a man asks the groom how it feels to know that he "will never sleep with another woman again, and wake up to the same face until the sweet release of death takes you away" (*Friends*). When a wife reminds her husband that they have pledged to be together forever in their wedding vows, he points out, "Technically, it ain't forever. It's just 'til death do us part.' Like, if you see me in heaven and I'm with Jennifer Lopez, you don't know me" (*The Hughleys*). Male infidelity was rampant and occurred irrespective of a couple's level of commitment to each other, their age or occupation, or the program's genre. In dramas, male infidelity was treated with solemnity; the cheating male character was often portrayed in a negative light and sympathy or pity was evoked for the female victim. In one teen-oriented drama, a male protagonist is deeply troubled to learn that his married boss is having an affair with a young waitress (*Dawson's Creek*). In sitcoms, however, male infidelity was treated in a humorous and light-hearted manner. A male robot in an animated sitcom has grown tired of his girlfriend. He reasons, "For now, I'll just resume dating floosies on the side" (*Futurama*). Two teenage boys visit a supermarket in an attempt to pick up older housewives. Reminiscing, one boy casually says to the other, "Back when I was cheating on Jackie, I used to meet a lot of older ladies here" (*That '70s Show*).

Male-oriented Homophobia

Although male-oriented homophobia represented only 3.26% of all codes, 45 it appeared at least once in over half of the programs in our sample. Sitcoms generally conveyed more male-oriented homophobia than did dramas, although perhaps due to the overall scarcity of these messages, this difference was not significant. MOH was invoked most frequently by jokes that implicitly or explicitly questioned a male character's sexual orientation. In a sitcom, a father and son are watching a football game together. The father becomes excited when his team scores a touchdown, but the young boy is unmoved and comments distastefully, "I've never seen someone get so excited about something so silly on TV." A sportscaster then announces that Cher will be performing, which makes the boy jump up and down in anticipation. The father is plainly concerned about his son's excitement due to Cher's status as a gay icon (*The Hughleys*). On *Friends*, Ross greets a childhood friend played by Brad Pitt with a hug, exclaiming, "Man, you look incredible! Hot stuff!" He then becomes visibly embarrassed by his phrasing and actions. In a drama, the male protagonist and his male friend are asked if they are "together." The friend places his hand on the protagonist's shoulder, proudly asserting, "Yes, two champions, here together." The protagonist quickly removes his friend's hand and qualifies, "We're not *together together*" (*Angel*).

Appropriation of Female Homosexuality

The least prevalent code applied in our sample, representing only 1.46% of all codes applied, depicted men becoming aroused by the thought or sight of attractive women touching each other in sexual ways. Sitcoms and dramas did not significantly differ in the number of AFH messages portrayed, and rarely did they involve genuine same-sex desire expressed among women. Instead they centered on men's efforts to persuade heterosexual women to engage in sexual touching with one another. A teenage boy comments to his girlfriend, "Donna, feel free—I mean, feel *encouraged*—to make out with all the slutty girls you want" (*That '70s Show*). In a drama, a young man is caught cheating on his girlfriend. Confronted by the two angry women at once, he offers a suggestion. "I like you," he says to one woman. "And I like you," he says to the other. "And once upon a time you both liked me. So, I propose, tell me if I'm crazy or not, that we all like each other at the same time" (*Dawson's Creek*).   46

DISCUSSION

In this article, we present the Heterosexual Script as a viable new approach for evaluating television's sexual content. We envision this analysis of sexual content being used in conjunction with previous coding schemes (e.g., Kunkel et al., 2005) to more fully understand the potential impact of television viewing on adolescent sexual behavior. By shifting the focus of inquiry from sex to sexuality, we find that in addition to showing sexual talk and behavior, television provides viewers with meaningful information guiding how girls/women and boys/men think, feel, and behave in romantic and sexual relationships. Portrayals of boys/men captured by these codes were pervasive, and the message was unilateral: Accumulating sexual experience with women is an important, desirable, and even necessary component of masculinity, and boys/men should attain sexual experience by any means possible. Indeed, in several programs, male characters used forceful or deceitful strategies to persuade girls/women to engage in sexual activity or to catch glimpses of them unclothed. Even more troubling was that these uninvited sexual overtures were often met with success. Compulsory heterosexuality provides a framework to make sense of girls'/women's mostly positive responses—indeed, according to this perspective, attracting boys'/men's attention is the primary way by which girls/women attain and assert (a form of) power.   47

Consistent with the contradictory dimensions of the Heterosexual 48
Script, portrayals of girls/women captured by these codes were more conflicting. For example, feminine courtship strategies encouraged girls/women
to seduce boys/men by exploiting their bodies and dressing in tight, revealing clothing, even though these same behaviors were devalued and seen as
a sign of their sexual indiscretion or impropriety. Such depictions reveal
the challenge that girls face when they are encouraged to both conform to
pervasive conventions of femininity (Bartky, 1990) and perform active gate-
keeping on boys' "uncontrollable" sexual desire. In the programs we sam-
pled, however, the challenging or problematic nature of this task was rarely
identified. From our theoretical perspective, it made sense to retain (and not
try to resolve) such contradictions within the Heterosexual Script coding
scheme. However, in practical terms, it is possible that these contradictions
will weaken the codes' predictive power in explaining adolescent sexual outcomes. It is possible, for example, that the two contradictory aspects of the
"Good Girls" code—that good girls set sexual limits and that good girls pas-
sively acquiesce to men's sexual needs—would be associated with different
sexual health outcomes (less sexual risk and more sexual risk, respectively).

Taken together, results suggest that via the Heterosexual Script, televi- 49
sion offers mutually impoverished constructs of male and female sexuality,
which may ultimately preclude boys' ability to say no to sex and girls' ability
to say yes. Our coding scheme captured the concrete ways male and female
characters were either punished for deviating from or rewarded for comply-
ing with the Heterosexual Script. Boys/men that acted feminine risked being
teased or labeled homosexual, and girls/women that expressed sexual desire
risked being called a slut. This policing did not occur just interpersonally
between characters. It was also portrayed as internalized. Indeed, when
characters caught themselves deviating from the Heterosexual Script, they
often exhibited shame, doubt, embarrassment, or regret. From television,
then, viewers learn that boys/men and girls/women need to be in a state of
constant vigilance and must regulate their sexuality. Whereas boys must
constantly work to construct and assert their masculinity, girls walk the
precarious line between making themselves sexually available to men and
being appropriately demure—the tension at the heart of femininity (Bartky,
1990). Furthermore, although girls' sexual gate-keeping may diminish the
risk for contracting an STD or becoming pregnant, our theoretical perspective questions whether a system that leaves girls with all of the responsibility and leaves boys with no accountability is a fair and/or effective system.
This point also raises the question of the "cost" of the Heterosexual Script
for girls when considering a broader conception of healthy sexuality that
includes the entitlement to be attentive to one's own sexual needs and
desires (SIECUS, 1995; Tolman, Striepe, & Harmon, 2001).

Although all 25 of the primetime network programs in the sample por-   50
trayed the Heterosexual Script to some degree, differences emerged between
and within genres. We found that sitcoms contained more than twice as
many references to the Heterosexual Script per hour as did dramas, a finding almost entirely explained by the prevalence of Sex as Masculinity messages on sitcoms. Why are sitcoms so saturated in scripted messages linking
sex to masculinity? We submit that it is the disproportionate presence of
male characters in leading roles, coupled with a tendency to exploit men's
anxieties about achieving (or failing to achieve) "real manhood" as a source
of humor. Notably, three of the programs most saturated in references
to Sex as Masculinity, *That '70s Show, Just Shoot Me*, and *Titus*, also contained the lowest number of references to Feminine Courtship Strategies.
This finding is interesting given that one of the most common ways Sex as
Masculinity was invoked was by men objectifying women and that one of
the most common ways Feminine Courtship Strategies was invoked was by
women willingly objectifying themselves. Might these particular programs
portray stereotypical male characters but female characters who resist or
reject the Script by relying on their intelligence and assertiveness in romantic and sexual relationships? Such portrayals that run counter to or defy the
Heterosexual Script suggest an important direction for future research.

Indeed, one limitation of this study is that it does not systematically   51
assess counter-scripted portrayals, including, for example, independent and
sexually assertive girls/women and boys/men who are emotionally invested
in romantic relationships. If portrayals of the Heterosexual Script have
explanatory value, it is also possible that portrayals of such counterscripts
could give credence to alternative ways of being and behaving that resist the
Script. Recently, we began tracking such counterscripts systematically, and
in future research, we intend to examine further the relationship between
counterscripted and scripted portrayals. Ultimately, using these two coding
schemes in tandem has tremendous potential to elucidate the meanings and
contexts in which sex talk and sex behavior occur. Using multiple coding
schemes for evaluating the impact of television's sexual content on adolescent sexual outcomes will likely prove fruitful.

It may be impossible for primetime television viewers to avoid the   52
Heterosexual Script entirely; however, the variability in scriptedness found
across different programs suggests that it *is* likely that viewers will be exposed
to it at different rates, making its potential explanatory power in predicting
sexual outcomes promising. In line with our broader conceptualization of
television's sexual content, we recommend that future researchers consider
a wider range of sexual outcomes than is typical in the literature (i.e., sexual
behavior), including adolescents' ability to make authentic, responsible, and
gratifying relational and sexual decisions. Although previous studies indicate

that the *amount* of sexual content consumed is a stronger predictor of adolescents' sexual behavior than the *type* of sexual content consumed (Collins et al., 2004; Pardun, L'Engle, & Brown, 2005), these studies did not consider adolescents' exposure to sexual content understood in terms of gendered sexuality and compulsory heterosexuality, which may be more meaningful than their exposure to types of sexual behaviors or specific body parts.

Because this content analysis was part of a much larger study that examined the impact of television viewing on adolescent sexual behavior, we selected television programs for our content analysis based on the actual viewing habits of a large sample of adolescents living in the Northeast (N = 703). Our decision to restrict our analysis to primetime network sitcoms and dramas limits the generalizability of our findings. Future studies would benefit from using comprehensive sampling techniques that encompass music lyrics, movies, teen magazines, the internet and a wider variety of television genres, including soap operas, music videos, reality programs, and cable television. The reality genre is particularly interesting, given recent evidence that reality programs contain particularly low levels of sexual talk and sexual behavior (Kunkel et al., 2005). Because many of these programs center on romantic and relational themes (e.g., *The Bachelor, Blind Date, Cheaters, Elimidate*), using this new coding system may reveal the significance of such programs in adolescents' sexuality development. Finally, research indicates that many homes are equipped with cable television (Roberts, 2000), and a substantial number of families subscribe to premium cable channels (e.g., HBO, Showtime, Cinemax). Although many made-for-cable television series may contain more sexually explicit content than network primetime programming, it is unclear how these programs would compare in their level of Heterosexual Scriptedness. The popular HBO program, *Sex and the City*, for example, featured a considerable amount of sexual talk and sexual behavior, but the series revolved around the lives of four single women who, more or less, defy the Heterosexual Script by exhibiting sexually agency, prioritizing their sexual pleasure, and valuing their independence from men. Thus, *Sex and the City* may rank high in sexual content but low in Heterosexual Scriptedness, serving as a stark example of how these constructs are conceptually distinct. Such an analysis may raise key questions about who is allowed to deviate from the Heterosexual Script without severe social consequences. The women in *Sex and the City* are white, heterosexual, upper-class, adult women—a very select group that we might expect to enjoy the most flexibility in this respect. In the end, these questions can and should be tested empirically.

One of the challenges we faced in this study, and indeed, one that confronts all media researchers, is keeping up with a television landscape that is constantly transforming. Although our analysis focused on episodes that

53

54

were originally aired in the 2001–2002 season, many continue to be aired in syndication now, appearing on multiple channels and at multiple times of the day. They are also increasingly available for rental or purchase on video and DVD. Nevertheless, monitoring how television's portrayal of the Heterosexual Script evolves over time is important, especially since rates of sexual talk and behavior have been shown to increase over time (Kunkel et al., 2005). A quick survey of the primetime network programs airing at the time of this publication leads us to believe that the Heterosexual Script persists in the 2005–2006 television season. Popular titles include *Desperate Housewives, Beauty and the Geek, Wife Swap, Two and a Half Men*, and *Yes, Dear*. Even more provocative titles are found on cable, including *Queer Eye for the Straight Guy, The L Word, Nip Tuck, The Man Show, WildBoyz, The Girls Next Door*, and *Queer as Folk*.

The results of this analysis have a number of important implications for parents and policy-makers who are concerned with the amount and type of television content children and adolescents consume. Whereas adults may recognize the importance of censoring, restricting, or mediating children's exposure to overtly sexual content, they may not detect or may perceive as benign children's viewing of content that is saturated with the Heterosexual Script. Although current federal advisories warn parents about the presence of sexual language or sexual behavior in television programs, no such warning system exists for scripted or gendered sexual content. One initial step is to expand media literacy for parents and children to help them identify the presence of the Heterosexual Script. This task is difficult because the Heterosexual Script is not the type of television content that strikes most people as problematic. Indeed, it is because the Heterosexual Script is so invisible and perceived to be so natural and normal that its potential impact on adolescents' sexual decision-making is so formidable. Media literacy programs can help parents and educators identify scripted sexual content, provide advice about instituting policies in the home that restrict children's viewing, and offer strategies for talking with children about what they are viewing in this domain. **55**

Our second set of recommendations target those in the media industry. Since network television faces increasing competition to attract viewers during primetime hours, it may be unrealistic to ask scriptwriters to reduce the amount of sexual content depicted in their programs or to add substantially more portrayals of sexual risk and responsibility. However, a plausible solution may be to provide viewers with more diverse alternatives to the Heterosexual Script, including powerful female characters who are assertive in dating and sexual relationships and monogamous male characters who value emotional intimacy. To a certain extent, television has already begun to provide such counter-scripted characters for (and **56** about) adolescent girls. In our sample, three popular primetime programs, *Buffy the Vampire Slayer, Charmed,* and *Dark Angel,* featured action heroines in leading roles. Notably, however, our results indicate that these women revert back to the Heterosexual Script in their romantic and sexual relationships with men, despite the strength and intelligence they exhibit when fighting demons and vampires (Sorsoli, Porche, & Tolman, 2004). The presence of any counter-scripted female characters also highlights the striking absence of counter-scripted characters for (and about) boys and men. Given recent evidence that television's messages about sexual responsibility can have positive and enduring effects on adolescents' beliefs and understandings (Collins et al., 2003), the inclusion of counter-scripted television characters may play a critical role in supporting adolescents' development of healthy sexuality.

REFERENCES

Bandura, A. (1977). *Social learning theory.* Englewood Cliffs, NJ: Prentice Hall.

Bartky, S. (1990). *Femininity and domination.* New York: Routledge.

Butler, J. (1993). *Bodies that matter: On the discursive limits of sex.* New York: Routledge.

Check, J. V. P. & Malamuth, N. (1985). An empirical assessment of some feminist hypotheses about rape. *International Journal of Women's Studies, 8,* 414–422.

Clark, R. D. & Hatfield, E. (1989). Gender differences in receptivity to sexual offers. *Journal of Psychology and Human Sexuality, 2,* 39–55.

Collins, R. L., Elliott, M. N., Berry, S. H., Kanouse, D. E., & Hunter, S. B. (2003). Entertainment television as a healthy sex educator: The impact of condom-efficacy information in an episode of Friends. *Pediatrics, 112,* 1115–1121.

Collins, R. L., Elliot, M. N., Berry, S. H., Kanouse, D. E., Kunkel, D. K., Hunter, S. B., & Miu, A. (2004). Watching sex on TV predicts adolescent initiation of sexual behavior. *Pediatrics, 114,* e280–e289.

Connell, R. W. (1987). *Gender and power: Society, the person and sexual politics.* Palo Alto, CA: Stanford University Press.

Cope-Farrar, K. M. & Kunkel, D. (2002). Sexual messages in teens' favorite primetime television programs. In J. D. Brown, J. R. Steele, & K. Walsh-Childers (Eds.), *Sexual teens, sexual media: Investigating media's influence on adolescent sexuality* (pp. 59–78). Mahwah, NJ: Lawrence Earlbaum Associates.

Diamond, L. (2005). "I'm straight but I kissed a girl": The trouble with American media representations of female-female sexuality. *Feminism and Psychology, 15,* 104–110.

Fredrickson, B. L. & Roberts, T. (1997). Objectification theory: Toward understanding women's lived experiences and mental health. *Psychology of Women Quarterly, 21,* 173–206.

Frith, H. & Kitzinger, C. (2001). Reformulating sexual script theory. Developing a discursive psychology of sexual negotiation. *Theory and Psychology, 11,* 209–232.

Gagnon, J. H. (1990). The explicit and implicit use of the scripting perspective in sex research. *Annual Review of Sex Research, 1,* 1–43.

Gagnon, J. H. & Simon, W. (1973). *Sexual conduct: The social sources of human sexuality.* Chicago, IL: Aldine.

Gerbner, G., Gross, L., & Morgan, M. (1994). Growing up with television. The cultivation perspective. In J. Bryant & D. Zillman (Eds.), *Media effects. Advances in theory and research* (pp. 17–41). Hillsdale, NJ: Lawrence Earlbaum Associates.

Hyde, J. S. & Oliver, M. B. (1993). Gender differences in sexuality: Results from meta-analysis. *Psychological Bulletin, 114,* 29–51.

Kaiser Family Foundation. (2004). *Parents, media, and public policy: A Kaiser Family Foundation Survey.* Menlo Park, CA: Kaiser Family Foundation.

Korman, S. K. & Leslie, G. R. (1982). The relationship of feminist ideology and date expense sharing to perceptions of sexual aggression in dating. *The Journal of Sex Research, 18,* 114–129.

Kunkel, D., Cope, K. M., Farinola, W. J. M., Beily, E., Rollin, E., & Donnerstein, E. (1999). *Sex on TV: Content and context. A Biennial report to the Henry J. Kaiser Family Foundation.* Menlo Park, CA: Kaiser Family Foundation.

Kunkel, D., Eyal, K., Biely, E., Cope-Farrar, K., & Donnerstein, E. (2003). *Sex on TV 3: A Biennial report to the Kaiser Family Foundation.* Menlo Park, CA: Kaiser Family Foundation.

Kunkel, D., Eyal, K., Finnerty, K., Biely, E., & Donnerstein, E. (2005). *Sex on TV 5. A Biennial report to the Kaiser Family Foundation.* Menlo Park, CA: Kaiser Family Foundation.

Lowry, D. T. & Shidler, J. A. (1993). Prime time TV portrayals of sex, "safe sex" and AIDS: A longitudinal analysis. *Journalism Quarterly, 70,* 628–637.

Lowry, D. T. & Towles, D. E. (1989). Soap opera portrayals of sex, contraception, and sexually transmitted diseases. *Journal of Communication, 39,* 76–83.

McCormick, N. B. (1979). Come-ons and put-offs. Unmarried students' strategies for having and avoiding sexual intercourse. *Psychology of Women Quarterly, 4,* 194–211.

McCormick, N. (1987). Sexual scripts: Social and therapeutic implications. *Sexual and Marital Therapy, 2,* 3–27.

McCormick, N. B. (1994). *Sexual salvation.* Westport, CT: Praeger.

McCormick, N. B., Brannigan, G. G., & LaPlante, M. N. (1984). Social desirability in the bedroom: Role of approval motivation in sexual relationships. *Sex Roles, 11,* 303–314.

O'Sullivan, L. F. & Byers, E. S. (1993). Eroding stereotypes: College women's attempts to influence reluctant male sexual partners. *The Journal of Sex Research, 30,* 270–282.

Pardun, C. J., L'Engle, K. L., & Brown, J. D. (2005). Linking exposure to outcomes: Early adolescents' consumption of sexual content in six media. *Mass Communication and Society, 8,* 75–91.

Reiss, I. L. (1960). *Premarital sexual standards in America.* New York: The Free Press.

Rich, A. (1980). Compulsory heterosexuality and lesbian existence. *Signs: Journal of Women in Culture and Society, 5,* 631–660.

Roberts, D. F. (2000). Media and youth: Access, exposure, and privatization. *Journal of Adolescent Health, 27,* 8–14.

Rosotsky, S. S. & Travis, C. B. (2000). Menopause and sexuality: Ageism and sexism unite. In C. B. Travis & J. W. White (Eds.), *Sexuality, society, and feminism* (pp. 181–209). Washington, DC: American Psychological Association.

Simon, W., & Gagnon, J. H. (1986). Sexual scripts: Permanence and change. *Archives of Sexual Behavior, 15,* 97–120.

Sorsoli, C. L., Porche, M., & Tolman, D. L. (2004). "He left her for the alien": Girls, television, and sex. In E. Cole & J. H. Daniel (Eds.), *Featuring females: Feminist analyses of media* (pp. 25–39). Washington, DC: American Psychological Association.

Sorsoli, L., Ward, L. M., & Tolman, D. L. (in press). De(coding) television's representation of sexuality: Beyond behaviors and dialogue. In D. Kunkel, A. Jordan, J. Manganello, & M. Fishbein (Eds.), *Media messages and public health: A decisions approach to content analysis.* Mahwah, NJ: Lawrence Erlbaum Associates.

Tolman, D. L. (1996). Adolescent girls' sexuality: Debunking the myth of the urban girl. In B. J. Leadbeater & N. Way (Eds.), *Urban girls: Resisting stereotypes, creating identities* (pp. 255–271). New York, NY: New York University Press.

Tolman, D. L. (2002). *Dilemmas of desire: Teenage girls talk about sexuality.* Cambridge, MA: Harvard University Press.

Tolman, D. L. (2006). In a different position: Conceptualizing female adolescent sexuality development within compulsory heterosexuality. *New Directions for Child and Adolescent Development, 2006,* 71–89.

Ward, L. M. (1995). Talking about sex: Common themes about sexuality in prime-time television programs children and adolescents view most. *Journal of Youth and Adolescence, 24,* 595–615.

Zylbergold, B. A. (2005). Heteroflexibility in North American Television and Film. Unpublished master's thesis, San Francisco State University, California.

QUESTIONS FOR COMPREHENSION, STUDY, AND DISCUSSION

1. In the third paragraph, the authors state, "Previous studies [of television's sexual content] are often anchored in cultivation or social learning theories." Define *cultivation, learning theory,* and *social learning theory.*

2. What is "scripting theory," and why is it important to this study? What is "the Heterosexual Script"?

3. How did the authors select the television programs they would view to conduct their study?

4. What did the results of the study indicate about the relationship that male characters on television programs perceive between masculinity and sexual prowess?

5. What did the results of the study indicate about the behavior of television female characters who are trying to attract male attention?

6. What did the results of the study indicate about the behavior of television female characters in sexually charged situations?

7. What did the results of the study indicate about the behavior of television male characters who are trying to attract female attention?

8. What did the results of the study suggest about the differences between men and women in attitudes toward committed relationships, as they are portrayed on television programs?

9. What did the results of the study suggest about the prevalence of homophobia among male television characters?

10. What did the results of the study suggest about male attitudes toward female homosexuality?

JOURNAL PROMPT

Write a 400- to 500-word response to the "Discussion" section of this article.

Academic Disciplines: Popular Culture; Film Studies
Citation Method: MLA
Rhetorical Modes: Exposition; Argument

This article is from the *Journal of Popular Film and Television,* published in Summer 2006. It follows the MLA method for source citation.

Resurrecting and Updating the Teen Slasher: The Case of *Scream*
Valerie Wee

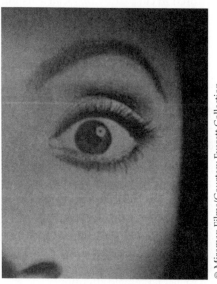
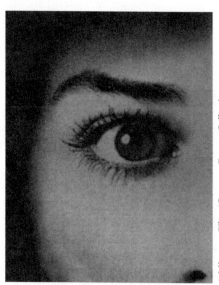

© Miramax Films/Courtesy Everett Collection

© Miramax Films/Courtesy Everett Collection

Abstract: The author examines the *Scream* trilogy and disputes the perception that the series is conservative and reactionary in its politics. She argues that the films reflect specific 1990s American concerns and contends that the distinctive treatment of the slasher villain and final female survivor reflect a progressive, revolutionary stance.

Key words: Final Girl, *Scream*, serial killer, slasher film, teen film(s)

In December 1996, Dimension Films, a subsidiary of Miramax Films, released   1
Scream, a slasher film that actively plays with the established conventions of

the familiar genre. *Scream* and its sequels went on to resurrect the dormant slasher flick,[1] spearhead the media industry's interest in the teen market, and reshape the teen movie for a new generation of paying moviegoers.

While the *Scream* trilogy has received its share of scholarly attention, many of the existing examinations focus primarily on its postmodern elements, with numerous discussions centering on the heightened self-reflexivity and intertextuality that characterize the three films in the series.[2] Less attention has been paid to the ways in which the films have updated the defining conventions of the slasher-film genre—in particular, how the series has revised the treatment of the monster-villain and the final female survivor, two of the key narrative elements central to the slasher-film genre. This article focuses on these two elements and considers how they have been reshaped to reflect the contemporary issues and concerns relevant to the teen generation that came of age during the final years of the twentieth century.

Of the existing studies that have focused on these two issues, the general trend has been to dismiss the *Scream* films for failing to sustain the established elements of indestructible villains and self-reliant female survivors. The films have also been criticized for their seemingly conformist stance with regard to mainstream ideologies. Sarah Trencansky, for instance, notes that the *Scream* trilogy's villains are distinct deviations from their predecessors; unlike the indestructible Freddy Kruger (*A Nightmare on Elm Street*, 1984) and Michael Myers (*Halloween*, 1978), *Scream*'s various villains are less-than-formidable adversaries who are comparatively more easily defeated. Trecansky has similarly argued that *Scream*'s female survivors represent a regression from the capable, self-determined, more politically progressive Final Girls (35) of earlier, classic slashers such as *Friday the 13th* (1980) and *A Nightmare on Elm Street*. According to Trencansky, Sidney Prescott (Neve Campbell), *Scream*'s heroine of a sort, harks back to an earlier version of the female survivor as victim who relied on others to save her life (72). Finally, in discussing the politics of the *Scream* films, Trencansky is particularly critical of the *Scream* series' depiction of a relatively benign, if ineffectual, range of authority figures, including fathers and members of the police force (72). *Scream*'s treatment of all three narrative elements has caused Trencansky to dismiss the series as largely conservative. While this may be one possible way of reading the series' characterization of the slasher villain and survivor, I believe that a more in-depth study of these elements, with a focus on relating their depiction/revision to contemporary issues and concerns, would be fruitful in highlighting the films' complex attempts at negotiating contemporary cultural and social anxieties. Rather than dismiss these recent incarnations as simply regressive or reactionary, I would suggest that these texts were actively engaged in commenting on and negotiating the threats, fears, and concerns that characterized 1990s American society in general, and American teenagers—the films' target market—in particular. Indeed, I would argue that a careful consideration of the *Scream* films' revision of the traditional conventions of the slasher genre, far from being conservative or reactionary, reflects a distinctly revolutionary stance.

To fully grasp the contemporary state of the teen slasher film and the ways in which the '90s versions represent a departure from its predecessors, we must first address the historical precedents set in the genre's earlier cycles. 4

THE TEEN SLASHER FILM: TRADITION AND EVOLUTION

The teen slasher film came into its own in the late 1970s and quickly became one of the most popular subgenres of horror in the decade that followed (Clover 24; Ryan and Kellner 191; Tudor 68–72). Scholars generally agree that *The Texas Chainsaw Massacre* (1974) and *Halloween* were the original films that generated the cycle (Clover 24; Tudor 198). Both pioneered films in a number of ways: 5

1. They featured imperiled, sexually attractive women being stalked by a knife-wielding serial killer and included scenes of unexpected and shocking violence and brutality—conventions that would eventually be associated with the slasher genre.[3]
2. They initiated the tradition of having a group of young, often teenage people as victims (Ryan and Kellner 191; Tudor 70), introducing the youth-focused element that marked the arrival of the teen-oriented slasher film.
3. They inaugurated the virtually indestructible, psychotic villains associated with the slasher film (Clover 30; Tudor 68).
4. They originated the trend toward spin-offs, sequels, and imitators, sparking off a rash of successful slasher-film franchises (Ryan and Kellner 191; Tudor 199).

The success of *The Texas Chainsaw Massacre* and *Halloween* paved the way for other slasher film series, including the *Friday the 13th* and *Nightmare on Elm Street* series. A study of the box-office gross of key slasher franchises highlights the popularity and profitability of these movie franchises. The first *Halloween* film cost $325,000 and grossed $47 million. The first *Friday the 13th* cost $700,000 and grossed $37.5 million, while *A Nightmare on Elm Street* cost $1.8 million and grossed $25.5 million. During the 1980s, the first few sequels in each franchise grossed as much as, if not more than, the original—the third and fourth installments of *Friday the 13th* (released in 1982 and 1984, respectively) grossed in excess of $30 million, while *A Nightmare on Elm Street, Part 2* (1985), *Part 3* (1987), and *Part 4* (1988) grossed 6

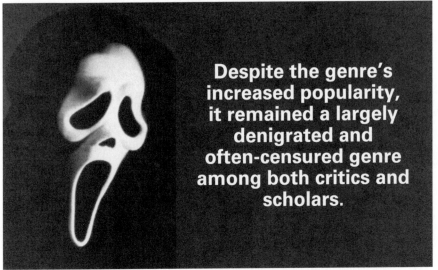

Despite the genre's increased popularity, it remained a largely denigrated and often-censured genre among both critics and scholars.

© Miramax/Courtesy Everett Collection

$30 million, $45 million, and $50 million, respectively, marking the heyday of the teen slasher genre. With the release of each installment in these film series, the conventions of the genre were repeated and consolidated in the late '70s and early '80s.

The popularity of these films has in fact been tied to the increasing   7
familiarity of these conventions. As Andrew Britton notes,

> It became obvious at a very early stage [in the slasher film's cycle] that every spectator knew exactly what the film was going to do at every point, even down to the order in which it would dispose of its various characters, [... yet,] the film's total predictability did not create boredom or disappointment [—at least not initially]. On the contrary, the predictability was clearly the main source of pleasure, and the only occasion for disappointment would have been a modulation of the formula, not a repetition of it. (qtd. in Clover 9)

Despite the genre's increased popularity, it remained a largely denigrated   8
and often-censured genre among both critics and scholars. "Drenched in taboo and encroaching vigorously on the pornographic, the slasher film lies [...] by and large beyond the purview of respectable criticism," notes Clover (21). Pinedo similarly observes that the slasher film is generally considered "the most disreputable form of the horror film" (71).

Despite the narrow constraints of the genre's familiar conventions and   9
the often controversial portrayals of violence and brutality, the films did attract some scholarly attention, particularly in terms of how they appeared to deal with a range of contemporary issues and concerns. Film scholars,

such as Ryan and Kellner, Pinedo, and Williams, have highlighted the link between slasher films and real life. Ryan and Kellner, for instance, argue that horror/slasher films, with their extreme depictions of violence and terror "indicate heightened levels of anxiety in the culture, particularly with regard to the family, children, political leadership, and sexuality" (168). Pinedo similarly remarks how "the horror film is an exquisite exercise in coping with the terrors of everyday life [...] the pain of loss, the enigma of death, the unpredictability of events, the inadequacy of intentions" (39). As Williams notes, "Although most commentators dismiss these films as worthless trash, they are symptomatic of their particular era and deserve attention" (183).

Pat Gill, Sarah Trencansky, and Tony Williams have argued that the   10
horror/slasher films of the late 1970s and early '80s reflected the zeitgeist of those eras by exhibiting a declining faith in family and the adult world. In "The Monstrous Years: Teens, Slasher Films and the Family," Gill examines a range of slasher films, including *Halloween, Friday the 13th,* and *A Nightmare on Elm Street* comparing the films' narrative themes to larger social developments in American society, including rising divorce rates, changing family structures, and evolving cultural emphases on adult needs at the expense of children and youths (18). According to Gill, *Halloween* and the other slasher films that followed appear to suggest that "the horror derives from the family and from the troubling ordeal of being a late-twentieth-century teenager" (16). These films "show teenagers in peril, with no hope of help from their parents" (Gill 17). As Trencansky points out, "A consistent theme in these slashers is the depiction of youth subjugated to an adult community that produces monsters" (68). Williams concurs, noting that films such as *A Nightmare on Elm Street* "indicts the adult world, presenting parents as weak, manipulative, and selfish" (229).

By the mid-1980s, however, the slasher film appeared to reach a point   11
of exhaustion. Many of the films released in the late 1980s and early 1990s were final installments of franchises that were popular during the previous decade, and a large number of these were straight-to-video releases. Unlike the profitable earlier installments, most of which earned significant box office, the franchises' later releases had significantly diminished box office grosses. *Halloween Part 6* (1995), the final installment before 1998's *Halloween: H20*, grossed $15 million. The last *Friday the 13th* (1993) grossed $16 million, and the final *A Nightmare on Elm Street* made $18 million at the box office in 1994. While these grosses are still considerable in light of their lower budgets, there was a significant drop-off in the films' box office compared with their peak grosses in the mid-1980s. It should also be noted that the films mentioned here belong to initially popular, and particularly high-profile, branded franchises. As such, they were able to sustain public interest and popularity for a longer period than lesser-known slasher films.

© Miramax/Courtesy Everett Collection

**"Mr. Ghostface," the indestructible, unrelenting villain, haunts the *Scream*
series.**

By the early 1990s, the number of slasher film releases had fallen   12
sharply. This decline was due to a combination of factors. The formulaic
nature of subsequent low budget, independently produced slashers—and
the excessive repetition in the form of sequels, remakes, and imitations—
inevitably led to the audience's overfamiliarity with the genre, so that
"by the end of the decade the form was largely drained" (Clover 23).
Furthermore, the teens who first embraced and nurtured the genre had
aged out of the demographic. Major studios were also turning their attention away from teen audiences at that point. In fact, as Leonard Klady noted
in *Variety* in 1997,

> The teen audience [. . . has] largely been ignored by the majors for the past
> five years. Major hits in recent memory aimed at 16- to 24-year-olds have
> been scarce [. . .]. Much more attention has been paid to creating event films
> meant to appeal to the full spectrum of filmgoers, or niche appeal family
> films and movies for thirty somethings and older that had crossover
> potential. (Klady 11–12)

Consequently, the teen slasher genre fell into dormancy between the late   13
1980s and mid-1990s. Dimension chief Bob Weinstein recalled that prior to
Scream's 1996 release, "There were no movies being made for teenagers anymore. It had become an adult oriented business. I knew there was an audience that was not being satisfied" (Orwall D15).

By the mid-1990s, however, the teen audiences that were largely ignored   14
by the movie studios and the entertainment industries in general, were stag-
ing a demographic comeback. Retailers, marketers, and other entertainment
industries began noticing the teen demographic's increasing numbers and
burgeoning spending power. At the end of the twentieth century, America
witnessed the emergence of a generation of teenagers who had few time
constraints, large disposable incomes and a growing need to assert their independence. As Universal's marketing president, Buffy Shutt, noted in 1997,
"Young people are beginning to assert themselves in a way that they haven't
for a long time" (Orwall D15). Studios began attending to population data
that showed "the North American teenage population rising to more than
55 million by 2005—larger than the original baby boom at its peak" (Orwall
D15). Entertainment corporations began to realize that these significant
demographic numbers meant that teenagers were again a viable niche market.

In December 1996, prompted by the entertainment industry's growing   15
interest in the teen demographic, Dimension released *Scream*.[4] The film
would eventually result in the resurrection of the slasher film and a reinterpretation of the genre's overfamiliar conventions for a new teen generation.
The film's phenomenal success also provided proof of the demographic's
significance and led to the reshaping of 1990s teen culture.[5]

In the mid-'90s, reviving the tired and disreputable slasher genre posed   16
a challenge. As a genre, the slasher film was languishing at the bottom
of the horror heap. Most slasher films had degenerated into straight-to-
video, B-grade releases with low production values and weak acting. If
Dimension hoped to resurrect the slasher film, it would need to find a
way to retain many of its conventions while simultaneously updating the
material and redefining the genre for a 1990s-era teenage audience. The
late 1990s teen was a new and distinct demographic. Media obsessed and,
hence, pop-culture literate, extremely self-aware, and cynical, this brand
of teen was very different from every previous teen cohort. Dimension
chief Bob Weinstein realized that the late-1990s teen generation was probably already overly familiar with the established conventions of the slasher
film and would never accept a mere retread of the old genre (Eller, "What
about Bob?" A1). Furthermore, while the previous conventional target
audience for slasher films was adolescent boys,[6] in the mid-1990s, adolescent girls were emerging as the more significant filmgoing demographic.

In 1995, teenage girls were largely responsible for the $57 million US box office success of *Clueless* (1995), a romantic comedy about a high school girl's romantic misadventures. A year later, *William Shakespeare's Romeo and Juliet* (1996), also targeted at the teen-girl demographic, grossed $46 million domestically.[7] While traditional wisdom argues that the slasher genre skewed toward adolescent male audiences, Weinstein, established horror-film director Wes Craven, and then-unknown scriptwriter Kevin Williamson were keen to revive the genre with the conscious intent of making it more relevant to female audiences, a point that I return to in the penultimate section of this article.

These considerations would ultimately impact the nature, content, and structure of the *Scream* films. How did the *Scream* films update the slasher genre for a new late-1990s teen audience? What identifying characteristics did these films possess? How did the *Scream* trilogy speak to its target demographic of teenagers in general and teen girls in particular?   17

REINVENTING THE SLASHER GENRE

With renowned horror auteur Wes Craven and scriptwriter Kevin   18
Williamson, Dimension embarked upon a project that consciously tried to reshape and update the genre. The creators decided to exploit the audience's familiarity with the genre's conventions by creating a film that would comment on the highly formulaic nature of the slasher films while simultaneously playing off of the established traditions. A significant portion of the films' aesthetic style and content are almost entirely derived from previous slasher films. One of the most overt strategies involved the deconstruction of the genre's conventions and the insertion of tongue-in-cheek intertextual and self-referential comments, highlighting the *Scream* trilogy's debt (and similarity) to earlier slasher film classics. This particular characteristic has received significant attention and discussion, with scholars like Pinedo and Tietchen commenting on the highly postmodern quality of the films. Many of the *Scream* trilogy's elements, therefore, functioned to highlight the films' own artificiality, acknowledging their status as popular culture and as consumable media products.

It should be noted, however, that *Scream*'s distinction as a '90s teen text   19
is not restricted to its postmodern qualities. While the films' postmodern elements are significant, the trilogy has also reconfigured some of the genre's more traditional, established elements—specifically, the trilogy's reinterpretation of the female victim-hero stereotype, as well as its reconsideration of the slasher villain. These two conventional elements have been reshaped in ways that redirect the traditional trajectory of the genre and offer interesting insights into contemporary social and cultural concerns and ideologies.

RECONSIDERING THE PSYCHOTIC SERIAL KILLER

One of the more distinctive ways in which the *Scream* trilogy breaks with   20
the slasher-film tradition involves the portrayal and reinterpretation of the
familiar slasher villain/monster. In films such as *Psycho* (1960) and *The
Texas Chainsaw Massacre*, through the *Halloween, Friday the 13th*, and
A Nightmare on Elm Street series, the traditional villains are almost consistently characterized as psychotic, virtually indestructible maniacs.

Tudor notes that a psychologically disturbed, "near superhuman, male,   21
masked killer who preys upon young people, mostly females" lays at the heart
of the traditional slasher film (68). According to Clover, typical villains are
often "misfits and outsiders.[…] They are usually large, sometimes overweight, and often masked. In short, they may be recognizably human, but
they are only marginally so […]" (30). Acccording to Trencansky, "Freddy,
Jason and Pinhead [of the *Hellraiser* series] are the rejected, marginalized
underbelly of society, the traits that suburban America represses and denies,"
and as such, they are representations of the abject (70).[8] As Kristeva argues,
the abject is defined as that which does not "respect borders, positions,
rules"; the abject "disturbs identity, system, order" and ultimately threatens
life (4). These slasher monsters, therefore, belong outside the normal, the
healthy, the safe, and the familiar. As representations of the abject, these
figures ignore the traditional boundaries that separate the living and the
dead. In almost every case, the traditional slasher villain is infinitely reviv-
able, effectively eluding death and destruction indefinitely, emerging as

The teen slasher genre fell into dormancy between the late 1980s and mid-1990s.

© Miramax/Courtesy Everett Collection

"supernaturally resurrected [...] monsters" in sequel after sequel (Williams 216). Gill labels "Michael and his compatriot slashers [...] the hobgoblins of childhood fantasy, indestructible beings who seem able to be everywhere and do anything" (24). Clover, similarly, notes the killers' "virtual indestructibility. Just as Michael (in *Halloween*) repeatedly rises from blows that would stop a lesser man, so Jason (in the *Friday the 13th* films) survives assault after assault to return in sequel after sequel" (30). Clearly, the convention of the undefeatable psychotic murderer/slasher has been reinforced historically across numerous films. *Scream*, a film that positions itself securely within the genre, would have been expected to recognize and replicate this most significant and consistent element of the genre. Interestingly, the film's creators adopted a novel reinterpretation of the convention.

In *Scream* (and its subsequent installments), the killers are not mar- 22 ginalized monsters in the tradition of Leatherface, or the supernatural Freddy Kruger, nor are they "seemingly invincible psychotics" (Tudor 69) in the tradition of Michael Myers and Jason. While still psychologically disturbed maniacs, *Scream*'s villains are not misfits or outsiders, nor are they the uncharacterized monsters typical of earlier slasher films. Instead, the killers in *Scream* are seemingly normal, attractive, popular people, often "insiders," boyfriends or friends who initially appear harmless until they go on a killing spree. Trencansky notes as much when she acknowledges that "in the *Scream* and [*I Know What You Did Last*] *Summer* (1997) series, the monster is changed from a supernatural force to a resolutely ordinary person, human, personally troubled, and usually a member of the heroine's close circle of friends" (71).

If, as has been noted earlier, slasher films articulate the fears and concern 23 prevalent in their respective eras, then *Scream*'s reinterpretation of the killers as the evil within, its portrayal of seemingly ordinary teenagers turned serial killers seems particularly contemporary and relevant in light of the real-life incidents of teenage violence occurring in American high schools at the end of the twentieth century. As Ryan and Kellner note,

> During times of social crisis, several sorts of cultural representations tend to emerge. Some idealize solutions or alternatives to the distressing actuality, some project worst fears and anxieties induced by the critical situation into metaphors that allow those fears to be absolved or played out, and some evoke a nihilistic vision of a world without hope or remedy. (168)

The *Scream* trilogy can certainly be read in the above terms. Like its 24 slasher predecessors, the trilogy acknowledges and confronts the key anxieties of its era. If the 1980s slasher films portrayed parents and family as ineffectual protection against evil, and in fact suggested that adults and authority figures were the source or cause of evil's emergence, the *Scream* trilogy offers a world in which evil is more closely aligned with the victims. In these later films, evil resides within the teenager's group of friends; in every case, it is the victims' close friends and lovers who are the unsuspected monsters. As Trencansky argues,

> each decade embraces the monsters that speak to it: If the villains of popular late 1990s slashers are embraced by the adolescents today, perhaps it is because, in a culture of sudden random violence, exemplified in the school shootings that originate from one of their own, a villain that looks just like them makes sense. (73)

Despite recognizing the possible link between *Scream* and actual high school violence, Trencansky does not go on to interrogate the connection in any detail, as the focus of her paper lies elsewhere. While I agree with Trencansky, I also believe that *Scream*'s reinterpretation of the evil within goes beyond offering its viewers a potentially recognizable and terrifyingly familiar villain. Pinedo maintains that "horror renaturalizes the repressed by transmuting the 'natural' elements of everyday life into the unnatural form of the monster [...]. This transmutation renders the terrors of everyday life at least emotionally accessible" (39). As such, the trilogy's portrayal of seemingly ordinary teenagers turned serial killers is a direct commentary on the demons and terrors that impact actual teenagers' lives in the light of real-life teenage violence in high schools across America, of which the tragic events in Pearl, Mississippi; Jonesboro, Arkansas; and Columbine, Colorado, are only the most publicized. The *Scream* trilogy, therefore, offers its teen viewers a form of cathartic release by exploring the terrors associated with high school, unexpected violence, and the difficulty of knowing or trusting one's peers. If, as Trencansky (71–72) argues, "the objective for the heroine becomes constant suspicion, a 'whodunit' of sorts in which the only way to survive is to constantly suspect one's fellow youth," then *Scream* must be credited for acknowledging and addressing the very real fear and paranoia experienced by high schoolers during the late twentieth century. Indeed, the trilogy's representation of seemingly average, ordinary teenagers whose transformation into disgruntled, dysfunctional youth who slaughter their unsuspecting friends is particularly relevant to the films' target audience.

Scream's exploration of the contemporary situation does not end there. Each film in the series also addresses the impact of media violence on the (teenage) individual, a topic that was hotly debated in the weeks following the tragic events in Columbine, and that continues to resonate with parents, legislators, and media watchdogs. Certainly, much of the trilogy's treatment of this particular issue tends to be ironic and tongue-in-cheek. In *Scream*, both the unmasked killers facetiously mention media violence as a possible influence while discussing their actions. In *Scream 2* (1997), one of the villains mentions that he intends to cite exposure to media violence as part of his legal defense. Far from approaching the topic seriously, the villains adopt an overtly smug attitude when discussing the situation, suggesting that media violence is, at best, a convenient scapegoat. Consequently, it is difficult not to be cynical and read the film's derisive response to the notion that the media play a role in shaping teen behavior as anything but self-serving. Yet, the opposite belief that violent films are solely responsible for the kind of high school violence that had become terrifyingly common in the late 1990s might also appear overly simplistic and reductive.

Interestingly, the *Scream* trilogy, unlike the traditional slasher film, refuses to provide a clear explanation or motivation for the characters' turn to violence. In the *Nightmare* and *Friday the 13th* series, we learn that Freddy and Jason, respectively, are motivated primarily by revenge, while Michael, in *Halloween*, is driven to kill as a result of his anger at his sister's neglect of him. In the *Scream* trilogy, such overt and apparent explanations are absent. While one of the killers claims to have been motivated initially by his father's extramarital affair, this explanation is only offered in passing and fails to adequately account for the multiple random murders he then goes on to gleefully commit in the first installment of the trilogy. The films thus seem reluctant to offer any clear motivation for the killers' actions and seem almost to imply that it is the acts of murder and terrorism themselves that amuse and excite the villains. In the sequel, Sidney's murderous classmate also offers a less-than-convincing explanation for his behavior: he says he was committing the murders as part of an experiment to test the effectiveness of citing media violence as his defense. While a range of familiar scapegoats are mentioned in the films, including dysfunctional families, the influence of media violence, and the undue influence of a psychologically deranged and murderous mentor, none of these ultimately emerge as unequivocal reasons for the ensuing carnage.

> In the same way, the *Scream* trilogy appears to break with the earlier slasher film tradition, in which larger social problems are indicted for creating the films' monsters. Classic slashers, including *Halloween*, the *Nightmare* series, and the *Friday the 13th* franchise have been praised for offering progressive critiques of society and its values. These earlier films tended to adopt a critical stance on reactionary patriarchal values, on authority figures, as well as on middle-class values. In contrast, the *Scream* trilogy has been criticized for its benign representations of society and authority.
>
> Society is presented as functioning well, in no need of change or transformation. Authorities, like the sympathetic cop Dewey who stars in each *Scream* and Sidney's loving father, are likely to be blameless; they too are on the side of the heroine against the "other." (Trencansky 72)

These observations have led Trencansky to dismiss the trilogy as   28
"conservative," suggesting that "these patterns serve to subvert [the] more
progressive ideology of the 1980s films" (72). I would suggest that rather
than espousing a conservative, reactionary ideology that supports established authority and existing social values, the *Scream* films may actually be
offering another comment on the real-life violence witnessed in the high
school shootings, in which clear-cut explanations and causes, let alone solutions, are unavailable. The *Scream* films' inability to offer a concise, convincing reason for how these monsters came to be, in a sense reflects American
society's inability to understand how seemingly ordinary teenagers can
morph into cold-blooded mass murderers.[9]

In fact, I would argue that far from being reactionary or regressive, the   29
trilogy may be revolutionary, particularly in its treatment of the monstrous
killer and the survivors. In a traditional slasher series, the killer survives
and orchestrates a return to torment and kill another group of teenagers. As Clover points out, "the killers are normally the fixed elements and
the victims the changeable ones in any given series of the 1970s and early
'80s slasher films" (30). In the *Nightmare* series for instance, Freddy works
his way through a series of female heroines: Nancy, from the first film, is
replaced by Lisa in the sequel, and in the third installment, Freddy battles
Kirsten, while Alice becomes his adversary in the fourth. While it is true that
"none of them dies without first training a new girl to carry on the fight they
have started" (Trencansky 66), the fact remains that these heroic women
consistently fail to defeat and outlive their tormentors. Although these

Renowned horror auteur
Wes Craven and
scriptwriter Kevin
Williamson decided to
exploit the audience's
familiarity with the
genre's conventions.

© Miramax/Courtesy Everett Collection

earlier women must be credited with ferociously fighting against the monster, the fact remains that they all succumb and are destroyed in the subsequent film. This familiar narrative trajectory is rejected in the *Scream* series. The trilogy, in contrast, *reverses* the tradition, maintaining the longevity of the victim/survivors and introducing new villains with each installment. This reversal is noteworthy and resonant because in doing so, the trilogy preserves the significance and importance of the (female) survivors over that of the killer, while inverting the genre's traditional conventions. The female survivors ultimately displace the killers as the recurring characters and effectively adopt the central narrative roles. This effectively allows the female characters to develop and evolve across the film's various installments.

REINTERPRETING THE FINAL GIRL

The slasher film has always maintained a complicated relationship with gender. As Clover observes, "the independent, low-budget [horror] film tradition has been central in the manufacture of the new 'tough girls' that have loomed so large in horror since the mid-seventies," a period that witnessed the rise of the feminist movement in the United States (6). At the same time, the slasher film's raison d'être is the torture and often brutal killing of nubile young women.   30

While we can trace the evolution of the 1990s slasher film's tough girl to her predecessors who populated the genre in the 1970s and early '80s, the '90s version has been revised to reflect more contemporary concerns. *The Texas Chainsaw Massacre* and *Halloween* are two of the early films that introduce the tough teenage girl who survives numerous violent attacks by the murderous, psychopathic villain. This girl's survival prompted Clover to dub her the "Final Girl," for she is commonly the last person left alive at the end of the film (35). It is worth noting that in both *The Texas Chainsaw Massacre* and *Halloween*, the Final Girl's survival is dependent on an external savior. In the final moments of *The Texas Chainsaw Massacre*, Leatherface and Hitchhiker's final victim manages to escape to a highway with the killers in pursuit. She is finally saved by a passing pickup that takes her to safety. Likewise, in *Halloween*, the Final Girl (Jamie Lee Curtis) is saved by Dr. Loomis (Donald Pleasence), the psychiatrist who treated the killer. Clover correctly suggests that horror-slasher films of the 1970s and early '80s tend to represent the female as both victim and hero simultaneously (4). In these early slasher films, female heroism is defined more in terms of the Final Girl's ability to survive and escape numerous attacks than in her ability to triumph independently over her tormentor(s). In the instances in which the female actually does triumph over her persecutors, Clover points out that the victory comes at a price. In a number of slasher films of the period, the depiction of the female hero/victim who   31 independently and successfully defends herself is negatively marked. Such a representation exists in a subgenre of horror that introduces the female victim as monster. Citing *Carrie* (1974) as one example, Clover explores the complex nature in which the title character morphs from victim to hero to monster, encompassing all these characteristics simultaneously (4).

By the 1980s, however, these earlier conceptions of the Final Girl had given way to a more capable and active version. According to both Clover and Trencasnky, "in the major 1980s slashers [...] the Final Girl is depicted as more powerful than ever before" (Trencansky 64). Films like *Friday the 13th, Slumber Party Massacre* (1982), *A Nightmare on Elm Street,* and *Texas Chainsaw Massacre 2* (1986) all present Final Girls who manage to both survive numerous attacks and dispatch the killers by themselves. These Final Girls are exceptions to the norm and are marked accordingly. As Clover points out, while the typical female victim is sexually active, the Final Girl is not; where the former is naive and oblivious, the latter is "watchful to the point of paranoia" (Clover 39). The Final Girl is also "intelligent and resourceful in a pinch [...]. The Final Girl is boyish, in a word" (Clover 39–40). These final girls are clearly the predecessors to the capable, brave, and active girls in the 1990s slasher cycle. However, there have been further developments in the more recent incarnations of the Final Girl.

Along with reenvisioning the monster/villain, *Scream* also rewrote the conventional representation of the Final Girl, offering viewers female characters who, while victimized, still manage to overcome their tormentors and emerge as heroes who triumph using their own merits and abilities. *Scream*

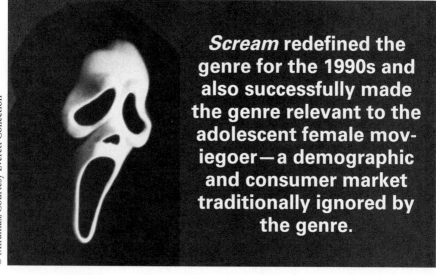

Scream redefined the genre for the 1990s and also successfully made the genre relevant to the adolescent female moviegoer—a demographic and consumer market traditionally ignored by the genre.

© Miramax/Courtesy Everett Collection

also deviates from the tradition by offering two Final Girls: Sidney Prescott and Gale Weathers (Courteney Cox-Arquette).[10] One of the more interesting aspects in *Scream* involves the representation of these Final Girls who break with a number of the genre's conventions. The traditional Final Girl is a "[figure] of rebellion against society, the heroine and other characters in films [such as *Halloween*, *A Nightmare of Elm Street*, and *Hellraiser*] are firmly entrenched as outsiders within their worlds, even among other adolescents" (Trencansky 68). In contrast, Sidney is an ordinary high school girl: she is popular, has a boyfriend, and a group of close-knit friends. While the traditional Final Girl is distinguished from the other characters by her virginity and seeming prudishness, Sidney, initially a virgin, eventually has sex, though the audience and the characters on the screen know that conventionally, "sex equals death." In keeping with the conventions, Sidney is consequently attacked and victimized. Yet, against the established rules, she escapes post-coital death and manages to overcome the villains. Conversely, the virgin, who, in classic slasher films, was always a female, the main character, and the sole survivor, was reconceptualized to renovate the genre's traditional gender conventions. In *Scream*, the requisite virgin is Randy (Jamie Kennedy), the male slasher-film fan who articulates the genre's rules and is a self-confessed virgin. While he is just as susceptible to violence, brutality, and death as the sexually experienced, he is little more than a sidekick in *Scream*. In a self-conscious twist to the format, when Randy is violently attacked and almost killed, he is saved by the no-longer-virginal Sidney. In addition to acknowledging (while simultaneously rejecting) the conventions of the slasher conventions, this particular development is a noteworthy advancement on the conventional sex-role stereotypes associated with the traditional slasher genre. Significantly, Sidney is not the outcast of the *Carrie* variety, nor is she the boyish virgin of *Halloween*.

Gale Weathers, the television journalist, is an even greater deviation from the Final Girl norm. She is career oriented, selfish, vain, ambitious, and largely amoral, yet she emerges as a Final Girl at the end, allying herself with Sidney and helping to destroy the killer. While these two women begin as adversaries, they are able to overcome their differences and work together to defeat their mutual demons. These Final Girls save themselves, and each other, without acquiring any monstrous connotations. More important, with the exception of Sidney's androgynous name, neither one is marked as particularly boyish nor are they actively differentiated from the other women in the film. Sidney and Gale, therefore, do not conform to the traditional characterization of the Final Girl, whom Clover describes as "compromised from the outset by her masculine interests, her inevitable sexual reluctance, her apartness from other girls" (48). Rather, both Sidney and Gale triumph over their ordeals and even forge a bond that includes the

other survivors from the first film. This group of survivors continues to support and aid each other as they attempt to put their traumatic experiences
behind them and go on with their lives. And they continue to help each
other through the continuing cycle of violent events that follow in the later
installments.

Scream also goes against a related genre convention in which the mon-   35
ster's victims and the Final Girl traditionally survive only to suffer from
"societal rejection" (Trencansky 69), which often entails some form of
physical confinement. As Trencansky highlights, the young people in
Freddy's Dead (1991) are incarcerated in a home for delinquent youth, while
A Nightmare on Elm Street exiles its Final Girl to a mental institution. In
contrast, the Final Girls in the *Scream* series not only triumph against their
persecutors but eventually transcend their terrifying experiences to emerge,
in the final installment, as independent, (relatively) well-adjusted, func-
tional individuals with a place in society. At the end of the trilogy, we see a
less-selfish Gale engaged to another survivor, while Sidney appears to have
finally laid her fears and demons to rest and appears determined to go for-
ward with her life surrounded by her friends.

The fact that these Final Girls survive through all three installments   36
is significant and represents a clear deviation from the traditional slasher
movie convention of killing off the Final Girl in each subsequent sequel.
One of the ironies of the conventional teen slasher film lies in the fact that
while the Final Girl is strong, resourceful, and powerful enough to seemingly defeat the monster, she almost never survives for long. In many cases,
she never succeeds in out-surviving the monster. As Williams points out,

> A Final Woman may fight and sometimes defeat the monster. But her ulti-
> mate victory is undercut either by eventual death in a sequel (Adrienne
> King in *Friday the 13th, Part II*; Heather Langencamp in *A Nightmare on
> Elm Street III: Dream Warriors*) or insanity (the heroines in *The Texas
> Chainsaw Massacre I* and *II*; *Friday the 13th: Part II* and *III*; and *Hollowgate*
> [1988]). (214)

In all of the films mentioned, it must be acknowledged that the depic-   37
tion of the Final Girl, while progressive, is also limited. In fact, the inevitable
death of the Final Girl in the traditional slasher series appears to represent
a very conservative ideology in which capable, independent young women
must inexorably be contained and/or destroyed for fear they trouble patri-
archy further (Ryan and Kellner 192). By comparison, the Final Girls in
the *Scream* trilogy subvert this trend. Sidney and Gale are not women who
survive a single film only to be summarily dispatched in the sequel. Unlike
previous Final Girls, Sidney and Gale outlive every psychotic killer they
encounter and in doing so, ultimately emerge physically, mentally, and

emotionally stronger. *Scream*, therefore, celebrates Sidney and Gale's abilities to survive and thrive.

Having Sidney and Gale remain as the central characters throughout the 38 trilogy and prompting audiences to follow them on their continuing journey also emphasizes the female-centered core of the films. Rather than build a series around an indestructible monster who constantly returns to wreak more destruction on new groups of women in each new cinematic installment, the creators of the *Scream* films have broken with tradition and chosen to highlight the strength, power, and resilience of the female survivors. This is a new treatment of the Final Girls, who emerge as women, are not defeated, do not die, and most important, continue to persevere against the various bogeymen/monsters that they encounter in their lives as depicted by each sequel.

Retaining the surviving Final Girls through the trilogy was also a par- 39 ticularly effective way of retaining audience loyalty because audiences kept returning to the subsequent releases to follow their favorite characters' growth, evolution, and development over the complete run of the series. Unlike the traditional slasher series, "*Scream* '[plays] more like a continuing serial because it's the same characters who survived the first movie, and people have an affinity for these characters,' Weinstein said, adding that test audiences cheered when cast members first appear on screen" (Eller, "Word of Mouth" D1).

In reconceptualizing the role of the Final Girl, *Scream* redefined the 40 genre for the 1990s and also successfully made the genre relevant to the adolescent female moviegoer—a demographic and consumer market traditionally ignored by the genre. The female audiences' responses to slasher films have been the subject of scholarly discussion, with the genre's ambiguous hostility toward women prompting debate on whether female viewers can legitimately find pleasure in such texts. Sarah Trencansky notes the tendency to dismiss "a female horror viewer [as either ...] blindly perpetuating oppressive norms, or else misunderstanding what she is seeing" (64). Isabel Pinedo has noted that "the female viewer [of slasher films is often] accused of masochism or the female fan [is] labeled an apologist for a woman-hating genre" (69). Clover, however, claims that the *A Nightmare on Elm Street* series had some success in attracting adolescent females (23). The traditional consensus, however, was that the slasher film remained a distinctly male-oriented genre.

This perception was revised in the late 1990s in the wake of a demo- 41 graphic that was becoming increasingly significant and influential. Much of *Scream*'s success came from appealing to this overlooked segment of the horror audience: teenage girls. According to Wes Craven, writer Kevin Williamson intentionally oriented *Scream*'s narrative toward concerns particularly relevant to teenage girls. Williamson explained, "I try to write very smart women [...who have to] deal with issues of betrayal and trust" (Weeks 1A).[11] One of the *Scream* trilogy's primary interests focuses upon the nature of boyfriends, who Williamson presents as "ordinary people [...] capable of great deception" (Weeks 1A). The films' plots essentially examine the issue of trust in romantic relationships, using the slasher film conventions as an allegory through which we explore the turmoil of female adolescence. Sidney's horror at discovering that she had unknowingly dated the boy who raped and killed her mother may be read as a metaphor for every teenage girl's fear that she does not really know her boyfriend. The fact that Sidney discovers this after she sleeps with him introduces another issue of concern to teenage girls: the boyfriend who turns against his girlfriend after sex. Craven in fact has remarked that the *Scream* series "has the emotional appeal of a soap opera, which he thinks plays better to woman than men. There are secret loves, haunting pasts, snobs, nerds and badly behaved boyfriends, twists that normally drive soaps" (Weeks 1A). That Sidney refuses to let these betrayals destroy her and that she learns self-reliance and independence and successfully overcomes the numerous events that threaten her is a particularly empowering message for teenage girls.

These generic revisions coincided with, and were perhaps a consequence   42
of, the rise of the teenage girl as a key target consumer. If young males were the target audience for the slasher genre in the past, the young female emerged as the ideal(ized) target audience at the box office in the 1990s, even for a genre as conventionally male oriented as the horror-slasher film. Neal Moritz, producer of teen films, including the teen slashers *I Know What You Did Last Summer* (1997) and its sequel *I Still Know What You Did Last Summer* (1998), as well as *Urban Legend* (1998), claims that "all our research led us to believe that it's best to target young females. The guys who want to go on dates will follow" (Wloszczyna 1D). Furthermore, according to CNN box office analyst Martin Grove, "[Teenage girls] tend to go to the movies in groups, which adds to the excitement of what's happening on screen" (Wloszczyna 1D). And as *Titanic* (1997) proved, teenage girls are willing to watch a film over and over again if it manages to capture their imagination.

It is clear that *Scream*'s female-oriented perspective contributed signifi-   43
cantly to its box office success. The film became a cult classic for young women and girls. *USA Today* reported that "Typically, only about 1% of moviegoers will pay to see a film more than once. With *Scream*, an estimated 16% of women age 25 and under who saw the film in theatres went more than once, according to polling by Miramax. By comparison, only 3% of young men who saw *Scream* returned for additional screenings" (Weeks 1A). By broadening the slasher film's appeal beyond the young male

demographic and actively appealing to young women, the three installments of the *Scream* series grossed $293.5 million domestically, the highest
combined box office for a horror franchise (Chetwynd and Seiler 4E), far
exceeding the combined box office of other series such as *Halloween* and
Friday the 13th, which had multiple sequels.

CONCLUSION

Scream and its two sequels deserve credit for breaking away from the tradi- 44
tional form of the slasher and updating several key conventions. In doing
so, the films received both critical and box office success and resurrected a
largely dormant genre, making it relevant to a new generation of teenagers.
Furthermore, the filmmakers successfully attracted the teenage girl audience, a demographic not associated with the genre historically. Finally, the
trilogy made a significant impact on the entertainment industry. *Scream*'s
success in 1996 proved that teenagers could be lured back to the multiplex
and sparked off a new cycle of slasher films for the late 1990s.

No longer neglected by the entertainment industries, teenagers returned 45
to the multiplex in droves. By 1998, *Variety* was reporting that 92% of teens
surveyed by the Artist Rights Foundation in Los Angeles and the Boston-
based Institute for Civil Society said they regard watching films as their
number-one pastime. The survey also revealed that 68% had seen a movie
within the previous week; a statistic considerably higher than in the spring
of 1993, when only 55% said that they had watched a film in a theater in
the preceding seven days. According to the survey, 82% of teenagers watch
at least one movie in a theater each month, while 87% watch one video
at home in the same period; 30% watch at least three theatrical releases a
month, while 65% rent at least the same number of videos; just 8% buy
tickets to five movies a month, although as many as 49% rent that many
films on tape (Madigan 3). In 1999, when the Motion Picture Association
reported huge box office numbers for 1998, with $1.48 billion in tickets
sold, it revealed that moviegoers aged 12 to 24 years accounted for 37.4%,
while audiences 25 to 39 years old accounted for 27.4% and those over 40
years, 35.3% (*Reality Check* M1).

This noteworthy increase in teen/youth film attendance was, in many 46
ways, a direct result of the increasing numbers of teen-oriented films that
the studios were actively releasing in the late 1990s. In the five years following *Scream*'s release, numerous other teen horror and slasher films followed,
including *I Know What You Did Last Summer*, *Disturbing Behavior* (1998),
Halloween: H20, *Urban Legend*, *I Still Know What You Did Last Summer*, *The
Faculty* (1998), *Final Destination* (2000), and *Urban Legend 2* (2000). These
subsequent releases provided an indication of the extent to which *Scream*
had revived the dormant slasher film.

NOTES

1. See Wloszczyna.

2. See Tietchen.

3. Certainly, *The Texas Chainsaw Massacre* and *Halloween* were not the originators of these narrative elements. As Clover points out, Hitchcock's *Psycho* (1960) is one of the earliest incarnations of the slasher film (14).

4. Brothers Harvey and Bob Weinstein launched Dimension Films fourteen years after they formed Miramax in 1979. Where Miramax focused on financing and distributing low-budget, independently produced, intelligent, art house fare largely ignored by the established studios in the 1980s, such as Steven Soderberg's *Sex, Lies and Videotape* (1989) and Neil Jordan's *The Crying Game* (1992), Dimension allowed the Weinsteins to pursue their alternative interests in producing low-budget, mainstream genre movies—particularly horror, sci-fi, and action films.

5. Prior to *Scream*, there were two other relatively high-profile live-action teen oriented films. One was *Clueless*, a 1995 high school romantic comedy starring Alicia Silverstone. Aimed at teenage girls, the film did very well at the box office, grossing $57 million (for some perspective, the 1989 teen "hit" *Heathers* grossed $1.1 million). A year later, *William Shakespeare's Romeo and Juliet*, starring Leonardo Di Caprio and Claire Danes, also did well at the box office. While these two films can be credited with indicating just how valuable and significant the teenage girl market could be, as well as hinting at the teen movie-going market's potential, I do not consider them the films that motivated the resurgence of the "teen pic" in the late 1990s. Neither *Clueless*, nor *Romeo and Juliet*, inspired studios to begin churning out teen films in bulk the way *Scream* did. It was only in the wake of *Scream* that the studios began producing a slew of slasher films intent on repeating their predecessors' success. In addition, neither *Clueless* nor *Romeo and Juliet* inspired the intense amount of media discourses declaring the resurgence of the teen market that *Scream* ultimately did.

6. As Clover notes, "the majority audience, perhaps even more than the audience for horror in general, was largely young and largely male [...]. Young males are also [...] the slasher film's implied audience, the object of its address" (23).

7. *Titanic* (1997) later confirmed the power of the teenage female demographic. A significant portion of the film's phenomenal $600 million domestic gross was the result of teenage girls who saw the film multiple times.

8. Please see Clover and Trencansky for a more developed discussion of the slasher villain's abjection.

9. According to a 1999 Gallup Poll at CNN.com, "America's teenagers put the blame for tragedies such as the Littleton school shooting directly on themselves rather than on parents, gun laws or media violence. An earlier poll of adults showed a markedly different result with most surveyed blaming parents and families for the tragedies."

10. I disagree with Trencansky, who argues that *Scream* is regressive in its portrayal of the Final Girl, claiming that Sidney harks back to the 1970s victim/hero who constantly relies on others to rescue her, suggesting that "these [...] films are not a process of emotional and physical independence for the heroines" (72). Furthermore, Trencansky restricts her discussion of the Final Girl to Sidney and fails to mention Gale in her discussion.

11. Certainly, Williamson's *Dawson's Creek* has found popularity with teenage girls with its presentation of female characters who are grounded, smart, brave, and mature.

WORKS CITED

Chetwynd, Josh, and Andy Seiler. "Expectations Rise for 'Scary' Body Count." *USA Today* 23 June 2000: 4E.

Clover, Carol. *Man, Women and Chainsaws: Gender in the Modern Horror Film*. Princeton: Princeton UP, 1992.

Eller, Claudia. "What about Bob?" *Los Angeles Times* 6 Apr. 2001: A1.

————"Word of Mouth; Sleeper Spawns a Franchise as Sequel to *Scream* Has Fans and Execs Abuzz." *Los Angeles Times* 12 Dec. 1997: D1.

Gallup Poll. CNN.com. 1999. <http:// edition.CNN.com/SPECIALS/1998/schools>.

Gill, Pat. "The Monstrous Years: Teens, Slasher Films, and the Family." *Journal of Film and Video* 54.4 (2002): 16–30.

Klady, Leonard. "Studios Focus on Teen Stream." *Variety* 9–13 Jan. 1997: 11–12.

Kristeva, Julia. *Powers of Horror: An Essay in Abjection.* New York: Columbia UP, 1982.

Madigan, Nick. "For Teens, Movies Are a Big Deal, Really Big." *Variety* 2–8 Nov. 1998: 3–4.

Orwall, Bruce. "Teen Tidal Wave Hits Hollywood in the Head." *Toronto Star* 19 Dec. 1997: D15.

Pinedo, Isabel Christina. *Recreational Pleasure: Women and the Pleasures of Horror Film Viewing.* Albany: State U of New York P, 1997.

"Reality Check—What's Up with All the Hot Teen Movies?" *Seattle Times* 4 Apr. 1999: M1.

Ryan, Michael, and Douglas Kellner. *Camera Politica: The Politics and Ideology of Contemporary Hollywood Film.* Bloomington: Indiana UP, 1988.

Tietchen, Todd F. "Samplers and Copycats: The Cultural Implications of the Postmodern Slasher in Contemporary American Film." *Journal of Popular Film and Television* 26.3 (1998): 98–107.

Trencansky, Sarah. "Final Girls and Terrible Youth: Transgression in 1980s Slasher Horror." *Journal of Popular Film and Television* 29.2 (2001): 63–73.

Tudor, Andrew. *Monsters and Mad Scientists: A Cultural History of the Horror Movie.* Oxford: Basil Blackwell, 1989.

Weeks, Janet. "*Scream* Movies Cultivate Special Audience: Girls." *USA Today* 12 Dec. 1997: 1A.

Williams, Tony. *Hearths of Darkness: The Family in the American Horror Film.* London: Associated UP, 1996.

Wloszczyna, Susan. "*Scream 2* Takes a Stab at Sophistication." *USA Today* 12 Dec. 1997: 1D.

VALERIE WEE is an assistant professor of English language and literature at the National University of Singapore. She has published articles in Kinema and Journal of ISSEI. She has also contributed chapters to Postcolonial Cultures and Literatures: Modernity and the (Un)Commonwealth (Peter Lang, 2002) and Teen Television: Genre, Consumption, Identity (BFI, 1998).

QUESTIONS FOR COMPREHENSION, STUDY, AND DISCUSSION

1. What, specifically, is the focus of this article?

2. The author notes, in the third paragraph, that "the general trend has been to dismiss the *Scream* films." What are the three narrative elements in the *Scream* films that some film scholars have criticized?

3. How does the author indicate she will, in her paper, refute the trend to dismiss the *Scream* films?

4. The author claims that the slasher films that preceded the *Scream* films "reflected the zeitgeist of those eras." How does she support this point?

5. Why did interest in slasher films decline in the early 1990s?

6. Why did interest in slasher films rekindle in the mid-1990s?

7. How did the *Scream* films change the nature of the psychotic serial killer, as he is portrayed in slasher films?

8. What is the "Final Girl"?

9. How did the *Scream* films change the nature of the "Final Girl" in slasher films?

10. How does the author argue that the *Scream* films are socially relevant?

JOURNAL PROMPT

Why are slasher films popular among teenagers?

Disciplines: History; Sociology; Psychology
Citation Method: *Chicago Manual of Style*
Rhetorical Mode: Argument

This article is from *Skeptic*, Volume 12, Number 4 (2006). It follows the *Chicago Manual of Style* method for source citation.

9/11 Conspiracy Theories:
The 9/11 Truth Movement in Perspective
Phil Molé

At the Hyatt Regency O'Hare near Chicago, a crowd of approximately   1
400 people has gathered on a pleasant summer evening. Some are old and
some are young; some are dressed in colorful tie-died shirts while others
wear dress shirts and slacks, but most seem cheerful and friendly. We are all
waiting for the opening of the main lecture hall for the evening's event, the
first of many scheduled talks during a weekend-long conference. We bide
some time by looking at the items for sale: DVD copies of Michael Moore's
Fahrenheit 9/11, the anti-Karl Rove documentary *Bush's Brain*, and the more
recent *Walmart: The High Cost of Low Price*.

There is nothing especially unusual here, since all of these are available   2
at the Borders or Best Buy near you. But then as the doors to the main hall
are about to open, one anxious attendee tries to start a chant of "9/11 was
an Inside Job." A few people join in before another attendee tells him, quite
emphatically, "we *already* know!" The weekend conference is the Chicago
meeting for 911truth.org, one of the most visible organizations within a
larger coalition known as the "9/11 Truth Movement," and most of the
crowd believes that the United States government planned and orchestrated
the terrorist attacks of September 11, 2001.

The statement "we already know!" well summarizes the attitude of the   3
conference attendees toward the material presented during the lectures.
Many at the conference do not seem to be looking for new information that
might lead to more accurate perspectives about the events of 9/11. A fellow
sitting near me admits, "We already know this stuff; we're here to reconfirm
what we already know." The conference is a way for attendees to consolidate
their group identity, and try to bring their message to those people at home
and abroad who believe the "official story" of 9/11. As someone who does
not share the views of the 9/11 Truth Movement, I have another objective.
I want to listen to their arguments and view their evidence, and understand
the reasons why so many likeable and otherwise intelligent people are convinced that the United States government planned the murder of nearly
3,000 of its own citizens.

THE COLLAPSE OF WORLD TRADE CENTER
BUILDINGS 1 AND 2

When most of us recall the events of 9/11, we think of the image of those   4
two seemingly indestructible World Trade Center towers crumbling to the
ground. Not surprisingly, their collapse is also a central issue for the 9/11
Truth Movement. An overwhelming amount of the organization's talks
and publicity materials address the fall of Buildings 1 and 2. But as these
materials show, 911truth.org does not believe the official story that the
primary damage to the WTC occurred when two airplanes hijacked by terrorists crashed into the towers. Rather, they maintain that the towers fell
due to a controlled demolition, planned in advance by the United States
government.

Why do they think this? A primary reason seems to be that the collapse   5
of the towers *looks* like the result of a controlled demolition. Since there is no
structural resistance to gravity in a controlled demolition, the building collapses straight into its own footprint, with each floor "pancaking" onto the
floors below at or near the speed of a free fall. Many of the presenters at the
Hyatt Conference compared videos of the collapse of the towers with videos
of known controlled demolitions, noting the similarity in both the appearance and speed of collapse, -911truth.org maintains that if actually hit by
an airplane, the steel structure of the WTC buildings should have provided
at least some resistance to the weight of the floors above, causing the falling
structure to pitch over to one side rather than pancake straight down. They
further argue that fires caused by burning jet fuel from the crashed planes
could not have caused the collapse, since jet fuel burns at a temperature of no
more than 1500° Fahrenheit,[1] while a temperature of approximately 2800° is
needed to melt steel. David Heller makes the point in a widely read article:

> The official story maintains that fires weakened the buildings. Jet fuel sup-
> posedly burned so hot it began to melt the steel columns supporting the
> towers. But steel-framed skyscrapers have *never* collapsed from fire, since
> they're built from steel that doesn't melt below 2750° Fahrenheit. No fuel,
> not even jet fuel, which is really just refined kerosene, will burn hotter than
> 1500° Fahrenheit.[2]

Since burning jet fuel is not hot enough by itself to melt steel, reports   6
that melted steel was observed at Ground Zero suggest to conspiracy theorists that some other incendiary substance must have been introduced.

Finally, many of the leaders of the movement claim that demolition   7
"squibs" can be seen in videos of the WTC collapse just before and during
the time the towers began to fall. In professional demolition lingo, a "squib"
is an explosive device used to weaken building structure during a controlled
demolition. Several presenters at the conference pointed out small bursts of

FIGURE 1
The circled area shows an alleged "squib"—actually air compressed by the falling tower.

FIGURE 2
The South Tower did not fall straight down. The top section above the fire tilted in the direction of the impact point. Photos courtesy of *Popular Mechanics* magazine.

debris spraying out horizontally from the towers during collapse, and identified these as "squibs" secretly detonated to fell the buildings.

What can we make of these allegations? First, let's examine the similar- 8
ity in appearance between the collapse of the World Trade Center towers
and the collapse of buildings destroyed through planned demolitions. In
controlled demolitions, detonating devices weaken or disrupt all major
support points in a building at the same time. Therefore, once the collapse
begins, all parts of the building are simultaneously in motion, free-falling
to the ground. However, this is definitely *not* what happens during the collapse of WTC Buildings 1 and 2. Carefully review footage of the collapses,
and you will find that the parts of the buildings above the plane impact
points begin falling *first*, while the lower parts of the buildings are initially
stationary.[3] The parts of the towers below the impact point do not begin
to fall until the higher floors have collapsed onto them. This is not what
we would expect if the towers collapsed from a controlled demolition, but
it is exactly what we would expect if the building collapse resulted from
damage sustained by the impact of the planes and subsequent fire damage.
A conspiracy theorist may counter that the buildings were rigged to begin
falling from the top down, but what are the chances that those planning
such a complicated demolition would be able to predict the exact location
the planes would impact the towers, and prepare the towers to begin falling
precisely there?

Additionally, footage of the collapse of the South Tower, or Building 9
2, reveals that the tower did *not* fall straight down, as the North Tower
and buildings leveled by controlled demolitions typically fall. Instead, the
tower tilted toward the direction of the impact point, and then began to
pancake downward with the top part of the building tilted at an angle. The
difference between the two collapses can be explained by the different way
each airplane struck the buildings. The first plane struck the North Tower
(Building 1) between the 94th to 98th floors and hit it head on, burrowing
almost directly toward the core of the building, The second airplane struck
the South Tower between the 78th and 84th floors, but sliced in at an angle,
severely damaging the entire northeast comer of the building.[4] Compared
with the North Tower, the South Tower sustained damage that was both less
evenly distributed and significantly lower on the building's frame, requiring
the weakened point to support more upper building weight than the corresponding crash site on the North Tower. This explains both the tilt of the
building as it fell toward the weakened corner, and the fact that the South
Tower fell first despite being struck after the North Tower was struck. Again,
this scenario makes good sense if the buildings fell due to damage inflicted
by the plane crashes, but makes very little sense if the buildings fell due to a
planned demolition.

The 9/11 Truth Movement often states or implies that steel would have   10
needed to melt in order for the structure to collapse at the speed of a free-
fall. While there are varying assessments of the temperature of the fire at
WTC, most agree that the temperature probably reached 1,000° Fahrenheit
and possibly higher than 1,800 °F. Flames of this temperature would be far
short of the approximately 2800 °F needed to melt steel, but they would have
been sufficient to severely reduce the structural integrity of the metal. Best
engineering estimates tell us that steel loses 50% of its strength at 650 °C.
(1,200 °F) and can lose as much as 90% of its strength at temperatures of
1,800 °F.[5] Even if we assume temperatures of no higher than 1,000 °F during
the fire, we would still have more than enough reasons to expect damage
severe enough to result in eventual collapse.

The unique structure of the WTC towers exaggerated the problems   11
caused by the weakened steel. The towers had a lightweight "perimeter
tube" design consisting of 244 exterior columns of 36cm square steel on
100 cm centers, with 95% of the structure's interior consisting of nothing
but air.[6] Within this perimeter tube design there was a 27 m by 40 m core,
designed to provide additional support to the tower. Steel trusses, or joists,
connected the outer beams to the core at each story, and provided much of
the overall support to the weight of each floor. The impact and explosion
of the airplane crashes probably knocked off most of the insulating material intended to fireproof the steel beams, considerably increasing their
vulnerability to flames. The heat of the flames reduced the steel to a fraction of its initial strength, while also causing the steel trusses to expand at
each end until they no longer supported the weight of the building's floors,
triggering the collapse. The expansion and warping of the steel would
have been particularly significant due to temperature differences within
the burning structure.[7] Thus, the trusses went limp much like a slackened
laundry line, providing little or no resistance to the weight of the floors
overhead.

What about the "melted steel" that 9/11 conspiracy theorists claim was   12
at Ground Zero? Dr. Steven Jones' popular article cites several anecdotal
sources speaking about flowing or pooled samples of melted steel found
at Ground Zero.[8] However, the sources in question are informal observations of "steel" at Ground Zero, not laboratory results.[9] To many people,
any grayish metal looks sufficiently like steel to call it "steel" when speaking
informally. To actually establish that the substance in question is steel, we
need analytical laboratory results using atomic absorption (AA) or another
suitable test. It seems far more likely that the metal seen by the contractors
was aluminum, a component of the WTC structural material that melts at a
much lower temperature than steel and can look superficially similar to it.
As for the "squibs" conspiracy theorists claim to see in videos of the WTC

collapse, these are plumes of smoke and debris ejected from the building due to the immense pressure associated with millions of tons of falling towers (see Figure 1). Videos of the WTC collapse show that these plumes do not begin until *after* the towers begin falling and increase in intensity as the collapse continues— this is not the scenario one would expect if the plumes were actually explosives used to *cause* the buildings to fall.

THE COLLAPSE OF WTC BUILDING 7

"Not so fast," the 9/11 Truth Movement might say. How do you explain   13
the collapse of WTC Building 7, which was *not* struck by an airplane? Many 9/11 conspiracy theorists maintain that the collapse of this building at about 5:20 PM on 9/11 would not have occurred unless it was already prepared for demolition. The conspiracy theorists assume that damage sustained by WTC 7 during the attack was not sufficient to trigger its collapse. The site wtc7.net claims that "fires were observed in Building 7 prior to its collapse, but they were isolated in small parts of the building, and were puny by comparison to other building fires." They further claim that any damage from falling debris from WTC 1 and WTC 2 would have needed to be symmetrical to trigger the pancaking collapse of WTC 7.[10]

These arguments only reveal the assumptions of their authors. First,   14
the fires burning in WTC 7 were extremely extensive. The reason this is not obvious from 9/11 Truth Movement presentations and documentaries is that they tend to only show the north side of WTC 7, selectively causing the building to appear both far less ravaged by fire and structural damage than it actually was.

Firefighter Richard Banaciski notes the difference in appearance between 15
the north and south sides of the building in his first-person account:

> We were told to go to Greenwich and Vesey and see what's going on. So we go there and on the north and east side of 7 it didn't look like there was any damage at all, but then you looked on the south side of 7 there had to be a hole 20 stories tall in the building, with fire on several floors.[11]

Emergency response workers at Ground Zero realized that extensive   16
damage to the lower south section of WTC 7 would cause collapse as early as 3 PM on 9/11, a fact reported on news broadcasts at the time.[12] Video footage shows that when collapse occurred, the south wall of the building gave in first, which is exactly what we would expect based on the location of the most extensive damage. As noted for the collapse of the South Tower, the mechanics of the building's fall are completely consistent with the nature of the damage sustained. The planned demolition hypothesis, on the other hand, fails to explain why collapse would begin at exactly the point where damage was inflicted, since the conspirators would have had to been able to

predict exactly where debris from the fallen North and South Towers would strike WTC 7. And while the makers of the documentary *Loose Change* comment that WTC 7 "fell straight down, into a convenient pile," the truth is that the pile of debris was 12 stories high and 150 meters across, hardly the kind of "convenient pile" described by conspiracy theorists.[13]

For those who believe that Building 7 fell due to controlled demolition, some of the most powerful "evidence" seemingly comes from WTC leaseholder Larry Silverstein's alleged "confession" that he authorized the tower's destruction. The quote in question comes from a September, 2002 PBS Special called *America Rebuilds*, in which Silverstein says: 17

> I remember getting a call from the, er, fire department commander, telling me that they were not sure they were gonna be able to contain the fire, and I said, "We've had such terrible loss of life, maybe the smartest thing to do is pull it." And they made that decision to pull and we watched the building collapse.[14]

To conspiracy theorists such as Alex Jones at prisonplanet.com, this quote seems to be a "smoking gun" because they interpret the phrase "pull it" to be "industry jargon for taking a building down with explosives."[15] Silverstein seems to be saying that he and the firefighters decided to pull (destroy) Building 7, and watched it fall after authorizing the demolition. No building could be controllably demolished so quickly, the conspiracy theorists go on to argue, so WTC 7 must have been prepared for demolition long in advance.   18

On closer inspection, this supposedly devastating evidence does not seem to mean what the 9/11 Truth Movement thinks it means. There is far from unanimous industry agreement that the phrase "pull it" always signifies a controlled demolition with explosives—more specific phrases such as "pull away" would be used to designate the specific operation to be performed.[16] And of course, "pull" has many common language uses quite separate from demolition lingo. But if Silverstein wasn't describing a decision to destroy WTC 7, what could the words "pull it" mean? A good place to seek the answer is this September 9, 2005 statement by Mr. Dara McQuillan. a spokesperson for Larry Silverstein: 19

> In the afternoon of September 11, Mr. Silverstein spoke to the Fire Department Commander on site at Seven World Trade Center. The Commander told Mr. Silverstein that there were several firefighters in the building working to contain the fires. Mr. Silverstein expressed his view that the most important thing was to protect the safety of those firefighters, including, if necessary, to have them withdraw from the building.
>
> Later in the day, the Fire Commander ordered his firefighters out of the building and at 5:20 p.m. the building collapsed. No lives were lost at Seven World Trade Center on September 11, 2001.

As noted above, when Mr. Silverstein was recounting these events for a television documentary he stated, "I said, you know, we've had such terrible loss of life. Maybe the smartest thing to do is to pull it." *Mr. McQuillan has stated that by "it" Mr. Silverstein meant the contingent of firefighters remaining in the building* (emphasis added).[17]

McQuillan's response also indicated that firefighters were present at   20
WTC 7 to evacuate tenants, and worked at the site until late in the afternoon shortly before the collapse occurred. There is in fact abundant evidence that firefighters were present in and around WTC 7 in evacuation and rescue missions until late in the day on 9/11. According to Fire Department Chief Daniel Nigro:

> The most important operational decision to be made that afternoon was [that] the collapse [of the WTC towers] had damaged 7 World Trade Center ...
> It had very heavy fire on many floors and I ordered the evacuation of an area sufficient around to protect our members, so we *had to give up some rescue operations that were going on at the time* (emphasis added) and back the people away far enough so that if 7 World Trade did collapse, we [wouldn't] lose any more people. We continued to operate on what we could from that distance and approximately an hour and a half after that order was [given], at 5:30 in the afternoon, World Trade Center collapsed completely.[18]

Another first responder adds that there were "tremendous, tremendous   21
fires going on. Finally they *pulled* (emphasis added) us out."[19] The first-hand accounts of rescue operations at WTC 7 tell a consistent story, and the latter quote also uses the word "pull" to describe the removal of firefighters from the vicinity of the building, just as McQuillan's statement does. Indeed, there is large agreement between McQuillan's response and the testimony of the firefighters, including the fact that: (a) firefighters were in fact in the vicinity of WTC 7 on 9/11; (b) their activities involved evacuation and rescue missions; (c) firefighters remained near WTC 7 until late in the afternoon of 9/11; (d) firefighters realized that WTC 7 would probably fall by approximately 3 PM on 9/11; and (e) firefighters pulled back from the building shortly after this realization, and watched the building collapse at approximately 5:20 PM. Despite the objections of conspiracy theorists, the "official story" is both logically coherent and supported by evidence.

By contrast, the story told by the 9/11 Truth Movement is riddled with   22
holes. It assumes that Larry Silverstein destroyed WTC Building 7, presumably in order to claim a huge insurance payoff. But if this is so, why would he tell the world of his plot on a PBS special? Furthermore, what relationship does Silverstein have with the United States government who, according to conspiracy theorists, destroyed the WTC buildings in order to terrorize its citizens into accepting domination by a police state?[20] And if

the government controlled the demolition of the WTC buildings in order to strike fear into its citizens, why in this one case would it wait until all of the tenants were evacuated from WTC 7 so that there were no reported casualties?[21] The government's strategy appears wildly inconsistent in the Truth Movement account—killing nearly 3,000 people in the destruction of the two main towers, while allowing an entire afternoon for the tenants of WTC 7 to escape. We should also note that the alleged 9/11 plot was needlessly complicated, since the building was wired for a controlled demolition *and* targeted to be hit by airplanes—why not just do the controlled demolition, ditch the airplanes and blame it on the terrorists of your choice?

There's also the problem that, as even the 9/11 Truth Movement admits,   23 prepping a building for demolition takes considerable time and effort. Usually a building targeted for demolition has been abandoned for considerable time and partially gutted to allow explosives intimate contact with the structure of the building. But since all of the WTC buildings were occupied right up to 9/11, how did the government gain access to wire 3 towers for complete demolition without anyone noticing? Imagine trying to sneak wires and bombs into buildings while thousands of people are working in offices, riding the elevators and milling about in the halls—that scenario is unlikely in the extreme.

THE PENTAGON

Many people in the 9/11 Truth Movement believe that the Pentagon was   24 not actually struck by Flight 77, as the "official story" claims. Instead, they believe that the United States government somehow staged the damage, perhaps through the use of a bomb or strategically fired missile. This claim first attracted attention in French author Thierry Meyssan's book, *Pentagate*, which claims that the damage done to the Pentagon was too limited to have resulted from the crash of a Boeing 757.[22] The documentary "Loose Change" claims that the hole left in the Pentagon by the alleged airplane was "a single hole, no more than 16 feet in diameter," and that no remains whatsoever of Flight 77 were found at the crash site.[23] To dramatically support this last point, conspiracy theorists cite CNN correspondent Jamie McIntyre's repot from the crash site on 9/11, which says, "From my close-up inspection, there's no evidence of a plane having crashed anywhere near the Pentagon."[24]

Like the previously discussed arguments about WTC 7 not being dam-   25 aged enough to fall on its own, complaints about the size of the hole in the Pentagon left by Flight 77 rely on selective choice of perspective. 9/11 conspiracy theorists like to reference pictures of the damaged Pentagon in which the hole made by the plane appears to be small, but aren't as fond of

AP Images/Navy Times, Mark Faram

FIGURE 3
One of many pictures that show recognizable airplane debris on the lawn of the burning Pentagon on 9/11. Photo courtesy of *Popular Mechanics* magazine.

the pictures accurately showing the full extent of the damage. Some conspiracy theorists also don't seem satisfied that the shape of the hole matches that expected for a crashed airplane. But the expectation that the plane should have left an immediately recognizable hole in the building is delusional—a speeding Boeing 757 will not leave a snow-angel style impression of itself in a concrete building (versus the mostly-glass exterior of the WTC buildings, which did leave an outline of a plane). And the contention that no remains of Flight 77 were found at the crash site is simply absurd. Many pictures taken of the area around the Pentagon crash site clearly show parts of an airplane in the wreckage. In an excellent article about 9/11 conspiracy theories in *Popular Mechanics*, blast expert Allyn E. Kilsheimer describes his own observations as the first structural engineer to arrive at the Pentagon after Flight 77 crashed:

> I saw the marks of the plane wing on the face of the building. I picked up parts of the plane with the airline makings on them. I held in my hand the tail section of the plane, and I found the black box.

Kilsheimer's eyewitness account is backed up by photos of plane   26
wreckage inside and outside the building. Kilsheimer adds: "I held parts of
uniforms from crew members in my hands, including body parts. Okay?"[25]

But if there is so much evidence that a plane crashed into the Pentagon,   27
why did CNN correspondent Jamie McIntyre report that he could find
none? The answer is that McIntyre did not report this at all, and the 9/11
Truth Movement is once again selectively manipulating evidence to fit their
conclusions. When McIntyre noted that no debris from a plane was observable near the Pentagon, he was responding to a specific question asked by
CNN anchor Judy Woodruff during the segment. Flight 77 came in flying
very low, and there had been speculation that the plane might have struck
the ground shortly before reaching the Pentagon. McIntyre's response, when
quoted in full, makes clear that he is saying that there was no evidence that
the plane hit the ground *before hitting the Pentagon*, but he certainly does
not deny that the plane struck the Pentagon itself.

> WOODRUFF: Jamie, Aaron was talking earlier—or one of our correspon-
> dence was talking earlier—I think—actually, it was Bob Franken—with
> an eyewitness who said it appeared that that Boeing 757, the American jet,
> American Airline jet, landed short of the Pentagon.
>
> Can you give us any better idea of how much of the plane actually impacted
> the building?
>
> MCINTYRE: You know, it might have appeared that way, but from my
> close-up inspection, there's no evidence of a plane having crashed anywhere
> near the Pentagon. *The only site is the actual site of the building that's crashed
> in* [emphasis added], and as I said, the only pieces left that you can see are
> small enough that you can pick up in your hand. There are no large tail
> sections, wing sections, fuselage, nothing like that anywhere around, *which
> would indicate that the entire plane crashed into the side of the Pentagon and
> then caused the side to collapse* [emphasis added].[26]

Note that McIntyre never questions that an airplane crash damaged the   28
Pentagon, and indeed describes seeing many pieces of the aircraft around
the crash site in an earlier section of the CNN transcript.[27] Of course, this
has not stopped conspiracy theorists from picking and choosing the evidence to push their own agendas.

FLIGHT 93 AND OTHER ALLEGED ANOMALIES

On April 5, 2006, the creators of the 9/11 conspiracy documentary "Loose   29
Change" and their supporters decided to attend the premiere of the film
"United 93," about the hijacked airplane that crashed on 9/11. They wanted
to take the opportunity to expose the alleged lies about this flight, and in

the words of one "Loose Change" forum member, to "bite these bastards where it hurts, and have this Flight 93 movie backfire on them."[28] To many Americans, the passengers on United 93 who fought back against the terrorists and caused it to crash before it could reach its target are heroes, but the 9/11 Truth Movement sees things differently. Depending on which conspiracy theorist you ask, you will either learn that Flight 93 actually landed safely, or that a US military jet shot the plane out of the sky.[29] The first claim stems from confusion in the initial Associated Press (AP) reports between Flight 93 and Flight 1989, the latter of which did land at Cleveland's Hopkins Airport on 9/11. The AP subsequently corrected the error, but many conspiracy theorists have not followed suit.[30] The second claim rests largely on unsupported assertions that the main body of the engine and other large parts of the plane turned up miles from the main wreckage site—too far away to have resulted from an ordinary crash. This is incorrect, because the engine was found only 300 yards from the main crash site, and its location was consistent with the direction in which the plane had been traveling.[31] Furthermore, the black box for the flight records the struggle onboard preceding the plane's crash. Conspiracy theorists are left with not only an evidentially worthless theory, but also a confusing one. Why would the same U.S. government that allegedly destroyed the WTC shoot down Flight 93 before it could cause similar damage to other buildings? Of course, this question assumes a standard of logical consistency that the 9/11 Truth Movement seems to lack.

Another alleged flight anomaly concerns the supposed "stand down" order given by the North American Aerospace Defense Command (NORAD) on 9/11 to allow the hijacked airplanes to reach their destinations without interference. The 9/11 Truth Movement believes that NORAD had the capability of locating and intercepting planes on 9/11, and its failure to do so indicates a government conspiracy to allow the attacks to occur. To support this assertion, they claim that NORAD could have quickly neutralized the hijacked planes because flight interceptions are routine, with 67 such intercepts occurring before 9/11.[32] Significantly, this claim does not specify the length of time over which these alleged intercepts occurred, or tell us whether they took place near major cities or over, say, miles of open ocean. More specific and accurate information comes from the *Popular Mechanics* article, which states:

> In the decade before 9/11, NORAD intercepted only one civilian plane over North America: golfer Payne Stewart's Learjet, in October 1999. With passengers and crew unconscious from cabin decompression, the plane lost radio contact but remained in transponder contact until it crashed. Even so, it took an F-16 1 hour and 22 minutes to reach the stricken jet. Rules in effect back then, and on 9/11, prohibited supersonic flight on intercepts.[33]

It is not a quick or easy matter to locate and intercept a plane behaving   31
erratically. NORAD personnel must first attempt repeated communication with the plane in question to rule out more mundane problems, and
then must contact appropriate military personnel to scramble fighters and
direct them to the appropriate location. The situation on 9/11 was further
complicated by the fact that terrorists on the hijacked jets had turned off
or disabled the onboard radar transponders. Without a transponder signal
identifying the airplanes, each hijacked airplane would have been only one
moving blip among many others on NORAD's screens, making it much
harder to track. Thus, even a direct NORAD decision to intercept any of
the hijacked planes on 9/11 would have still entailed a significant amount of
time to reach the jet—time that was simply not available on 9/11.

Various other conspiracy theories focus on the government's alleged   32
foreknowledge of the terrorist attacks. One popular theory suggests there
was a suspiciously high volume of "put" trading of airline stocks in the days
just before 9/11. Since "put" trading is effectively a gamble that the price of
a stock will decrease, conspiracy theorists surmise that trading "insiders"
knew about the coming events of 9/11 and placed their bets accordingly.
While this may look suspicious in isolation, the general volume of put trading on these stocks reached similar levels at earlier points in the year. The
spike in American Airlines trading was the highest of all the airline companies involved, but that's hardly surprising considering that the company had
just released a major warning about possible losses.[34] Indeed, general bad
news about the airline industry prompted investment companies to advise
their clients to take the put options, removing any need to blame the trading
options on foreknowledge of the attacks.

Another theory alleges that the Federal Emergency Management Agency   33
(FEMA) arrived at the World Trade Center on September 10, 2001, thus
showing that the government knew about the coming disaster. This claim is
based on a statement by Tom Kenney of the Massachusetts task force, who
told CBS news anchor Dan Rather on September 13, 2001, "We're currently,
uh, one of the first teams that was deployed to support the city of New York
for this disaster. We arrived on, uh, late Monday night and went into action
on Tuesday morning. And not until today did we get a full opportunity to
work, uh, the entire site."[35] The rather mundane explanation for this quote is
that Mr. Kenney confused his days—not an unusual occurrence for someone
who had been working for more than two long days in emergency response
activities. Thus, a straightforward interpretation of Kenney's response is
that he arrived at Ground Zero on 9/11 (which he incorrectly identified as
Monday, rather than Tuesday), went into action on 9/12 (mistakenly identified as Tuesday) and did not get a chance to work the whole WTC site until
"today" (the day he was speaking to Rather, or Thursday, 9/13) Additionally,

many sources document the arrival of FEMA on 9/11, and Kenney's wife confirmed the day her husband was dispatched to Ground Zero as 9/11.[36] The degree to which the 9/11 Truth Movement will exaggerate and exploit simple misunderstandings does not speak well of their concern for truth.

Much of this discussion has focused on explanations given by the 9/11 Truth Movement, but we should note that the explanations they *don't* give are just as problematic. I have not been able to locate any significant discussion of al Qaeda, radical Islamic terrorists or the modern history of the Middle East in any of the 9/11 Truth Movement's writings. The most likely reason for this is that, like most other Americans, many of them simply didn't pay very much attention to the Middle East before 9/11. Yet, it is impossible to understand the threat of terrorism unless we also understand how the fall of the Ottoman empire, the fragmentation of much of the Middle East into new nations with largely arbitrary boundaries after WW II, Muslim reaction to the creation of the state of Israel, the birth of Islamic fundamentalism, conflict with and influence by Soviet Russia, and frustration over America's support for Israel have shaped the ideology and mission of groups like al Qaeda. Islamic terrorist groups arose in this context, and have actively and repeatedly targeted American interests for over two decades. The idea that Islamic terrorists would target U.S. buildings for attack fits well with recent events over the past two decades, including:

- an attack by the radical Hezbollah faction on Marine barracks in Lebanon in 1983;
- the hijacking of the *Achille Lauro* in 1985;
- a truck bomb attack on the World Trade Center in 1993, killing 6 people and injuring over 1,000 more;
- a thwarted attempt to blow up 12 planes heading from the Philippines to the U.S. in January, 1995;
- an attack on Khobar Towers in Saudi Arabia in 1996, killing 19 U.S. military personnel and injuring hundreds more;
- the bombings of U.S. Embassy buildings in Kenya and Tanzania in 1995, killing 12 Americans and 200 Kenyans and Tanzanians;
- a thwarted attempt by Ahmed Ressam to attack Los Angeles International airport in late 1999;
- a suicide boat bombing against the U.S.S. Cole on October 12, 2000, killing 17 sailors and injuring 39 others.[37]

Additionally, there is well-documented evidence that Osama Bin Laden has repeatedly organized and prompted attacks against the United States. His role as a financier for major terrorist organizations and the leader of al Qaeda is well-established. Bin Laden issued a 1996 fatwa officially declaring a jihad against the United States, and a second fatwa in 1998 declaring "to kill the Americans and their allies—civilian and military is an individual duty for any Muslim who can do it in any country in which it is possible to do it."[38] Since bin-Laden and al Qaeda have officially claimed responsibility for the attacks of 9/11, and the evidence points in their direction there is no point in seeking alternative theories.[39]

The best explanation for the events of 9/11 is that it was the latest and most damaging attack yet in a series of attacks by radical Islamic terrorists who wish to end what they believe is an evil U.S. foreign policy. As a nation, we were psychologically and strategically unprepared for this attack due to our failure to acknowledge the seriousness of the threat. Sadly, the 9/11 Truth Movement continues to divert its gaze from the real problems, preferring the solace of delusions to reality.   36

CONCLUSION: THE POWER OF CONSPIRACY THEORIES

This article has analyzed the arguments of the 9/11 Truth Movement and found them lacking. Yet, the 400 people who attended the conference and the thousands of others who support their efforts find these theories convincing, and the reason does not necessarily seem to be grounded in common political ideology. Based on my informal survey of the crowd at the Hyatt conference, I noted that attendees seemed to come from each extreme of the political spectrum. There were representatives of the far right who decry any form of government authority, but there were also members of the far left waging a tireless campaign against the perceived evils of capitalism and imperialism. We need to return to a question posed near the beginning of this discussion: Why do so many intelligent and promising people find these theories so compelling?   37

There are several possible answers to this question, none of them necessarily exclusive of the others. One of the first and most obvious is distrust of the American government in general, and the Bush administration in particular. This mistrust is not entirely without basis. The American government deceived its citizens about the real human costs of Vietnam, and resorted to military tactics that were ethically questionable even by the standards of war. The revelations of Watergate, the Iran-Contra scandal, and other nefarious schemes great and small have understandably eroded public confidence in government. Couple that with an administration that took office after the most controversial presidential election in more than a century, and one that backed out of international agreements such as the Kyoto Protocol, misled citizens about the science of global warming and stem cell research, initiated a war in Iraq based on unsupportable "intelligence" about weapons   38 of mass destruction, and failed to respond adequately to the effects of hurricanes in the Gulf Coast, and you have strong motivations for suspicion.[40] (Suffice it to say, admiration for George W. Bush is not my motivation for defending him against the claims of conspiracy theorists.)

However, there are a few things to be said about suspicion. First, there is   39 the simple philosophical point that suspicion alone demonstrates nothing—any theory needs evidence in its favor if it is to be taken seriously. Second, the mistakes made by our government in the past are qualitatively different from a conscious decision to kill thousands of its own citizens in order to justify the oppression of others. Most importantly, there is the fact that most of what we know about the bad decisions made by our government is only knowable due to the relative transparency with which our government operates, and the freedom to disseminate and discuss this information.

The full irony of this last point hit me while I was at the conference. Here   40 was a group of about 400 people gathered to openly discuss the evil schemes of the U.S. government, whom they accuse of horrible atrocities in the service of establishing a police state. But if America really was a police state with such terrible secrets to protect, surely government thugs would have stormed the lecture halls and arrested many of those present, or would at the very least have conducted behind the scenes arrests and jailed the movement's leaders. Yet even the most vocal leaders of the 9/11 Truth Movement are still going strong, and no one at the conference seemed very worried about government reprisals. This fact seemingly indicates that at some level, the conspiracy theorists themselves don't really believe what they are saying.

Another reason for the appeal of 9/11 conspiracies is that they are easy to   41 understand. As previously mentioned, most Americans did not know or care to know much about the Middle East until the events of 9/11 forced them to take notice. (The brilliant satirical newspaper *The Onion* poked fun at this fact with its article "Area Man Acts Like He's Been Interested In Afghanistan All Along".)[41] The great advantage of the 9/11 Truth Movement's theories is that they don't require you to know anything about the Middle East, or for that matter, to know anything significant about world history or politics. This points to another benefit of conspiracy theories—they are oddly comforting. Chaotic, threatening events are difficult to comprehend, and the steps we might take to protect ourselves are unclear. With conspiracy theory that focuses on a single human cause, the terrible randomness of life assumes an understandable order.

The great writer Thomas Pynchon memorably expressed this point in   42 his novel *Gravity's Rainbow:* "If there is something comforting—religious, if you want—about paranoia, there is still also anti-paranoia, where nothing is connected to anything, a condition not many of us can bear for long."[42] The promiscuity of conspiracy theories toward evidence thus becomes part of their appeal—they can link virtually any ideas of interest to the theorist into a meaningful whole. This point was illustrated nicely during the Q & A session following the conference screening of Rick Siegel's *Eyewitness: Hoboken*. An attendee wanted to know what role the Freemasons played in the plot, and seemed very concerned that Siegel's account had neglected them. After waffling on the answer for a few moments without appeasing his questioner, Siegel finally relented and said, "Sure, they're involved." And why not? With the standards of evidence used by conspiracy theorists, there is no reason why the Freemasons, the Bavarian Illuminati, or the Elders of Zion cannot also be involved in the 9/11 plot—it just depends on what you find the most solace in believing. As it turns out, some conspiracy theorists do throw one or more of these other parties into the mix, as a popular and bogus rumor that 4,000 Jews mysteriously failed to come to work on 9/11 shows.[43]

Solace is something all of us needed after the horrible events of 9/11, and each of us is entitled to a certain degree of freedom in its pursuit. However, there is no moral right to seek solace at the expense of truth, especially if the truth is precisely what we most need to avoid the mistakes of the past. Truth matters for its own sake, but it also matters because it is our only defense against the evils of those who cynically exploit truth claims to serve their own agendas. It is concern for the truth that leads us to criticize our own government when necessary, and to insist that others who claim to do so follow the same rigorous standards of evidence and argument. 9/11 was a powerful reminder of how precious and fragile human life and liberty are— the greatest possible rebuke to those who would live in service to delusions.

REFERENCES

1. 2005. "9/11; Debunking the Myths." *Popular Mechanics*. March. 2005.
2. Heller, David. 2005. "Taking a Closer Look: Hard Science and the Collapse of the World Trade Center." *Garlic & Grass*, Issue 6. Available at http://www.garlicandgrass.org/issue6/Dave_Heller.cfm.
3. This is clearly visible in the PBS NOVA Documentary *Why The Towers Fell*.
4. 2005. "9/11: Debunking the Myths." *Popular Mechanics*. March. 2005.
5. Eager, Thomas and Musso, Christopher. 2001. "Why Did the World Trade Center Collapse: Science, Engineering and Speculation." *JOM*. 53(12), 8–11.
6. Ibid.
7. Ibid.
8. Jones, Steven. 2006. "Why Indeed did the WTC Buildings Collapse?" Available at http://www.physics.byu.edu/research/energy/htm7.html
9. A good discussion of this issue can be found at http://911myths.com/html/wtc_motten_steel.html
10. This claim can be found at http://wtc7.net/b7fires.html
11. "World Trade Center Task Force Interview: Richard Banaciski." Interview conducted on December 6. 2001. Transcribed by Elisabeth F. Nason. Available at http://graphics8.nytimes.com/packages/pdf/nyregion/20050812_WTC_GRAPHIC/9110253.PDF#search=%22Banaciski%22 Ibid.
12. Ibid.

13. http://www.loosechangeguide.com/LooseChangeGuide. html

14. "America Rebuilds," PBS Home Video, ISBN 0-7806-4006-3, is available from http://shop. pbs.org/products/AREB901/.

15. http://www.prisonplanet.com/011904wtc7

16. A discussion of the "pull it" phrase by professional demolition workers is at http://web. archive.org/web/20050327052408/http://home.planetnl/~reijd050/911_my_own_review. htm#222

17. See "9/11 Revealed? A New Book Repeats False Conspiracy Theories." At http://usinfo.state. gov/media/Archive/2005/Sep/16-241966.html

18. "World Trade Center Task Force Interview: Daniel Nigro." Interview conducted on October 24. 2001. The text of the interview is available at http://www. nytimes.com/packages/html/ nyregion/20050812_WTC_GRAPHIC/Nigro_Daniel.txt

19. "World Trade Center Task Force Interview: Richard Banaciski." Interview conducted on December 6. 2001. Transcribed by Elisabeth F. Nason. Available at http:// graphics8.nytimes.com/packages/pdf/nyregion/20050812_WTC_GRAPHIC/9110253. PDF#search=%22Banaciski%22 Ibid.

20. Read almost anything at http://www.prisonplanet.com for this idea.

21. The FEMA report on WTC 7 is available at http://usinfo.state.gov/media/Archive/2005/ Sep/16-241966.html

22. Meyssan, Thierry. 2002. *Pentagate*. New York USA Books.

23. http://www.loosechangeguide.com/LooseChangeGuide.html

24. The transcript: http://transcripts.cnn.com/TRANSCRIPTS/0109/11/bn.35.html

25. 2005. "9/11: Debunking the Myths." *Popular Mechanics*. March, 2005.

26. http://transcripts.cnn.com/TRANSCRIPTS/0109/11/bn.35.html

27. Ibid.

28. http://www.loosechangeguide.com/LooseChangeGuide.html

29. The claim that Fligt 93 landed safely is at http://www.rense.com/general56/flfight.htm. The claim that it was shot by a missile can be found at http://www.serendipity.li/wot/pop_mech/ shanksville.htm

30. A description of the confusion between the planes is in Kropko, M.R. 2002. "September 11 Tension Vivid to Controller." *Associated Press,* August 15, 2002. The story is also available online at http://www.enquirer.com/editions/2002/08/15/loc_sept_11_tension.html

31. 2005. "9/11: Debunking the Myths." *Popular Mechanics*. March, 2005.

32. One such claim can be found at http://911research.wtc7.net/essays/pm/

33. 2005. "9/11: Debunking the Myths." *Popular Mechanics*. March. 2005.

34. See "AMR Corp Issues 3Q' 2001 Profit Warning." *Airline Industry Information*, September 11, 2001. Available at http://www.highbeam.com/library/docFree.asp?DOCID=1G1:78127985. For a general contemporary assessment of the viability of airline industry in the months before 9/11, see Hamilton, Adam. 2001. "Plummeting Profits." Zeal Speculation and Investment. June 22. 2001, available at http://www.zealllc.com/2001/plummet.htm

35. Schorow, Stephanie. 2002. "Independent Research." *Boston Herald*, 5 September (Arts & Life). A sound recording of Kenney's statement can be heard at http://www.snopes.com/ rumors/sound/kenney.ram

36. Ibid.

37. This list is based on information in Strasser, Steven (ed.). 2004. *The 9/11 Investigations: Staff Reports of the 9/11 Commission*. New York: Public Affairs Books. More information about radical Islam can be found in Rashid, Ahmed. 2001. *Taliban: Militant Islam, Oil and Fundamentalism in Central Asia*. New York: Yale University Press.

38. This quote can be found in many sources, including Strasser, Steven (ed.). 2004. *The 9/11 Investigations: Staff Reports of the 9/11 Commission*. New York: Public Affairs Books.

39. Bamer, David. 2001. "Bin Laden: Yes, I Did It." *The Telegraph*. November 11.

40. One source among many possible for this information is Alterman, Eric and Green, Mark. 2004. *The Book on Bush: How George W. (Mis)leads America*. New York: Penguin.
41. This hilarious article is at http://www.theonion.com/content/node/28079
42. Pynchon, Thomas. 1973. *Gravity's Rainbow*. New York: Viking Press.
43. See, for instance, "Absent Without Leave" at the Urban Legends Reference Pages: http://www.snopes.com/rumors/israel.htm

In addition to the specific sources cited above, readers seeking responsible analysis of the claims of the 9/11 Truth Movement can use the following general sources:

www.911myths.com
A great general source for all manner of conspiracy claims.

www.snopes.com
The Urban Legends Reference Pages, containing entries about conspiracy claims such as the put options, the alleged early arrival of FEMA and the Pentagon attack. The forum also contains some intelligent discussion of conspiracy theories.

http://www.loosechangeguide com/LooseChangeGuide.html
This is a viewer's guide to the documentary "Loose Change," which contains many of the conspiracy claims discussed in this article.

QUESTIONS FOR COMPREHENSION, STUDY, AND DISCUSSION

1. According to 9/11 conspiracy groups, why did World Trade Center Buildings 1 and 2 collapse?

2. How does the author rebut their argument?

3. How do the 9/11 conspiracy groups explain the collapse of World Trade Center Building 7?

4. How does the author rebut this argument?

5. According to the 9/11 conspiracy groups, why was the Pentagon damaged?

6. How does the author rebut this argument?

7. What do the 9/11 conspiracy groups believe happened to Flight 93?

8. How does the author rebut this argument?

9. What key argument against a 9/11 conspiracy does the author believe the conspiracy theorists ignore?

10. What reasons does the author offer to explain why "so many intelligent and promising people" believe 9/11 was a government conspiracy?

JOURNAL PROMPT

Why are certain groups, such as the Roman Catholic Church, the American government, and the British royal family, often the focus of conspiracy theories?

Academic Discipline: History
Citation Method: *Chicago Manual of Style* (Footnotes)
Rhetorical Mode: Exposition; Argument

This article is from the *Journal of American History,* September 2006. It follows the *Chicago Manual of Style* method for source citation using footnotes.

Global Anti-Americanism and the Lessons of the "French Exception"
Philippe Roger

It would be hard not to agree with Rob Kroes's strong, emotional depiction [1] of the growing European hostility toward American policies in the wake of the Iraq crisis. All polls confirm what seems obvious: America's image abroad has been rapidly deteriorating in direct connection with a policy seen as (check one or more): ill motivated, politically naïve, hazardous for the region and the rest of the world, not to speak of illegitimate in the eyes of international law. Does that mean that Europeans, at least "old Europeans," are now unified under the banner of anti-Americanism? The answer would have to be a qualified one.

Empirical data drawn from numerous opinion polls taken in the past [2] five years show a general surge in negative opinions and feelings. But when read more carefully, the data also show interesting discrepancies or exceptions. It is worth noting, for instance, that in the polls taken by the U.S. State Department in the fall of 2002 (which showed strong evidence of the surge of adversarial views in Germany and Great Britain), France, which was in the forefront of political opposition to the Bush administration, showed no sign of aggravated anti-Americanism, with negative opinions staying at the same level as before the diplomatic crisis (a 1 percent variation, irrelevant in such polls).[1] I recall this episode to suggest that although the international crisis over Iraq did damage public views of the United States in (almost) all countries (Russia was a remarkable exception) and seemed to cast Europe in a single mold, it would be premature and probably unwise to speculate about the long term. The high negative ratings of 2002 have fluctuated, sometimes dramatically, in countries such as Great Britain or even Italy, as

Philippe Roger is a senior research fellow at the French National Center for Scientific Research and a professor at the Ecole des Hautes Etudes en Sciences Sociales in Paris; he also teaches at the University of Virginia.
Readers may contact Roger at philippe.roger@ehess.fr.

[1] Philippe Roger, *The American Enemy: A Story of French Anti-Americanism,* trans. Sharon Bowman (Chicago, 2005), 450.

a consequence of the countries' stages and forms of involvement in the war and the no less fluctuating ratings of their respective leaders. Opinion polls taken at times of crisis and phrased in the most simplified terms (approve/disapprove, good image/bad image) are hasty pictures of a fast-moving situation. Are those high negative ratings here in Europe to stay, or will they deflate like so many speculative bubbles? Will the negative image of America linger on, say, in Germany or Italy or even Spain (which has become a serious contender for first place in its hostility toward the United States, above the all-time leader: France) if and after the American presidency changes hands? The reelection of George W. Bush has deprived us of a quick answer.

Even more interesting, in my view, is the French and, to a lesser extent, 3 European perception of a widening gap between America and Europe in values. A poll taken in France in 2004 (ironically, in connection with a symposium on "shared values" held at the French National Assembly during the commemoration of D day) confirmed what we had learned in 2000, *before* the Iraq crisis, from a State Department survey: The French regarded themselves as *not* sharing Americans' ideas about family (58 percent), ethics (69 percent), work (76 percent) and, of course, life-style (81 percent), with democracy faring a little better at 49 percent and religion becoming a major topic of contention (in a 2002 survey, 65 percent of the French regarded the Americans as "too religious"). Looking back at pre–Iraq war polls is a good safeguard against falling prey to historical amnesia; in France the war only added collateral damage to a preexisting bleak picture of America.[2]

The core of the problem, however, does not lie in the fine-tuning of 4 damage assessment, but in the very notion of anti-Americanism, which should not be confused with such expressions of anger or disgust over the Iraq war as we have been witnessing in Europe and elsewhere. That is where I part ways with Rob Kroes: not on data analysis, but on the very definition of anti-Americanism. "If we choose to retain the term at all," wrote Rob Kroes, who did not seem quite sure we should, then we have to draw the line between politically articulated disagreement and a global rejection.[3] I would call the latter "imaginary," though that may sound awkward in English, since it is a complex of (mis)representations, stereotypes, and projections cemented into a tradition that in turn shapes our judgments. Granted, the distinction between arguable political disagreement and Pavlovian anti-American reactions is not always clear-cut: the most sophisticated and seemingly rational line of argumentation may be rife with

[2]U.S. Department of State, Office of Research, "West Europeans Positive toward U.S.," Nov. 2, 2000, p. 5 (in Richard Kuisel's possession); Pew Center, "Views of Changing Words," Nov. 2002, *ibid.*

[3]Rob Kroes, "European Anti-Americanism: What's New?," *Journal of American History*, 93 (Sept. 2006), 426.

misguided or misleading preconceptions. But difficult as it is, the task has to be confronted if we are to make sense, political and otherwise, of anti-Americanism as a driving and thriving force in the world today.

Anti-Americanism, as I see it, is not a doctrinal opposition to "Americanism." Americans themselves were always unable to define "Americanism," so you cannot blame the Europeans, who had shown some interest in the notion in the 1920s and 1930s, for discarding it altogether as early as the 1950s. In French, the word simply does not exist anymore, which certainly tells us something about its antonym. Anti-Americanism is and has been for two centuries, in the French case, a multilayered sedimentation of negative discourses. Although often contradictory, those discourses are treated as compatible and received as such. While rekindled by specific conflicts, anti-Americanism has thus become a permanent feature of France's national self-definition, not to say identity. In that regard, French anti-Americanism is and will remain different from German or Italian hostility; it has more in common with Spanish anti-Americanism, which is also deeply rooted in Spanish history—the 1898 conflict has not been forgotten there—and is reemerging today after decades of forced suppression under Francisco Franco.

French "exceptionalism" is the product of a long history, with three major factors (and a few minor ones) to account for it: (1) the rivalry between the two major democratic models, which turned into bitter competition with the decline of French influence and the rise of American hegemony; (2) the absence of significant French emigration to the United States, which deprived the French both of a sense of America as a land of promise and of direct, raw information, through family channels, about America; (3) the formation, as early as the nineteenth century, of an intellectual coalition against cultural Americanization, ranging from the far right to the far left, which was a formidable instrument for consensus in an otherwise deeply divided intelligentsia. In the French context, where intellectuals wielded a powerful influence, such a consensus had laid the groundwork for anti-Americanism, both cultural and political, by the turn of the last century. As Rob Kroes reminded us, Charles Baudelaire coined the word *américanisation* as early as the mid-nineteenth century; but Baudelaire was also responsible for expanding its meaning from sheer technophobia to an apocalyptic prediction of the total destruction of nature and society, art and religion, family ties and moral sense. That "prophecy," as he called it, which was probably written in 1861 and appeared posthumously in *Fusées*, had an enormous impact on the intelligentsia.[4] Time here is a key factor.

[4]*Ibid.*, 427; Charles Baudelaire, *Fusées; Mon coeur mis à nu; La Belgique déshabillée: Suivi de Amoenitates Belgicae* (Rockets; My heart laid bare; Belgium undressed: Followed by Belgian pleasures), ed. Andre Guyaux (Paris, 1985), 82–85.

Anti-Americanism has shorter roots in the rest of Europe, with the very special exception of Great Britain, and even shorter ones in the Middle East, for instance, where anti-Americanism is something from the 1950s (in Iran) or the 1960s (among Israel's neighbors).

Because of the different definition I hold of anti-Americanism, I differ with 7 Kroes's opinion that "anti-Americanism typically proceeds from specific areas of disagreement to larger frameworks of rejection." My anti-Americanism works the other way round: a globally negative reading of everything American constantly preempts isolated analyses in specific fields and circumstances. When in 1999 President Bill Clinton (not George W. Bush) finally decided to intervene militarily to stop the genocidal war in Bosnia—an intervention that had been called for by French public opinion for months and months—the same French people were quick to tell pollsters (by the huge margin of 60 percent) that "the Americans did it for their own political and military interests," with a meager 24 percent granting the possibility that they might have done it "for human rights and democracy." Clearly, for most French people, even in the ragged, oil-free hills of Kosovo, the greedy Yankees were conducting war and business as usual—that is, according to the preset global perception that French anti-Americanism has nurtured for so many decades.[5]

As another consequence of our diverging definitions, I tend to disagree 8 with Kroes's optimistic definition of anti-Americanism as "a weak and ambivalent complex of anti-feelings." Anti-feelings—alas!—have often proven to be very efficient and powerful feelings. Negativity exists and takes its toll; I am not much of a Platonist on that matter. Indeed, what some philosophers have called "negative synthesis" might well be the order of the day in our postmodern societies, where rallying people around positive notions (be it the Nation, the Free Market, or the Revolution) has become a dismal task for politicians, if not a mission impossible. We in France have been the quiet anti-Americans of Europe: loud and often foulmouthed, to be sure, but content with speech. (By the by, Jean-Marie Colombani's editorial in the French newspaper *Le Monde*, headed "We are all Americans," was immediately countered by a deluge of protesting articles and letters, even in his own paper.[6] Coming back to France at the end of October 2001, after seeing the twin towers fall with my own eyes from my New York University lodgings, I was struck by the short-lived solidarity and lack of interest in the victims shown by the French media.) One of the most interesting and puzzling questions ahead of us is the possible switch in the very nature of

[5]Kroes, "European Anti-Americanism," 419. On the 1999 poll, see Roger, *American Enemy*, trans. Bowman, 451.

[6]Kroes, "European Anti-Americanism," 426; Jean-Marie Colombani, "Nous sommes tous Americains" (We are all Americans), *Le Monde* (Paris), Sept. 13, 2001, p. 1; Roger, *American Enemy*, trans. Bowman, 448.

anti-Americanism, from elitist, intellectual rejection of a boisterous rival to populist-extremist hatred and resentment against the ultimate enemy, half Terminator, half golden calf.

Rob Kroes is not likely to renounce his own vision of anti-American-   9
ism. However, adopting mine would carry some advantages: he would no longer need to worry about charges of having become anti-American. Conscientiously opposing a policy one deems wrong is not anti-American-ism. To conclude with a memory of my own, I remember demonstrating in Paris and in Washington (during an exchange year at Yale University) against the Vietnam War. I never felt anti-American at the time. In fact, I rarely felt so close to America as when riding in a ramshackle old school bus to the Capitol with my American friends.

QUESTIONS FOR COMPREHENSION, STUDY, AND DISCUSSION

1. What does the author say about the extent to which Americans and the French share values?

2. How does the author define the term *anti-Americanism*?

3. The author argues that the French have been consistently negative in their attitude toward America. How does he support this argument?

4. What does the author tell his readers about the great French writer Charles Baudelaire's attitude toward America?

5. How does the author say his conception of anti-Americanism differs from that of Rob Kroes?

6. What effect did America's intervention in Bosnia in 1999 have on French anti-Americanism?

7. How, in the author's opinion, did the French react to the attack on the twin towers on September 11, 2001?

8. The title of this article contains the phrase "and the Lessons of the 'French Exception.'" Is this phrase misleading in any way?

9. Why, according to this article, is anti-Americanism rampant in Europe?

10. Why, if at all, should Americans be concerned with the ways in which people from other countries perceive them?

JOURNAL PROMPT

Do you think anti-American sentiments among other nations will diminish under the Obama administration? Explain your answer.

Academic Disciplines: History; Political Science; International Relations
Citation Method: *Chicago Manual of Style* (Endnotes)
Rhetorical Mode: Argument

This article is from the *World Policy Journal*, Winter 2006/2007. It follows the *Chicago Manual of Style* method for source citation using endnotes.

Fixing the Borders (Without a Wall)
Michele Wucker

Last year witnessed mass demonstrations in favor of legalizing unauthorized   1
immigrants juxtaposed with ongoing border patrols by Minuteman Project
volunteers and strident punditry decrying our "broken borders." Disparate
as they were, this combination of voices sent a clear and unified message:
"Something must be done."

After a year of debate and a set of competing bills in the House of   2
Representatives and the Senate, both the pro-immigration and restrictionist
camps were disappointed with the utter failure of Congress to do virtually
anything except approve a border fence, which most likely will never be
built in its entirety, if at all. Congress left unanswered how to deal with the
estimated 12 million unauthorized immigrants living in the United States
and how to reduce the future flow of illegal immigration.

With strong momentum for change, a mandate for bipartisan coop-   3
eration, and a brief window of opportunity before the 2008 presidential
elections, the time is now to address these questions. To create an orderly,
sustainable flow of immigration, Congress would do well to embrace issues
that received little attention over the past year, yet will be crucial to the
success of any reform project: how to decide whom to let in, how to fix a
deeply flawed immigration bureaucracy, and how coordination with sending countries might help to ease migration pressure.

What Congress decides on immigration policy will have a wide-ranging   4
impact on the health of communities, on tax revenue, on the businesses
and individual Americans who employ foreign-born workers, on competitiveness in high-skilled industries, on the ability of immigrants' children
and future generations to succeed in America, and on America's identity
as a nation of immigrants. The immigration policies that America pursues
resonate around the world. As a superpower whose identity is rooted in
the notion of itself as an immigrant nation, the United States stands as an

*Michele Wucker is a senior fellow at the World Policy Institute and research fellow at the
Immigration Policy Center. She is the author of* Lockout: Why America Keeps Getting Immigration
Wrong When Our Prosperity Depends on Getting it Right *(PublicAffairs, 2006).*

example—both good and bad—to countries that only recently have begun to wrestle with the question of how to integrate large foreign-born populations. Indeed, the talk of building a border fence has sparked plans for new barriers in places as diverse as the Caribbean, Europe, the Middle East, and Asia. Should the United States choose a mainly restrictionist path, it is highly likely that many other nations would follow suit and crack down on their immigrant populations, intensifying ethnic conflict.

Changes in U.S. immigration policy will have not only a symbolic   5
effect around the globe, but also a real economic impact. Nations like the Philippines and Mexico, which depend on remittances sent home by migrant workers, would be hard hit if the gates close. In countries without the universities or industries where skilled immigrants and talented students can pursue their scientific or professional interests, human capital would be wasted—hurting not just the home country but the rest of the world.

This interconnectedness also means that the United States cannot stop   6
at its own borders when conceiving a new immigration policy; slowing the flow of illegal immigration means addressing the root causes of the desperation that drives people into the shadows.

THE "PUSH" FACTOR

Much is made of the "push" and "pull" factors driving migration: the rea-   7
sons people leave their homelands and those that draw them to host countries. A sustainable immigration policy must address both.

It is essential to address the migration problem at its source: the despera-   8
tion that impels people to believe that the only way to feed their families is to leave them behind. Joint talks with Mexico—as well as other countries that send large numbers of migrants—could create partnerships intended to address the causes of illegal migration at their root. Recently, in a televised debate, I proposed diverting money intended for the border fence to potentially more productive purposes, such as development aid to create jobs in Mexico. Jim Gilchrist of the Minuteman Project—the private citizens' group that monitors border crossings—responded in agreement. "We can help Mexico build a Mexican Dream, just like we in the U.S. have an American Dream," he said, showing that such a plan is far from politically impossible, even among groups pushing to maximize enforcement. Yet, even if cross-border plans to change "push" factors are developed immediately, it will take some time for results to show. Policies to diminish the "pull" can have an impact much sooner.

CHANGING THE "PULL"

Thus far, the debate on how to reduce the "pull" for illegal immigrants—   9
and perhaps even reverse it by encouraging immigrants to return—has

focused on enforcement measures and policies to deny immigrants access to driver's licenses, bank accounts, housing, and other necessities of daily life. Yet right now, the push factor for many unauthorized immigrants is so strong that people will continue to migrate illegally no matter how harsh the conditions may be in the host country. This has combined with a powerful pull factor—the U.S. economy.

Here is where the problem starts. There are only enough legal visas to   10 accommodate about two-thirds of the immigrants who come to the United States each year seeking work. Shortage of visas has not slowed immigration; it has merely prompted people to find ways to come illegally, whether with the help of a smuggler or by overstaying a legitimate visa. The resulting flood of illegal immigration has overwhelmed the government's ability to enforce the existing law. In the past decade, a fivefold increase in the enforcement budget and a threefold staff increase have failed to slow illegal immigration. This is largely because the number of visas available is so far out of touch with reality that migrant-dependent businesses face the choice of breaking the law—with the pain of any consequences falling hardest on the unauthorized workers—or following the law and not being able to survive. Many employers fail even to check if a worker's identification is credible. This is part of a pervasive "don't ask, don't tell" mentality that surrounds the hiring of foreign-born workers. A big loophole holds employers legally responsible only if they "knowingly" hire undocumented immigrants. And, for employers who try to follow the law, sophisticated forgeries that proliferate in a billion-dollar market in faked documents make it difficult to tell legitimate papers from bogus ones.

VERIFYING EMPLOYEES

Employers must ask for identification showing that an employee is autho-   11 rized to work in the United States and provide the corresponding Social Security number when payroll deductions are taken. If the information provided is not valid (often because the name does not match the number), the Social Security Administration then sends the employer a letter of notification, a process that takes weeks. Several thousand businesses participate in the government's Basic Pilot program, which supposedly allows them to immediately verify a worker's eligibility. But that technology often fails to establish whether a worker has legal papers or not. The system produces a high number of false negatives, identifying a worker as unauthorized when he or she is, in fact, legal.[1] False positives also occur frequently. In June 2006, a Swift & Company official testified before the House Small Business Committee that the Basic Pilot program—in which it had participated since 1997—could not accurately establish whether or not a Social Security number was being used elsewhere. Six months later, despite Swift's history of cooperation, U.S. Immigration and Customs Enforcement police raided its

meat-packing plants in several states and arrested more than 1,000 unauthorized immigrants.² Ironically, in 2002, the government had attempted to
fine Swift $2.5 million for too aggressively trying to verify workers' status;
the case was settled for $200,000 with no admission of guilt.

The conundrum facing companies that have no reliable way of fol-   12
lowing the law illustrates the importance of creating a reliable system for
verifying worker identities. It would not come cheap; the Social Security
Administration estimates that simply creating a worker eligibility card
would cost between $3.9 and $9.2 billion.³ Then there are the ongoing
annual costs (estimated in the low tens of millions) of creating and maintaining an accurate database to promptly correct false positives or negatives.
But, compared to a border fence—which the Congressional Research Service
has estimated would cost nearly $50 billion to cover perhaps one-third of
the U.S.-Mexico border—such a database would be far more cost effective.
By making it much harder to find work without authorization, this single
measure could do more than any fence to slow the flow of illegal immigration. But it will only work if employers can be reasonably sure that there will
be enough work visas available to ensure a stable labor supply.

WHO COMES IN

Although the demand for labor and jobs is what clearly drives migration,   13
the United States fails to take that reality adequately into account when it
decides whom to let in. In 2005, 58 percent of permanent-resident visas,
or green cards, were awarded to family members of U.S. citizens (many of
whom are naturalized), while only 22 percent were awarded based on jobs.
Our immigration policy would be far more effective if it corresponded with
the market dynamics that drive people across borders. Right now, there are
nearly as many visas allotted to adult extended-family relatives as there are
to would-be immigrants with valuable job skills.

This requires overhauling the family preferences system that has long   14
been the formula for deciding who may come here and eventually apply
for citizenship. The goal of uniting families is worthy, but in practice, the
innocuously named family preferences system results in dividing the nuclear
families of legal permanent residents, and leaving adult siblings in limbo for
decades. It also has exponentially increased immigration, partly because it
raises potential migrants' expectations that they will be able to get visas once
a family member has found a toehold in America. When one family member
arrives and is naturalized, he or she can petition for admission of an adult
sibling or child—who, in turn, often brings children and a spouse, who then
sponsors his or her own parents and siblings, and so on.

Legal permanent residents can bring spouses and children under this   15
provision—but (unlike spouses and children of naturalized citizens) subject
to a per-country visa cap, which often breaks up nuclear families because

visas run out, particularly for high-emigration countries like Mexico, India, and China. Once the number of visas allocated to a particular country has exceeded 7 percent of the total visas available for that year, no new applications are processed until new visas become available, typically when the quota is opened the following year. If, for example, you were an adult sibling from the Philippines and wanted a green card, as of December 2006 the government would not process your application unless you had filed it before June 1, 1984—a wait of nearly 22 years.

Despite interminable delays, the family preferences system has created   16
expectations that adult family members will be able to follow their siblings and parents. Over time, the process uproots and transplants entire extended families, with significant consequences for the sending country. Most important, family preferences tends to accelerate the exodus of a nascent middle class. Migration scholars have long noted that as incomes rise above abject poverty, migration increases because people can afford transportation and, if needed, smugglers' fees—and does not decrease again until sending-country incomes have risen to the point where it does not make sense to leave. If a country's population leaves as soon as incomes are high enough to permit them to do so, it risks the loss of a healthy middle class that is essential to building consumption, production, and investment.

By eliminating preferences for adult siblings and adult children for   17
naturalized citizens and permanent residents, the United States could free up 138,066 visas. Moving these to job-based visa categories based on immigrants' skills (which currently totals only 140,000 visas), would nearly double employment-based green cards. Adult siblings and children could still come under job-based visas. But the increase in the foreign-born population—and the exodus from migrant-sending countries—would be closer to linear, instead of exponential. That would permit further increasing the number of employment-based visas and exempting green card holders' nuclear family members from quotas.

In particular, the number of visas available for high-skilled workers   18
should be raised. The United States depends on these workers—who make up half of the nation's research and development employees, as well as significant percentages of doctors, nurses, and science and engineering professionals—even more heavily than it does on low-skilled workers. Unlike low-wage workers, high-skilled professionals are unlikely to be hired for (or accept) jobs under the table, and current bottlenecks in visa processing often mean that they take their skills elsewhere.

The tradition of family preferences as the basis for U.S. policy is deeply   19
rooted, so any cutback is bound to be controversial. Opposition could be offset by speeding up approvals of adult siblings and offspring of naturalized citizens, as well as the spouses and minor children of permanent residents, who are backlogged because of current policy.

FIX THE SYSTEM

The least contentious action Congress can take is to authorize an effective   20
overhaul of immigration processing and information systems. Everyone—
including the hard-working men and women in government immigration agencies—agrees that the system malfunctions. U.S. Citizenship and
Immigration Services is notorious for losing visa applications and for its
processing errors. The government "help line" for visa applicants—staffed by
privately contracted telephone operators who must familiarize themselves
with 1,800 pages of tortuous and often out-of-date regulations—is almost
comically unreliable.

American management theories are a hot commodity around the   21
world, so why is our immigration bureaucracy reminiscent of the old East
Bloc? The system's dismal performance owes much to neglect and micro-
management. Because the agency's $2 billion budget is funded entirely by
user fees, it is perpetually plagued by shortfalls that have prevented an overhaul of its computer network and a staff reorganization.[4] Congress should
allocate funds essential for a technological upgrade of the U.S. Citizenship
and Immigration Services (an estimated $400 million to $1.4 billion). While
Congress slowly reaches a consensus on broader-reaching immigration
reform, it should enact stricter accountability and performance standards, a
step that can be taken immediately.

Congress has not only starved the bureaucracy of resources but has   22
imposed laws that needlessly burden the system. It has legislated conflicting mandates for agencies whose work overlaps, and it has micro-managed
immigration down to mandating specific formats for forms used by immigration agencies. Streamlining immigration regulations may not be a short-
term project, but it is a worthy one, especially if immigration agencies were
allowed enough leeway to do their jobs.

Congress should immediately pass a comprehensive immigration   23
reform that allows unauthorized immigrants to gain legal status and apply
for earned citizenship. It can dramatically increase the number of employment-based visas while cutting family preference visas for adult siblings and
adult children. To end the long-standing wink-wink-nudge-nudge approach
to workplace enforcement (whereby unscrupulous employers get away with
lawbreaking and businesses that comply have no realistic way to do so), it
should authorize and fund the creation of a database—with a realistic dead-
line for implementation—that would allow employers to verify worker eligibility. And it should allocate funds to upgrade the immigration bureaucracy
to standards worthy of America's management prowess and of the vital
importance of immigrants to the economy.

NOTES

1. Marc R. Rosenblum, "Immigration Enforcement at the Worksite: Making it Work," Washington, DC: Migration Policy Institute, November 2005. See also Tamar Jacoby, "An Idea Whose Time Has Finally Come? The Case for Employment Verification," Washington, DC: Migration Policy Institute, November 2005.

2. Sue Kirchhoff, "Raids at Swift Raise Questions about Employers' Ability to Check Status." *USA Today*, December 13, 2006.

3. Kevin Jernegan, "Eligible to Work? Experiments in Verifying Work Authorization," Washington, DC: Migration Policy Institute, November 2005.

4. Spencer S. Hsu, "Immigrant Processors Fall Behind," *Washington Post*, January 4, 2007.

QUESTIONS FOR COMPREHENSION, STUDY, AND DISCUSSION

1. How, according to the author, will U.S. government decisions about immigration affect the immigration policy of other countries?

2. What is the thesis of this article?

3. On what key point does the author of this article agree with the Minuteman Project?

4. What does the author mean by the "push" factor and the "pull" factor?

5. What is the effect on "migrant-dependent businesses" of current visa requirements?

6. What is wrong with the government's program to verify a worker's eligibility?

7. What are the advantages and disadvantages of requiring a worker eligibility card?

8. What is wrong with the family preference system, and how does the author recommend it be overhauled?

9. According to the author, why should the number of visas for high-skilled workers be raised?

10. In the author's view, why should the government allocate more funds to U.S. Citizenship and Immigration Services?

JOURNAL PROMPT

Do you think the federal government should build a wall to help control illegal immigration?

Academic Discipline: Earth Sciences
Citation Method: *Chicago Manual of Style*
Rhetorical Mode: Persuasion

This article is from *American Scientist*, Volume 95 (July–August 2007). It follows the *Chicago Manual of Style* method for source citation.

The Shrinking Glaciers of Kilimanjaro: Can Global Warming Be Blamed?

Philip W. Mote and Georg Kaser

The Kibo ice cap, a "poster child" of global climate change, is being starved of snowfall and depleted by solar radiation.

The shrinking glacier is an iconic image of global climate change. Rising   1
temperatures may reshape vegetation, but such changes are visually subtle on the landscape; by contrast, a vast glacier retreated to a fraction of its former grandeur presents stunning evidence of how climate shapes the face of the planet. Viewers of the film *An Inconvenient Truth* are startled by paired before-and-after photos of vanishing glaciers around the world. If those were not enough, the scars left behind by the retreat of these mountain-grinding giants testify to their impotence in the face of something as insubstantial as warmer air.

But the commonly heard—and generally correct—statement that   2
glaciers are disappearing because of warming glosses over the physical processes responsible for their disappearance. Indeed, warming fails spectacularly to explain the behavior of the glaciers and plateau ice on Africa's Kilimanjaro massif, just 3 degrees south of the equator, and to a lesser extent other tropical glaciers. The disappearing ice cap of the "shining

---

Philip W. Mote is a research scientist at the University of Washington in the Climate Impacts Group, and an affiliate professor in the Department of Atmospheric Sciences. His research interests include Northwest climate and its effects on snowpack, stream flow and forest fires. A frequent public speaker, he has written about 60 scientific articles and edited a book on climate modeling published in 2000. He and Georg Kaser met when both served as lead authors for the Fourth Assessment Report of the Intergovernmental Panel on Climate Change. Kaser, a glaciologist, is a professor at the University of Innsbruck in Austria. He has studied glaciers around the world, focusing on tropical glaciers, and has conducted field work on Kilimanjaro in Tanzania, Rwenzori in Uganda, the Cordillera Blanca in Peru and the European Alps. He is in the middle of a four-year term as president of the Commission for the Cryospheric Sciences of the International Union of Geodesy and Geophysics. He is coauthor of Tropical Glaciers, *published by Cambridge University Press in 2002. Address for Mote: CSES Climate Impacts Group, Box 354235. University of Washington, Seattle, WA 98195. Internet: philip@atmos.washington.edu*

mountain," which gets a starring role in the movie, is not an appropriate poster child for global climate change. Rather, extensive field work on tropical glaciers over the past 20 years by one of us (Kaser) reveals a more nuanced and interesting story. Kilimanjaro, a trio of volcanic cones that penetrate high into the cold upper troposphere, has gained and lost ice through processes that bear only indirect connections, if any, to recent trends in global climate.

GLACIAL CHANGE

The fact that glaciers exist in the tropics at all takes some explaining.   3
Atmospheric temperatures drop about 6.5 degrees Celsius per kilometer of altitude, so the air atop a 5,000-meter mountain can be 32.5 degrees colder than the air at sea level; thus, even in the tropics, high-mountain temperatures are generally below freezing. The climber ascending such a mountain passes first through lush tropical vegetation that gradually gives way to low shrubs, then grasses and finally a zone that is nearly devoid of vegetation because water is not available in liquid form. Tropical mountaintop temperatures vary only a little from season to season, since the sun is high in the sky at midday throughout the year. With temperatures this low, snow accumulates in ice layers and glaciers on Kilimanjaro, Mount Kenya and the Rwenzori range in East Africa, on Irian Jaya in Indonesia and especially in the Andean cordillera in South America, where 99.7 percent of the ice in tropical glaciers is found.

A simple, physically accurate way to understand the processes creating   4
and controlling these and other glaciers is to think in terms of their *energy balance* and *mass balance.*

Mass balance is merely the difference between accumulation (mass   5
added) and ablation (mass subtracted); in this case mass refers to water in its solid, liquid or vapor form. A glacier's mass is closely related to its volume, which can be calculated by multiplying its area by its average depth. When a glacier's volume changes, a change in length is usually the most obvious and well-documented evidence. Alaska's vanishing Muir Glacier, an extreme case, shrank more than 2 kilometers in length over the past half-century.

Glaciers never quite achieve "balance" but rather wobble like a novice tightrope walker. Sometimes a change in climate throws the glacier   6
substantially out of balance, and its mass can take decades to reach a new equilibrium.

Added mass comes largely from the atmosphere, generally as snow-   7
fall but also as rainfall that freezes; in rare cases mass is added by *riming*, in which wind carries water droplets that are so cold that they freeze on contact.

A.   B.

Photographs supplied by the U.S. Geological Survey

FIGURES 1A and 1B

Glaciers around the world have been retreating in recent decades. The most-studied glacier in North America may be the South Cascade Glacier in Washington state, where photographs taken by U.S. government scientists in 1928 (A) and 2006 (B) provide visible evidence of the glacier's loss of half its mass. Solid evidence implicates global warming in the retreat of South Cascade and other glaciers in temperate zones. There is scant evidence, however, of a direct connection between current global climate trends and the shrinking of the ice cap atop Kilimanjaro in tropical East Africa despite its new role as a climate-change poster child. However hot the dry plains below, temperatures atop the massif remain below freezing; observations suggest the ice faces are being scoured by solar radiation rather than heated by warm air. Today a river of meltwater flows from the toe of South Cascade, whereas on Kilimanjaro observations of runoff are scant. (Photographs courtesy of the U.S. Geological Survey Glacier and Snow Program.)

    The most obvious subtractive process is the runoff of melted water from   8 a glacier surface. Another process that reduces glacial mass is *sublimation*, that is, the conversion of ice directly to water vapor, which can take place at temperatures well below the melting point but which requires about eight times as much energy as melting. Sublimation occurs when the moisture in the air is less than the moisture delivered from the ice surface. It is the process responsible for "freezer burn," when improperly sealed food loses moisture.

AIR, ICE AND EQUILIBRIUM

Melting, sublimation and the warming of ice require energy. Energy in the   9 high-mountain environment comes from a variety of energy fluxes that interact in complex ways. The Sun is the primary energy source, but its direct effect is limited to daytime; other limiting factors are shading and the ability of snow to reflect visible light. Energy can nevertheless reach the

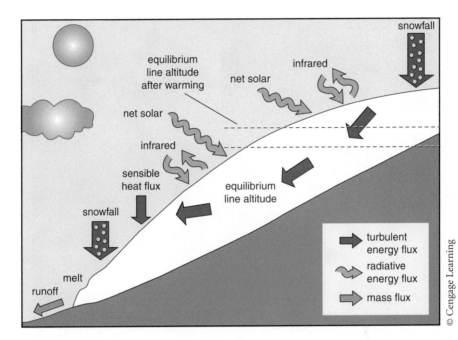

FIGURE 2
Most glaciers gain mass chiefly from snowfall and lose it primarily through the runoff of meltwater. A variety of factors can affect the mass balance of a glacier, and a glacier's location plays a major role in this balancing act. A typical midlatitude glacier (shown in the summertime in this cartoon) gains mass in its higher parts and loses it at the tongue. The glacier's equilibrium-line altitude is the point where these processes balance. Above this line, the glacier gains energy from solar radiation but loses it through infrared radiation toward the air. Below the line, sensible-heat transfer from warmer air into the glacier adds energy. With environmental warming, the equilibrium line moves up; inputs of sensible-heat flux and infrared radiation increase, with the result that melting is enhanced. Wind-driven water droplets, or rime, make small contributions to mass.

glacier through *sensible-heat flux*—the exchange of heat between a surface and the air in contact with it, in this case heat taken directly from the air in contact with the ice—and via infrared emission from the atmosphere and land surface. Energy can also leave glacier ice in several ways: sensible-heat flux from the glacier to cold air, infrared emission from snow and ice surfaces, and the "latent heat" required for water to undergo a phase change from solid to liquid (melting) or gas (sublimation).

Mountain glaciers accumulate snow at high altitudes, slide downhill—   10
some at speeds approaching 2 meters a day—and melt at low altitudes in

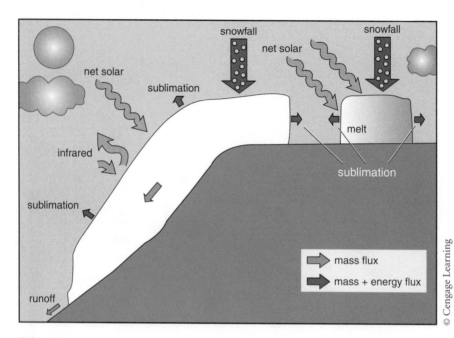

FIGURE 3
Kilimanjaro's location in a dry and cold tropical climate zone changes its mass-balance equation. In the tropics glaciers do not move between winter and summer, snowfall and melting; temperatures vary more from morning to afternoon than from season to season. The ice cap on Kilimanjaro consists of ice on the 5,700-meter-high flat summit, some with vertical edges, and several slope glaciers, mostly at altitudes where temperatures stay well below freezing and the major source of energy is solar radiation. Considerable infrared radiation is emitted from the glacier surface into the surrounding air, and the glaciers lose the most mass through sublimation—the direct conversion of ice to water vapor. Observers have seen only a trickle of meltwater

summertime. Some midlatitude glaciers reach sea level in part because of copious snowfall, exceeding the liquid equivalent of 3 meters per year.

Somewhere between the top and bottom of a glacier on a mountain slope, there is an elevation above which accumulation exceeds ablation and below which ablation exceeds accumulation. This is called the *equilibrium line altitude* or ELA. Rising air temperatures increase the sensible–heat flux from the air to the glacier surface and the infrared radiation absorbed by the glacier, so that melting is faster and is taking place over a larger portion of the glacier. 11

Thus rising temperatures also raise the equilibrium-line altitude. In latitudes with pronounced seasons, this expands the portion of the glacier that 12 melts each summer and may even, in some cases, reduce the portion of the glacier that can retain mass accumulated in the winter. Virtually all glaciers in the world have receded substantially during the past 150 years, and some small ones have disappeared. Warming appears to be the primary culprit in these changes, and indeed glacial-length records have been used as a proxy for past temperatures, agreeing well with data from tree rings and other proxies.

In many respects, however, conditions are quite different for glaciers in   13 the tropics, where temperature varies far more from morning to afternoon than from the coldest month to the warmest month. The most pronounced seasonal pattern in the tropics is the existence of one or two wet seasons, when glacial accumulation is greater and, owing to cloud cover, solar radiation is less.

Because there is almost no seasonal fluctuation in the ELA of tropical   14 glaciers, a much smaller portion of the glacier lies below the ELA. That is, because the processes causing depletion of the glaciers operate almost every day of the year, they are effective over a much smaller area. This smaller area also means that the terminus or bottom edge of tropical glaciers tends to respond more quickly to changes in the mass balance.

An additional important distinction among tropical glaciers divides wet   15 and dry regimes. In wet regimes, changes in air temperature are important in mass-balance calculations, but for dry regimes like East Africa, changes in atmospheric moisture are more important. Connections between such changes and global increases in greenhouse gases are more tenuous in tropical regimes. Year-to-year variability and longer-term trends in the seasonal distribution of moisture are influenced by the surface temperatures of the tropical oceans, which, in turn, are influenced by global climate. On many tropical glaciers, both the direct impact of global warming and the indirect one—changes in atmospheric moisture concentration—are responsible for the observed mass losses. The mere fact that ice is disappearing sheds no light on which mechanism is responsible. For most glaciers, detailed observations and measurements are missing, adding to the difficulty of distinguishing between the two agents.

THE SHINING MOUNTAIN

What about Kilimanjaro? Tropical glacier-climate relations are different, but   16 among them Kilimanjaro's glacial regime is unique. Its ice consists of an ice cap (up to 40 meters thick) sitting on the relatively flat summit plateau of its tallest volcanic peak, Kibo, about 5,700 to 5,800 meters above sea level and, below this, several slope glaciers. The slope glaciers extend down to about 5,200 meters (one, in a shady gully, extends to 4,800 meters). The ice cap is too thin to be deformed, and the plateau is too flat to allow for gliding. The summit's flanks are plenty steep—with angles averaging 35 degrees—but the slope glaciers move little compared with midlatitude, temperate glaciers. The slope glaciers gain and lose mass along their inclined surfaces. The plateau ice, by contrast, has two faces that each interact quite differently with the atmosphere and therefore with climate: near-horizontal surfaces and near-vertical cliffs, the latter forming the edges of the plateau ice.

What factors may explain the decline in Kilimanjaro's ice? Global warm- 17 ing is an obvious suspect, as it has been clearly implicated in glacial declines elsewhere, on the basis of both detailed mass-balance studies (for the few glaciers with such studies) and correlations between glacial length and air temperature (for many other glaciers). Rising air temperatures change the surface energy balance by enhancing sensible-heat transfer from atmosphere to ice, by increasing downward infrared radiation and finally by raising the ELA and hence expanding the area over which loss can occur. The first and only paper asserting that the glacier shrinkage on Kibo was associated with rising air temperatures was published in 2000 by Lonnie G. Thompson of Ohio State University and co-authors.

Another possible culprit is a decrease in accumulation combined with an 18 increase in sublimation, both possibly driven by a change in the frequency and quantity of cloudiness and snowfall. This argument traces its roots to 19th-century European explorers, and has been substantially improved after field work by Kaser, Douglas K. Hardy of the Climate System Research Center at the University of Massachusetts, Amherst, Tharsis Hyera and Juliana Adosi of the Tanzania Meteorological Agency and others.

In 2001 Hardy had invited Kaser to join him and some television journal- 19 ists in the filming of a documentary on the ice retreat on Kibo. For about a year and a half, Hardy's instruments had been deployed on the Kibo summit, measuring weather; Kaser had been studying tropical glaciers for almost a decade and a half. The team set up tents just below one of the most impressive ice cliffs that delineates the Northern Ice Field on its southern edge. During a full five days and nights on the plateau, we observed the ice and discussed the mechanisms that drive the changes, a discussion stimulated from time to time by penetrating questions from the two journalists. Kibo's volcanic ash provided a drawing board, and a ski pole served as the pencil as a picture of the regime of the glaciers on Kibo grew clearer. Thus was formed the basic hypothesis that still drives our research and that our subsequent field measurements of mass and energy balance have largely confirmed, one in which local air temperature and its changes would play only a minor role. Here is the evidence.

TIME AND TEMPERATURE

Observations of Kilimanjaro's ice from about 1880 to 2003 allow us to 20 quantify changes in area but not in mass or volume. The early European explorers Hans Meyer and Ludwig Purtscheller were the first to reach the summit in 1889. Based on their surveys and sketches, but mainly from moraines identified with aerial photographs, Henry Osmaston reconstructed (in 1989) an 1880 ice area of 20 square kilometers. In 1912, a precise 1:50,000 map based on terrestrial photogrammetry done by Edward Oehler and Fritz Klute placed the area at 12.1 square kilometers. By 2003 that area had declined to 2.5 square kilometers, a shrinkage of almost 90 percent. Much of that decline, though, had already taken place by 1953, when the area was 6.7 square kilometers (down 66 percent from 1880). Over the same period, ice movement has been almost nil on the plateau and slight on the slopes. There are indications that the slope glaciers at least are coming into equilibrium.

This pacing of change is at odds with the pace of temperature changes globally, which have been strongly upward since the 1970s after a period of stasis. Other glaciers share this pacing, with many coming into equilibrium or even advancing around the 1970s before beginning a sharp retreat.   21

Temperature trends are difficult to evaluate, owing to the paucity of relevant measurements, but taken together the data presented in the 2007 report from the IPCC (Intergovernmental Panel on Climate Change) suggest little trend in local temperature during the past few decades. In the East African highlands far below Kilimanjaro's peaks, temperature records suggest a warming of 0.5–0.8 degree during 1901–2005, a nontrivial amount of warming but probably larger than the warming at Kibo's peak. For the free troposphere, a deep layer including Kibo's peak, the warming rate during the period 1979–2004 for the zone 20 degrees latitude north and south of the equator was less than 0.1 degree per decade—smaller than the surface trend for that time and not statistically different from zero. Averages over a deep layer of the atmosphere, however, may be a poor estimate of the warming at Kilimanjaro's peak, although it has been argued that the warming must be nearly the same at all longitudes in the tropics, given that rotational effects are small, imposing strong dynamical constraints.   22

Focusing on measurements of air temperatures at the 500-millibar air-pressure level (roughly 5,500 meters altitude) from balloons, one paper suggests a warming trend in the tropical middle troposphere from about 1960 to 1979, followed by cooling from 1979 to 1997, although this study has not been updated.   23

Two of the data sets used to derive the tropical averages above are "reanalysis" data sets, in which observations are fed into a global dynamical model, thereby providing dynamically consistent fields of temperature, winds and so on, even where there are no observations. At the reanalysis point closest to Kilimanjaro's peak, there seems to be no trend since the late 1950s. But like the balloon and satellite data, the reanalysis data can be unsuitable for documenting trends over time.   24

When pieced together, these disparate lines of evidence do not suggest   25
that any warming at Kilimanjaro's summit has been large enough to explain
the disappearance of most of its ice, either during the whole 20th century or
during the best-measured period, the last 25 years.

STUCK IN THE FREEZER

Another important observation is that the air temperatures measured at   26
the altitude of the glaciers and ice cap on Kilimanjaro are almost always
substantially below freezing (rarely above −3 degrees). Thus the air by itself
cannot warm ice to melting by sensible-heat or infrared-heat flux: On the
occasions when melting takes place, it is produced by solar radiation in conditions of very light wind, which allows a warm layer of air to develop just
next to the ice.

A related line of evidence concerns the shape and evolution of ice.   27
Stunning vertical walls of astonishing height (greater than 40 meters in
places) tower over the visitor to Kibo's summit. These edges cannot grow
horizontally but lose mass constantly to ablation (primarily to sublimation
and intermittently to melting) when they are exposed to the sun—even
when the air temperature is below freezing. Once developed, the near-vertical edges will retreat until the ice is gone, since no snow can accumulate on
these walls.

The careful observer notes another striking fact about these walls: They   28
are predominantly oriented in the east-west direction. This too implicates
solar radiation, whose intensity is modulated by a seasonal and daily pattern
of cloudiness: The daily cycle of deep convection over central Africa means
that afternoons, when the Sun is to the west, are typically cloudy. The equi-
nox seasons when the Sun is overhead are also cloudy, whereas when the
Sun is to the south or north (solstices), the summit is typically cloud-free.
For the same reason, the edges of the ice are retreating more slowly on the
west, southwest and northwest sides.

The role of solar radiation in shaping the ice edges is evident in other   29
features as well. As the ice retreats horizontally, it can leave behind knife-
thin vertical remnants that eventually become so thin that they fall over and
disintegrate. Like other explorers who came before them, Kaser and Hardy
also noted the sculpted features called *penitentes* in the Kibo ice cap on
several occasions. Penitentes are seen also in many places in the Andes and
the Himalaya, where they are sometimes much larger. These finger-like features arise when initial irregularities in a flat surface result in the collection
of dust in pockets, which accelerates melting in those places by enhancing
absorption of solar radiation. The cups between the *penitentes* are protected
from ventilation even as wind brushing the peaks of the developing spires
enhances sublimation, which cools the surface.

If infrared radiation and sensible heat transfer were the dominant factors, these sculpted features would not long survive. Solar radiation and sublimation are sculptors; infrared radiation and sensible heat transfer are diffuse, coming equally from all directions, and so they are smoothers. The prevalence of sculpted features on Kilimanjaro's peak provides strong evidence against the role of smoothers, which are energetically closely related to air temperature. 30

MASS IN THE BALANCE

What is known about the mass balance of Kibo's ice? Detailed studies of mass and energy fluxes have shown that the mass balance on Kibo's horizontal surfaces is driven by the occurrence or lack of frequent and abundant 31

© Georg Kaser

FIGURE 4
Visitors to the summit of Kilimanjaro are greeted by ice cliffs as tall as 40 meters in places. (For scale, note the scientist checking instruments at the top of a 30-meter wall.) The south face of the Northern Ice Field, shown here, retreats when the Sun is to the south; the north face retreats when the Sun is to the north. A daily cycle of deep convection over central Africa makes most afternoons, when the Sun is to the west, cloudy, and the west, southwest and northwest edges are retreating more slowly. This pattern supports the notion that solar radiation is the culprit. The shrinking leaves separated ice features that eventually become small enough to fall over. (Photograph courtesy of Georg Kaser.)

snowfall. On Kilimanjaro, Hardy has measured the annual layering of snow directly since 2000 using snow stakes. These measurements show that the horizontal surface of the mountain's Northern Ice Field has experienced two years of near-neutral mass balance. The largest net gain observed was in 2006 when the calendar year over East Africa ended with exceptional heavy and extended rains, associated with sea-surface temperature anomalies over the Indian Ocean, and snow blanketed much of the summit of Kilimanjaro for several months.

Obviously snowfall is the main way to increase the mass of ice, but snowfall also has a role in the energy balance, one made even more important by the prominent role of solar radiation. The loss side of the balance is very much affected by the amount and even more by the frequency of snowfall: The surface of aged or polluted snow is dark and absorbs 32

© George Kaser

FIGURE 5
Sculpted finger-like features called "penitentes" are a striking feature on the Kibo ice cap, providing further evidence that warming is not at work there. Solar radiation and sublimation tend to create such features; infrared radiation and sensible-heat transfer smooth them. Nicolas Cullen of the University of Otago in New Zealand is silhouetted in this photograph taken by Georg Kaser during a recent field season.

considerably more energy from solar radiation than does a white surface of fresh snow. When there is more energy available to a glacier's surface, sub-limitation increases. But even in below-freezing air temperatures, the same energy can increase melting if there is no wind. Meltwater from the surface is thought to be refrozen in lower ice layers; thus such melting does not necessarily constitute a loss for the ice cap as a whole. Indeed, an observer watching a slope glacier will rarely see more than a trickle of meltwater from the toe.

Comparison of historic photographs indicates that over the past century the thinning of the plateau ice has amounted to perhaps 10 meters—a rate of loss that can be explained by snowfall insufficient to balance sublimation. The observed reduction of the ice's surface area has taken place mainly at the vertical edges, however, which is not explained by snowfall patterns.   33

The mass balance of the slope glaciers is somewhat different from that of the plateau ice. Retreating midlatitude glaciers typically lose most mass below the ELA and little or none above. The Kibo slope glaciers, though, show shrinkage at both top and bottom. Their history suggests that in 1900 they were already far from equilibrium, but their retreat appears to be slowing; that and their convex shape suggests that they are approaching a new smaller equilibrium between the (relatively constant) loss term and the smaller accumulation term.   34

GLACIERS AND GLOBAL CLIMATE

The observations described above point to a combination of factors other than warming air—chiefly a drying of the surrounding air that reduced accumulation and increased ablation—as responsible for the decline of the ice on Kilimanjaro since the first observations in the 1880s. The mass balance is dominated by sublimation, which requires much more energy per unit mass than melting; this energy is supplied by solar radiation.   35

These processes are fairly insensitive to temperature and hence to global warming. If air temperatures were eventually to rise above freezing, sensible-heat flux and atmospheric long-wave emission would take the lead from sublimation and solar radiation. Since the summit glaciers do not experience shading, all sharp-edged features would soon disappear. But the sharp-edged features have persisted for more than a century. By the time the 19th-century explorers reached Kilimanjaro's summit, vertical walls had already developed, setting in motion the loss processes that have continued to this day.   36

An additional clue about the pacing of ice loss comes from the water levels in nearby Lake Victoria. Long-term records and proxy evidence of   37 lake levels indicate a substantial decline in regional precipitation at the end of the 19th century after some considerably wetter decades. Overall, the historical records available suggest that the large ice cap described by Victorian-era explorers was more likely the product of an unusually wet period than of cooler global temperatures.

If human-induced global warming has played any role in the shrinkage   38
of Kilimanjaro's ice, it could only have joined the game quite late, after the result was already clearly decided, acting at most as an accessory, influencing the outcome indirectly. The detection and attribution studies indicating that human influence on global climate emerged some time after 1950 reach the same conclusion about East African temperature far below the peak.

The fact that the loss of ice on Mount Kilimanjaro cannot be used as   39
proof of global warming does not mean that the Earth is not warming. There is ample and conclusive evidence that Earth's average temperature has increased in the past 100 years, and the decline of mid- and high-latitude glaciers is a major piece of evidence. But the special conditions on Kilimanjaro make it unlike the higher-latitude mountains, whose glaciers are shrinking because of rising atmospheric temperatures, Mass- and energy-balance considerations and the shapes of features all point in the same direction, suggesting an insignificant role for atmospheric temperature in the fluctuations of Kilimanjaro's ice.

It is possible, though, that there is an indirect connection between the   40
accumulation of greenhouse gases and Kilimanjaro's disappearing ice: There is strong evidence of an association over the past 200 years or so between Indian Ocean surface temperatures and the atmospheric circulation and precipitation patterns that either feed or starve the ice on Kilimanjaro. These patterns have been starving the ice since the late 19th century—or perhaps it would be more accurate to say simply reversing the binge of ice growth in the third quarter of the 19th century. Any contribution of rising greenhouse gases to this circulation pattern necessarily emerged only in the last few decades; hence it is responsible for at most a fraction of the recent decline in ice and a much smaller fraction of the total decline.

Is Kilimanjaro's ice cap doomed? It may be. The high vertical edges of   41
the remaining ice make a horizontal expansion of the ice cap more difficult. Although new snowfall on the ice can accumulate over the course of months or years, new snowfall on the rocky plateau usually sublimates or melts in a matter of days (with the notable exception of the period of several months of continuous snow cover in late 2006 and into 2007), partly because thin snow above dark rock cannot long survive as the loss processes reduce the reflective snow and expose the sunlight-absorbing rock. If the cap ice were much thicker and shaped in a way that allowed ice to creep

outward, gentle slopes could develop along the edges; new snow would be buffered against loss and would accumulate. But steep edges do not allow such expansion.

Imagine, though, a scenario in which the atmosphere around Kilimanjaro were to warm occasionally above 0 degrees. Sensible and infrared heating of the ice surface would gradually erode the sharp corners of the ice cap; gentler slopes would quickly develop. If, in addition, precipitation increased, snow could accumulate on the slopes and permit the ice cap to grow. Ironically, substantial global warming accompanied by an increase in precipitation might be one way to save Kilimanjaro's ice. Or substantially increased snowfall, like the 2006–07 snows, could blanket the dark ash surface so thickly that the snow would not sublimate entirely before the next wet season. Once initiated, such a change could allow the ice sheet to grow. If the Kibo ice cap is vanishing or growing, reshaping itself into something different as you read this, glaciology tells us that it's unlikely to be the first or the last time.

BIBLIOGRAPHY

Cullen, N. J., T. Mölg, G. Kaser, K. Hussein, K. Steffen and D. R. Hardy. 2006. Kilimanjaro Glaciers: Recent areal extent from satellite data and new interpretation of observed 20th century retreat rates. *Geophysical Research Letters* 33:L16502. doi:10.1029/2006GL027084.

Gaffen, D. J., B. D. Santer, J. S. Boyle, J. R. Christy, N. E. Graham and R. J. Ross. 2000. Multidecadal changes in the vertical temperature structure of the tropical troposphere. *Science* 287:1242–1245.

Kaser, G. 1999: A review of modern fluctuations of tropical glaciers. *Global and Planetary Change* 22 (1–4):93–103.

Kaser, G., D. R. Hardy, T Mölg, R. S. Bradley and T. M. Hyera. 2004. Modern glacier retreat on Kilimanjaro as evidence of climate change: observations and facts. *International Journal of Climatology* 24:329–339. doi: 10.1002/joc.1008.

Mölg, T., D. R. Hardy and G. Kaser. 2003. Solar-radiation-maintained glacier recession on Kilimanjaro drawn from combined ice-radiation geometry modeling. *Journal of Geophysical Research* 108(D23):4731. doi:10.1029/2003JD003546.

Mölg, T., and D. R. Hardy, 2004. Ablation and associated energy balance of a horizontal glacier surface on Kilimanjaro. *Journal of Geophysical Research* 109:D16104.

Oerlemans, J. 2005. Extracting a climate signal from 169 glacier records. *Science* 308:675–677.

Osmaston, H. 1989. Glaciers, glaciation and equilibrium line altitudes on Kilimanjaro. In *Quaternary and Environmental Research on East African Mountains*, ed. W. C. Mahaney. Rotterdam: Brookfield, pp. 7–30.

Thompson, L. G., E. Mosley-Thompson and K. A. Henderson. 2000. Ice-core paleoclimate records in tropical South America since the Last Glacial Maximum. *Journal of Quaternary Science* 15:377–394.

Thompson, L. G., *et al.* 2002. Kilimanjaro ice core records: Evidence of Holocene climate change in tropical Africa. *Science* 298:589–593.

Trenberth, K. E., *et al.* 2007. Observations: Surface and atmospheric climate change. Chapter 3 in *Climate Change 2007: The Physical Science Basis.* Contribution of Working Group 1 to the Fourth Assessment Report of the Intergovernmental Panel on Climate Change. Cambridge, U.K., and New York: Cambridge University Press.

QUESTIONS FOR COMPREHENSION, STUDY, AND DISCUSSION

1. What is the thesis of this article?

2. Define *mass balance* and *sublimation* in the context of this article.

3. Why, according to the authors, are glaciers in nontropical climates shrinking?

4. Why, according to the authors, are glaciers in tropical climates shrinking?

5. How are the glaciers of Kilimanjaro unique?

6. What is the role of solar radiation in the shrinkage of the Kilimanjaro glaciers?

7. What is significant about the fact that the "sharp-edged features" of the Kilimanjaro glaciers "have persisted for more than a century"?

8. What does the water level of Lake Victoria suggest about the decline of the Kilimanjaro glaciers?

9. What role *might* global warming play in the decline of the glacier?

10. Why might the Kilimanjaro ice cap be doomed?

JOURNAL PROMPT

See (or see again) Al Gore's movie *An Inconvenient Truth,* and comment on how this article supports or refutes Gore's arguments.

Credits

Amiti, Mary, and Kevin Stiroh. "Is the United States Losing Its Productivity Advantage?" *Current Issues in Economics and Finance* 13.8 (2007): 1–7. Reprinted by permission of The Groningen Growth and Development Centre and the Federal Reserve Bank of New York.

Grossbard, Joel, Irene Markman Geisner, Clayton Neighbors, Jason R. Kilmer, and Mary E. Larimer. "Are Drinking Games Sports? College Athlete Participation in Drinking Games and Alcohol-Related Problems." *Journal of Studies on Alcohol and Drugs* 68 (2007): 97–105. Reprinted with permission from Journal of Studies on Alcohol and Drugs. Copyright by Alcohol Research Documentation, Inc., Rutgers Center of Alcohol Studies, Piscataway, NJ 08854.

Hard, Stephen F., James M. Conway, and Antonia C. Moran. "Faculty and College Student Beliefs about the Frequency of Student Academic Misconduct." *Journal of Higher Education* 77 (2006): 1058–80. Copyright 2006 The Ohio State University Press. Reprinted with permission.

Kim, Janna L., C. Lynn Sorsoli, Katherine Collins, Bonnie A. Zylbergold, Deborah Schooler, and Deborah L. Tolman. "From Sex to Sexuality: Exposing the Heterosexual Script on Primetime Network Television." *Journal of Sex Research* 44 (2007): 145–57. Reprinted by permission of Taylor & Francis Group, http://www.informaworld.com.

Ladin, Jay. "Meeting Her Maker: Emily Dickinson's God." *Cross Currents 56.3,* Fall 2006. Reprinted by permission of Wiley-Blackwell.

Manuel, Laura, and Eugene P. Sheehan. "Getting Inked: Tattoos and College Students." *College Student Journal* 41 (2007): 1089–97. Reprinted by permission.

Molé, Phil. "9/11 Conspiracy Theories: The 9/11 Truth Movement in Perspective." *Skeptic* 12.4 (2006): 30–42. © 1992–2009 Skeptic and its contributors.

Mote, Philip W., and Georg Kaser. "The Shrinking Glaciers of Kilimanjaro: Can Global Warming Be Blamed?," *American Scientist,* Volume 95, July/August 2007. Reprinted by permission of *American Scientist,* magazine of Sigma Xi, The Scientific Research Society.

Pritchard, Mary E., Gregory S. Wilson, and Ben Yamnitz. "What Predicts Adjustment Among College Students? A Longitudinal Panel Study." *Journal of American College Health* 56.1 (2007): 15–21. Reprinted with permission of the Helen Dwight Reid Educational Foundation. Published by Heldref Publications, 1319 Eighteenth St., NW, Washington, DC 20036-1802. © 2007.

Roger, Philippe. "Global Anti-Americanism and the Lessons of the 'French Exception.'" *Journal of American History* (Sept. 2006): 448–51. Copyright 2006 by Organization of American Historians. Reproduced with permission of Organization of American Historians in the format Textbook via Copyright Clearance Center.

Wee, Valerie. "Resurrecting and Updating the Teen Slasher: The Case of *Scream.*" *Journal of Popular Film and Television* 34.2 (2006): 50–61. Reprinted with permission of the Helen Dwight Reid Educational Foundation. Published by Heldref Publications, 1319 Eighteenth St., NW, Washington, DC 20036-1802. © 2006.

Wucker, Michele. "Fixing the Borders (Without a Wall)." *World Policy Journal* 23.4 (2006–07): 55–59. Reprinted by permission of the author.

Index